THE SEEDS OF POLITICS

THE SEEDS
OF POLITICS

Youth and Politics in America

Edited by
ANTHONY M. ORUM

Prentice-Hall, Inc., Englewood Cliffs, New Jersey

© 1972 by Prentice-Hall, Inc., Englewood Cliffs, New Jersey

ISBN: 0-13-799585-7 p
 0-13-799593-8 c

Library of Congress Catalog Card Number: 70-37635

PRINTED IN THE UNITED STATES OF AMERICA

10 9 8 7 6 5 4 3 2 1

PRENTICE-HALL INTERNATIONAL, INC., *London*
PRENTICE-HALL OF AUSTRALIA, PTY. LTD., *Sydney*
PRENTICE-HALL OF CANADA, LTD., *Toronto*
PRENTICE-HALL OF INDIA PRIVATE LIMITED, *New Delhi*
PRENTICE-HALL OF JAPAN, INC., *Tokyo*

CONTENTS

v

IV
STRATIFICATION AND SOCIALIZATION 165

V
THE DEVELOPMENT OF ACTIVISM 213

PREFACE

A question often asked of young political activists is: How can one plan and build a new society without heeding the lessons and experiences of the past? A parallel kind of query might be made of those students and scholars who take a dispassionate interest in the political behavior of American youth: How can one comprehend the character of contemporary political activism of youth without giving some attention to the historical and social psychological roots of young peoples' politics? This is one of the questions that has prompted me to assemble the present collection of readings. I have tried, in particular, to bring together several seemingly disparate bodies of thought about the nature of young peoples' political beliefs and behavior in America. Two groups seem to dominate contemporary discussion and scholarship more than others. On the one hand, there are those observers who have fastened on current political protest among youth, examining it almost *in vacuo*, paying little attention to its origins or possibly unique character. On the other hand, there are those scholars who have become interested in tracing the social psychological foundations and development of political beliefs and, in the process, seem to have lost sight of the groundswell of political activity among young Americans today. This book tries to weave these two strands of interest together into a framework that makes sense of conventional and unusual political styles alike.

In selecting articles for inclusion in this reader, I have been guided by several principles. For one thing, I have chosen from among those works that represent analyses of the political patterns of youth, avoiding papers that are simply descriptions. There is an abundance, indeed surfeit, of the latter. For another, I have selected articles that represent some of the most recent thinking by scholars. The readings also have been chosen with an eye to their ability to convey important ideas on a topic in a manner that the student will find concise, instructive, and stimulating. And finally, I have sought to represent the different ideological perspectives that have been brought to bear on the origins and character of political beliefs among young people. This is particularly true in the case of the articles that deal with student protest.

There are several people whom I wish to acknowledge for their contributions to this reader. In particular, I would like to thank the following students, all of whom furnished the right blend of both criticism and encouragement of the ideas conveyed in this book: Gregory Arling, Roberta Cohen, Kay Darnell, McKinlay Jones, Marilyn Klohr, Gordon Lurie, Janice Perrier, Dennis Roncek and Leonard Thornton. Leonard Thornton is owed a special thanks for his very helpful and instructive comments with regard to different models of socialization. Gregory Arling and Roberta Cohen also provided thoughtful criticisms of the Introduction.

And, lastly, there is my wife, Amy, who provided her usual wise counsel and warm encouragement in all phases of the preparation of this reader.

THE SEEDS OF POLITICS

INTRODUCTION:
PERSPECTIVES ON YOUTH
AND POLITICS IN AMERICA

Only a matter of a few years ago, in the 1950s, no one was especially interested in writing, much less reading, a book about young people and their politics. Youth, adolescence in particular, was thought to be a way station lying between infancy and adulthood, and the political expressions of youth were therefore considered transitory, passing phenomena. With the exception of Erik Erikson and a few others, most social scientists dealt with the phenomenon of youth and politics only within a framework of life-cycle changes in behavior or the general maturation process, but certainly not as a distinct subject matter.

Time and interests have changed. In the 1960s, young people throughout the world seemed to develop a distinctive style of political dissent, involving an inquiry into all manner and kind of issues. Since then, one reads almost daily of a political activity by some group of young people, regardless of whether they reside in a communist or democratic nation and without regard to cultural boundaries. To those of us with some measure of curiosity about these events, questions abound. How different, for instance, are the political styles of young people today from those of their counterparts in distant times and places? How new are the conditions that have given rise to the discontent? And what are the ways in which youth learn to express themselves in politics?

This book is designed to furnish some answers to such questions about young people and their politics. The magnitude of the topic naturally calls for some boundaries, and I have chosen to concentrate on the United States. In so doing, I hope to show what is both unique and common about the politics of youth in this country.

THREE PERSPECTIVES ON YOUTH AND
POLITICS IN THE UNITED STATES

The most accurate and comprehensive picture of young people and their politics in the United States will emerge only from a consideration of the insights and knowledge provided by three perspectives. They, in fact, form the basis for the organization of this reader. The first is the *historical* which is concerned chiefly with pinpointing the sources and scope of political activity of American youth now in relation to that of youth in earlier times. The *social psychological*, or political socialization, perspective seeks to determine the general principles underlying the transmission of political beliefs. Finally the *comparative,* or cross-cultural, point of view tries to discover the similarities and differences between the politics of American youth and that of their young counterparts elsewhere in the world.

Historical

There are several important observations to be drawn from the historical perspective regarding youth and their politics in the United States. The first and perhaps the most important is that other nations experienced vigorous political activity by young people and, in particular, by students, long before the United States. Numbers of young students took part in the Revolution of 1848 in Germany.[1] Similarly, there was fairly widespread political activity among young people in Russia in the 1860s and 1870s, the activity being noted particularly for its emphasis on populism. Parallel activities were the preoccupation of many Russian students in the years immediately prior to the Bolshevik Revolution in 1917, although Lenin, seeking to broaden the base of the movement, deliberately discouraged efforts by the young intelligentsia.

One of the more notable youth movements in the twentieth century took place in Germany after the end of World War I. According to some observers, it played an important part in Hitler's eventual rise to power.[2] One observer notes that

> many young people thought that parental religion was largely sham, politics boastful and trivial, economics unscrupulous and deceitful, education stereotyped and lifeless, art trashy and sentimental, literature spurious and commercialized, drama tawdry and mechanical . . . . family life repressive and insincere, and the relations of the sexes, in marriage and without, shot through with hypocrisy.[3]

The movement embracing so many German youth embodied a variety of intriguing themes, among them an emphasis on the importance of the German *Volk*—similar to the place of the *narod* in the Russian movement of the 1860s and 1870s—a high-minded idealism, and an aimlessness that eventually was salvaged by the emergence of a strong charismatic leader in the person of Adolf Hitler.

There have been similar efforts by youth in other nations as well, although they have not had such ominous results. In many Latin American countries, young people, especially university students, long have tried to modernize the educational system while also serving to blunt, if not totally derail, the political ambitions of military elites. And spearheading many of the independence movements in the countries of Asia and Africa in the 1950s and 1960s were members of the young intelligentsia.

---

[1] For a discussion of this and other European student movements, see, for example, Lewis Feuer, *The Conflict of Generations: The Character and Significance of Student Movements* (New York: Basic Books, 1969).

[2] See Howard Becker, *German Youth: Bond or Free* (London: K. Paul, Tronch, Trubner & Co., Ltd., 1946) and Robert G. L. Waite, *Vanguard of Nazism: The Free Corps Movement in Postwar Germany 1918–1923* (Cambridge, Mass.: Harvard University Press, 1952).

[3] Becker, *German Youth*, p. 51.

The second important conclusion to be drawn from the historical perspective is that genuine youth political movements in the United States were, until the 1960s at least, quite uncommon. Indeed, no previous efforts matched the diversity or scale of the political groups and activities of the 1960s. In the nineteenth century, certain minor revolts engaged the energies of young students on college and university campuses, but on the whole young people tended to be passive recipients of the political fate prescribed for them by their elders. Politics at the turn of the century was a bit livelier for American youth. In 1905, for example, the Inter-Collegiate Socialist Society (ISS), which ultimately became the League for Industrial Democracy (LID), was founded. Lipset reports that the ISS possessed a dues-paying membership of about 2000 in 1912–1913, or about five percent of the college population.[4] The themes of protest of this and similar groups resemble those of today: peace, free speech, and concern with the alienating aspects of the university.

Not until the turbulence of the 1930s did anything resembling a genuine youth political movement develop in the United States. Like countless other disenchanted Americans in the 1930s, young people, and students in particular, joined a variety of political groups that advocated radical restructuring of the political and economic system. Among these groups were the Communist and Socialist parties. The youth branch of the LID, the Student League for Industrial Democracy (SLID), was revived by the tensions and clamor of the times. In 1935, the American Student Union, a coalition of different left-wing political organizations, reported a membership of 20,000 students among almost one million people in college at the time.[5] War and the other alleged defects of modern capitalistic society were again the preoccupation of young people, matching those of youth in the early twentieth century and the 1960s. Yet, in contrast to the current era, these activities remained largely the youth branch of adult organizations and, for that reason, had only limited independent political impact.

During the 1940s and 1950s there were few, if any, visible political movements by young people in the United States. In the 1940s, the war and political infighting among the Communists and Socialists undermined the thrust of radical dissent. Many young men, moreover, fought abroad and few had the time or desire to engage in specifically political activities. Those who did not fight overseas either were attending to their education or were busily employed in the wartime industries. The political lassitude of the 1940s became even more pronounced among youth—and others as well—in the 1950s, encouraged partly by the almost single-minded economic ambitions of many and partly by the fear produced by Senator McCarthy's witchhunts. For the most part, the 1950s were years of political quiescence, and youth became known as the Silent Generation. Dissent, when it arose, assumed a cultural rather than political form, represented specifically in the literature and life styles of the Beatniks.

Almost on the very eve of the 1960s, the Silent Generation gave way to a resurgence of political consciousness among American youth. On February 1,

---

[4] Seymour Martin Lipset, "The Dimensions of Student Involvement," in Seymour M. Lipset and Gerald Schaflander, *They Would Rather Be Left* (Boston: Little, Brown, 1971).

[5] Lipset, "The Dimensions of Student Involvement."

1960, in a small North Carolina town, four young black students unwittingly initiated a massive wave of protest demonstrations against racial discrimination by refusing to leave a lunch counter meant only for whites. Eventually, thousands of white and black youth were caught up in the black student efforts and by 1962, according to Southern Regional Council estimates, more than 70,000 people had participated in demonstrations throughout the country.[6] Numbers were not the only salient thing about the new politics; diversity was represented as well. In addition to the Student Nonviolent Coordinating Committee (SNCC), which arose to coordinate the black student movement in 1961, the Students for a Democratic Society (SDS) and the right-wing Youth Americans for Freedom (YAF) became a part of the political landscape.

The politics of young people in the United States in the 1960s were notable for more than their diversity. Most importantly, they seemed to help shape policies and public opinion, something which had not happened in the movements of the 1930s. Among those occasions when youth, per se, played a prominent role in politics were the Mississippi Freedom Democratic Party in 1964, and Eugene McCarthy's presidential campaign in 1968. The antiwar effort, which ultimately became the cause of a large majority of the population, in large measure owed its origins to the continuous concern of a few young people and peace groups. And some have suggested that even the unparalleled success of George Wallace's third party movement in the 1968 election owed much to the efforts of young people.[7]

There is another, final observation which results from using the historical perspective on youth and their politics in the United States. It is that there are important recurrent characteristics of those young people who have chosen throughout history to be the activists of their generation. Most of them have been well educated, members of the young intelligentsia of the nation. Further, many have been members of the middle or upper classes, the urban middle classes in particular, rather than the working classes. Whether because they permit a kind of liberation from basic needs, as Richard Flacks suggests in one of his essays in this collection (Reading 17), or because they foster a kind of intellectual enlightenment, wealth and education are important preconditions of political protest among youth, regardless of social conditions or historical epoch. This same theme will reappear later in our discussion of the Comparative Perspective. (In Reading 23, Lewis Feuer dwells at length on these aspects of youth movements.)

There are, in sum, three important conclusions that emerge from observing youth and their politics in the United States through historical lenses. The first is that American youth in the 1960s and more recent times were by no means the first generation of young people in the world to be active in politics. The second is that there have been prior occasions in American history when youth were especially active in politics, although none involved the magnitude of the movement in the 1960s. And the final one is that, regardless of epoch, wealth and education seem to characterize the young activists.

---

[6] Southern Regional Council, "The Student Protest Movement: A Recapitulation" (September 1961), 16 pp., mimeo., p. 3.

[7] Seymour Martin Lipset and Earl Raab, "The Wallace Whitelash" *Trans-Action* 7, no. 2 (December 1969): 23–32, 34 and 35.

Social Psychological Perspective

In comparison with the historical point of view, which can reveal to us what is unique and not so unique about the political style of American youth today, the social psychological approach can show us some of the general principles involved in the transmission of political beliefs from one generation to another. The scheme is not quite so simple as it might appear. In fact, there are four main ways of looking at political learning: the psychoanalytic; the cognitive development; the social learning; and the role theory.

Four models of socialization. The origins of the first model, the *psychoanalytic,* rest of course with Sigmund Freud and his concern with the development of the separate facets of the personality—the *id, ego,* and *superego*—in the context of the family. Recently, the psychoanalyst Erik Erikson has modified the thrust of some of Freud's original ideas and focused greater attention on the problems involved in achieving an integrated identity, among adolescents in particular. To Erikson, the central concern of psychoanalysis is the ego process, "the organizational principle by which the individual maintains himself as a coherent personality with a sameness and continuity both in his selfexperience and in his actuality for others." [8]

The psychoanalytic model has had special impact on the views of political learning, especially with regard to assumptions about the developmental basis of political beliefs in the family, the role of authority figures in political learning, and the potential expression of so-called "identity crises" in different political forms. There are those, for instance, who believe that the quality of the relationship between a child and his parent, in particular between son and father, will help shape the child's attitude towards political authority. Some feel that a positive and warm relationship will enhance the child's respect for political authority, while others claim just the opposite.[9] In addition, certain followers of the Erikson tradition have sought to interpret recent political actions by young people in ways compatible with his framework of analysis, among them Jacob Fishman and Frederic Solomon who developed the notion of "prosocial" group identity to describe the political activities by young people "on behalf of ideals, the social good, and towards the benefit of others." [10]

The *cognitive development* model of learning, which owes its origins to the Swiss psychologist-philosopher Jean Piaget, focuses on the development of the

---

[8] Erik Erikson, *Identity, Youth and Crisis* (New York: W. W. Norton, 1968), p. 73.

[9] For a discussion of the possible impact of authority in relationship to the family political socalization process, see Robert Hess and Judith Torney, *The Development of Political Attitudes in Children* (Chicago: Aldine Press, 1967), especially Chapter 5; Dean Jaros, Herbert Hirsch, and Frederic J. Fleron, Jr., "The Malevolent Leader: Political Socialization in an American Sub-Culture," Reading 12 in this book; and Robert LeVine, "Political Socialization and Culture Change," in *Old Societies and New States*, ed. Clifford Geertz (New York: Free Press, 1963), pp. 280–303.

[10] Jacob Fishman and Frederic Solomon, "Youth and Social Action: An Introduction," *Journal of Social Issues* 20, no. 1 (Winter 1964): 5. Portions of this article appear in Reading 15.

cognitive mental processes by which people structure their experience.[11] Cognitive developmentalists believe that there are certain stages through which people invariably will pass in the development of their mental processes. The distinctive characteristics of these stages, according to Lawrence Kohlberg, are: each stage is qualitatively different from every other one; individuals must move sequentially from a lower to a higher stage; each higher stage incorporates the learning and complexity of every lower stage; and each higher stage is more differentiated than each lower stage in terms of thought processes and cognitive development.[12] This emphasis on mental processes means that the environment, broadly speaking, plays a far less central role in learning than in other models of socialization. Recently, however, Kohlberg has modified the scheme to better account for the effects of environment, in particular its ability either to accelerate or impede learning.

Most germane to political learning is that facet of cognitive developmental research and theory which has dealt with the moral growth and development of children. Piaget, in a very early work, claims that there are two major steps in the development of moral judgment or conscience.[13] The first involves learning standards of right and wrong, while the second entails incorporating these principles into an actual experience of guilt or anxiety in committing prohibited acts. The development of these steps in the child is viewed as a change from moral realism to moral relativism. Until he is about seven or eight years old, during the "egocentric" period, the child's view of morality simply is a black and white one: certain acts are right, others are wrong; one must do the former, but not the latter. At this stage, the child is unable to distinguish between laws and the acts they govern. In the second stage, that of "relativism," the child is capable of discriminating laws from acts, as well as being able to judge the advantages and disadvantages of laws. Laws no longer are seen by him as having originated at the beginning of human history and having remained unaltered forever. Later in his life, the child develops an even greater sense of the relative values of laws and rules so that he is able to identify the kinds of circumstances which permit their violation. A somewhat more refined version of this stage-model of moral growth has been formulated by Kohlberg.

Different observers of political learning among young people have applied parts of the cognitive developmental model in interpreting children's conceptions of law, government, and politics, several of whom are represented in Readings 3 and 4.

A third major model of learning is the *social learning* point of view. Inasmuch as there is no single school of social learning, our discussion must needs be simplified, emphasizing the similarities in outlooks.[14] Generally speaking, learning theorists conceive of two types of processes in the acquisition of social

---

[11] For those readers unfamiliar with Piaget's work an excellent introduction is to be found in Herbert Ginsburg and Sylvia Opper, *Piaget's Theory of Intellectual Development: An Introduction* (Englewood Cliffs, N.J.: Prentice-Hall, 1969).

[12] Lawrence Kohlberg, "Stage and Sequence: The Cognitive Developmental Approach to Socialization," in *Handbook of Socialization Theory and Research,* ed. David Goslin (Chicago: Rand McNally, 1969).

[13] Jean Piaget, *The Moral Judgment of the Child* (New York: Harcourt, Brace & World, 1932).

[14] For a discussion of the different kinds of learning theory, see Edward Zigler and Irvin L. Child, "Socialization," *Handbook of Social Psychology,* vol. 3, ed. Gardner Lindzey, rev. ed. (Boston: Addison-Wesley, 1968).

behavior by the child. The first comprises learning based on direct training whereby particular agents, for instance parents or teachers, attempt to train the child to adopt certain types of behavior through the reinforcement of that behavior. This type of teaching is explained in terms of such notions as stimulus-response, discrimination, and generalization. The second process simply is observational learning and involves notions like imitation, identification, and modeling. The child learns by matching his response to cues provided by the responses of the other person, a "model." The development of a conscience also proceeds differently depending on the process: in the first case, it proceeds by direct training, while in the second it develops by virtue of observational learning, identification, and internalization.

Despite its evident applicability to political socialization, not until recently has the social learning model been systematically applied to this area. The interested reader may want to examine Herbert Hirsch's *Poverty and Politicization* (New York: Free Press, 1970). (Hirsch, incidentally, is the coauthor of Reading 12 in this book.)

The fourth and final model of socialization is *social role* theory, first introduced in the writings of two sociologists, George Herbert Mead and Charles Horton Cooley.[15] This model, like social learning theory, claims that a child learns by means of identifying with, as well as imitating, the behavior of important people in his environment. The elements of interest, however, are the social role and the ways in which the child learns through role-taking and role-playing. Mead, like Piaget, employs a developmental sequence to explain this learning process. In the first stage of development, the child acquires the "rules of the game" by imitating the behavior associated with the roles of single "significant others" in his environment, for instance his father or mother. In the second stage, the child develops a general conception of how each and every person important to him acts and reacts, a conception Mead calls the "generalized other." The idea is similar to Freud's concept of *superego,* and to our commonsense idea of a conscience.[16] Of special importance, according to Cooley, are the small, intimate groups that provide the setting for most social learning and otherwise are known as "primary groups." Examples of these are the family, the play group, and the work group.

In the area of political learning, social role theory has been specifically applied to problems entailed in young people's ability to identify with, and respond to, salient political figures, such as the President. Reading 3 in this reader deals directly with some of these matters.

These are, then, the four principal ways for looking at how people acquire their political attitudes and behavior. It should be evident that there are some important similarities and differences among the models. Three of them—the psychoanalytic, the social learning, and the social role—place a common emphasis on the influence of important figures in socialization. The social learn-

---

[15] The works by the two authors that are most pertinent to this discussion are: Charles Horton Cooley, *Human Nature and the Social Order* (Boston: Scribner, 1902), and George Herbert Mead, *Mind, Self, and Society* (Chicago: University of Chicago Press, 1934).

[16] Frederick Elkin, *The Child and Society: The Process of Socialization* (New York: Random House, 1960), p. 40. This book, by the way, provides an excellent introduction to socialization mainly via social role theory. The author not only writes plainly, but also makes systematic comparisons among the several types of socialization schemes.

ing and social role theories differ radically from the cognitive development model inasmuch as they place a great deal of stress on the environment.[17] And social role theory differs from the others since it accepts the idea that socialization may be a lifelong process, while the others tend to view socialization as being concentrated primarily in the early years of a person's life.[18] In the absence of any clear and systematic theory of political socialization per se, however, these differences and others as well tend to be overshadowed by basic similarities and by the gain achieved in using the four approaches together.

Agencies of socialization. Most of the political socialization that occurs in the United States seems to take place through the efforts of three agencies: the family, the peer group, and the school system. The first two of these tend to rely on informal mechanisms for transmitting knowledge, including role-models. Variations in the cohesiveness and warmth of the family and comparable aspects of the peer group seem to play an important part in the efficacy of socialization as well. The school, in contrast, has both informal and formal techniques of training at its disposal. The first comprise such things as the characteristics of teachers, who may act as role-models for students, and the general social composition of the school. And the second consists principally of the content of the curriculum.

The most important aspect of the agencies of socialization is the degree and scope of their influence over the child's learning. In the United States, the family has the most pervasive influence on political learning, according to Herbert Hyman's pioneering work, *Political Socialization* (New York: Free Press, 1969) and many of the early studies reported therein. Hyman's claim was based largely on the consistently high statistical correlations uncovered between the party preference of adults and their children. Recent studies imply, however, that the influence of the family in the United States is limited perhaps just to the transmission of party preference.[19] One such investigation suggests that most political learning occurs within the school, elementary school in particular, while others report that neither the family nor the school have an especially significant effect on political learning.[20] (See Readings 5 and 7.)

It seems likely that shifts in influence from the family to other agencies have

---

[17] An excellent discussion of the differences between cognitive development and social learning theories with special regard to the process of moral growth is presented in Eleanor Maccoby, "The Development of Moral Values and Behavior in Children," in *Socialization and Society*, ed. John A. Clausen (Boston: Little, Brown, 1968), pp. 227–69.

[18] Orville Brim and Stanton Wheeler pay particular attention to this facet of social role theory in Orville Brim, Jr., *Socialization After Childhood* (New York: John Wiley, 1966).

[19] Besides the article by M. Kent Jennings and Richard Niemi, "Transmission of Political Values from Parent to Child," which deals with this subject and is included in this collection, Reading 5, the reader should examine the several papers in *Harvard Educational Review, Special Issue on Political Socialization* 38, no. 3 (Summer 1968).

[20] For a study which suggests the importance of the school, see Robert Hess and Judith Torney, *The Development of Political Attitudes in Children* (Chicago: Aldine Press, 1967). Studies demonstrating little effect on the part of either the family or the school include those cited in Footnote 19, together with the article by M. Kent Jennings and Kenneth Langton, "Political Socialization and the High School Civics Curriculum in the United States," included here as Reading 7.

taken place in the past few decades in the United States, matching those in other realms. At the same time, new agencies seem to be emerging, such as the mass media, that presage important changes in the political transmission process.

Stratification and socialization. Socialization is a conservative force in the United States as in other societies. It insures that beliefs of one generation pass, almost untouched and unaltered, to another generation. In no case is this principle more clearly demonstrated than in the way in which social stratification is reinforced by the political socialization process, in particular in terms of the influence of social class, race, and sex-role differences on political learning.

Consider social class. For a long time, social scientists have been aware of the substantial differences in the political orientation and participation of members of different social classes in the United States. People in the middle and upper classes tend to be Republicans, conservative on economic matters, liberal on civil rights issues, active in groups, political organizations in particular, and among the prominent civic leaders of their communities.[21] Just the opposite set of traits characterize people in the working classes: a tendency to be Democrats, liberal in economic and welfare issues, conservative on civil rights, and pretty much inactive in politics.

Almost without exception, parallel findings are revealed among youngsters, as early as the seventh and eighth grades. According to Fred Greenstein, in Reading 10:

> the New Haven findings . . . suggest that there are even more deeply imbedded psychological impediments to the participation in politics of lower-status groups. These barriers to participation seem to result from lack of self-direction and self-confidence and from inability and unwillingness to express personal feelings and ideas. It is especially notable that lower socioeconomic status children do not share the explicit unwillingness to participate in politics found among adults of the same background. But they *do* show a greater deference toward political leadership; unlike upper-status children they do not begin to display in sixth, seventh, and eighth grades a sense that political choices are theirs to make—that *their* judgments are worth acting upon. And this seems part of a much larger pattern in the socialization practices of American status groups. (p. 178)

The substance and spirit of Greenstein's findings have been seen elsewhere, in other American communities and at other times.[22]

Differences in political orientations are passed from one generation to another in areas of stratification other than social class. Disparities in the levels of political interest and knowledge between men and women in the United States, for instance, are matched at an early age by those between boys and girls.[23] Boys, for instance, tend to know more about political affairs and to pay closer attention to them than girls.

---

[21] Many different studies report these and similar findings. A good summary is found in Lester Milbraith, *Political Participation* (Chicago: Rand McNally, 1965).

[22] Hess and Torney, *The Development of Political Attitudes in Children*; Herbert Hyman, *Political Socialization* (Glencoe, Ill.: Free Press, 1959).

[23] Fred I. Greenstein, *Children and Politics* (New Haven, Conn.: Yale University Press, 1965); Hyman, *Political Socialization.*

More than just attitudes and knowledge are passed along, however. This becomes especially evident in the case of racial and other subcultural differences in political learning. In addition to setting aside the mistaken conception that political socialization in the United States is a uniform process throughout society, studies of blacks suggest a widespread, deeply felt sense of distrust towards the United States government. As Eugene Green reveals in Reading 11, this cynicism extends even to such presumably revered symbols as the President. In effect, a culture of poverty in the United States seems to have bred its political counterpart, a culture of cynicism.

There are many political movements now afoot in the United States, and one wonders how these might affect the process of political transmission by different social groups. Will the women's liberation movement affect the sex-role differences between boys and girls, for instance? Or will the black protest movement radically alter the content of political learning among black youngsters? Even more to the point, can any of these contemporary political movements be successful without radically changing political socialization practices?

Comparative Perspective

By themselves, the historical and social psychological perspective cannot convey the full complexity of young people's politics in the United States, mainly because they are not meant or able to probe variations in contemporary social structures and cultures. This gap is filled by the comparative, or cross-cultural, approach. In particular, the approach incorporates two related strategies. One involves a search for similarities and differences, independent of cultural boundaries. This permits one to arrive at principles common to all young people's politics. The other entails relating any similarities or differences to the characteristics of nations, thereby enabling one to pinpoint the structural and cultural conditions productive of particular styles or levels of political activity.

Consider some of the major similarities in the politics of youth across the world first. Most of the current activism of youth has been concentrated among those in attendance at universities, for reasons noted below.[24] Within the universities, in industrialized countries especially, most of those students who engage in activism concentrate in the social sciences and humanities, a result no doubt of the content of these disciplines and their appeal to students of certain political persuasions. Activism also seems to be concentrated among students from middle-class backgrounds, or with middle-class aspirations, a lesson of the historical perspective too. In the industrialized nations this seems to occur because such students are a "liberated generation," without special material wants, while in developing nations this appears to result from unknown job opportunities as well as unclear career paths. Ethnic minority members also seem to have a special attraction to contemporary political activism as, for in-

---

[24] An excellent comparative piece on these and similar issues is provided by Donald K. Emmerson in his conclusion to the reader he edited on student politics in developing nations. See Donald K. Emmerson, ed., *Students and Politics in Developing Nations* (New York: Frederick A. Praeger, 1968).

stance, in the case of Jewish students as well as that of black students in the United States. And the rallying cries of most young activists throughout the world seem to be the same as well: the increasing impersonalization of life, together with growing technology and bureaucracy. (See Reading 20 by Raymond Aron.)

The one similarity that overshadows all others is the salience of education, a point also revealed by the historical perspective. Whether one looks at the experience of the developing or the developd nations, the political awakening of the contemporary era is experienced most frequently and forcefully by the young intelligentsia. The specific reasons for this are many. In general, education provides a common social location as well as a means of communication among youth. It thus helps to facilitate an awareness of similar dissatisfactions at the same time as it allows for the easy transmission of tactics of revolt. Reasons also differ from one country to another. In some instances, education has meant the creation of marginal values inasmuch as it entails traveling to other cultures for university training. In other cases, it has created an acute realization of the limitations of social institutions, government in particular, as well as suggesting the need to alter the material basis of society.

But there are also substantial differences in the politics of youth throughout the world. Comparing young people in Latin American countries with those in the United States, one finds a much more fully-developed tradition of activism among the Latin American youth coupled with a greater share in the administration of the universities. A somewhat similar observation emerges from contrasting Japan with the United States. Not only have Japanese youth been politically organized for a longer period of time, since the formation of the *Zengakuren* in 1948, but they also have played a more central role in shaping Japanese policy.[25] A different observation can be drawn from comparing French and American youth, the former of whom were able in 1968 to create a temporary alliance with workers, thereby creating the basis for a nationwide strike. Doubtless, such an event is unlikely to occur soon in the United States.

Differences like these as well as others noted in Readings 19 and 20, prompt a search for cultural and structural variations, and lead us into a discussion of the second major strategy of the comparative approach. Among the most suggestive analyses of the correspondence between societal variations and styles of youth politics is that of Kalman Silvert. Based on the correspondences he observed in Latin American nations, he writes as follows:

> *Situations of Stable Traditional Societies.* In very rudimentary, almost bi-class social structures, necessarily governed under crude dictatorial forms, students normally play a very limited role in innovation and political activity . . .
>
> *Situations of Beginning Modernization and Disarray.* As the city begins to grow, as an industrially oriented middle class emerges, and as the politics of change begin to operate, students assume a most important role in the importation and adaptation of ideology, in the organization of power as well as of ideas, and in government itself . . .

---

[25] See Michiya Shimbori, "Comparison Between Pre- and Post-War Student Movements in Japan," *Sociology of Education* 37, no. 1 (Fall 1963): 59–70.

More Mature Situations of Temporary Resolution. When the social structure is relatively complex, politics turbulent, and at least interim political decisions are made with the immediate future in mind, student groups are usually very active but limited in their role by other established interests . . . usually the university as an institution begins to turn inward, preparing to meet the demand for professionalism that always arises in times of rapid economic and political development . . .

Situations of Institutional Complexity and Relative Strength. Where the student finds himself in a plural-interest structure and complex class system, his relative power becomes even more limited. . . . In these situations the students may and usually do have much influence over university policy and affairs, but in national politics their role must of necessity depend on other, more primary definitions of interest.[26]

Silvert's analysis probably can be extended and used in other situations where major differences are to be observed in the state of economic and social development of countries. In the case of large, so-called post-industrial societies, other analyses are more fruitful, especially some of those suggested by Aron (Reading 20) and Flacks (Reading 17).

There are, in sum, both similarities and differences between the politics of young people in the United States and those of youth elsewhere. The overriding similarity is found in the concentration of activism among the young intelligentsia, while the differences seem largely to be ones of degree rather than style. Most of the major differences seem due, as Silvert suggests, to the stage of social and economic development of respective nations.

Development of Activism and Protest in America

The three perspectives—the historical, the social psychological, and the comparative—share a common concern with youth and politics, namely, a focus on the roots of young people's political activism. Recall, in particular, the principal observations of the historical and social psychological perspectives. The historical view taught us that the political activism of contemporary youth is unprecedented in America. And the social psychological perspective pointed to the impressive strength of socialization in perpetuating political styles and levels of political activism. Inevitably, we are led to inquire: What are the specific sources of young people's political activism in contemporary America?

By merging these three perspectives, we arrive at four possible sources of activism among youth in the United States. First there are certain *subcultural pockets of political cynicism* that during the 1960s contributed disproportionate numbers of young activists, among them families in the black middle class and white middle class of "Old Left" persuasion. The selections by Dean Jaros and his colleagues and by David Westby and Richard Braungart (Readings 12 and 16) discuss some of the possible dynamics underlying this source. Next are *socialization mechanisms*—for instance, permissive as compared with strict disci-

---

[26] Kalman H. Silvert, *The Conflict Society: Reaction and Revolution in Latin America*, rev. ed. (New York: American Universities Field Staff, 1966), pp. 123–24.

pline styles—that might produce activism. This matter is taken up in Reading 13. Third are *broad social changes,* such as the increasing availability of higher education to large numbers of young people, as well as important *historical events* like the Supreme Court ruling in 1954 on school desegregation. Jacob Fishman and Frederic Solomon, in Reading 15, argue for the importance of these types of conditions in prompting activism by young people. And finally there are certain *variations in college and university settings* that seem to prompt activism, among which are the size and quality of the school. John Orbell, in Reading 14, treats these in terms of black student activism.

The readings I have suggested here, together with others in Section V, are sufficiently comprehensive so that any discussion of mine would be quite superfluous. But it is useful to note, in broadest outlines, the portrait of the typical youth activist in the contemporary United States that emerges from these readings. He is a member of a subculture notable for its cynicism towards the larger society; a product of a warm and loving set of middle-class parents who fostered his independence and self-assertiveness; a student at a large, high quality university; white, but sometimes black; and most frequently a member of leftwing political organizations.

CONCLUDING REMARKS

This brief survey of perspectives on youth and their politics in the United States has been designed to illustrate the complexity of this area and, at the same time, to reveal both the distinctive and traditional qualities characteristic of this phenomenon. Recently, as we all know, the activism among young people in this country has raised some important questions. Before we turn to the selections of the reader, I wish to dwell briefly on two of these.

The first is one of long-standing interest to social scientists, especially those concerned with the appearance and development of political movements. Since the time of Karl Marx, many have believed that the underlying impetus to change is economic in origin and nature. My review of the historical and comparative materials on the origins of contemporary youth movements in the United States ought to dispel this myth. Not only has poverty—absolute or relative—been generally uncharacteristic of the social origins of the activists, it seems to have played little real part in the rallying cries of their dissent. Middle-class students, for the most part, comprise the young activists, children born of affluence with little interest in material goods or ambitions. Even in other nations, less wealthy and industrialized than the United States, economics has not appeared to be the single driving force of revolution.

Instead, we are witnessing a revolution by young people in which education plays the key role, serving to enlighten youth and to make them aware of the limitations of their societies, as I have noted already. In the broadest sense, political activism has emerged among the young intelligentsia, regardless of national and cultural boundaries. Education and its institutional wrappings have become the source of political dissent, in particular the university and its impersonality, the gap between those with access to education and those without it, and the frequent overtraining of the highly educated and their resulting inability to locate jobs commensurate either with their skills or values. Perhaps, from the point of view of those who still adhere to Marx's economic analysis, the central question nowadays in the United States is whether the young intelligentsia ever can overcome the chasm which separates them from the truly deprived, those genuinely in need of the fruits of revolution.

This brings me to my second point. Observers differ on the future course of the political activism of youth in the United States. Some, like Lewis Feuer, argue that these efforts will remain chiefly at the stage of "generational revolt," and thus ultimately be self-defeating. Others, like Richard Flacks, believe that these efforts represent only the beginnings of dissent that will develop in societies at advanced stages of technological development. At the heart of the matter, I believe, is the ability of the new style of youth politics in the United States to sustain itself, in particular to be able to recruit future generations of young people to replenish the membership, a problem faced by any group. To my mind, the question largely is one of organization; in the absence of any genuine organization, youth will be unable to have a permanent voice in politics, thus no base for changing society. The presence of organizations, whether of the type suggested by Flacks, or others, may well be the single thing on which hinges the ultimate fate of contemporary youth activism.

HISTORICAL SECTION

The political activism by American youth in the 1960s was not without historical precedent. Other nations at other times had witnessed political dissent by young people which sometimes served to shape national policy. But the protest by American youth in the 1960s was in many ways new for this nation. Youth qua youth began to demand and receive a larger voice in political affairs in this country.

The two articles in this section trace some of the historical roots of political activism by American young people. In the first one, Norman Birnbaum and Marjorie Childers briefly discuss the history of the American university and its relationship to the emergence of student political activism. They believe, among other things, that until recently the American university system acted to deprive students of their rightful power and responsibility on the campus. Their discussion of events in the 1930s and later is augmented by Hal Draper's intensive analysis of the American student movement in the 1930s. In a most interesting and informative article, Draper outlines the history of some of the different political groups that arose during this period as well as some of the controversies and national events that led to the rise and decline of the movement.

Both these articles should serve to remind us of the recent emergence of political activism by American young people, while also revealing to us the bearing of social conditions on these events.

1

THE AMERICAN
STUDENT MOVEMENT

NORMAN BIRNBAUM / MARJORIE CHILDERS

I

The present situation of the American student movement, and in particular of its militantly critical elements, seems very favourable. It has a large public outside the universities and a considerable following within them. Students and not their teachers determine the political atmosphere of the universities; administrators can no longer treat teachers and students alike as totally domesticated for fear of student protest. . . . The student movement, seems to be at the apex of the vast and often inchoate force of dissent which is engaged in a fundamental revision of American politics. However, an appreciation of its nature and possibilities (by contrast with the student movement in other societies) can only come as a result of an examination of its historical peculiarities.

The American university system in its present form is a system of historically, culturally, and socially stratified elements. The origins of the American universities in the seventeenth and eighteenth centuries were private. The universities (in those days and for most of the nineteenth century, in fact, "colleges" rather than universities in the modern sense) were almost invariably founded by and supervised by the several churches. Their aims were not the imparting of an elite culture characterised by knowledge, even by ritualised knowledge, nor yet the formation of an academic stratum (England and Germany representing the two types in question), but rather the induction of the young into the manners and morals proper to the American *bourgeoisie*. "Character" and not "intellect" were the marks of the educated man: Richard Hofstadter has shown how much of American anti-intellectualism can be traced back to a Protestant emphasis on the righteousness of the heart. As a consequence, the early American universities were concerned with discipline, with the regulation of the private lives of the students in the minutest details. The conception of the university as standing *in loco parentis*,

From *Student Power,* ed., Julian Nagel (London: Merlin Press, 1968), pp. 125–34; reprinted and abridged by permission of the authors and publisher.

still today an object of contention between students and universities, was born.

The juridical status of these private foundations was unequivocal: they were the property of their "trustees," united in a directorial body which owned the physical plant, made the rules, and could appoint and dismiss teachers at will as well as give degrees and regulate the lives of the students. The "trustees" were generally men of standing in church and community. Unable to regulate the daily working of the universities, they were represented in these by the presidents, appointed to serve at their pleasure, but exercising their authority over teachers and students. The strong position of the American university presidents, later to be described by Thorstein Veblen as "captains of erudition," cannot be explained by the necessity of coordinating complex modern academic institutions. It was strong before the American universities became either complex or modern, and is a derivative of the power of the "trustees." The initial status of the teachers, meanwhile, was often miserable: defective in status and remuneration, they often lacked genuine scholarly attainment and almost always showed a want of corporate self-consciousness and self-respect. The American university professoriat in the twentieth century is defective in almost none of these respects. Nevertheless, it is the lineal descendant of powerless ancestors: its own failure of corporate organisation against president and "trustees" is a mark of the continuation of a certain tradition.

The first American universities, or colleges, were scattered through the country. Their sites were determined by the movement of population, particular foundations often enough by confessional secessions within particular churches. With such variations as attached to the social composition of particular denominations or regions, they had a relatively uniform student body: young men drawn from mercantile and professional families, and destined for similar careers. The first major modification of this situation occurred after the Civil War, with the foundation of the land grant universities. The grant of land in question came from the federal government, and the Congressional act authorising the foundations referred to the necessity for the states to have institutions offering instruction in the practical arts. The land grant institutions were public, and they charged no tuition or little tuition. They did offer instruction in practical disciplines (the agricultural sciences, applied science in general) as contrasted to the more classical curricula of the established colleges. Administered by the several states, they set a pattern for public higher education which was to continue for nearly a century: greatly enlarged access to a practical higher education for the benefit of social groupings hitherto excluded from the universities. Despite the new form of public ownership of these universities, they generally followed the older ones in their systems of governance: state appointed trustees replaced church appointed ones.

The actual introduction of a university system in the European sense (with universities as sites of instruction and scholarship, as places of formation for future university teachers and scholars) waited upon the introduction of German models (the doctorate, the research seminar) at the end of the nineteenth century. From this has followed the pervasive American distinction between postgraduate and undergraduate instruction, the peculiar character of the American university as a fusion of English (collegiate) and German (university organised) types. The absence in America of a fully developed bourgeois idea of classical education made the introduction of a fully rationalised postgraduate education that much easier. The transformation of some of the older private foundations (Columbia, Harvard, and Yale), of newer private universities (Chicago and Stanford) and of the land grant institutions (California, Michigan, and Wisconsin) into great international centres of learning proceeded uninterruptedly from the end of the nineteenth century. The present world position of the American graduate schools has, at its origins, the feeble resistance of an older type of education to a newer conception of the division of intellectual labour. The American scholar and scientist has been free to develop extremely specialised skills, without worrying about their relationship to a defined general culture. Put in another way, we may say that a defined general culture in Europe expressed the political position of the educated middle class (liberal and empirical in Britain, positivistic and formally libertarian in France, metaphysical and bureaucratic in Germany). The educated middle class in America having by the end of the nineteenth century no political position of its own, a scholarship and a science without cultural content was possible. This in turn made possible the pragmatism, the adaptability, of science and scholarship in America: participants in an unreflective general consensus, the scholarly and scientific representatives of the educated middle class viewed the utilisation of the results of their work by other agencies with a certain detachment, in part compounded of resignation, in part of agreement. This gradually changed, at the beginning of the twentieth century, as we shall see subsequently.

II

What about actual student life in the colleges and universities up to the emergence of the modern American universities? There were disturbances and revolts, but these were mainly protests at familial tyrannies, and petty irritations attendant upon the assumption by the institutions of a generalised parental role. Two nineteenth century exceptions to this tendency are noteworthy. In the first instance, the formation in the nineteenth century of literary societies may be likened to a critical universities or free universities movement. The societies discussed those matters deemed important by the students, drawn from current intellectual controversy, which were not encompassed or insufficiently encompassed by the institutional curriculum. The societies arranged for lectures and discussions and even in some cases maintained libraries. Secondly, some American student bodies had an important role in the movement for the abolition of slavery which preceded the Civil War. Some colleges were actually stations on the

"Underground Railway," by which slaves were smuggled to Canada and freedom; others were centres of abolitionist agitation. In general, as access to universities widened, one political tendency was notable: critical thought and activity was often confined to established institutions with students bodies of relatively high social standing. Where, in general, institutions were newer and the generation studying there the first to do so, protest was rarely political.

With the movement of middle class social reform at the turn of the century and Woodrow Wilson's "New Freedom," the political role of the universities took on some of its present characteristics. The universities became reservoirs of governmental and administrative expertise: the interchange of personnel between the faculties of law, economics, politics and government began. The view that this somehow began with Franklin Roosevelt, diminished under Truman, was dropped under Eisenhower, and resumed under John Kennedy is factually incorrect. The present interrelation of government and the universities in America is a stage in a long-term development. More, the present interrelation of the universities and corporate enterprise—frequently mediated by the state and federal governments in their roles as patrons of the universities and of research programmes—was prefigured in the late nineteenth and early twentieth centuries. Wealthy industrialists endowed the private and sometimes the state universities on the implicit condition that they prove "useful" in the education of future elites and their technical subordinates, or in the pursuit of applied research. The composition of boards of "trustees" of the private and public universities, as new wealth replaced older forms of inherited property and status, reflected these changes.

The spiritual climate of the universities changed, as well, as the twentieth century progressed. The cultural domination of a Protestant elite whose cultural centre was Boston was shaken. Other, newer Protestant groups pushed forward—including a considerable contingent with a German national background, and many from the middle west of unquestioned Protestant moral earnestness but with no conspicuously high social status. After the first world war, the universities (especially the public ones in the cities) began to receive the offspring of the eastern European Jewish emigration: socially of limitless ambition, and culturally (on account of the traditions of learning institutionalised in Judaism) well able to master university work. The Catholic educated, meanwhile, were enclosed in their own institutions—which are only now (following those Catholic middle class and elite families who have refused to patronise the Catholic universities to the exclusion of the others) ending their isolation. Briefly, the atmosphere of the universities, both as a result of changes in their composition, in their tasks, and in the prevailing cultural climate, was rapidly secularised.

It was within this general setting that the modern, stratified, American university system emerged. At its apex were the great eastern private universities, of undisputed social prestige on account of their close association with the old elite, and also in the front rank in scholarship. Allied to them in prestige if not invariably in scholarship were the smaller elite colleges, and some of the newer women's institutions. The newer private universities, especially Chicago, were often distinguished with respect to scholarship. Chicago, indeed, provided university teachers for a whole range of institutions in the west—including great state universities like Wisconsin which were centres of learning in their own right. The new urban universities under local, public or private sponsorship developed especially in the 1920s (like the City College of New York). Grouped after these were an extreme miscellany of private and public institutions, with the institutions for Negro students—alas—unquestionably at the very bottom of the academic pyramid. The entire system of course exhibited extraordinary variety with respect to cultural and intellectual level, the degree of provincialism or cosmopolitanism manifest on the separate campuses, and the openness or otherwise of student bodies to new political and intellectual currents. In general, we shall be concerned with the institutions towards the top of the system—since these were the only ones, until recently, in which any student political activity was manifest at all.

III

Insofar as the question of student power entails student autonomy with respect to student affairs, or student participation in the wider governance of the universities, the United States has had a strikingly authoritarian university system. The assumption or usurpation by the universities of functions *in loco parentis* has meant that presidents and deans (generally not professors, who either have refused or have not been entrusted with such responsibilities) have dealt with matters which include the purely private sphere and which extend to questions of housing, student clubs and the like. The definition of the private sphere (inter-personal relationships, dress, sexuality) as fit matters for university supervision reflected, of course, the socialising task assigned to the universities (as well as the parvenu character of the population from which, increasingly, the students were recruited). With some exceptions for some of the socially elite institutions (where student participation has been confined to a gentlemanly policing of student honesty on examinations) discipline has been a resort of instances imposed on the students from above. As for student participation in matters of educational policy, this has been conspicuous by its absence. It is true that in some institutions students comment freely and publicly on the quality of the teaching they have received, but here again, no institutional mechanisms for student participation in the determination of educational policy have been devised. Student comment, in these circumstances, has been a parody of American consumer behaviour: the consumer is free to select amongst goods, but not to alter the structure of the market. It seems paradoxical that this general state of affairs has been accompanied by a relative ease of social relationship between teachers and students, free discussion in the class room, and other phenomena reflecting a social atmosphere different than that found in the European universities. In part, these phenomena reflect the obsessive pseudoegalitarianism of American society: real relationships of power, as well as real distinctions of cultural attainment, must remain unspeakable, since to name them would cause an ideological crisis. In part, this sort of social ease is possible precisely because it has had no political consequences: students may discuss all they like, but they have been powerless to act. Further, the relatively powerless status of the professoriat on the campuses has resulted in a genuine social rapprochement with the students, who know that their professors are in fact employees. Where professors themselves hardly share in the critical decisions relative to their institutions, finally, questions of student participation can hardly arise.

IV

It is interesting that recent challenges to this state of affairs have been inextricably bound to a conscious political onslaught on the entire American system of authority. It is to the student political movement, therefore, that we now turn. We have inimated that the politicisation of the campuses began with the movement of middle-class reform at the beginning of this century. Horrified by the excesses and crudities of primitive American capitalism, the educated middle class (which had its own interests in the development of employment for those with educational qualifications, in government, and the institutions of opinion formation) very early demanded the modification of capitalism in the direction of an American welfare state. This movement had its first broad student resonance on the campuses, as far as we can see, precisely when in the 1930s it was challenged on its left by a socialist student movement.

The recruitment of the educated middle class to important political functions, from the universities, proceeded individually from the beginning of the twentieth century. It is true that there were groups of teachers and students with political interests, even with scholarly programmes with political implications (those allied with Beard, or Veblen, or Commons), certain campuses, moreover, were centres of political thought (Wisconsin, for instance, from before the first world war). The organisation of the students into large political groupings waited upon the social convulsions of the 1930s and the attendant changes in American consciousness.

The New Deal brought thousands of the American educated into the governmental and political process. The general economic crisis of which the New Deal was a part radicalised thousands of others in the learned professions and in the universities. The Soviet Union, depicted in characteristically American terms as the "Soviet experiment," became an object of interest, indeed, fascination. A certain, if generally superficial, knowledge of Marxism developed alongside of further work in more indigenous traditions of social criticism. The influence of the European emigration was considerable in this respect. It is true that there had been a small if influential Intercollegiate Socialist Society before the first world war (including as members Walter Lippmann, John Reed and Upton Sinclair), which later became the adult League for Industrial Democracy. Mass student organisation, engaged in political conflict with university authority, first developed in the 1930s. It is significant that amongst the chief issues of contention was the students' right to political activity at all: bans on speakers, censorship of student newspapers, punishments for demonstrations, were frequently *causi bellicum*. By the middle of the 1930s a large popular front grouping, the American Student Union, claimed some 20,000 members—small in comparison with the total number of students but absolutely and relatively larger than that claimed by its spiritual successor, the Students for a Democratic Society, today. The group united Communists, progressivists, and a far larger number who might be described as left liberals. It mounted campaigns against military training on campus, against repressive authorities, but was significantly silent on many issues of university governance and policy. Its interest was in the daily politics of the American left, not in the alteration of university structures as such. Its tactics and strategy bespoke the twin influences upon it: the reformist liberalism of the left wing of the New Deal, and the popular front conceptions of the American Communist Party. Its long-term influence may be found in the political experience it gave to tens of thousands of students who passed through it en route to careers in government, the professions, the media of communications, or the universities themselves. A significant number of victims of McCarthyism (including those who victimised and degraded themselves by "confessing" and denouncing their former associates) were to be found in this group. A significant number of them came from the eastern European Jewish emigration, although a large number were of impeccably American lineage. The A.S.U. decomposed in 1939 with the Hitler-Stalin pact. Having concentrated exclusively upon issues of daily politics, it succumbed to these when the progressive-left liberal coalition broke up. It had implicitly made a breach in the apoliticism of many of the campuses, and it had established radical traditions at certain universities (Wisconsin, Berkeley, Michigan, Harvard, Columbia) which were to be revived a generation later—often by the very children of A.S.U. members.

The war, and America's subsequent imperial ascendancy, accelerated the social integration of the American intellectual generation which had studied in the 30s. It also was the occasion for an amplification and consolidation of the ties between the state and the universities. In the circumstances, the universities generally resisted the McCarthyite ideology of the late 40s and early 50s, but accepted the more refined anti-communism of the cold war. Student political activity diminished continuously from the late 40s onward; radical professors in the universities could be counted (not for particular universities but for the entire country) on the fingers of one set of hands. Others with latent radical dispositions thought it more discreet to conceal their critical intentions. Characteristically, the dominant political group in this period was an apolitical one, the union of student governments—governments which governed no one—known as the National Students' Association. This was mainly a vehicle for careerists in politics and government, and the recent publicity given to the subsidisation of the N.S.A. by the Central Intelligence Agency can hardly have surprised many who had to do with it. In this apolitical period, the student groupings attached to the regular political parties were not entirely dormant, and Young Democrats and Young Republicans solemnly mouthed the clichés of their elders. (This was a period, it must be recalled, in which Senator Hubert Humphrey was thought of as a man of the left . . .) The origins of the present wave of student protest, nonetheless, lie in this period: they are not alone political in a global sense but have to do with the new or heightened political functions of the universities.

The great expansion of the American universities, which now educate some 40 percent of the age group 18–22, began in the late 40s and 50s. This was the period of the rise of the University of California to national and international scholarly eminence, of great changes in the status and salaries of the professoriat (without corresponding changes in university government), of a vast increase in research funds at the disposal of the professors, of the final integration of the universities—in brief—in the system of administration and production as one of its key factors. Public commissions, recruited from the universities but responsive to the needs of government and industry, decided on the general allocation of research funds, on the nation's requirements for the "production" of manpower. The private universities receded in importance before the public ones, and even the private ones became increasingly dependent upon public monies. To accommodate these tasks, the internal organisation of the universities was increasingly rationalised: an assembly line system for the fabrication of graduates was devised, and the actual tasks of education were forgotten or themselves became the concern of a few specialists amongst other specialists—thought by many of their colleagues to be wasting their time in view of the opportunities for advancement and enrichment accessible in the new academic cornucopia.

2

THE STUDENT MOVEMENT
OF THE THIRTIES:
A POLITICAL HISTORY

. . . Most of the references one hears to the student movement of the thirties, and most published references, too, are quite wrong in one basic respect: they speak as if "the thirties" represented a single, homogeneous period for the student movement. But the biggest single fact about the history of this movement is that it went through a sweeping change in spirit, methods, and politics, which changed its face completely in midcourse. The present sketch will concern itself mainly with that transformation.[1]

1

This movement was newborn in 1931; it was not the continuator of a previously existing one. During the twenties there had been a small movement around a magazine called *The New Student,* but it had never created much of a stir. The "Lost Generation" reflected in F. Scott Fitzgerald's novels was (as he wrote in one of them) "a new generation . . . grown up to find all gods dead, all wars fought, all faiths in men shaken."

From *As We Saw the Thirties,* ed. Rita J. Simon (Urbana: University of Illinois Press, 1967), pp. 153–82; reprinted by permission of the publisher.

1 There is no published material on this, but a sound treatment can be found in the unpublished Ph.D. dissertation by George P. Rawick, "The New Deal and Youth" (University of Wisconsin, 1957). This is without doubt the only attempt at an outline history of the movement that is worth reading; it has the added advantage of including also the closely related story of the American Youth Congress as well as of the New Deal youth agencies. Also still worth reading is the 1935 book by the National Student League leader James Wechsler, *Revolt on the Campus* (New York: Covici-Friede, 1935), even though it deals with only the first period of the movement and of course is written entirely from the then NSL viewpoint. For this first period, it is especially good for great detail on the issues and battles of the student movement, about which I have put very little into this essay. I have leaned heavily on both Rawick and Wechsler's accounts for the factual framework.

The rebels too reflected the malaise of the society they rebelled against, as is so often true. *The New Student* thought that what was needed was a revolt in "manners and morals"; youth had to save the broken-down old world; some kind of change was necessary, something had to be done; "spiritually, this is an age of ruin and nausea." By 1923–24 there were a number of campus battles; but by 1924–25 "normalcy" and prosperity were returning, and *The New Student's* interests turned amorphously toward moral indignation with such phenomena as the growing "gigantism" of the universities, the evils of commercialized education, and the "quality of life." With increasing depoliticalization, the movement decayed into Menckenism, particularly enamored of Mencken's derision of bourgeois society from an elitist standpoint—one which was as contemptuous of the mass of people as it was of the "booboisie." By 1927 the magazine was confessing that "Where we used to dream of new faith and new communities developing out of colleges and flowering through a thankful country, now the main hope is that students will be less bored by lecturing. . . ." And by 1928 it was through. For the bulk of students, what reigned supreme were football, fraternities, and sex.

Then in 1929 the bottom fell out. It seemed as if the bottom had fallen out of the whole economic system. For there was no natural famine, no devastating war, no plague: it was as if the social machine simply broke inside and had ground to a halt. There was something referred to as "overproduction," which meant that too much wealth had been produced; and since there was too much wealth, millions were unemployed, factories were shut down, and breadlines grew. Apple sellers became a street sight; vaudeville entertainers sang "Buddy, Can You Spare a Dime?" The bodies of financial magnates rained down from upper stories of Wall Street executive suites; and other tycoons, like Charles M. Schwab, were convinced that the Social Revolution was just around the corner.

The social group hardest hit by the depression was the youth. In 1930, the census figure for unemployed of all ages was 3,187,647, and about one-fourth of these were in the fifteen to twenty-four age range. (According to other estimates, over one-third.) As of January, 1935, there were 2,876,800 youths between sixteen and twenty-four years of age who were on relief; and this was about 14 percent of the total for this age group. In 1938, one out of every five youths in the labor market was either totally unemployed or on work relief (not counting those working only part-time). This was the youth problem of the thirties: "unemployment for between 20 percent and 30 percent of all youth; scanty education for the great bulk of youth from families in the lower-income brackets; and an extreme intensification of all problems for Negro youth. Youth made up more than its share of the one-third of a nation ill-clothed, ill-housed and ill-fed." [2]

For this "Locked-Out Generation," the prospects of the student youth were correspondingly dim.

In 1935 one college president told a student assembly that the 150,000 students with degrees were emerging into a world which did not want

---

[2] Rawick, "The New Deal and Youth."

them. A Columbia University official said: "the social order is unable to absorb those who are annually graduated from our colleges and professional schools." (This was often true even for the highest-ranking men.) Another well-known educational institution, the U.S. Army, was getting a stream of college graduates at its Whitehall Street recruiting station in New York, and the New York *Post* explained that the attraction was "grub, prosaic grub." In 1934, the year I was graduated, it was estimated that one-third of the previous graduating class had been able to obtain no employment at all, and that another third had gotten jobs for which they had no interest, talent, or training. One college journal addressed an editorial to the graduating class headed "Into the Wasteland." There was an "Ode to Higher Education," of which one variation went like this:

> I sing in praise of college,
> Of M.A.s and Ph.D.s,
> But in pursuit of knowledge
> We are starving by degrees.

All this meant two other things, too: first, it was increasingly difficult to work one's way through college; and second, retrenchment in educational budgets reduced the opportunity for other students to go to college. A *Harper's* article of 1935 said: "In many respects, the post-1929 college graduate is the American tragedy. He is all dressed up with no place to go. . . ."

A whole section of the American middle class was being declassed; and the student movement was in part a result of this declassment.

2

The student movement that arose was initiated and launched by two radical youth groups, working separately: the Young Socialists and the Young Communists. This fact determined its whole history. Let us begin with the Socialist wing.

There had been a socialist student organization in existence since 1905, when Jack London, Upton Sinclair, and others formed the Intercollegiate Socialist Society. The I.S.S. later became the League for Industrial Democracy, an adult organization which maintained an intercollegiate department. But after the First World War, the college section of the LID was small and amounted to very little during the 1920s. It was only with the onset of the depression that it began to grow. Two years after the stock market crash the LID's annual student conference, held at Union Theological Seminary on the theme of "Guiding the Revolution," assembled 200 representatives from 44 colleges. In the presidential election of 1932 the Socialist candidate was Norman Thomas, whose campaign drew in a considerable number of students (including myself) and helped to build the LID's student organization.

By December, 1932, the college arm of the LID—at this point called the Intercollegiate Student Council—was chafing at being merely a department of an adult organization; and it was also facing competition from the Communists, as we shall see. Reorganization as an autonomous Student League for Industrial Democracy (SLID) gave it its own structure and a more independent life, but it never achieved independence in one respect: financially. The adult LID continued to pay its officers, whom it had originally appointed, and these remained, as before, Joseph P. Lash and Molly Yard. Lash, a graduate of The City College of New York in his early twenties, remained on as executive secretary of the SLID, and later of the American Student Union, right through the thirties, with Miss Yard as his first lieutenant. Both were members of the Socialist party. Lash also became editor of the SLID's new magazine, first called *Revolt* but quickly toned down to the *Student Outlook*.

It must be explained that the SLID was an amalgam of two fairly different kinds of socialist students: the "Yipsels" and the "LID types." The "LID types" were essentially liberal-social-democratic in their approach to politics, and sometimes not very political at all; they often tended to be colored by pacifist, Christian socialist views, and not infrequently were more liberalistic than socialistic. A young man at Swarthmore named Clark Kerr could fit into the SLID chapter there. In their own way, both Lash and Molly Yard were "LID types."

Numerically more important than the "LID types" were the student members of the Young Peoples Socialist League (YPSL—youth section of the Socialist party), commonly called "Yipsels." In the larger cities, where there were substantial young socialist groups, the Yipsels tended to dominate the SLID chapters, especially in New York City. (As student director of the New York organization of YPSL for several years, I was largely concerned with mobilizing Yipsels to help build the SLID chapter in the city.)

It is important to understand that, by and large, at this time the young Socialists constituted the left wing of a Socialist party which was itself rapidly going left throughout this period. The YPSL leaders, and an overwhelming majority of its membership, considered themselves to be revolutionary socialists, and, far from being influenced by the Communists in this regard, were utterly contemptuous of them, especially when the communist movement swung right after 1935. The Socialist party also swung sharply left in the thirties, though not enough to please the Yipsels. By 1935, as a result of the increased radicalization of its members and the influx of younger, more militant recruits, the party's extreme right wing (the "Old Guard") walked out. Later that year, the party accepted into its ranks the whole Trotskyist group (Workers party, with its youth group, the Spartacus Youth League, many of whom were already active in the student movement). Both the loss and the gain served to shift the balance of politics in the party even more to the left—until the latter part of 1937 when another split took place in the party along left-right lines, with the large majority of the youth organization going along with the left wing.

As long as the tone of the student movement remained militant, i.e., up to 1935, the tension implicit in the coexistence of these two socialist strains within the SLID occasioned little or no hostility. Besides, particular SLID chapters were usually either Yipsel-dominated or else "LID-ish," and went their own ways in practice, as "hards" and "softs," respectively. It was only with the rightward turn in 1935 that a clash developed.

3

The other source of the student movement came from the Communist students, and eventuated in the building of the National Student League. This part of the story is usually represented under the heading, "Communist Conspiracy Decides to Capture the College Campuses," etc. What actually happened is a good deal more interesting and more complex. Both for this initiatory period and for the later turns and changing course of the student movement's leadership, it is indispensable to understand the coeval turns of the Communist party line, which constitute the background. On the basis of this background, the story of what happened to the student movement is as clear as crystal; without this background, it is an insoluble mystery.

In 1929 the Communist International had launched all of its parties into what it baptized the "Third Period," a period of wildly ultraleft and ultrasectarian policies. The motivation came from the needs of the Russian regime. Having already liquidated the Trotskyist left opposition, the Stalin dictatorship now consolidated itself by turning against the Bukharin "right wing," and was driving hard toward the crystallization of the new Stalinist society in the image of the new ruling class. Internally, the turn toward mass bureaucratic collectivization of the land meant the adoption of terroristic policies toward the peasantry, and a rigidification of the party leadership's autocracy in all aspects of life.

Translated into terms of the satellite parties' tactics, the result was lunatic-fringe politics. (Maoist China, together with its faithful Maoist parties in other countries, is going through a sort of modified "Third Period" development today, for analogous reasons.) The revolution was officially announced to be just around the corner. Roosevelt was a fascist. The A.F. of L. and all of its trade unions were fascist, and the party line was to split the unions to form dual "Red" unions, like the National Miners Union. The socialists were another kind of fascists, called "social-fascists." There was nothing more important than to destroy their organizations, and no united front with them was permissible—except something called "the United Front from Below," which meant that "honest" socialist rank-and-filers were called on to support Communist activities in defiance of their own "social-fascist" leaders. Of all socialists, the left-wing socialists were the worst "social-fascists" of all. Party organizations were oriented toward underground secrecy whether necessary or no, and discipline was conceived in military terms.

The "Third Period" line was still going strong as official policy in 1931 and 1932, when the student movement got started. In 1933 the Communist International was giving signs of softening the line; by 1934 it was clearly on the way out; and in 1935 the decisive flipflop took place when the

Franco–Soviet military assistance pact was signed in May. (The French Communist party began voting for war budgets and militarization, and the line spread to other countries immediately.) Later that year, the new Popular Front line was formally inaugurated at the Seventh Congress of the Comintern.

The Popular Front line meant a 180-degree swing in Communist policy from ultraleft to ultraright. It, like the preceding course, was decisively motivated by Moscow's orientation in foreign policy. Having helped to stymie resistance to Hitler's seizure of power, the Kremlin now took fright at the Nazis' threats of a holy war against Communism. The widest possible military alliance against Germany, in anticipation of World War II, became the crash-program objective, to which all other considerations were subordinated. To push this perspective, the American Communist party, like others, spared no effort to convince Washington and the American power structure that Moscow, together with the Communist parties it kept in tow, was no longer a Red Menace, no longer even interested in revolution. That, in fact, it could be depended on as a respectable defender of the status quo—as long as America participated in a system of "collective security" (world bloc) against the danger from Hitler's Germany that might conceivably serve to "defend the Soviet Union" from attack from that quarter. All pretense at prosecuting a Leninist class-struggle policy was sold out in exchange for wooing the government into a foreign policy satisfactory to Moscow, naturally under anti-Nazi slogans.

Before the Popular Front period was over, nothing was too extreme for the Communist party to use to destroy its image as a Red Menace, including the dissolution of the party itself into a "Communist Political Association." Every bit of radical language in the Communists' program and propaganda was carefully translated into vague liberalese or unceremoniously abandoned or repudiated. The slogan became "Communism is Twentieth Century Americanism," and quotations from Marx and Lenin gave way to passages from Jefferson or Franklin or folksy evocations of Abraham Lincoln. President Roosevelt was transmogrified from a sinister fascist into a People's Hero, and every good Communist became the most fanatical New Dealer within ten miles. Communist front organizations were hastily retailored to the new style: for example, the "anti-imperialist" American League Against War and Fascism became the pro—"collective-security" American League for Peace and Democracy.

Not all of this happened at once. For example, by early 1936 when the Communist party nominated Earl Browder for President, the new line had not yet completely crystallized, but by fall it was clear that the party was advocating a vote for Roosevelt. Since Browder continued formally to run, the Communist press of September—October, 1936 presented one of the weirdest pictures in its checkered history.

While the Communist party was moving all the way right with bewildering speed, the Socialist party, as we have seen, was steadily going left. In 1936, for example, the Socialist party adopted statements against the danger of imperialist war and for a revolutionary transformation of American capitalism which marked an extreme leftward point for the movement, with the approval even of Norman Thomas. (Incidentally, Thomas was no longer a "fascist" or "social-fascist" in Communist treatments. He was now more likely to be denounced as an ultra-left adventuristic Trotskyite.) The YPSL was one of the important ingredients in the leftward pressure within the Socialist party, and pushed for more. Politically speaking, the Socialists and Communists crossed each other, going in opposite directions.

During the first part of the Popular Front period (1935–36), the obsessive concern of the Communist party was for "unity" with the Socialists in any way whatsoever. (This too was an internationalization of the Communist parties' course in Europe, where unity with the mass social-democratic parties could bring the desired respectability.) But by 1937–38 the Communists passed beyond this stage to wooing the real powers of the Establishment, from the Democratic party machines to the National Association of Manufacturers, about whom Browder made unctuous speeches "holding out the hand of friendship" to the "progressive capitalists" who understood the Menace of Hitlerism. Popular Front changed to "Democratic Front" and then to "National Front," as also in Europe where the Italian Communists reached the point of offering common cause with Mussolini's "good" fascists as against the bad Nazi fascists.

This part of the story came to an end with the Hitler-Stalin Pact of 1939, which gave the green light to the Nazis' launching of the Second World War. The nature of the Communists' concern with the menace of Hitlerism was adequately demonstrated when Molotov announced that "fascism is a matter of taste." But this was politically inconceivable to the student movement that was built during the "Third Period" and Popular Front days.

4

We can now return to the year 1931, when the student movement was beginning to stir. This was still in the murky depths of the fantastic "Third Period" line of the communist movement; and naturally the Young Communist League (YCL) was a tiny organization. The YCL's leadership, typified by Gil Green, had been handpicked for woodenheaded docility to the party line, now that every slightly critical element had been driven out as a "Trotskyite" or "Lovestoneite."

This leadership had no interest in orienting toward the organization of students, who were "petty-bourgeois" by definition and unstable intellectuals by occupation (just the kind who had caused so much trouble in the recent factional splits and expulsions). The "Third Period" dogma was that Communists were interested only in "proletarians," although the interest was not reciprocal, and the YCL leaders flatly feared intellectuals, with whom they could not cope in any discussion of their own phantasmagorical politics.

It can be flatly stated that the YCL did not initiate the organization of the National Student League (NSL) and did not want it. Yet it is also true that the NSL was formed by communist students. That these two statements are both true is a testimonial to the misleading simplism of the "conspiracy" theory of radical history.

In New York, where it got started, there were two hostile groups of communist students. The YCL hardliners, in agreement with their leaders, simply went to school and then hurried away to do their stint for the party or the International Workers Order or one of the other party fronts. The other group, consisting of some YCL'ers and a number of Communist sympathizers and fellow-travelers, held to a "student orientation"; that is, they believed in the possibility and utility of Communist organization of students on campus, in the teeth of the party line.

It was the latter group which initiated the New York Student League (predecessor of the National Student League), while the YCL leadership remained cold to the enterprise but did not prohibit the participation of YCL members in it. It was not until 1933 that the leaders went over wholeheartedly to the "student orientation," in part because of the salient success it had scored in making student Communists through the NSL's activities, and in part because (as we have mentioned) the "Third Period" line was already thawing by this time. By 1934 if not before, there was a complete rapprochement between the strategy and tactics of the YCL factions and the course of the NSL leaders; in fact, in this year the YCL inaugurated a comparable project of its own in the shape of the American Youth Congress.

The only teacher prominent in the organization of the National Student League was a young economics instructor at Columbia named Donald Henderson, who became the NSL's first executive secretary. When the university refused to renew his contract, a student strike on campus made the case a *cause célèbre*. (He later threw himself into work for the Communist-dominated Farm Equipment Workers Union, which absorbed his energies until his death.)

The NSL was one of the most successful of the Communist-led movements of the thirties, and it was also one of the most competently led. Among its top leaders were Joseph Starobin, Joseph Cohen (Joseph Clark), James Wechsler—all of New York—and, from the West Coast, Serril Gerber and Celeste Strack. In general, they were more imaginative and less muscle-bound in style than the cliché-ridden hacks who presided over other Communist party enterprises in the earlier years; in a real sense the NSL pioneered the Popular Front pattern which, after 1935, paid off so well for the Communist movement.

One of the first attention-drawing actions of the NSL was its sponsorship of a student delegation to Harlan County, Kentucky, where a desperate miners' strike was taking place, under the aegis of the National Miners Union, against brutal conditions and "legal" terror. The students were turned back from Harlan County by armed intimidation—in a manner somewhat reminiscent of what happened in the sixties to the Freedom Riders in the South. This was not the only attempt by student leaders to link the student movement with the labor movement (as their ideology demanded) but no other case garnered so much notice.

Then in 1932 came the Reed Harris case. Harris, the crusading liberal editor of the Columbia *Spectator*, ran stories exposing the bad conditions in the campus dining hall with regard to the preparation of food and treatment of student waiters. He was clumsily expelled, in the course of a series of events which highlighted the high-handedness and hypocrisy of the Columbia administration. (There have been some parallels since then.) This was the administration of Nicholas Murray Butler—"Nicholas Miraculous Butler," he was called—who was widely thought to have his eyes fixed on tenancy in the White House rather than Morningside Heights. Harris' expulsion precipitated a sort of small-scale free speech movement, with thousands of students coming out in a one-day strike to manifest their indignant protest. The result was mainly a victory; Harris was reinstated, although he had first to make some concessions. The affair was a boost to the NSL, which had organized and led it, and to the student movement in general, particularly in New York City.

The arrival of the Roosevelt administration in 1933 had the effect of heightening political consciousness among the students, as it also did among the general population. A "National Conference of Students in Politics," sponsored by the SLID, took advantage of and reflected this development. The NSL participated in it too, as did the student divisions of the YMCA and YWCA, student Christian associations, and some student service groups. There was a substantial list of eminent professors who allowed their names to be used as sponsors: Charles Beard, Morris R. Cohen, Jerome Davis, John Dewey, and Reinhold Niebuhr. Politicians on the list included Norman Thomas, Philip La Follette, and two senators. It was typical of such gatherings that, although there was a large number of liberals present, it was the Socialists and Communists whose discussions (and disputes) dominated the proceedings, not (in this case) by manipulation but simply because the liberals had nothing distinctive to say. They tended to follow in the wake of the radicals, who set the ideological tone.

5

Perhaps the greatest impetus to the student movement came from the war question.

There is no question but that there has never been a generation of youth more concerned about the danger of war than this one. Their attitude toward this danger was unmistakable: some of the polls and surveys showed a depth of opposition among large masses of youth which was unprecedented. In 1933 a sampling of 920 Columbia students included 31 percent who considered themselves absolute pacifists—almost one-third; another 52 percent stated they would bear arms only if the country were invaded; only 8 percent said they were willing to fight for the United

States under any circumstances. A national poll showed 39 percent who said they would not participate in any war, and another 33 percent who would do so only if the United States were invaded.

The students obviously did not share the attitude of some of their mentors, like the Fordham dean who denounced student antiwar activity with these words: "They are making fools of themselves. . . . What war are they worrying about anyway?"

The mounting consciousness of the danger of war crystallized politically around the "Oxford Pledge," an English import. In February, 1933, the Oxford Union, following a debate, had passed a resolution which announced that under no circumstances would they "fight for King and country." This was adopted by a vote of 273 to 153; when Randolph Churchill made a motion at the next meeting to expunge this offense to patriotism, the pledge was sustained by an even higher vote, 750 to 175. The sentiment was echoed at other English universities, including Leicester, Manchester, and Cambridge.

In the United States the Oxford Pledge, while retaining the name, was quickly translated into American as a refusal "to support the United States government in any war it may conduct." For the next period the Oxford Pledge was the platform of the student antiwar movement.

It will be noted that the American version does not say quite the same thing as the Oxford version of the Oxford Pledge. The difference was deliberate. It was formulated here by student leaders who, both Socialist and Communist, regarded themselves as Marxists and did not want to make the pledge a statement of absolute pacifism—a viewpoint which was virtually nonexistent among the Communist leaders of the NSL and infrequent in the leaderhip of the SLID nationally or locally. Hence the American pledge was pointedly *not* worded to read as a refusal "to support any war which the U.S. government might conduct." Instead, it was politically directed against support of the *government* in any war.

In 1934 the two radical student organizations launched what seemed to many at first a rather wild idea, but which turned out to be the most successful single action of the movement: a "Student Strike Against War." The date was set to commemorate the entrance of the United States into the World War, and it took place on April 13, 1934. It was actually only a "demonstration strike," scheduled for one hour, from 11:00 to noon, but it did call on all students to "walk out" of their classrooms. (This was intended literally; students were asked not to cut classes but to go to their scheduled class and leave with as many others as possible.)

At this point the political orbits of the Socialist and Communist students were at perigee. The Communists had already pulled out of the "revolutionary" buffoonery of the "Third Period" but had not yet entered on the complete abandonment of revolutionary tactics which was going to characterize the Popular Front period. On their side, not only the YPSL but even the Socialist party itself had adopted resolutions on the war question which were thoroughly revolutionary-socialist in content and phraseology (in fact, this was one of the main reasons why its "Old Guard" right wing split away). If, as we have said, the Socialists and Communists were crossing each other as they went in opposite political directions, it was during the period from 1934 to the middle of 1935 that they were closest.

There was therefore little difficulty in achieving complete NSL-SLID cooperation in the organization of the first student antiwar strike. To the surprise of its sponsors, it also achieved a considerable measure of success, especially in its public impact. In spite of a barrage of threats and pressure from administrations, about 25,000 students participated in 1934. To be sure, about 15,000 of these were in New York City—and of these, in turn, nearly half were probably accounted for by the three city colleges, City College of New York (CCNY), Brooklyn College, and Hunter. At other campuses the number was not impressive as yet, but the public sat up and took notice. Attempts to intimidate the student strikers at CCNY, Harvard, and Johns Hopkins added to the headlines.

The number of participants took a big jump on April 12 of the following year. The second Student Strike Against War in 1935—focused, like the first, on the Oxford Pledge—drew about 150,000 students nationally, according to the student organizations. This claim was probably not much exaggerated provided one notes the qualification that not all of these 150,000 actually participated in a "strike," that is, a walkout from classes. In some places a more usual form of demonstration or meeting was substituted.

The figures were still highest in New York City, with Brooklyn College easily leading again with 6,000; CCNY and Columbia each had 3,500 out. Philadelphia did well, with 3,000 at the University of Pennsylvania and 2,500 at Temple. In the Middle West, the biggest strikes took place at the Universities of Chicago, Minnesota, and Wisconsin. On the West Coast, Berkeley came in, at 4,000, with the second largest demonstration in the country; but even Stanford had 1,500. This time the movement was nationwide: there was some kind of manifestation on over 130 campuses in all regions of the country, including nearly 20 in the South.

This was a great shot in the arm for the student movement, but the fact is that this image of a national mass movement had been projected by the work of comparatively small groups of radical students. To take the example of my own campus, Brooklyn College, which had seen the largest strike in the country for both years: there were probably about thirty active members each in both the SLID and NSL chapters, give or take another dozen. If about 95 percent of the student body came out on the strike, in the face of administration threats of disciplinary action and the violent opposition of the student newspaper, this was an index not to the size of the *direct* organizational influence of either group but rather to the climate of social and political opinion among the students generally. I doubt whether there was at any time during this period a number of student-movement activists greater than there are today (1965), though there are two important qualifications to be added: the total student population in the universities and colleges was much smaller then and the student leaderships insisted on more compact and efficient organization than is common today. The main difference was in the times.

6

The years 1934—35 were not only those in which the Communists and Socialists came closest together politically, but also those in which the Communists, having abandoned the doctrine that Socialists were "social-fascists," started going all-out for "unity" with those whom it had so recently stigmatized. On the student field, the NSL started proposing unity with the SLID in 1934. With cooperation in two student strikes behind them, and increasing cooperation in other projects, the SLID began to look favorably upon the proposal. By 1935, as their own line toward "unity" blossomed internationally, the Communists seemed ready to make almost any concession to get agreement. Within the SLID, the left-wing YPSL also was favorable to merger, feeling that in a united student movement their own politics would have a larger field to operate in. Another source of pressure toward merger was the growth of the NSL, which threatened to overshadow the SLID.

In June the national executive committee of the SLID voted for fusion, and the unity convention was held during Christmas week in Columbus, Ohio. The new organization formed there was called the American Student Union.

There was a considerable bloc of previously unaffiliated liberals at this convention, but, as before, they played no independent role. The agreements, disputes, and discussions emanated from the Socialist and Communist blocs. By this time, not only the Franco-Soviet Pact but also the speeches and documents of the Seventh Congress of the Comintern had begun to make clear the direction of the Popular Front policy. The entire international Communist movement, including the American party with its usual automatism, had already by this time abandoned its anti-war policy and, in all countries earmarked for the anti-German alliance, was headed in the direction of classic jingoism. Soon there were going to be no more shrill "patriots" than the Communists.

The NSL line had not yet been overtly affected. Even though, outside the student field, the Young Communist League had dutifully made clear that the Oxford Pledge was now obsolete, the leaders of the NSL formally stated that the Oxford Pledge would be maintained, in answer to a challenge from the Socialists. In fact the process of coordinating the student movement with the new Communist prowar line was going to take two years, up to the Vassar convention of the ASU at Christmas-time 1937, whereas elsewhere Communist-dominated organizations were able to carry out the flipflop in weeks or months. The difference was due entirely to the bitter fight made against this turn by the Yipsel forces in the SLID.

At the fusion convention, therefore, all was not sweetness and light, as might have been the case if the merger had taken place a few months earlier. One sticky question was the attitude of the ASU toward the Russian regime. In a compromise, a resolution referred to the Soviet Union only as an example of a "non-imperialist" nation whose "peace policy" deserved support—a formulation which was then satisfactory to the left-wing Socialists too. Another problem, the relationship of the ASU to the Communist front organization which then still called itself the American League Against War and Fascism, was settled by an agreement not to affiliate with any such body except by a three-quarters vote of the national committee.

The main dispute took place over the question of war policy. In line with the preconvention pledge of the NSL leadership, the Oxford Pledge was re-endorsed, by a vote of 244—49 (the 49 were liberals who agreed with the *new* Communist line of "collective security" and had no reason to weasel over it). But when the Socialist bloc introduced a resolution which included the idea that the Oxford Pledge would still be applicable even if the United States were aligned with Russia in the war-for-democracy toward which the Communists now looked, this was defeated 155—193 by the combined votes of the Communists and pro—collective-security liberals against the Socialist left wing. But this was still only a negative action, as compared with the later complete endorsement of American foreign policy when the ASU came under unchallenged Communist domination.

The leadership of the new organization was divided according to preconvention agreement. Three "LID types" became national officers: Lash as executive secretary, George Edwards as national chairman, and Molly Yard as treasurer. NSL'ers took the posts of high school chairman, field secretary, and editor of the magazine (*Student Advocate*). The national committee was divided into three blocs, with an equal number named by the SLID and NSL, leaving a number of seats for "unaffiliated liberals." There was only one hitch in these proceedings: the morning of the vote, the YCL faction decided that they would not accept one name on the SLID list—mine—in spite of the previous agreement that each of the merging organizations would name its own people to the national committee. The infuriated SLID'ers informed them that this would explode the agreement, and the YCL finally backed down, muttering darkly about the "disruptive" role I had played by presenting the Socialist antiwar resolution on the Oxford Pledge.

7

The typical issues on which the student movement fought and around which it organized were mainly the following six, given roughly in order of importance:

(1) Anti-war activity and opposition to compulsory ROTC.
(2) Violations of academic freedom and student rights on campus.
(3) Issues involving economic aid to students (tuition fees, free textbooks, etc.).

(4) Reform of college administrations, particularly changes in the boards of trustees who ruled the campuses.

(5) Aid to the labor movement.

(6) Antifascist activity—which could be concretized only now and then, as when a delegation of Italian Fascist student leaders were welcomed at CCNY by the administration in one way and by the student body in another.

There were, of course, the usual cries of alarm from all quarters as the student movement grew and impressed the public mind with the fact that something was happening in the colleges. The pulp writer H. Bedford-Jones—emulating Calvin Coolidge's 1921 article, "Are the Reds Stalking Our College Women?"—published an article in *Liberty* under the pen name of J. G. Shaw, asking "Will the Communists Get Our Girls in College?", purporting to explain the terrible dangers to which his daughter had been subjected by sinister Red conspirators. The following week the *New Masses* headlined a reply, "My Father Is a Liar!", by Nancy Bedford-Jones, the daughter, who shortly thereafter atoned for her sins by marrying Lash.

A recurrent image of the student movement of the thirties as "ideological" rather than "activist" needs qualification. It certainly was "ideological," being under the thorough leadership of Communists and Socialists, but it was also at least as "activist" as campus radicals today; the difference was that it did not counterpose one to the other. Probably all wings would have agreed on the following statement from the SLID's *Blueprints for Action—A Handbook for Student Revolutionists:* "The radical movement has too many sideline commentators; the great need is for participants. Besides, action is one of the best ways of getting clarification."

But the second period of the student movement was now beginning, in which the highly ideological leadership of the Communist students made a turn toward "de-ideologizing" and depoliticalizing the movement in line with their new orientation. The "non-ideological" mask that was to be adopted was incompatible even with ideology in a liberal form. What was beginning was the cant of speaking in the name of "The Students," whose aspirations and most secret thoughts always somehow coincided with the latest pronouncements of the YCL. Already before the ASU merger convention, the *NSL Organizer* (organizational bulletin) for December, 1935 had inveighed against the belief that the new student organization would be "radical": "For what purpose is the Union formed? We say, simply, to protect our welfare, to advance our interests, to give us strength. Then why do some NSL'ers still view the Union in terms of the 'radical,' 'liberal,' 'liberal-radical' etc. students in their particular schools? Is it not because these NSL'ers see the Union primarily in terms of vague 'social problems,' political discussions, etc., and not in terms of student problems, campus issues." [3] This dichotomy between "social prob-

---

[3] *NSL Organizer,* December 1935.

lems" and "student problems, campus issues" was a fraudulent one, for the approach of the NSL—as of the SLID—had been to direct activity and education to bridging the gap between the two, showing the connection between campus issues and broader social problems, and the relevance of society-wide radical solutions to student life. What the NSL-YCL line was now demanding was the dropping of an overtly radical approach to *both* social problems and campus issues, in the interest of maximum unity of all men of good will for an anti-German alliance.

This was acted out most obviously in the student antiwar actions of 1936 and 1937. There were two influences at work now, only one of which was the new Communist line against militancy. The other was that many of the campus administrations sharply changed their tone. Instead of denouncing the strike and threatening draconic punishment, they rolled with the punch and tried to clinch. They offered auditorium facilities, called off classes for the hour, and proposed to make it all official: only, of course, "why should it be called a strike, since you aren't really striking against us, are you?" And "antiwar" is *so* negative: why not "for peace?" Increasingly, "Peace Assemblies" replaced the antiwar strikes, and, swathed in respectability, the students listened to peaceful rhetoric in the same pews where they were accustomed to hearing commencement addresses.

The Communists eagerly accepted every such offer by administrations, and the statistics of participants rose mightily, as whole campuses went through the motions of a "Peace Assembly." There were strikes of the 1934–35 variety, and evocations of the Oxford Pledge, mainly in those places where the left-wing Socialists dominated the ASU chapter. Liberal students in the ASU followed in the wake of the Communist line, which suited them to a T; in fact, they could feel, with justice, that it was the Communist line which had come over to them, not the other way around. By 1937 the guts had been taken out of what had once been the Student Strike Against War.

At the Christmas 1936 convention of the ASU, the time was not yet propitious to unload the Oxford Pledge formally, as was shown by the fact that a YPSL-sponsored resolution attacking the collective-security (prowar) line lost by only thirty-seven votes. What did happen, however, was that the two "LID types" who had become ASU national officers, Lash and Yard, went over to the Popular Front and collective-security line and became staunch fellow-travelers of the Communist bloc. At a Socialist caucus meeting during the convention itself, a furious denunciation of these two was the main feature, and in effect the national staff of the ASU became monolithic.

During 1937 prowar feeling in the country grew apace. The New Deal moved more openly toward interventionism, as Roosevelt came out in October with his "Quarantine the Aggressor" speech. The Socialist antiwar minority in the ASU had a harder row to hoe. By the end of 1937 the Communists, in bloc with Lash, were in position to dump the last vestiges of the student movement's militant politics and antiwar activity. At the convention, a well-organized Socialist bloc of delegates carried on a last-ditch fight to save the Oxford Pledge, but lost, 282—108. By the 1938 convention, with the Socialist left wing out, the complete Popular-Frontization of the organization bore fruit: the Roosevelt administration finally gave its official blessing to the ASU, in a letter of greetings to the convention from the President; the convention also got messages from the mayor of New York and its Board of Higher Education, from the president of CCNY, from the women's director of the Democratic National Committee, and other notables. The student movement was now completely respectable, completely pro-administration, and completely emasculated.

The new atmosphere that enveloped the ASU can be gathered, in part, from the following comment by a friend of the movement, Bruce Bliven, writing in the *New Republic* for January 11, 1939 on the convention that had just taken place:

> Their enthusiasm reached its peak at the Jamboree in the huge jai-alai auditorium of the Hippodrome (seating capacity 4500) which was filled to its loftiest tier. There were a quintet of white-flanneled cheer leaders, a swing band, and shaggers doing the Campus Stomp ("everybody's doing it, ASU'ing it")—confetti. There were ASU feathers and buttons, a brief musical comedy by the Mob Theatre and pretty ushers in academic caps and gowns. All the trappings of a big-game rally were present and the difference was that they were cheering, not the Crimson to beat the Blue, but Democracy to beat Reaction. To me, it bordered just alongside the phony.[4]

It *was* phony, of course, whatever one might think of football-rally exercises. This was making like Joe College according to the detailed instructions of the *YCL Organizer* on "How to Be American."

Later on in 1939 there was a second excellent example of what had happened. This one is directly from the *Young Communist League Bulletin* at the University of Wisconsin: "Some people have the idea that a YCL'er is politically minded, that nothing outside of politics means anything. Gosh, no. They have a few simple problems. There is the problem of getting good men on the baseball team this spring, of opposition from other pingpong teams, of dating girls, etc. We go to shows, parties, dances, and all that. In short, the YCL and its members are no different from other people except that we believe in dialectical materialism as the solution to all problems." [5]

This is what the student movement had become. The last chapter was written after September, 1939. After four years of eviscerating the student antiwar movement for the sake of the grand alliance against Nazism, the Second World War was inaugurated with the Hitler-Stalin Pact. The Communist leaders of the ASU ground all gears into reverse, and some of the passengers got shaken out, particularly Lash, who really believed what he had been saying about collective security. At the Christmas 1939 convention, the rug was pulled from under the "innocents." The Com-

---

4 Bruce Bliven, *New Republic,* 11 January 1939.
5 *Young Communist League Bulletin,* University of Wisconsin, 1939.

munists held it in iron control, rolling up huge majorities even on pro-
cedural questions whenever necessary. A motion condemning the Soviet
attack on Finland was defeated 322—49. It was announced that the war
was "imperialist," and ASU propaganda echoed the slogan that "The
Yanks Are Not Coming." A motion for a national membership referen-
dum on this line was overwhelmingly turned down. Lash was replaced
in the executive secretary's office by the YCL apparatus-man, Bert Witt.
At the 1940 convention there was no opposition at all—also no cheer-
leaders, confetti, or shaggers; the major speakers were all Communists or
fellow-travelers. But by this time it scarcely mattered, for the ASU was a
shell. When the line changed again, after the German attack on Russia,
and the Communists became shrill patriots again, it was too late to save
the student movement even in its Popular Front form. The student movement was dead. . . .

part II

BASIC PROCESSES IN THE ACQUISITION OF POLITICAL KNOWLEDGE AND BEHAVIOR

Throughout history human nature has been shaped by institutions and agencies in society. Man has been both the creator and recipient in this process, creating new institutions and values, receiving the heritage of old and ancient customs. Political socialization—the transmission of political values and beliefs—is part of this process. In some respects it is more crucial than other parts of the process because it involves learning obedience to the political system which, in turn, keeps society running smoothly. In the first selection, Robert Hess and Judith Torney talk about several of the principal mechanisms involved in political socialization as well as about the main content of politics. They emphasize that political learning occurs in stages, moving, respectively, from simple identification of political objects to participation in political activities. The reader should note the resemblance between their several models of political socialization and the four general models of socialization outlined in the Introduction to this book.

In the eyes of the Greek philosophers, all political activity in a society occurred within the *polis,* or political community. The *polis* attracted men's commitments to a greater or lesser degree and provided the arena in which political battles were waged. Modern society does not differ in this regard from its predecessors. The community and our conception of it serve to orient our political thinking and action. Yet, community is in this sense an idea, an abstraction, and can be more or less quickly grasped by people. How rapidly and when do we acquire it? Joseph Adelson and Robert O'Neil set themselves the task of answering this question. They find that children are unable to grasp the idea of the community before the age of fifteen, although they are able to think of it in very concrete and specific terms. They also discover that adolescents' political images and ideas tend to become less authoritarian and more philosophical with age, thereby confirming certain of Jean Piaget's ideas on the growth of moral and abstract thought.

3

PATTERNS OF GROWTH
IN EMERGENCE OF
POLITICAL ATTITUDES

ROBERT D. HESS | JUDITH V. TORNEY

The most prominent feature of political socialization is the rapidity with which attitudes change during the elementary-school years. Not all attitudes develop at the same time or show the same types of growth, however. One of the aims of the study was to understand more completely these different patterns of growth and change.

How should we think about this process? One model is offered by Piaget who in his classic work on the growth of logic conceptualized children's movement away from infantile patterns of thought toward adult thought processes. [1] Perhaps political socialization may be viewed as proceeding along similar lines, assuming that children are moving toward the political concepts, attitudes, and expectations which are characteristic of adults. It is clear from previous work that changes in political attitudes occur as age increases; the character of adult participation and the images of government and citizenship prevalent in the adult population are among the most influential forces guiding these changes.[2]

There are several aspects common to the child's and the adult's image of the political systems. The adult holds ideal standards with which to evaluate the political system and its representatives. He also has information about the way the system does in fact operate, and he makes judgments about whether it attains the ideal standards (for example, most government officials are or are not honest; most laws are or are not administered fairly).

The individual also has an image of himself as a citizen: how he *should*

Reprinted from Robert D. Hess and Judith V. Torney, *The Development of Political Attitudes in Children,* pp. 12–22 (Chicago: Aldine Publishing Co., 1967); copyright © 1967 by Robert D. Hess and Judith V. Torney.

[1] Jean Piaget, *The Psychology of Intelligence* (London: Routledge and Kegan Paul, 1947).

[2] Fred I. Greenstein, *Children and Politics* (New Haven: Yale University Press, 1965); and Robert Hess and David Easton, "The Child's Changing Image of the President," *Public Opinion Quarterly* 24 (1960): 632–44.

act in relation to the government and how he *does* act. There is consensus in the population about most ideals of citizen behavior (for example, citizens should obey laws; they should vote in elections). The particular forms of citizen behavior are also influenced by ideal norms and by other factors (for example, individuals possess varying amounts of knowledge about the most effective ways to channel their influence and about the most fruitful sources of information about candidates).

Children begin early in life to accept ideals about how the system should operate. There is agreement in the society about many of these norms; ideals about government frequently result from a transfer of more general behavior standards, which the child has already applied to himself, onto the political system (for example, children should be honest and public officials should also be honest; rules in children's games should be fair, and laws should also be fair). These ideal perceptions of the system appear to be established easily. In fact, for many children a gap between what is ideal and what is real does not exist; in the child's view of the adult world, what is *ideal* is. The values that encourage citizen activity in influencing the government are not so apparent to the young child, in part because the idea that a citizen should interfere in the operation of a group to which he belongs is a relatively complex concept.

At the present time there is not sufficient information available on the adult population to make precise and careful comparisons between the attitudes of children and adults. However, it was possible as part of the study to assess some of the attitudes of teachers. Although their attitudes are probably not a faithful representation of the attitudes of adults in general, teachers are important representatives of the attitudes toward which children are socialized. In this country, teachers transmit a large share of information about the governmental system, presenting and discussing examples of governmental actions which fulfill or fail to fulfill the accepted ideals. They also transmit ideals of citizen behavior and teach some of the skills necessary to fill these requirements—how to get information for choosing a candidate, how to band together with others in a common cause. While teachers are restrained from partisan controversy, they are held responsible for presenting material about the government's organization and operation and for inculcating norms of citizen behavior. They also play a vital role in organizing many other kinds of experiences which contribute to cognitive development, even though the experiences may not have explicit political content.

PHASES OF EARLY POLITICAL INVOLVEMENT

A study of the child's progressive involvement in the political system of his country could be limited to behavior and attitudes of adults which are appropriate for children—talking about political subjects, reading about political issues, commitment to a party. Much previous research with children and adolescents has described involvement from this point of view, but such an approach leaves unexplored the initial phases of political socialization.[3]

It is useful to consider political involvement starting from the point where no attitudes or cognitions about the political system exist and to define four aspects of engagement with the system. The first is *identification of political objects,* becoming aware of them and recognizing them as part of the political realm. As the child learns more, comes into contact with more aspects of the political system and forms his own opinions about it, he becomes more involved in the system than the child who knows nothing of political objects or processes.[4]

There were great individual differences in the information children in the study had about various aspects of government and political processes. During one interview with a second-grade boy, the following exchange was recorded:

"Jimmy, do you know about the Supreme Court, have you heard anyone mention it?"
"No, nothing at all."
"How about Congress, have you heard of Congress?"
"Nope."
"United States Senate?"
"Nope."
"United States House of Representatives?"
"No."
"County Agent?"
"Nope."
"School Board? City or town government?"
"Nope, nothing at all."

The difficulty encountered in trying to elicit attitudes about political objects from Jimmy is obvious. . . .

Another child revealed impressions of the President and the courts in spite of the fact that his information was exceedingly limited:

"Johnny, what is the United States Senate?"
"I know what the United States is—United States is a country where there is lots of people and presidents. That's all I know—the Senate part makes it too hard."
"What is the United States House of Representatives?"
"You mean the White House?"
"No, not quite the same. How about courts?"
"Courts is a place like a house or something like a building that is big

---

3 Herbert Hyman, *Political Socialization* (Glencoe, Ill.: Free Press, 1959).

4 Oeser and Emery have similarly conceptualized the child's absorption of the country's ideology, measuring it by the number of times questions about political matters are omitted when the child has the choice of answering or leaving out the question. See O. Oeser and F. Emery, *Social Structure and Personality in a Rural Community* (New York: Macmillan, 1954).

and the man's name is, I can't say his name very well, but you know, he has a cap and he's big. And he sits down on a big desk, and when they want to talk to him, they say—uni— uni—"

"*Your honor?*"

"Yeah, yeah, yeah."

"*Where did you hear about that?*"

"Well, a lot of times on television. And this man says to the policeman, do this and do that."

"*Oh, I see. How does somebody get to do that, do you think?*"

"If they be real good."

"*What about the School Board?*"

"No."

"*The state government?*"

"No, I don't know. . . ."

"*The White House?*"

"Well, I heard that the White House is real big, and it's got a lot of rooms—the teacher told us the number, but it is a big number and I can't even say it. There's a gray room, a gold room, a green room, and the President lives in the White House. . . . It is real big and nice. It is big and has two chairs, and if the King and Queen wants to come and visit, they sit down on the chairs."

From the extraordinary range in level of information revealed in interviews as well as more structured data-gathering instruments, we came to regard the number of attitudes a child is able to express as one index of the amount of his political socialization. Although it touches only one aspect of a multidimensional cluster of attitudes, knowledge, and overt behavior, it is a useful concept, especially at young age levels.

A second aspect of engagement with the political system is the acquisition of more elaborated *conceptualizations* of it, of the norms of appropriate citizen behavior, and of the ways in which the citizen can deal with the system. Interviews with children show their increasing information about the institutions and procedures of government. An exchange with an eleven-year-old boy illustrates this awareness of the complexity of the President's activities.

"*What can you tell me about the President?*"

"Well, the President has quite a direct handling of the country. First, any bill—he can veto just about any bill. I don't really know too much about this. From what I've heard it's correct. He can veto any bill and he has the power—I mean he can make bills. I mean not all of them, but well, they pass, and he has something to do with it. And if he can get the people's support in him—well, that will help the country a lot."

A third aspect stresses emotional or *subjective involvement* with political objects—particularly positive or negative feelings about authority figures and political issues. Subjective involvement is most easily seen in the child's support for a candidate, as in this excerpt from a conversation with an eleven-year-old boy:

"I was for Nixon in this past election, but I feel that Kennedy has . . . well, I'm certainly going to give him any support I can give him if I got a chance. I'm sure I probably won't get a chance, out of 200 million citizens, but if I do I'll support him fully. But if there was another election I'd still be for Nixon."

The fourth aspect—step—is that of *overt activity*, which approximates to a limited extent the political activity of adults. These activities include wearing buttons for a candidate, talking with friends about political matters, reading and listening to political presentations, and working for an organization at election time.

The four steps—awareness, conceptualization, subjective involvement, and active participation—indicate the components of political involvement in children. There is some question about the sequence in which these phases occur. From the interviews quoted above, there is clearly a mingling of aspects of involvement in the several excerpts. Possibly some children begin to participate as button wearers before having any real sense of the meaning of elections. Participation without meaning is also typical of other political activities of children—reciting the pledge of allegiance and singing the national anthem. An interview with Billy, age seven, illustrates this point:

"What do you do here at school when you see the flag?"
"Oh, we say the pledge."
"The pledge. Do you know what a pledge is?"
"Well, it's a kind of a prayer."
"A prayer. And who are you speaking to when you say the pledge?"
"To God."
"To God. I see. And what are you asking Him to do?"
"Take care of people."
"Do you ever sing when you see the flag?"
"Yeah."
"Can you tell me what that song is for?"
"Oh, . . . I don't know."

This sort of activity is not the voluntary, self-motivated participation described as the last of the phases above. Rather it might be regarded as *pseudo-participation*—used by adults to teach attitudes and information about the political world. But adult participation in elections and other activities of government and political life can also occur without subjective involvement. Persons may vote without any knowledge of the candidate—as a favor to a friend or relative, in response to urging by an organization or a promise of a bribe. In our view, such activities represent deviant socialization. They obviously affect election outcomes and in this sense must be regarded as political behavior. However, from the standpoint of induction of the individual into behavior appropriate to the system, they are deviant in the normative sense—in that there is evidence that most adults do have a personal concern with political affairs. They are also deviant ideologically, in that the election process assumes a personal preference and interest on the part of the voter. In pre-adults, as with adults, there are frequent instances of participation without subjective involvement. One girl, age twelve, expressed it in this way:

> *"Sally, you said you don't think that the teacher, your father, or the postman are as important as senator or judge in making laws. Why?"*
> "Because their jobs aren't high enough—I guess that's all."
> *"What do you mean when you said their jobs aren't high enough?"*
> "Well, like the postman—he doesn't have as much to do as the senator or the President."
> *"These questions are not something you think about too much during the daytime—isn't that so?"*
> "Well. . . ."
> *"Now don't just tell me what you think you should tell me. Right now, what are you really mostly interested in?"*
> "Well, my boyfriend."
> *"Well, now, that explains it. Let's go on. What do you and your friends in class do together?"*
> "Just talk."
> *"Do you talk about politics?"*
> "No."
> *"Did you wear a button or anything like that in the [Presidential] election?"*
> "Yes, but I wore one just for the heck of it. I didn't really care which one."
> *"But most of the time you didn't talk about any of this stuff, huh?"*
> "No."
> *"Did your folks ever mention it?"*
> "Well, just a little bit."
> *"Do you watch the news?"*
> "No."

This interview continues, revealing a good deal of information about current hit records, movie actors and Oscar awards, features on the women's page of the local newspaper. The lack of interest in politics is not part of a more general apathy but is specific.

POLITICAL SOCIALIZATION AS THE DEVELOPMENT OF RELATIONSHIPS BETWEEN CITIZEN AND GOVERNMENT

Citizenship is not only a matter of legal status. It is also a pattern of interaction between the individual and the political system. The relative roles played by the citizen and the government and other features of the system are reciprocal. For example, the small child believes that it is his obligation to obey laws, and he usually believes that in return the policeman will protect him. Political socialization can be regarded as the process by which reciprocal relationships such as this are developed.

The term *role* refers to certain specified behavior of individuals within a social system. Roles are defined by the expectations set up by the system (such as rules, laws, and customs) and by the expectations of other individuals. Mutuality is a crucial element in the definition of roles and of role expectations. This has been stated more comprehensively by Parsons and Bales who used the term *reciprocal role interaction pattern* to indicate roles which are mutually defined by and dependent upon two interacting units or individuals.[5] Reciprocity in these role relationships implies that each partner in the relationship has rights and duties with regard to the other partner.[6] Social systems are stable and predictable to the degree that persons involved conform to each other's expectations. To produce conformity to reciprocal obligations there must be strong norms and values which are generally shared throughout the social system.

There are two important aspects in the development of the *citizen role*. First, the child must see his own behavior in relation to that of some other person or institution. Before one's behavior can be regulated by a role, one must learn the expectations of that role—that is, one's rights and duties in relation to the rights and duties of the system. For example, the student's role involves the obligation to study and the right to receive academic credit; the teacher's role includes the obligation to present material for learning and the right to attention from his students. Second, the child, in viewing each social object in terms of reciprocal roles, defines it as an object of his own action or potential action. That is, the child's image of a person or element of a system focuses particularly upon those qualities of the object which are important for the child's interaction with it.

The child is taught expectations and values about political matters in preparation for *future* behavior, not primarily for guiding his current behavior. Given the proper situation and supports, these expectations will orient the child's behavior when he reaches adulthood. For example, a child who develops expectations of his own competence and of the responsiveness of the system to citizen influence, will be likely as an adult to attempt to influence the government when an issue arises which is of concern to him. The concept of reciprocal role relationship also implies that an adult expects different kinds of response from the system than does a child, and the adult acts accordingly; the role relationship between a senator and a voter who writes to him is different from the role relationship between the senator and a school child who writes to him.

Socialization of political involvement proceeds through several phases. At different times in a child's development, different attributes of the national government are salient to him. The initial image of the system and the ground rules for dealing with it comprise the first category for presenting data in the following chapters. Because the data in this book are organized around the child's perception of his relationship with the political system, the second category includes his expectations of the system's response to him as well as his behavior toward it. These two

---

5 Talcott Parsons and Robert F. Bales, *Family, Socialization and Interaction Process* (Glencoe, Ill.: Free Press, 1955).

6 Alvin Gouldner, "The Norm of Reciprocity," *American Sociological Review* 25 (1960): 161–79.

poles of interactive exchange—the child's image of what he can expect from the system and his own attitudinal and behavioral response to this image of the system—will be the bases of discussion.

MODELS OF POLITICAL SOCIALIZATION

Four models are suggested which describe in different ways the acquisition, change, and stabilization of political attitudes. These are not formal explanatory models but devices for examining the attitudes the child brings to the socialization process and the ways he utilizes experience in the development of political roles. Political socialization apparently follows several models: socialization in one attitude area may be understood best by using one model, while socialization in another area or at a different time is best understood in terms of a different conception. The data presented in this and succeeding chapters may be best understood by referring to these four general patterns.

The Accumulation Model

This view assumes that the acquisition of political role expectations proceeds by the addition of units of knowledge, information, attitudes, and activities. Teaching and experience are direct and specific; the units may be small and simple or larger and more complex. Johnny's response quoted earlier ("I know what the United States is . . . the Senate part makes it too hard.") offers an example of this type of learning: some knowledge has been gained but other information is lacking. The basic feature of this mode of socialization is that it involves direct teaching, usually by adults, in which the capabilities of the child and the nature of the materials are assumed to be irrelevant. The child's attitudes, involvement, and behavior are seen as an accumulation of the specific and direct learning which has taken place. These discrete acquisitions are not necessarily transmitted to the child as consistent conceptual systems. For example, the child may fail to see connections among contemporary problems of the civil rights of minorities and the principles of the Bill of Rights.

Inconsistencies of a similar type appear with some frequency in the data reported in this book; many of the items showed less correlation with each other than would be expected on a priori grounds.[7] In the Accumulation Model there need not be any logical connection among the attitudes and information acquired, although there may be consistency. Also, there need not be any particular sequence in which attitudes are learned. This model makes no assumptions about the properties of the child as limiting or facilitating the socialization process. That is, the

---

[7] Judith V. Torney, *Structural Dimensions of Children's Political Attitude-Concept Systems: A Study of Developmental and Measurement Aspects.* Ph.D. dissertation, University of Chicago, 1965.

4

GROWTH OF POLITICAL IDEAS
IN ADOLESCENCE:
THE SENSE OF COMMUNITY

JOSEPH ADELSON | ROBERT P. O'NEIL

During adolescence the youngster gropes, stumbles, and leaps towards political understanding. Prior to these years the child's sense of the political order is erratic and incomplete—a curious array of sentiments and dogmas, personalized ideas, randomly remembered names and party labels, half-understood platitudes. By the time adolescence has come to an end, the child's mind, much of the time, moves easily within and among the categories of political discourse. The aim of our research was to achieve some grasp of how this transition is made.

We were interested in politcial ideas or concepts—in political philosophy—rather than political loyalties per se. Only during the last few years has research begun to appear on this topic. Earlier research on political socialization, so ably summarized by Hyman (1959), concentrated on the acquisition of affiliations and attitudes. More recently, political scientists and some psychologists have explored developmental trends in political knowledge and concepts, especially during childhood and the early years of adolescence; the studies of Greenstein (1965) and of Easton and Hess (1961, 1962) are particularly apposite.

Our early, informal conversations with adolescents suggested the importance of keeping our inquiry at some distance from current political issues; otherwise the underlying structure of the political is obscured by the clichés and catchphrases of partisan politics. To this end, we devised an interview schedule springing from the following premise: Imagine that a thousand men and women, dissatisfied with the way things are

From *Journal of Personality and Social Psychology*, 4, no. 3 (1966): 295–306; copyright 1966 by the American Psychological Association and reproduced by permission.

The research was supported by grants to the first author from the H. H. Rackham Faculty Research Fund of the University of Michigan and from the Social Science Research Council. It constituted a portion of the second author's doctoral dissertation submitted to the University of Michigan.

going in their country, decide to purchase and move to an island in the Pacific; once there, they must devise laws and modes of government.

Having established this premise, the interview schedule continued by offering questions on a number of hypothetical issues. For example, the subject was asked to choose among several forms of government and to argue the merits and difficulties of each. Proposed laws were suggested to him; he was asked to weigh their advantages and liabilities and answer arguments from opposing positions. The interview leaned heavily on dilemma items, wherein traditional issues in political theory are actualized in specific instances of political conflict, with the subject asked to choose and justify a solution. The content of our inqury ranged widely to include, among others, the following topics: the scope and limits of political authority, the reciprocal obligations of citizens and state, utopian views of man and society, conceptions of law and justice, the nature of the political process.

This paper reports our findings on the development, in adolescence, of *the sense of community.* The term is deliberately comprehensive, for we mean to encompass not only government in its organized forms, but also the social and political collectivity more generally, as in "society" or "the people." This concept is of course central to the structure of political thought; few if any issues in political theory do not advert, however tacitly, to some conception of the community. Hence the quality of that conception, whether dim, incomplete, and primitive, or clear, complex, and articulated, cannot fail to dominate or temper the child's formulation of all things political.

The very ubiquity of the concept determined our strategy in exploring it. We felt that the dimensions of community would emerge indirectly, in the course of inquiry focused elsewhere. Our pretesting had taught us that direct questions on such large and solemn issues, though at times very useful, tended to evoke simple incoherence from the cognitively unready, and schoolboy stock responses from the facile. We also learned that (whatever the ostensible topic) most of our questions informed us of the

TABLE 1.   **Distribution of Sample by Grade, Sex, and Intelligence**

	Boys		*Girls*	
	Average IQ	*Superior IQ*	*Average IQ*	*Superior IQ*
5th grade: N	10	5	10	5
Mean IQ	106.1	127.8	105.1	128.4
7th grade: N	10	5	10	5
Mean IQ	104.1	140.0	104.5	134.4
9th grade: N	10	5	10	5
Mean IQ	106.6	133.2	105.1	134.0
12th grade: N	10	5	10	5
Mean IQ	106.1	140.8	103.8	134.8

child's view of the social order, not only through what he is prepared to tell us, but also through what he does not know, knows falsely, cannot state, fumbles in stating, or takes for granted. Consequently we approached this topic through a survey of questions from several different areas of the schedule, chosen to illuminate different sides of the sense of community.

METHOD

Sample

The sample was comprised of 120 youngsters, equally divided by sex, with 30 subjects at each of 4 age-grade levels—fifth grade (average age, 10.9), seventh (12.6), ninth (14.7), and twelfth (17.7). The sample was further divided by intelligence: At each grade level, two thirds of the subjects were of average intelligence (95-110) and one third of superior intelligence (125 and over), as measured by the California Test of Mental Maturity. Table 1 shows the distribution by grade, intelligence, and sex. For each grade, school records were used to establish a pool of subjects meeting our criteria for age, sex, and IQ; within each of the subgroups so selected, names were chosen randomly until the desired sample size was achieved. Children more than 6 months older or younger than the average for their grade were excluded, as were two otherwise eligible subjects reported by their counselor to have a history of severe psychological disturbance.

This paper will report findings by age alone (to the next nearest age) and without regard to sex or intelligence. We were unable to discover sex differences nor—to our continuing surprise—differences associated with intelligence. The brighter children were certainly more fluent, and there is some reason to feel that they use a drier, more impersonal, more intellectualized approach in dealing with certain questions, but up to this time we have not found that they attain political concepts earlier than subjects of average intelligence.

The interviews were taken in Ann Arbor, Michigan. We were able to use schools representative of the community, in the sense that they do not draw students from socioeconomically extreme neighborhoods. The children of average IQ were preponderantly lower-middle and working class in background; those of high intelligence were largely from professional and managerial families. Academic families made up 13% of the sample, concentrated in the high IQ group; 5% of the "average" children and somewhat over one quarter of the "brights" had fathers with a professional connection to the University of Michigan. In these respects—socioeconomic status and parental education—the sample, which combined both IQ groups, was by no means representative of the American adolescent population at large. Yet our inability to find differences between the IQ groups, who derive from sharply different social milieux, makes us hesitate to assume that social status is closely associated with the growth of political ideas as we have measured them, or that the findings deviate markedly from what we would find in other middle-class suburbs.

Interview

The aims, scope, and form of the interview schedule have already been described. In developing the schedule we were most concerned to find a tone and level of discourse sufficiently simple to allow our youngest subjects to understand and respond to the problems posed, yet sufficiently advanced to keep our older interviewees challenged and engaged. Another aim was to strike a balance between the focused interview—to ease scoring —and a looser, more discursive approach—to allow a greater depth of inquiry and spontaneity of response. Our interviewers were permitted, once they had covered the basic questions of a topic, to explore it more thoroughly.

The interviews were conducted at the school. There were six interviewers, all with at least some graduate training in clinical psychology. The interviews were tape-recorded and transcribed verbatim. Those conducted with younger subjects were completed in about 1 hour, with older subjects in about 1½ hours.

Reliability

In order to appraise the lower limits of reliability, only the more difficult items were examined, those in which responses were complex or ambiguous. For five items of this type, intercoder reliabilities ranged from .79 to .84.

RESULTS

When we examine the interviews of eleven-year-olds, we are immediately struck by the common, pervasive incapacity to speak from a coherent view of the political order. Looking more closely, we find that this failure has two clear sources: First, these children are, in Piaget's sense, egocentric, in that they cannot transcend a purely personal approach to matters which require a sociocentric perspective. Second, they treat political issues in a concrete fashion and cannot manage the requisite abstractness of attitude. These tendencies, singly and together, dominate the discourse of the interview, so much so that a few sample sentences can often distinguish eleven-year-old protocols from those given by only slightly older children.

The following are some interview excerpts to illustrate the differences: These are chosen randomly from the interviews of eleven- and thirteen-year-old boys of average intelligence. They have been asked: "What is the purpose of government?"

11A. To handle the state or whatever it is so it won't get out of hand, because if it gets out of hand you might have to . . . people might get mad or something.

11B. Well . . . buildings, they have to look over buildings that would be . . . um, that wouldn't be any use of the land if they had crops on it or something like that. And when they have highways the government would have to inspect it, certain details. I guess that's about all.

11C. So everything won't go wrong in the country. They want to have a government because they respect him and they think he's a good man.

Now the thirteen-year-olds:

13A. So the people have rights and freedom of speech. Also so the civilization will balance.

13B. To keep law and order and talk to the people to make new ideas.

13C. Well, I think it is to keep the country happy or keep it going properly. If you didn't have it, then it would just be chaos with stealing and things like this. It runs the country better and more efficiently.

These extracts are sufficiently representative to direct us to some of the major developmental patterns in adolescent thinking on politics.

Personalism

Under *personalism* we include two related tendencies: first, the child's disposition to treat institutions and social processes upon the model of persons and personal relationships; second, his inability to achieve a sociocentric orientation, that is, his failure to understand that political decisions have social as well as personal consequences, and that the political realm encompasses not merely the individual citizen, but the community as a whole.

1. "Government," "community," "society" are abstract ideas; they connote those invisible networks of obligation and purpose which link people to each other in organized social interaction. These concepts are beyond the effective reach of eleven-year-olds; in failing to grasp them they fall back to persons and actions of persons, which are the nearest equivalent of the intangible agencies and ephemeral processes they are trying to imagine. Hence, Subject 11A seems to glimpse that an abstract answer is needed, tries to find it, then despairs and retreats to the personalized "people might get mad or something." A more extreme example is found in 11C's statement, which refers to government as a "he," apparently confusing it with "governor." Gross personalizations of "government" and similar terms are not uncommon at 11 and diminish markedly after that. We counted the number of times the personal pronouns "he" and "she" were used in three questions dealing with government. There were instances involving six subjects among the eleven-year-olds (or 20 per cent of the sample) and none among thirteen-year-olds. (The most striking example is the following sentence by an eleven: "Well, I don't think she should forbid it, but if they, if he did, well most people would want to put up an argument about it.")

Although personalizations as bald as these diminish sharply after eleven, more subtle or tacit ones continue well into adolescence (and in all likelihood, into adulthood) —the use of "they," for example, when "it" is appropriate. It is our impression that we see a revival of personalization among older subjects under two conditions: when the topic being discussed is too advanced or difficult for the youngster to follow or when it exposes an area of ignorance or uncertainty, and when the subject's beliefs and resentments are engaged to the point of passion or bitterness. In both these cases the emergence of affects (anxiety, anger) seems to produce a momentary cognitive regression, expressing itself in a loss of abstractness and a reversion to personalized modes of discourse.

2. The second side of personalism is the failure to attain a sociocentric perspective. The preadolescent subject does not usually appraise political events in the light of their collective consequences. Since he finds it hard to conceive the social order as a whole, he is frequently unable to understand those actions which aim to serve communal ends and so tends to interpret them parochially, as serving only the needs of individuals. We have an illustration of this in the data given in Table 2.

3. Table 2 reports the answers to the following item: "Another law was suggested which required all children to be vaccinated against smallpox and polio. What would be the purpose of that law?"

A substantial majority—about three quarters—of the eleven-year-olds see the law serving an individual end—personal protection from disease. By thirteen there has been a decisive shift in emphasis, these children stressing the protection of the community. At fifteen and after, an understanding of the wider purposes of vaccination has become nearly universal.

Parts and Wholes

Another reflection of the concreteness of younger adolescents can be found in their tendency to treat the total functioning of institutions in terms of specific, discrete activities. If we return to the interview excerpts,

TABLE 2.   Purpose of Vaccination

	Age			
	11	*13*	*15*	*18*
Social consequences (prevention of epidemics, etc.)	.23	.67	1.00	.90
Individual consequences (prevention of individual illness)	.70	.33	.00	.10

Note.— $\chi^2(3) = 46.53$, $p < .001$. In this table and all that follow $N = 30$ for each age group. When proportions in a column do not total 1.00, certain responses are not included in the response categories shown. When proportions total more than 1.00, responses have been included in more than one category of the table. The p level refers to the total table except when asterisks indicate significance levels for a designated row.

we find a good example in the answer given by Subject 11B on the purpose of government. He can do no more than mention some specific governmental functions, in this case, the inspecting of buildings and highways. This answer exemplifies a pattern we find frequently among our younger subjects, one which appears in many content areas. Adolescents only gradually perceive institutions (and their processes) as wholes; until they can imagine the institution abstractly, as a total idea, they are limited to the concrete and the visible.

Table 3 is one of several which demonstrates this. The subjects were asked the purpose of the income tax. The responses were coded to distinguish those who answered in terms of general government support from those who mentioned only specific government services. (In most cases the services referred to are both local and visible—police, firefighting, etc.) We observe that the percentage of those referring to the government in a general sense rises slowly and steadily; all of the high school seniors do so.

Negatives and Positives

Before we leave this set of interview excerpts, we want to note one more important difference between the eleven- and thirteen-year-olds. Two of the former emphasize the negative or coercive functions of government ("To handle the state . . . so it won't get out of hand"; "So everything won't go wrong . . ."). The thirteen-year-olds, on the other hand, stress the positive functions of the government—keeping the country happy or working properly. This difference is so important and extensive that we will treat it in depth in a later publication, but it should be discussed at least briefly here. Younger subjects adhere to a Hobbesian view of political man: The citizenry is seen as willful and potentially dangerous, and society, therefore, as rightfully, needfully coercive and authoritarian. Although this view of the political never quite loses its appeal for a certain proportion of individuals at all ages, it nevertheless diminishes both in frequency and centrality, to be replaced, in time, by more complex views of political arrangements, views which stress the administrative sides of government (keeping the machinery oiled and in repair) or which emphasize melioristic ends (enhancing the human condition).

TABLE 3.   Purpose of Income Tax

	Age			
	11	*13*	*15*	*18*
General support of government	.23	.33	.47	1.00*
Specific services only	.23	.17	.23	.00
Do not know	.53	.50	.30	.00

Note.— p level refers to row designated by asterisk.
*$\chi^2(3) = 9.54$, $p < .05$.

The Future

The adolescent years see a considerable extension of time perspective. On the one hand, a sense of history emerges, as the youngster is able to link past and present and to understand the present as having been influenced or determined by the past. On the other, the child begins to imagine the future and, what may be more important, to ponder alternative futures. Thus the present is connected to the future not merely because the future unfolds from the present, but also because the future is *tractable;* its shape depends upon choices made in the present.

This idea of the future asserts itself with increasing effect as the child advances through adolescence. In making political judgments, the youngster can anticipate the consequences of a choice taken here and now for the long-range future of the community and can weigh the probable effects of alternative choices on the future. The community is now seen to be temporal, that is, as an organism which persists beyond the life of its current members; thus judgments in the present must take into account the needs of the young and of the unborn. Further, the adolescent becomes able to envision not only the communal future, but himself (and others) in possible statuses in that future as well.

The items which most clearly expose the changing meaning of the future are those dealing with education. When we reflect on it, this is not surprising: Education is the public enterprise which most directly links the generations to each other; it is the communal activity through which one generation orients another toward the future. Several questions of public policy toward education were asked; in the answers to each, the needs of the communal future weigh more heavily with increasing age. One item runs: "Some people suggested a law which would require children to go to school until they were sixteen years old. What would be the purpose of such a law?" One type of answer to this question was coded "Continuity of community"; these responses stress the community's need to sustain and perpetuate itself by educating a new generation of citizens and leaders. Typical answers were: "So children will grow up to be leaders," and "To educate people so they can carry on the government." Looking at this answer alone (analysis of the entire table would carry us beyond this topic), we find the following distribution by age (see Table 4).

Another item later in the interview poses this problem: "The people

TABLE 4.   Purpose of Minimum Education Law

	Age			
	11	13	15	18
Continuity of community	.00	.27	.33	.43

Note. $-\chi^2(3) = 11.95, p < .01$.

TABLE 5.   Should People Without Children Pay School Taxes?

	Age			
	11	*13*	*15*	*18*
Continuity of community	.10	.10	.47	.60

Note.— $\chi^2(3) = 18.61, p < .001$.

who did not have children thought it was unfair they would have to pay taxes to support the school system. What do you think of that argument?" Again the same category, which stresses the community's continuity and its future needs, rises sharply with age as shown in Table 5.

Finally, we want to examine another education item in some detail, since it offers a more complex view of the sense of the future in adolescent political thought, allowing us to observe changes in the child's view of the personal future. The question was the last of a series on the minimum education law. After the subject was asked to discuss its purpose (see above), he was asked whether he supports it. Almost all of our subjects did. He was then asked: "Suppose you have a parent who says 'My son is going to go into my business anyway and he doesn't need much schooling for that.' Do you think his son should be required to go to school anyway? Why?"

Table 6 shows that as children advance into adolescence, they stress increasingly the communal function of education. Younger subjects respond more to the father's arbitrariness or to the economic consequences of the father's position. They are less likely to grasp the more remote, more general effects of a curtailed education—that it hinders the attainment of citizenship. Representative answers by eleven-year-olds were: "Well, maybe he wants some other desire and if he does maybe his father is forcing him"; and ". . . let's say he doesn't like the business and maybe he'd want to start something new." These children stress the practical and familial aspects of the issue.

Older subjects, those fifteen and eighteen, all but ignored both the struggle with the father and the purely pragmatic advantages of remain-

TABLE 6.   Should Son Be Required To Attend School Though Father Wants Him To Enter Business?

	Age			
	11	*13*	*15*	*18*
Yes, education needed to function in community	.00	.23	.43	.77***
Yes, education good in itself	.03	.23	.20	.27
Yes, education needed in business	.40	.47	.23	.13
Yes, prevents parental coercion	.57	.47	.43	.23

Note.—*p* level refers to row designated by asterisk.
***$\chi^2(3) = 25.54, p < .001$.

ing in school. They discoursed, sometimes eloquently, on the child's need to know about society as a whole, to function as a citizen, and to understand the perspectives of others. Here is how one eighteen-year-old put it:

> . . . a person should have a perspective and know a little bit about as much as he can rather than just one thing throughout his whole life and anything of others, because he'd have to know different things about different aspects of life and education and just how things are in order to get along with them, because if not then they'd be prejudiced toward their own feelings and what *they* wanted and they wouldn't be able to understand any people's needs.

Older subjects see education as the opportunity to become *cosmopolitan,* to transcend the insularities of job and kinship. For the older adolescent, leaving school early endangers the future in two ways. On the personal side, it threatens one's capacity to assume the perspective of the other and to attain an adequate breadth of outlook; thus, it imperils one's future place in the community. On the societal side, it endangers the integrity of the social order itself, by depriving the community of a cosmopolitan citizenry.

Claims of the Community

We have already seen that as adolescence advances the youngster is increasingly sensitive to the fact of community and its claims upon the citizen. What are the limits of these claims, the limits of political authority? To what point, and under what conditions can the state, acting in the common good, trespass upon the autonomy of the citizen? When do the community's demands violate the privacy and liberty of the individual? The clash of these principles—individual freedom versus the public welfare and safety—is one of the enduring themes of Western political theory. Many, perhaps most, discussions in political life in one way or another turn on this issue; indeed, the fact that these principles are so often used purely rhetorically (as when the cant of liberty or of the public good is employed to mask pecuniary and other motives) testifies to their salience in our political thinking.

A number of questions in the interview touched upon this topic tangentially, and some were designed to approach it directly. In these latter we asked the subject to adjudicate and comment upon a conflict between public and private interests, each of these supported by a general political principle—usually the individual's right to be free of compulsion, on the one hand, and the common good, on the other. We tried to find issues which would be tangled enough to engage the most complex modes of political reasoning. A major effort in this direction was made through a series of three connected questions on eminent domain. The series began with this question:

Here is another problem the Council faced. They decided to build a road to connect one side of the island to the other. For the most part they had no trouble buying the land on which to build the road, but one man refused to sell his land to the government. He was offered a fair price for his land but he refused, saying that he didn't want to move, that he was attached to his land, and that the Council could buy another piece of land and change the direction of the road. Many people thought he was selfish, but others thought he was in the right. What do you think?

Somewhat to our surprise, there are no strong developmental patterns visible, though we do see a moderate tendency (not significant statistically, however) for the younger subjects to side with the landowner (see Table 7). The next question in the series sharpened the issue somewhat between the Council and the reluctant landowner:

TABLE 7.   Which Party is Right in Eminent-Domain Conflict?

	Age			
	11	*13*	*15*	*18*
Individual should sell; community needs come first	.30	.20	.30	.40
Detour should be made; individual rights come first	.60	.47	.27	.37
Emphasis on social responsibility; individual should be appealed to, but not forced	.10	.17	.17	.07
Ambivalence; individual is right in some ways, wrong in others	.00	.13	.27	.17

The Council met and after long discussion voted that if the landowner would not agree to give up his land for the road, he should be forced to, because the rights of all the people on the island were more important than his. Do you think this was a fair decision?

The phrasing of the second question does not alter the objective facts of the conflict; yet Table 8 shows decisive shifts in position. It is hard

TABLE 8.   Should Landowner be Forced to Sell His Land?

	Age			
	11	*13*	*15*	*18*
Yes, rights of others come first	.40	.37	.63	.70
No, individual rights come first	.57	.50	.33	.07**
No, social responsibility should suffice	.03	.10	.00	.23

Note.– *p* level refers to row designated by asterisk.
**$\chi^2(3) = 12.17, p < .01$.

to be sure why: perhaps because the second question states that the Council has considered the matter at length, perhaps because the Council's decision is justified by advancing the idea of "the people's rights." Whatever the reason, we now see a marked polarization of attitude. The younger subjects—those eleven and thirteen—continue to side with the landowner; those fifteen and eighteen almost completely abandon him, although about one quarter of the latter want to avoid coercion and suggest an appeal to his sense of social responsibility.

The final question in the series tightened the screws:

> The landowner was very sure that he was right. He said that the law was unjust and he would not obey it. He had a shotgun and would shoot anyone who tried to make him get off his land. He seemed to mean business. What should the government do?

The landowner's threat startled some of the subjects, though in very different ways depending on age, as Table 9 shows: The younger subjects in these cases did not quite know what to do about it and suggested that he be mollified at all costs; the older subjects, if they were taken aback, were amused or disdainful, saw him as a lunatic or a hothead, and rather matter-of-factly suggested force or guile to deal with him. Nevertheless, this question did not produce any essential change in position for the sample as a whole. Those older subjects who had hoped to appeal to the landowner's social conscience despaired of this and sided with the Council. Otherwise, the earlier pattern persisted, the two younger groups continuing to support the citizen, the older ones favoring the government, and overwhelmingly so among the oldest subjects.

These findings seem to confirm the idea that older adolescents are more responsive to communal than to individual needs. Yet it would be incorrect to infer that these subjects favor the community willy-nilly. A close look at the interview protocols suggests that older adolescents choose differently because they reason differently.

Most younger children—those thirteen and below—can offer no justification for their choices. Either they are content with a simple statement of preference, for example: "I think he was in the right"; or they do no more than paraphrase the question: "Well, there is really two sides to it. One is that he is attached and he shouldn't give it up, but again he

TABLE 9. **What Should Government Do if Landowner Threatens Violence?**

	Age			
	11	*13*	*15*	*18*
Detour	.60	.63	.37	.10
Government coercion justified	.23	.27	.57	.83

Note.— $\chi^2(3) = 29.21, p < .001$.

should give it up for the country." These youngsters do not or cannot rationalize their decisions, neither through appeal to a determining principle, nor through a comparative analysis of each side's position. If there is an internal argument going on within the mind of the eleven- or thirteen-year-old, he is unable to make it public; instead, he seems to choose by an intuitive ethical leap, averring that one or the other position is "fair," "in the right," or "selfish." He usually favors the landowner, because his side of the matter is concrete, personal, psychologically immediate, while the Council's position hinges on an idea of the public welfare which is too remote and abstract for these youngsters to absorb. Even those few children who try to reason from knowledge or experience more often than not flounder and end in confusion. A thirteen-year-old:

> Like this girl in my class. Her uncle had a huge house in ———, and they tore it down and they put the new city hall there. I think they should have moved it to another place. I think they should have torn it down like they did, because they had a law that if there was something paid for, then they should give that man a different price. But then I would force him out, but I don't know how I'd do it.

What we miss in these interviews are two styles of reasoning which begin to make their appearance in fifteen-year-olds: first, the capacity to reason consequentially, to trace out the long-range implications of various courses of action; second, a readiness to deduce specific choices from general principles. The following excerpt from a fifteen-year-old's interview illustrates both of these approaches:

> Well, maybe he owned only a little land if he was a farmer and even if they did give him a fair price maybe all the land was already bought on the island that was good for farming or something and he couldn't get another start in life if he did buy it. Then maybe in a sense he was selfish because if they had to buy other land and change the direction of the road why of course then maybe they'd raise taxes on things so they could get more money cause it would cost more to change directions from what they already have planned. [Fair to force him off?] Yes, really, just because one person doesn't want to sell his land that don't mean that, well the other 999 or the rest of the people on the island should go without this road because of one.

In the first part of the statement, the subject utilizes a cost-effectiveness approach; he estimates the costs (economic, social, moral) of one decision against another. He begins by examining the effects on the landowner. Can he obtain equivalent land elsewhere? He then considers the long-range economic consequences for the community. Will the purchase of other land be more expensive and thus entail a tax increase? Though he does not go on to solve these implicit equations—he could hardly do so, since he does not have sufficient information—he does state the variables he deems necessary to solve them.

The second common strategy at this age, seen in the last part of the statement, is to imply or formulate a general principle, usually ethico-political in nature, which subsumes the instance. Most adolescents using this approach will for this item advert to the community's total welfare, but some of our older adolescents suggest some other governing principle —the sanctity of property rights or the individual's right to privacy and autonomy. In either instance, the style of reasoning is the same; a general principle is sought which contains the specific issue.

Once a principle is accepted, the youngster attempts to apply it consistently. If the principle is valid, it should fall with equal weight on all; consequently, exceptions are resisted:

> I think that the man should be forced to move with a good sum of money because I imagine it would be the people, it said the rights of the whole, the whole government and the whole community, why should one man change the whole idea?

And to the question of the landowner's threatening violence: "They shouldn't let him have his own way, because he would be an example. Other people would think that if they used his way, they could do what they wanted to." Even a child who bitterly opposes the Council's position on this issue agrees that once a policy has been established, exceptions should be resisted:

> Well, if the government is going to back down when he offers armed resistance, it will offer ideas to people who don't like, say, the medical idea [see below]. They'll just haul out a shotgun if you come to study them. The government should go through with the action.

The Force of Principle

Once principles and ideals are firmly established, the child's approach to political discourse is decisively altered. When he ponders a political choice, he takes into account not only *personal* consequences (What will this mean, practically speaking, for the individuals involved?) and pragmatic *social* consequences (What effect will this have on the community at large?), but also its consequences in the realm of *value* (Does this law or decision enhance or endanger such ideals as liberty, justice, and so on?). There is of course no sharp distinction among these types of consequences; values are contained, however tacitly, in the most "practical" of decisions. Nevertheless, these ideals, once they develop, have a life, an autonomy of their own. We reasoned that as the adolescent grew older, political principles and ideals would be increasingly significant, and indeed would loom large enough to overcome the appeal of personal and social utility in the narrow sense.

To test this belief we wanted an item which would pit a "good" against a "value." We devised a question proposing a law which, while achieving a personal and communal good, would at the same time violate a political ideal—in this case, the value of personal autonomy. The item ran: "One [proposed law] was a suggestion that men over 45 be required to have a yearly medical checkup. What do you think of that suggestion?"

The answer was to be probed if necessary: "Would you be in favor of that? Why (or why not)?" Table 10 shows the distribution of responses.

The findings are interesting on several counts, aside from offering testimony on the degree to which good health is viewed as a summum bonum. The eleven-year-olds, here as elsewhere, interpret the issue along familial and authoritarian lines. The government is seen in loco parentis; its function is to make its citizens do the sensible things they would otherwise neglect to do. But our primary interest is in the steady growth of opposition to the proposal. The basis for opposition, though it is phrased variously, is that the government has no business exercising compulsion in this domain. These youngsters look past the utilitarian appeal of the law and sense its conflicts with a value that the question itself does not state. These data, then, offer some support to our suggestion that older adolescents can more easily bring abstract principles to bear in the appraisal of political issues. Strictly speaking, the findings are not definitive, for we cannot infer that all of those supporting the law do so without respect to principle. Some of the older adolescents do, in fact, recognize the conflict implicit in the question, but argue that the public and personal benefits are so clear as to override the issue of personal liberties. But there are very few signs of this among the younger subjects. Even when pressed, as they were in a following question, they cannot grasp the meaning and significance of the conflict; they see only the tangible good.

TABLE 10.   Should Men Over 45 be Required to Have a Yearly Medical Checkup?

	Age			
	11	13	15	18
Yes, otherwise they would not do it	.50	.07	.00	.03***
Yes, good for person and/or community	.50	.80	.70	.60
No, infringement on liberties	.00	.13	.27	.37**

Note.— p level refers to rows designated by asterisk.
**$\chi^2(3) = 11.95, p < .01$.
***$\chi^2(3) = 33.10, p < .001$.

DISCUSSION

These findings suggest that the adolescent's sense of community is determined not by a single factor, but by the interaction of several related developmental parameters. We should now be in a position to consider what some of these are.

1. *The decline of authoritarianism.* Younger subjects are more likely to approve of coercion in public affairs. Themselves subject to the author-

ity of adults, they more readily accept the fact of hierarchy. They find it hard to imagine that authority may be irrational, presumptuous, or whimsical; thus they bend easily to the collective will.

2. With advancing age there is an increasing grasp of the *nature and needs of the community*. As the youngster begins to understand the structure and functioning of the social order as a whole, he begins to understand too the specific social institutions within it and their relations to the whole. He comes to comprehend the autonomy of institutions, their need to remain viable, to sustain and enhance themselves. Thus the demands of the social order and its constituent institutions, as well as the needs of the public, become matters to be appraised in formulating political choices.

3. *The absorption of knowledge and consensus.* This paper has taken for granted, and hence neglected, the adolescent's increasing knowingness. The adolescent years see a vast growth in the acquisition of political information, in which we include not only knowledge in the ordinary substantive sense, but also the apprehension of consensus, a feeling for the common and prevailing ways of looking at political issues. The child acquires these from formal teaching, as well as through a heightened cathexis of the political, which in turn reflects the generally amplified interest in the adult world. Thus, quite apart from the growth of cognitive capacity, the older adolescent's views are more "mature" in that they reflect internalization of adult perspectives.

4. We must remember that it is not enough to be exposed to mature knowledge and opinion; their absorption in turn depends on the growth of *cognitive capacities*. Some of the younger subjects knew the fact of eminent domain, knew it to be an accepted practice, yet, unable to grasp the principles involved, could not apply their knowledge effectively to the question. This paper has stressed the growth of those cognitive capacities which underlie the particular intellectual achievements of the period: the adolescent's increasing ability to weigh the relative consequences of actions, the attainment of deductive reasoning. The achievement of these capacities—the leap to "formal operations," in Piaget's term —allows him to escape that compulsion toward the immediate, the tangible, the narrowly pragmatic which so limits the political discourse of younger adolescents.

5. In turn the growth of cognitive capacity allows *the birth of ideology*. Ideology may not be quite the right word here, for it suggests a degree of coherence and articulation that few of our subjects, even the oldest and brightest, come close to achieving. Nevertheless there is an impressive difference between the younger and older adolescents in the orderliness and internal consistency of their political perspectives. What passes for ideology in the younger respondents is a raggle-taggle array of sentiments: "People ought to be nice to each other"; "There are a lot of wise guys around, so you have to have strict laws." In time these sentiments may mature (or harden) into ideologies or ideological dispositions, but they are still too erratic, too inconsistent. They are not yet principled or gen-

eralized and so tend to be self-contradictory, or loosely held and hence easily abandoned. When younger subjects are cross-questioned, however gently, they are ready to reverse themselves even on issues they seem to feel strongly about. When older subjects are challenged, however sharply, they refute, debate, and counterchallenge. In some part their resistance to easy change reflects a greater degree of poise and their greater experience in colloquy and argument, but it also bespeaks the fact that their views are more firmly founded. The older adolescents, most conspicuously those at 18, aim for an inner concordance of political belief.

These then are the variables our study has suggested as directing the growth of political concepts. We must not lean too heavily on any one of them: The development of political thought is not simply or even largely a function of cognitive maturation or of increased knowledge or of the growth of ideology when these are taken alone. This paper has stressed the cognitive parameters because they seem to be so influential at the younger ages. The early adolescent's political thought is constrained by personalized, concrete, present-oriented modes of approach. Once these limits are transcended, the adolescent is open to influence by knowledge, by the absorption of consensus, and by the principles he adopts from others or develops on his own.

A Developmental Synopsis

We are now in a position to summarize the developmental patterns which have emerged in this study. It is our impression that the most substantial advance is to be found in the period between eleven and thirteen years, where we discern a marked shift in the cognitive basis of political discourse. Our observations support the Inhelder and Piaget (1958) findings on a change from concrete to formal operations at this stage. To overstate the case somewhat, we might say that the *eleven-year-old* has not achieved the capacity for formal operations. His thinking is concrete, egocentric, tied to the present; he is unable to envision long-range social consequences; he cannot comfortably reason from premises; he has not attained hypothetico-deductive modes of analysis. The thirteen-year-old has achieved these capacities some (much?) of the time, but is unable to display them with any consistent effectiveness. The *thirteen-year-olds* seem to be the most labile of our subjects. Depending on the item, they may respond like those older or younger than themselves. In a sense they are on the threshold of mature modes of reasoning, just holding on, and capable of slipping back easily. Their answers are the most difficult to code, since they often involve an uneasy mixture of the concrete and the formal.

The *fifteen-year-old* has an assured grasp of formal thought. He neither hesitates nor falters in dealing with the abstract; when he seems to falter, it is more likely due to a lack of information or from a weakness in knowing and using general principles. His failures are likely to be in content and in fluency, rather than in abstract quality per se. Taking our data as a whole we usually find only moderate differences between fifteen and eighteen. We do find concepts that appear suddenly between eleven and thirteen, and between thirteen and fifteen, but only rarely do we find an idea substantially represented at eighteen which is not also available to a fair number of fifteen-year-olds.

The *eighteen-year-old* is, in other words, the fifteen-year-old, only more so. He knows more; he speaks from a more extended apperceptive mass; he is more facile; he can elaborate his ideas more fluently. Above all, he is more philosophical, more ideological in his perspective on the political order. At times he is consciously, deliberately an ideologue. He holds forth.

part III

AGENCIES OF SOCIALIZATION

Induction into society is not a random process allocated to whomever or whatever group has time. Indeed, certain specific groups are concerned almost wholly with training young people to be members of society. In America and most other industrialized nations, four main agencies handle this responsibility: the family, the peer group, the high school, and the college.

The first reading in this section by M. Kent Jennings and Richard Niemi, takes up the matter of the family's role in the political socialization process. Ordinarily the family plays a major part in teaching us how to behave and think. This is almost inevitable since we are born, helpless and dependent, into this group and spend about twenty years, or a little less than one-third of our lifetime, here. Nevertheless, the family may have a very minor role in the political transmission process, according to Jennings and Niemi. Only in the realm of party identification, in fact, do they uncover a substantial correspondence between the politics of parents and their children.

In the absence of any appreciable influence by the family, one may wonder where most political views and ideas are learned. One important setting, at least in modern America, is the peer group, which acts to sift the views of parents and the media and eventually to transform them into a form appreciated by youth. Theodore Newcomb's classic study at Bennington College suggests how the peer group can influence political behavior. Newcomb finds that students who adopted their friends at college as a reference group were more likely to take on the political coloration of this group than those students who remained strongly attached to their families.

Although it deals ostensibly with only the influence of peers on political opinions, Newcomb's article also implicates the college and, more broadly, the educational system, in the political socialization process. The next reading in this section, by Kenneth Langston and M. Kent Jennings, deals at length with the effect of the high school curriculum on young people's political attitudes. Except in the case of black school children, it appears that formal political instruction has little effect on the political views of American youth. The authors note, however, that, "while the formal curriculum may have little effect there is still the acquisition of conceptual skills, the social climate of the school, and the presence of peer groups, all of which may play a significant role in the political socialization process."

Whether because of its alleged impersonality or sheer importance in modifying one's life chances in America, the university has become a target of much contemporary protest among youth. The last two readings in this section note the ways in which the university and its institutional apparatus can mold the political opinions of young people. The article by Hanan Selvin and Warren Hagstrom shows that the influence of the family on political opinions diminishes the longer a student spends at a university and, at the same time, that university experiences, such as involvement in campus groups, help to shape young peoples' political orientations. Burton Clark and Martin Trow discuss the university in terms of its structural features such as its size and authority structure. Clark and Trow's analysis, like that of Selvin and Hagstrom, suggests that the university may have a special and independent influence on students' views, and that differences in university structures are apt to produce different types of political orientations in the student body.

5

THE TRANSMISSION
OF POLITICAL VALUES
FROM PARENT TO CHILD

M. KENT JENNINGS | RICHARD G. NIEMI

In understanding the political development of the preadult one of the
central questions hinges on the relative and differentiated contributions
of various socializing agents. The question undoubtedly proves more difficult as one traverses a range of polities from those where life and learning
are almost completely wrapped up in the immediate and extended family
to those which are highly complex social organisms and in which the socialization agents are extremely varied. To gain some purchase on the role
of one socializing agent in our own complex society, this paper will take
up the specific question of the transmission of certain values from parent
to child as observed in late adolescence. After noting parent-child relationships for a variety of political values, attention will be turned to some
aspects of family structure which conceivably affect the transmission flows.

I. ASSESSING THE FAMILY'S IMPACT

"Foremost among agencies of socialization into politics is the family." So
begins Herbert Hyman's discussion of the sources of political learning.[1]
Hyman explicitly recognized the importance of other agents, but he was
neither the first nor the last observer to stress the preeminent position of
the family. This viewpoint relies heavily on both the direct and indirect
role of the family in shaping the basic orientations of offspring. Whether

From *American Political Science Review* 62, no. 1 (March 1968): 169–84; reprinted
by permission of the authors and the American Political Science Association.

Revised version of a paper delivered at the annual meeting of the American Political
Science Association, New York, September 1966. Financial support for the study reported here comes from the Danforth Foundation and the National Science Foundation. We wish to acknowledge the assistance of Michael Traugott in the preparation
of this paper.

[1] Herbert Hyman, *Political Socialization* (New York: Free Press, 1959), p. 69.

the child is conscious or unaware of the impact, whether the process is role-modelling or overt transmission, whether the values are political and directly usable or "nonpolitical" but transferable, and whether what is passed on lies in the cognitive or affective realm, it has been argued that the family is of paramount importance. In part this view draws heavily from psychoanalytic theory, but it is also influenced by anthropological and national character studies, and by the great emphasis on role theory in sociological studies of socialization. In part the view stems also from findings in the area of partisan commitment and electoral behavior indicating high intergenerational agreement. Unfortunately for the general thesis, such marked correlations have been only occasionally observed in other domains of political life. Indeed, other domains of political life have been rarely explored systematically with respect to the central question of articulation in parent-child political values.[2] Inferences, backward and forward extrapolations, and retrospective and projective data have carried the brunt of the argument.

A recent major report about political socialization during the elementary years seriously questions the family's overriding importance. In contrast to the previously-held views that the family was perhaps preeminent or at least co-equal to other socializing agents stands the conclusion by Robert Hess and Judith Torney that "the public school is the most important and effective instrument of political socialization in the United States," and that "the family transmits its own particular values in relatively few areas of political socialization and that, for the most part, the impact of the family is felt only as one of several socializing agents and institutions."[3] Hess and Torney see the primary influence of the family as the agent which promotes early attachment to country and government, and which thus "insures the stability of basic institutions."[4] Hence, "the family's primary effect is to support consensually-held attitudes rather than to inculcate idiosyncratic attitudes."[5] The major exception to these conclusions occurs in the area of partisanship and related matters where the family's impact is predictably high.

The Hess and Torney argument thus represents a major departure from the more traditional view. They see the family's influence as age-specific and restricted in its scope. In effect, the restriction of the family's role removes its impact from much of the dynamic qualities of the political system and from individual differences in political behavior. The consensual qualities imparted or reinforced by the family, while vital for comprehending the maintenance of the system, are less useful in explaining adjustments in the system, the conflicts and accommodations made, the

---

2 Most of these few studies, cited by Hyman, *Political Socialization*, pp. 70–71, are based on extremely limited samples and nearly all took place between 1930–1950.

3 Robert D. Hess and Judith V. Torney, *The Development of Basic Attitudes and Values Toward Government and Citizenship During the Elementary School Years, Part I* (Cooperative Research Project No. 1078, U.S. Office of Education, 1965), pp. 193, 200.

4 Ibid., p. 191.

5 Ibid., p. 192.

varied reactions to political stimuli, and the playing of diverse political roles. In short, if the family's influence is restricted to inculcating a few consensual attributes (plus partisan attachment), it means that much of the socialization which results in individual differentiation in everyday politics and which effects changes in the functioning of the political system lies outside the causal nexus of the parent-child relationship.

The first and primary objective of the present article will be to assay the flow of certain political values from parent to child. Our attention will be directed toward examining the variation in the distributions of the offsprings' values as a function of the distribution of these same values among their parents. This is not to say that other attitudinal and behavioral attributes of the parents are unimportant in shaping the child's political orientations. For example, children may develop authoritarian or politically distrustful attitudes not because their parents are authoritarian or distrustful but because of other variables such as disciplinary and protection practices.[6] Such transformations, while perhaps quite significant, will not be treated here. Rather, we will observe the degree to which the shape of value distributions in the child corresponds to that of his parent. Most of the values explored do not reflect the basic feelings of attachment to the political system which supposedly originate in the early years,[7] but much more of the secondary and tertiary values which tend to distinguish the political behavior of individuals and which contribute to the dynamics of the system.

Study Design

The data to be employed come from a study conducted by the Survey Research Center of the University of Michigan in the spring of 1965. Interviews were held with a national probability sample of 1669 seniors distributed among 97 secondary schools, public and nonpublic.[8] The response rate for students was 99 percent. For a random third of the students the father was designated for interviewing, for another random third the mother was designated, and for the other third both parents were assigned. In the permanent absence of the designated parent, the other parent or parent surrogate was interviewed. Interviews were actually completed with at least one parent of 94 percent of the students, and with both parents of 26 percent of the students, or 1992 parents altogether.

---

6 Illustrative of this argument is Frank A. Pinner's careful rendering in "Parental Overprotection and Political Distrust," *The Annals* 361 (September 1965): 58–70. See, in the same issue, Fred I. Greenstein, "Personality and Political Socialization: The Theories of Authoritarian and Democratic Character," pp. 81–95.

7 In addition to the Hess and Torney report, evidence for this is supplied by, *inter alios,* Fred I. Greenstein, *Children and Politics* (New Haven, Conn.: Yale University Press, 1965); and David Easton and Jack Dennis, "The Child's Image of Government," *The Annals* 361 (September 1965): 40–57.

8 Of the original ninety-eight schools, drawn with a probability proportionate to their size, eighty-five (87%) agree to participate; matched substitutes for the refusals resulted in a final total of ninety-seven out of 111 contacted altogether (87%).

Among parents the response rate was 93 percent.[9] Two features of the student and parent samples should be underscored. First, since the sample of students was drawn from a universe of 12th graders, school drop-outs in that age cohort, estimated at around 26 percent for this time period, were automatically eliminated. Second, due mainly to the fact that more mothers than fathers constitute the head of household in single-parent families, the sample of parents is composed of 56 percent mothers.[10]

Our basic procedure will be to match the parent and student samples so that parent-student pairs are formed. Although the actual number of students for whom we have at least one parent respondent is 1562, the base number of pairs used in the analysis is 1992. In order to make maximum usage of the interviews gathered, the paired cases in which both the mother and father were interviewed (430) are each given half of their full value.[11] A further adjustment in weighting, due to unavoidably imprecise estimates at the time the sampling frame was constructed, results in a weighted total of 1927 parent-student pairs.[12]

Using 12th graders for exploring the parental transmission of political values carries some distinct characteristics. In the first place, most of these pre-adults are approaching the point at which they will leave the immediate family. Further political training from the parents will be minimal. A second feature is that the formal civic education efforts of society, as carried out in the elementary and secondary schools, are virtually completed. For whatever effect they may have on shaping the cognitive and cathectic maps of individuals, these various formal and informal modes of citizenship preparation will generally terminate, although other forms of educational preparation may lie ahead, especially for the college bound. A final consideration is that while the family and the educational system have come to some terminal point as socializing agents, the pre-adult has yet to be much affected by actual political practice. Neither have other potentially important experiences, such as the establishment of his own nuclear family and an occupational role, had an opportunity to exert their effects. Thus the 12th grader is at a significant juncture in his political

---

9 Additional interviews were conducted with 317 of the students' most relevant social studies teachers and with the school principals. Some 21,000 paper-pencil questionnaires were administered to all members of the senior class in 85 percent of the sample schools.

10 In any event, initial controls on parent (as well as student) sex suggest that parent-student agreement rates on the values examined here differ little among parent-student combinations. This will be discussed in more detail below.

11 The alternative to half-weighting these pairs is to subselect those cases where both mother and father were interviewed. Half weighting tends to reduce the sampling variability because it utilizes more data cases.

12 It proved impossible to obtain accurate, recent figures on 12th grade enrollment throughout the country. Working with the data available and extrapolating as necessary, a sampling frame was constructed so that schools would be drawn with a probability proportionate to the size of the senior class. After entry was obtained into the sample schools and precise figures on enrollments gathered, differential weights were applied to correct for the inequalities in selection probabilities occasioned by the original imprecise information. The average weight equals 1.2.

life cycle and it will be instructive to see the symmetry of parental and student values at this juncture.

Adolescent Rebellion

It should be emphasized that we are not necessarily searching for patterns of political rebellion from parental values. Researchers have been hard-pressed to uncover any significant evidence of adolescent rebellion in the realm of political affairs.[13] Pre-adults may differ politically from their parents—particularly during the college years—but there is scant evidence that the rebellion pattern accounts for much of this deviance. Data from our own study lend little support to the rebellion hypotheses at the level of student recognition. For example, even of the 38 percent of the student sample reporting important disagreements with their parents less than 15 percent placed these disagreements in a broadly-defined arena of political and social phenomena. And these disagreements do not necessarily lie in the province of rebellion, as one ordinarily construes the term.

There is, furthermore, some question as to whether adolescent rebellion as such occurs with anything approaching the frequency or magnitude encountered in sociological writings and the popular literature. As two scholars concluded after a major survey of the literature dealing with "normal" populations:

> In the large scale studies of normal populations, we do not find adolescents clamoring for freedom or for release from unjust constraint. We do not find rebellious resistance to authority as a dominant theme. For the most part, the evidence bespeaks a modal pattern considerably more peaceful than much theory and most social comment would lead us to expect. 'Rebellious youth' and 'the conflict between generations' are phrases that ring; but, so far as we can tell, it is not the ring of truth they carry so much as the beguiling but misleading tone of drama.[14]

To say that rebellion directed toward the political orientations of the parents is relatively rare is not to say, however, that parent and student values are consonant. Discrepancies can occur for a variety of reasons, including the following: 1) Students may consciously opt for values, adopted from other agents, in conflict with those of their parents without falling

---

13 Hyman, *Polticial Socialization,* p. 72, and n. 6, p. 89. See also Robert E. Lane, "Fathers and Sons: Foundations of Political Belief," *American Sociological Review* 24 (August 1959): 502–11; Eleanor E. Maccoby, Richard E. Matthews, and Anton S. Morton, "Youth and Political Change," *Public Opinion Quarterly* 18 (Spring 1954): 23–39; Russell Middleton and Snell Putney, "Political Expression of Adolescent Rebellion," *American Journal of Sociology* 68 (March 1963): 527–35; and Robert H. Somers, "The Mainsprings of the Rebellion: A Survey of Berkeley Students in November, 1964," in *The Berkeley Student Revolt,* ed. Seymour M. Lipset and Sheldon S. Wolin (Garden City, N.Y.: Doubleday, 1965), p. 547.

14 Elizabeth Douvan and Martin Gold, "Modal Patterns in American Adolescence," in *Review of Child Development Research,* eds. Lois and Martin Hoffman (New York: Russell Sage Foundation, 1966), vol. II, p. 485.

into the rebellion syndrome. 2) Much more probable are discrepancies which are recognized neither by the parent nor the offspring.[15] The lack of cue-giving and object saliency on the part of parents sets up ambiguous or empty psychological spaces which may be filled by other agents in the student's environment. 3) Where values are unstable and have low centrality in a belief system, essentially random and time-specific responses to stimuli may result in apparent low transmission rates. 4) Another source of dissonant relationships, and potentially the most confounding one, is that life cycle effects are operative. When the pre-adult reaches the current age of his parents, his political behavior might well be similar to that of his parents even though his youthful attitudes would not suggest such congruency. This is an especially thorny empirical question and nests in the larger quandry concerning the later life effects of early socialization.

II. PATTERNS OF PARENT-CHILD CORRESPONDENCES

Confronted with a number of political values at hand we have struck for variety rather than any necessary hierarchy of importance. We hypothesized a range of correlations dependent in part on the play of factors assumed to alter the parent-student associations (noted above). We have purposely deleted values dealing with participative orientations and, as noted previously, those delving into sentiments of basic attachment and loyalty to the regime. The values selected include party identification, attitudinal positions on four specific issues, evaluations of socio-political groupings, and political cynicism. For comparative purposes we shall glance briefly at parent-student congruences in the religious sphere.

To measure agreement between parents and students we rely primarily on correlations, either of the product-moment or rank-order variety. While the obvious alternative of percentage agreement may have an intuitive appeal, it has several drawbacks. Percentage agreement is not based on the total configuration of a square matrix but only on the "main diagonal." Thus two tables which are similar in percentage agreement may represent widely differing amounts of agreement if deviations from perfect agreement are considered. Moreover, percentage agreement depends heavily on the number of categories used, so that the degree of parent-student similarity might vary for totally artificial reasons. Correlations are more resistant to changes in the definition of categories. Finally, correlations are based on relative rankings (and intervals in the case of product-moment correlations) rather than on absolute agreement as percentage agreement usually is. That is, if student scores tend to be higher (or lower) than parent scores on a particular variable, but the students are ranked similarly to their parents, a high correlation may be obtained with very little perfect agreement.

---

15 For an analysis of students' and parents' knowledge of each other's political attitudes and behavior, see Richard G. Niemi, "A Methodological Study of Political Socialization in the Family" (Ph.D. thesis, University of Michigan, 1967).

Party Identification

Previous research has established party identification as a value dimension of considerable importance in the study of political behavior as well as a political value readily transmitted from parents to children. Studies of parent-youth samples as well as adult populations indicate that throughout the life cycle there is a relatively high degree of correspondence between respondents' party loyalites and their parents'. Our findings are generally consistent with those of these earlier studies.

The substantial agreement between parent and student party affiliations is indicated by a tau-b (also called tau-beta) correlation of .47, a statistic nearly unaffected by the use of three, five, or all seven categories of the party identification spectrum generated by the question sequence.[16] The magnitude of this statistic reflects the twin facts of the presence of a large amount of exact agreement and the absence of many wide differences between students and parents. When the full 7×7 matrix of parent-student party loyalties is arrayed (Table 1), the cells in which parents and students are in unison account for a third of the cases. The cells representing maximum disagreement are very nearly empty. Despite our earlier contention, collapsing categories and considering percentage agreement in the resulting table does make good substantive sense with regard to party identification. In this instance the collapsed categories have a meaning beyond just broader segments of a continuum, and are associated with a general orientation toward one party or the other or toward a neutral position between them. Thus arrayed, 59 percent of the students fall into the same broad category as their parents, and only 7 percent cross the sharp divide between Republicans and Democrats.

The observed similarity between parents and students suggests that transmission of party preferences from one generation to the next is carried out rather successfully in the American context. However, there are also indications that other factors (temporarily at least) have weakened the party affiliations of the younger generation. This is most obvious if we compare the marginal totals for parents and students (Table 1). The student sample contains almost 12 percent more Independents than the parent sample, drawing almost equally on the Republican and Democratic proportions of the sample. Similarly, among party identifiers a somewhat larger segment of the students is but weakly inclined toward the chosen party. Nor are these configurations simply an artifact of the restricted nature of the parent sample, since the distribution of party identification among the parents resembles closely that of the entire adult electorate as observed in November, 1964 (SRC 1964 election study).

---

16 This figure is based on parent-student pairs in which both respondents have a party identification; eliminated are the 2 percent of the pairs in which one or both respondents are apolitical or undecided. The product-moment correlation for these data is .59. The standard SRC party identification questions were used: see Angus Campbell, Philip E. Converse, Warren E. Miller, and Donald E. Stokes, *The American Voter* (New York: John Wiley, 1960), Ch. 6.

TABLE 1.   Student-Parent Party Identification

Parents	Strong Dem.	Weak Dem.	Ind. Dem.	Ind.	Ind. Rep.	Weak Rep.	Strong Rep.	*Total*
Party Identification								
Strong Dem.	9.7%	8.0	3.4	1.8	.5	.9	.5	24.7%
Weak Dem.	5.8	9.0	4.2	2.6	.7	1.6	.7	24.7
		(32.6)[a]		(13.2)		(3.6)		(49.4)
Ind. Dem.	1.6	2.1	2.1	1.7	.8	.7	.2	9.3
Ind. Ind.	1.1	1.6	1.6	2.7	1.2	.9	.5	9.7
Ind. Rep.	.1	.5	.8	.9	.9	1.3	.5	4.9
		(7.0)		(12.7)		(4.1)		(23.9)
Weak Rep.	.3	2.1	1.6	2.3	1.9	5.0	1.9	15.0
Strong Rep.	.2	.9	.8	.8	2.4	3.3	3.5	11.7
		(3.4)		(9.7)		(13.6)		(26.7)
Total	18.8%	24.2	14.5	12.8	8.4	13.6	7.7	100.0%
		(43.0)		(35.7)		(21.3)		

tau-b = .47   N = 1852

[a]The full 7 X 7 table is provided because of the considerable interest in party identification. For some purposes, reading ease among them, the 3 X 3 table is useful. It is given by the figures in parentheses; these figures are (within rounding error) the sum of the numbers just above them.

A number of factors might account for the lesser partisanship of the students, and we have only begun to explore some of them. On the one hand, the students simply lack their parents' long experience in the active electorate, and as a consequence have failed as yet to develop a similar depth of feeling about the parties.[17] On the other hand, there are no doubt specific forces pushing students toward Independence. The experience of an ever-widening environment and the gradual withdrawal of parental power may encourage some students to adopt an Independent outlook. The efforts of schools and of teachers in particular are probably weighted in the same direction. If these forces are at work, high school students may be gradually withdrawing from an earlier position of more overt partisanship. But, whatever the exact nature of the causes, they clearly draw off from the partisan camp a small but significant portion of the population as it approaches full citizenship.

Opinions on Specific Issues

One way in which political values are expressed is through opinions on specific issues. However, as Converse has shown, many opinions or idea elements not only tend to be bounded by systems of low constraint but are also quite unstable over relatively short periods of time among mass publics.[18] Hence in comparing student responses with parent responses the problem of measurement may be compounded by attitude instability among both samples. Rather than being a handicap instabilities actually sharpen the test of whether significant parent-to-child flows occur. One would not expect unstable sentiments to be the object of any considerable political learning in the family. It seems unlikely that many cues would be given off over matters about which the parents were unsure or held a fluctuating opinion. Even in the event of numerous cues in unstable situations, the ambivalent or ambiguous nature of such cues would presumably yield instability in the child. In either case the articulation between parent and child beliefs would be tempered.

We have selected four specific issues for examination. Two involve public schools; given the populations being studied, schools are particularly relevant attitude objects. Furthermore these two issues envelop topics of dramatic interest to much of the public—integration in the schools and the use of prayers in schools. After an initial screening question weeded out those without any interest at all on the issues, the respondents were

---

17 This is suggested by an analysis of different age groups among the active electorate: see Ibid., pp. 161ff. For evidence that the depth of adult attachment to party is not necessarily uniform across electoral systems see M. Kent Jennings and Richard G. Niemi, "Party Identification at Multiple Levels of Government," *American Journal of Sociology* 72 (July 1966): 86–101.

18 Philip E. Converse, "The Nature of Belief Systems in Mass Publics," in *Ideology and Discontent*, ed. David E. Apter (New York: Free Press of Glencoe, 1964), pp. 206–61. The following section borrows from Converse's discussion. Robert E. Agger takes a somewhat different view of instabilities in "Panel Studies of Comparative Community Political Decision-Making," in *The Electoral Process*, ed. M. Kent Jennings and L. Harmon Zeigler (Englewood Cliffs, N.J.: Prentice-Hall, 1966), pp. 265–89.

asked if they thought the government in Washington should "see to it that white and Negro children go to the same schools" or if the government should "stay out of this area as it is none of its business." On the prayers in school question the respondents were asked if they believed "schools should be allowed to start each day with a prayer" or that "religion does not belong in the schools." [19] Taken in the aggregate the high school seniors proved less likely to sanction prayers in school than did the parents (although a majority of both answered in the affirmative) and more willing to see the federal government enforce segregation than were the adults (with both yielding majorities in favor). These differences are moderate; no more than 14 percentage points separate like-paired marginals on the prayer issue and no more than 10 points on the integration issue. The cross-tabulation of parent and student responses produces moderately strong coefficients, as shown in the first two entries of Table 2.

Combining as they do some very visible population groupings along with topics of more than usual prominence in the mass media and local communities, it would be surprising if there were not at least a moderate amount of parent-student overlap. The wonder is not that the correlations are this high, but rather that they are not higher. If correlations no higher than this are produced on issues which touch both generations in a manner which many issues assuredly do not, then one would speculate that more remote and abstract issues would generate even less powerful associations.

This hypothesizing is borne out by the introduction of two other issues. Both parents and students were asked to agree or disagree with these two statements: "If a Communist were legally elected to some public office around here, the people should allow him to take office"; and "If a person wanted to make a speech in this community against churches and religion, he should be allowed to speak." In general, the pre-adults took a slightly

TABLE 2.   **Correlations Between Parent-Student Attitudes on Four Issues**

Federal government's role in integrating the schools	.34[a]
Whether schools should be allowed to use prayers	.29
Legally elected Communist should be allowed to take office	.13
Speakers against churches and religion should be allowed	.05

[a]Each of the correlations (tau-b) in this table is based on at least 1560 cases.

[19] Sizeable proportions of both parents and students elected to state a middle or "depends" response, particularly on the first question. Such responses occupy a middle position in our calculation of the rank order correlations. On the first issue 10 percent of the pairs were dropped because either the parent or child opted out on the initial screen; the corresponding figure for the second issue is 19 percent.

more libertarian stance on the two issues than did the parents, but the differences in any of the like-paired marginals do not exceed 14 percent. These similarities mask extremely tenuous positive correlations, however, as the second pair of items in Table 2 reveals.

These two issues carry neither the immediacy nor the concreteness which may be said to characterize the two issues dealing with integration and prayers in the schools. Indeed, one might question whether the two statements represent issues at all, as the public normally conceives of issues. At any rate it is improbable that the students are reflecting much in the way of cues emitted from their parents, simply because these topics or related ones are hardly prime candidates for dinner-table conversation or inadvertent cue-giving. Nor do they tap some rather basic sentiments and attitude objects which permeate the integration and prayers issues. Such sentiments are more likely to be embedded in the expressive value structure of the parents than are those having to do with some of the more abstract "fundamental" tenets of democracy as exemplified in the free speech and right to take office issues. That adults themselves have low levels of constraint involving propositions about such fundamental tenets has been demonstrated by McClosky, and Prothro and Grigg.[20] Given this environment, the lower correlation for the two more abstract propositions is predictable.

Although the issues we have examined by no means exhaust the variety of policy questions one might pose, they probably exemplify the range of parent-student correspondences to be found in the populace. On all but consensual topics—which would perforce assume similar distributions among virtually all population strata anyway—the parent-student correlations obtained for the integration and prayer issues probably approach the apex. In part this may be due to unstable opinions and in part to the effects of agents other than the family. It is also possible that the children will exhibit greater correspondences to their parents later in the life cycle. But for this particular point in time, the articulation of political opinions is only moderately strong on salient, concrete issues and virtually nil on more abstract issues.

Evaluations of Socio-Political Groupings

Collectivities of people which are distinguished by certain physical, locational, social, religious, and membership characteristics (the list is obviously not exhaustive) often come to serve as significant political reference groups for individuals. While distinguishable groups may carry affective neutrality, it seems to be in the nature of mass behavior that these groups most often come to be viewed with greater or lesser esteem. The intersection of group evaluations and the political process comes when claims or demands are made by or upon significant portions of such group-

---

20 Herbert McClosky, "Consensus and Ideology in American Politics," *American Political Science Review* 58 (June 1964): 361–82; and James W. Prothro and Charles W. Grigg, "Fundamental Principles of Democracy: Bases of Agreement and Disagreement," *Journal of Politics* 22 (May 1960): 276–94.

ings. The civil rights movement of the past decade is perhaps the most striking contemporary example. As Converse has suggested, social groupings are likely to have greater centrality for mass publics than abstract idea elements per se.[21] Thus when particular issues and public policies become imbued with group-related properties, the issues acquire considerably more structure and concreteness for the mass public than would be the normal case.

To what extent is the family crucial in shaping the evaluations of social groupings and thus—at a further remove—the interpretation of questions of public policy? Some insight into this may be gained by comparing the ratings applied by the parents and students to eight socio-political groupings. While the groups all carry rather easily recognized labels, they do differ in terms of their relative visibility and their inclusive-exclusive properties. They include Protestants, Catholics, Jews, Negroes, Whites, Labor Unions, Big Business, and Southerners.

To measure the attitudes toward these groups, an instrument dubbed the "feeling thermometer" was used. The technique was designed to register respondents' feelings toward a group on a scale ranging from a cold 0 to a warm 100. In the analysis we will treat this scale as interval level measurement. We have also examined the data using contingency tables and ordinal statistics; our conclusions are the same regardless of the method used.

Turning first to the mean ratings, given in Table 3, we find a striking similarity in student and parent aggregate scores. The largest difference is five points and the average difference is only 2.2 points. Additionally, the standard deviations for the two samples (not shown) are extremely similar across all groupings. Nor were there significant tendencies for one sample to employ more than the other the option of "unawareness" or "no feelings" (a reading of 50 on the thermometer) about the groupings.

TABLE 3.   Correlations Between Parent-Student Group Evaluations

Group Evaluated	Parent-Student Correlations	Mean Ratings	
		Parent	*Student*
Catholics	.36[a]	72	70
Southerners	.30	66	62
Labor Unions	.28	60	60
Negroes	.26	67	69
Jews	.22	67	63
Whites	.19	84	83
Protestants	.15	84	79
Big Business	.12	64	63

[a]Each of the product-moment correlations in this table is based on at least 1880 cases. The corresponding tau-b's are (top to bottom) .28, .22, .22, .20, .18, .19, .13, .08.

---

[21] Converse, "The Nature of Belief Systems in Mass Publics."

Moreover, the aggregate differences which do occur are not immediately explicable. For example, students rate Southerners slightly lower than parents, as we expected, but the difference in ratings of Negroes is negligible, which was unanticipated. Students rate Whites and Protestants somewhat lower than parents. This is not matched, however, by higher evaluations of the minority groups—Jews, for example.

Given these extraordinarily congruent patterns it is rather startling to see that they are patently not due to uniform scores of parent-child pairs. As shown in Table 3, the highest correlation between the parent and student ratings is .36 and the coefficients range as low as .12. Even the highest correlation is well below that found for party identification (where the product-moment coefficient was .59 for the seven-fold classification), and for several groupings the relationships between parent and student scores are very feeble. If the child's view of socio-political groupings grows out of cue-giving in the home, the magnitude of the associations should exceed those observed here.

It is beyond the task of this paper to unravel thoroughly these findings. The range of correlations does provide a clue as to the conditions under which parent-student correspondences will be heightened. In the first place the three categories producing the lowest correlations appear to have little socio-political relevancy in the group sense. Whites and Protestants are extremely inclusive categories and, among large sectors of the public, may simply not be cognized or treated in everyday life as groupings highly differentiated from society in general. They are, in a sense, too enveloping to be taken as differentiated attitude objects. If they do not serve as significant attitude objects, the likelihood of parent to child transmission would be dampened. In the third case—Big Business—it seems likely that its visibility is too low to be cognized as a group qua group.

As the parent-student correlations increase we notice that the groupings come to have not only highly distinguishable properties but that they also have high visibility in contemporary American society. Adding to the socio-political saliency thereby induced is the fact that group membership may act to increase the parent-student correlations. One would hypothesize that parent-student pairs falling into a distinguishable, visible grouping would exhibit higher correlations in rating that same grouping than would nonmembers. Taking the four groupings for whom the highest correlations were obtained, we divided the pairs into those where both the parent and the child—except in the case of labor unions—were enveloped by the groupings versus those outside the groupings. Although none of the hypothesized relationships was contravened, only the coefficients for evaluations of Southerners provided a distinct demarcation between members and nonmembers (tau-b = .25 for Southern pairs, .14 for non-Southerners). It is quite possible that measures capturing membership identification and intensities would improve upon these relationships.

As with opinions on specific issues, intrapair correlations on group evaluations are at best moderately positive, and they vary appreciably as a result of socio-political visibility and, to a small degree, group membership characteristics. What we begin to discern, then, is a pattern of congruences which peak only over relatively concrete, salient values susceptible to repeated reinforcement in the family (and elsewhere, perhaps), as in party identification and in certain issues and group evaluations. It is conceivable that these results will not prevail if we advance from fairly narrow measures like the ones previously employed to more global value structures. We now turn to an illustrative example. It so happens that it also provides an instance of marked aggregate differences between the two generations.

Political Cynicism

Political cynicism and its mirror image, trust, offer an interesting contrast to other variables we are considering. Rather than referring to specific political issues or actors, cynicism is a basic orientation toward political actors and activity. Found empirically to be negatively related to political participation, political cynicism has also been found to be positively correlated with measures of a generally distrustful outlook (personal cynicism).[22] Political cynicism appears to be a manifestation of a deep-seated suspicion of others' motives and actions. Thus this attitude comes closer than the rest of our values to tapping a basic psycho-political predisposition.

Previous research with young children suggests that sweeping judgments, such as the essential goodness of human nature, are formed early in life, often before cognitive development and information acquisition make the evaluated objects intelligible. Greenstein, and Hess and Easton, have reported this phenomenon with regard to feelings about authority figures; Hess and Torney suggest similar conclusions about loyalty and attachment to government and country.[23] Evaluative judgments and affective ties have been found among the youngest samples for which question and answer techniques are feasible. This leads to the conclusions that the school, mass media, and peer groups have had little time to influence these attitudes.

It seems to follow that the family is the repository from which these feelings are initially drawn. Either directly by their words and deeds or indirectly through unconscious means, parents transmit to their children basic postures toward life which the children carry with them at least until the development of their own critical faculties. Although our 12th graders have been exposed to a number of influences which could mitigate the initial implanting, one should expect, according to the model, a rather

---

22 Robert E. Agger, Marshall N. Goldstein, and Stanley A. Pearl, "Political Cynicism: Measurement and Meaning," *Journal of Politics* 23 (August 1961): 490; and Edgar Litt, "Political Cynicism and Political Futility," *Journal of Politics* 25 (May 1963): 312–23.

23 Greenstein, *Children and Politics*, Ch. 3; Robert D. Hess and David Easton, "The Child's Changing Image of the President," *Public Opinion Quarterly* 24 (Winter 1960): 632–44; and Hess and Torney, *The Development of Basic Attitudes . . .* , pp. 73ff.

strong correspondence between parent and student degrees of political cynicism.

To assess the cynicism of parents and students, a Guttman scale was constructed from five questions asked of both samples. All questions dealt with the conduct of the national government.[24] In each sample the items formed a scale, with coefficients of reproducibility of .93 and .92 for parents and students, respectively. The aggregate scores reflect a remarkably lesser amount of cynicism among students than among parents. This is apparent in the marginal distributions in Table 4, which show the weight of the parent distribution falling much much more on the cynical end of the scale. Similarly, while a fifth of the students were more cynical than their parents, three times this number of parents were more cynical than their children. The students may be retreating from an even more trusting attitude held earlier, but compared to their parents they still see little to be cynical about in national political activity.

Here is a case where the impact of other socialization agents—notably the school—looms large. The thrust of school experience is undoubtedly on the side of developing trust in the political system in general. Civic training in school abounds in rituals of system support in the formal curriculum. These rituals and curricula are not matched by a critical examination of the nation's shortcomings or the possible virtues of other political forms. Coupled with a moralistic, legalistic, prescriptive orientation to the study of government is the avoidance of conflict dimensions and controversial issues.[25] A direct encounter with the realities of political life is thus averted or at least postponed. It would not be surprising, then, to find a rather sharp rise in the level of cynicism as high school seniors move ahead in a few years into the adult world.

Students on the whole are less cynical than parents; relative to other students, though, those with distrustful, hostile parents should themselves be more suspicious of the government, while those with trusting parents

---

24 The items are as follows:

1) Do you think that quite a few of the people running the government are a little crooked, not very many are, or do you think hardly any of them are?

2) Do you think that people in the government waste a lot of the money we pay in taxes, waste some of it, or don't waste very much of it?

3) How much of the time do you think you can trust the government in Washington to do what is right—just about always, most of the time, or only some of the time?

4) Do you feel that almost all of the people running the government are smart people who usually know what they are doing, or do you think that quite a few of them don't seem to know what they are doing?

5) Would you say that the government is pretty much run by a few big individuals looking out for themselves or that it is run for the benefit of all the people?

25 These are old charges but apparently still true. After a survey of the literature on the subject and on the basis of a subjective analysis of leading government textbooks in high schools, Byron G. Massialas reaches similar conclusions: see his "American Government: 'We are the Greatest'," in *Social Studies in the United States: A Critical Appraisal*, ed. C. Benjamin Cox and Byron G. Massialas (New York: Harcourt Brace Jovanovich, 1967), pp. 167–95.

TABLE 4.   Relationship Between Parent-Student Scores on the Cynicism Scale

Parents	Students Least Cynical 1	2	3	Most Cynical 4	5	6	Row Totals	Marginal Totals[a]
Least Cynical — 1	25%	27	33	13	1	2	101%	8%
2	19	28	38	9	1	5	100	12
3	18	28	37	10	3	4	100	33
4	16	23	41	13	3	4	100	17
5	15	19	35	19	3	9	100	9
Most Cynical — 6	12	22	36	18	4	8	100	21
Marginal Totals[a]	17%	25	37	13	3	5		100%

tau-b = .12   N = 1869

[a]The marginal totals show the aggregate scaler patterns for each sample.

should find less ground for cynicism. Against the backdrop of our discussion, it is remarkable how low the correspondence is among parent-student pairs. Aside from faint markings at the extremities, students' scores are very nearly independent of their parents' attitudes (Table 4). The cynicism of distrustful parents is infrequently implanted in their children, while a smaller group of students develops a cynical outlook despite their parents' views. Political cynicism as measured here is not a value often passed from parent to child. Regardless of parental feelings, children develop a moderately to highly positive view of the trustworthiness of the national government and its officials.

These findings do not mean that parents fail to express negative evaluations in family interaction nor that children fail to adopt some of the less favorable attitudes of their parents. What is apparently not transmitted is a *generalized* cynicism about politics. Thus while warmth or hostility toward specific political objects with high visibility may be motivated by parental attitudes, a more pervasive type of belief system labelled cynicism is apparently subject to heavy, undercutting influences outside the family nexus. These influences are still operative as the adolescent approaches adult status.

Working with another encompassing set of values we encountered much the same patterns as with cynicism. After obtaining their rank orderings of interest in international, national, state, and local political matters the respondents were allocated along a 7-point scale of cosmopolitanism-localism through an adaptation of Coombs' unfolding technique.[26] On the whole the students are considerably more cosmopolitan than the parents, and the paired correlation is a modest .17. Both life cycle and generational effects are undoubtedly at work here,[27] but the central point is that the students' orientations only mildly echo those of their parents.

---

[26] A description of this operation and some results are given in M. Kent Jennings, "Pre-Adult Orientations to Multiple Systems of Government," *Midwest Journal of Political Science* 11 (August 1967): 291–317. The underlying theory and technique are found in Clyde Coombs, *A Theory of Data* (New York: John Wiley, 1964), esp. Ch. 5.

[27] This is discussed in more detail in Jennings, "Pre-Adult Orientation . . . ,"

What results from juxtaposing parents and their children on these two measures of cynicism and cosmopolitanism-localism is the suspicion that more global orientations to political life do not yield parent-student correspondences of greater magnitude than on more specific matters. If anything, the opposite is true—at least with respect to certain specifics. It may be that the child acquires a minimal set of basic commitments to the system and a way of handling authority situations as a result of early experiences in the family circle. But it appears also that this is a foundation from which arise widely diverse value structures, and that parental values are an extremely variable and often feeble guide as to what the pre-adult's values will be.

Religious Beliefs

Up to this point we have traversed a range of political and quasi-political values, and have witnessed varying, but generally modest degrees of parent-student correspondences. To what extent does this pattern also characterize other domains of social values? For comparative purposes we can inject a consideration of religious beliefs. Like party preference, church affiliation among pre-adults is believed to be largely the same as parental affiliation. Such proves to be the case among our respondents. Of all parent-student pairs 74 percent expressed the same denominational preference. That this percentage is higher than the agreement on the three-fold classification of party identification (Democrat, Republican, Independent) by some 15 percent suggests that by the time the pre-adult is preparing to leave the family circle he has internalized the church preference of his parents to a moderately greater extent than their party preference.

There are some perfectly valid reasons for this margin. To a much greater extent than party preference, church preference is likely to be reinforced in a number of ways. Assuming attendance, the child will usually go to the same church throughout childhood, the behavior is repeated at frequent intervals; it is a practice engaged in by greater or lesser portions of the entire family and thus carries multiple role-models; formal membership is often involved; conflicting claims from other sources in the environment for a change of preference are minimal except, perhaps, as a result of dating patterns. Religious affiliation is also often imbued with a fervid commitment.

In contrast, party preference is something which the child himself cannot transform into behavior except in rather superficial ways; reinforcement tends to be episodic and varies according to the election calendar; while the party preference of parents may vary only marginally over the pre-adult years, voting behavior fluctuates more and thus sets up ambiguous signals for the child; other sources in the environment—most noticeably the mass media—may make direct and indirect appeals for the child's loyalty which conflict with the parental attachments. Given the factors facilitating intrafamilial similarities in church preference, and the absence of at least some of these factors in the party dimension, it is perhaps remarkable that congruity of party identification approaches the zone of church-preference congruity.

We found that when we skipped from party identification to other sorts of political values the parent-student correlations decreased perceptibly. May we expect to encounter similar behavior in the realm of religious values? One piece of evidence indicates that this is indeed the case. Respondents were confronted with a series of four statements having to do with the literal and divine nature of the Bible, ranging from a description of the Bible as "God's word and all it says is true" to a statement denying the contemporary utility of the book.

Both students and parents tended to view the Bible with awe, the parents slightly more so than the students. But the correlation (tau-beta) among parent-student pairs is only a moderately strong .30. As with political values, once the subject matter moves out from central basic identification patterns the transmission of parental values fades.[28] And, as with political values, this may be a function of instability—although this seems less likely for the rendering of the Bible—the impingement of other agents —particularly likely in this case—or the relative absence of cue-giving on the part of the parents. The more generalizable proposition emerging from a comparison of political and religious orientations is that the correlations obtained diminish when the less concrete value orientations are studied.

III. FAMILY CHARACTERISTICS AND TRANSMISSION PATTERNS

We have found that the transmission of political values from parent to child varies remarkably according to the nature of the value. Although the central tendencies lie on the low side, we may encounter systematic variations in the degree to which values are successfully transmitted according to certain properties of family structure. That is, whether the transmittal be conscious and deliberate or unpurposive and indirect, are there some characteristics of the family unit which abet or inhibit the child's acquisition of parental values? We shall restrict ourselves to a limited set of variables having theoretical interest.

In order to dissect the parent-student relationships by controlling for a variety of independent variables, we shall retain the full parent-student matrices and then observe correlations within categories of the control variables.[29] The political values to be examined include party identifi-

---

28 To compare directly the amount of correspondence on interpretation of the Bible with church membership information, which is nominal-level data, we used the contingency coefficient. Grouping parent and student church affiliations into nine general categories, the coefficient is .88, compared to .34 for the Bible question.

29 A more parsimonious method is to develop agreement indexes and to relate the control variables to these indexes. This results in a single statistic and contingency table for each control variable rather than one for each category of the control variable. Experience with both methods indicates that similar conclusions emerge, but retaining the full matrices preserves somewhat better the effects of each category of the control variable.

cation, political cynicism, political cosmopolitanism, four specific political issues, and the ratings assigned to three minority population groupings— Catholics, Negroes, and Jews. This makes ten variables altogether, but for some purposes the issues and the group ratings are combined into composite figures.

Parent and Student Sex Combinations

Various studies of adolescents have illustrated the discriminations which controls for sex of parent and sex of child may produce in studying the family unit.[30] Typically these studies have dealt with self-development, adjustment problems, motivational patterns, and the like. The question remains whether these discriminations are also found in the transmission of political values.

Part of the common lore of American political behavior is that the male is more dominant in political matters than the female, in his role both of husband and of father. And among pre-adults, males are usually found to be more politicized than females. While our findings do not necessarily challenge these statements, they do indicate the meager utility of sex roles in explaining parent-student agreement. The correlations between parent-student values show some variation among the four combinations of parent and student sex, but the differences are usually small and inconsistent across the several values. Of the sixty possible comparisons for the ten political variables (i.e., $\binom{4}{2} = 6$ pairs of correlations for each variable), only eight produce differences in the correlations greater than .10, and thirty-three fall within a difference of less than .05. The average parent-student correlations for these variables are: Mother-Son, .22; Mother-Daughter, .24; Father-Son, .20; Father-Daughter, .22. Thus the values of the father are not more likely to be internalized than those of the mother; nor do sons register consistently different rates of agreement than daughters. Finally, the particular sex mix of parent and child makes little difference. We also found that the use of sex combinations as controls on other bivariate relationships usually resulted in minor and fluctuating differences. Whatever family charcteristics affect differential rates of value transmission, they are only marginally represented by sex roles in the family.

Affectivity and Control Relationship

Another set of family characteristics employed with considerable success in studies of the family and child development has to do with the dimension of power or control on the one hand, and the dimension of

---

30 See, e.g., Charles E. Bowerman and Glen H. Elder, "Adolescent Perception of Family Power Structure," *American Sociological Review* 29 (August 1964): 551–67; E. C. Devereaux, Urie Bronfenbrenner, and G. J. Suci, "Patterns of Parent Behavior in the United States of America and the Federal Republic of Germany: A Cross-National Comparison," *International Social Science Journal* 14 (UNESCO, 1963), 1–20; and Morris Rosenberg, *Society and the Adolescent Self-Image* (Princeton, N.J.: Princeton University Press, 1965), Ch. 3.

attachment or affectivity on the other.[31] One salient conclusion has been that children are more apt to use their parents as role models where the authority structure is neither extremely permissive nor extremely autocratic and where strong (but not overprotective) supportive functions and positive affects are present.

Although these dimensions have been employed in various ways in assessing the socialization of the child, they have rarely been utilized in looking at value transmission per se. In the nearest approach to this in political socialization studies, college students' reports suggested that perceived ideological differences between parent and child were higher when there was emotional estrangement, when the parental discipline was perceived as either too high or too low, and when the parent was believed to be interested in politics.[32] Somewhat related findings support the idea that affective and power relationships between parent and child may affect the transferral of political orientations.[33]

Affectivity and control relationships between pre-adults and their parents were operationalized in a number of ways, too numerous to give in detail. Suffice it to say that both parent and offspring were queried as to how close they felt to each other, whether and over what they disagreed, the path of compatibilities over the past few years, punishment agents, perceived level of parental control, parent and student satisfaction with controls, the nature and frequency of grievance processing, and rule-making procedures.

In accordance with the drift of previous research we hypothesized that the closer the student felt to his parent the more susceptible he would be to adopting, either through formal or informal learning, the political values of the parent. This turned out to be untrue. The closeness of parents and children, taking either the parent's report or the child's report, accounts for little variation in the parent-student correlations. This is true whether closeness to mother or father is considered and regardless of the student's sex. Similarly, other measures of affective relationships give little evidence that this dimension prompted much variation in the correlations among pairs.

Turning to the power relationships between parent and child we hypothesized two types of relationships: 1) the more "democratic" and permissive these relationships were the greater congruency there would be; and 2) the more satisfied the child was with the power relationships the greater would be the congruency. Where patterning appears it tends to

---

[31] A discussion of these dimensions is found in Murray Straus, "Power and Support Structure of the Family in Relation to Socialization," *Journal of Marriage and the Family* 26 (August 1964): 318–26. See also Wesley C. Becker, "Consequences of Different Kinds of Parental Discipline," in *Review of Child Development*, ed. Martin and Lois Hoffman (New York: Russell Sage Foundation, 1964), vol. 1, pp. 169–208; William H. Sewall, "Some Recent Developments in Socialization Theory and Research," *The Annals* 349 (September 1963): 163–81; Glen H. Elder, Jr., "Parental Power Legitimation and its Effects on the Adolescent," *Sociometry* 26 (March 1963): 50–65; and Douvan and Gold, "Modal Patterns in American Adolescence."

[32] Middleton and Putney, "Political Expression of Adolescent Rebellion."

[33] Lane, "Fathers and Sons . . ."; and Maccoby et al., "Youth and Political Change."

support the first hypothesis. For example, those students avowing they have an "average" amount of autonomy agree slightly more often with their parents than do those left primarily to their own resources and those heavily monitored by their parents. More generally, however, the power configuration—either in terms of its structure or its appraised satisfactoriness—generated few significant and consistent differences. This proved true whether we relied on the parent's account or the student's.

As with sex roles, the affective and control dimensions possess weak explanatory power when laid against parent-to-student transmission patterns. In neither case does this mean that these characteristics are unimportant for the political socialization of the young. It does mean that they are of little help in trying to account for the differential patterns of parent-student congruences.

Levels of Politicization

Another set of family characteristics concerns the saliency and cue-giving structure of political matters within the family. One would expect parents for whom politics is more salient to emit more cues, both direct and indirect. Other things being equal, the transmission of political values would vary with the saliency and overt manifestations of political matters. Cue-giving would structure the political orientations of the child and, in the absence of rebellion, bolster parent-student correspondences. The absence of cue-giving would probably inject considerable instability and ambiguity in the child's value structure. At the same time this absence would invite the injection of other socializing agents whose content and direction might vary with parental values. In either event parental-offspring value correspondences should be reduced in the case of lower political saliency and cue-giving.

Turning to the data, it is evident that while the hypothesis receives some support for party identification and political cynicism, it does not hold generally. Illustratively, Table 5 provides the parent-student correlations for party identification, cynicism, cosmopolitanism, averaged group evaluations, and two pairs of issues. The two politicization measures capture different elements of family politicization—the extent of husband-wife conversations about politics (reported by parents) and the frequency of student-parent conversations related to political affairs (reported by students). The correspondence between parent and student cynicism is mildly related to both of these measures, while party identification is clearly affected by parental conversations, but not by student-parent political discussions. The other opinions and values show no consistent relationships with either measure of politicization. Similar results were obtained when politicization was measured by the general political interest among parents and students, parent-student disagreements regarding political and social matters, and parents' participation in political campaigns.

That the level of family politicization affects somewhat the flow of party identification and cynicism but is unrelated to the transmission of other variables should not be ignored. The extremely salient character

TABLE 6. Family Politicization and Parent-Student Agreement on a Range of Political Values[a]

Frequency of:	Party Identi- fication	Politi- cal Cyn- icism	Cosmopoli- tanism Localism	Group Ratings[b]	Prayer and Integra- tion Issues[c]	Free- dom Issues[c]
Husband-Wife						
Political						
Conversations						
Very often	.54	.19	.22	.20	.36	.13
Pretty often	.49	.15	.11	.20	.30	.10
Not very often	.45	.11	.14	.24	.28	.06
Don't talk	.32	.08	.22	.23	.32	.08
Student-Parent						
Political						
Conversations						
Several times/week	.49	.16	.17	.22	.32	.08
Few times/month	.45	.12	.16	.21	.35	.14
Few times/year	.41	.10	.18	.30	.18	−.05
Don't talk	.47	.02	.12	.20	.26	.06

[a]Each tau-b correlation in this table is based on at least 82 cases.
[b]Average ratings of Negroes, Catholics, and Jews on the "feeling thermometer."
[c]See p. 175 for a description of these issues.

of party loyalties, which results in the higher overall parent-student correlation, and the summary nature of the cynicism variable suggest characteristics that may determine the relevancy of family politicization for the transmission of political values. The essential point, though, is that the level of politicization does not uniformly affect the degree of parent-student correspondence. Students with highly politicized backgrounds do not necessarily resemble their parents more closely than students from unpoliticized families. Whether it is measured in terms of student or parent responses, taps spectator fascination with or active engagement in politics, or denotes individual-level or family-level properties, varying amounts of politicization do not uniformly or heavily alter the level of correspondence between parent and offspring values.[34]

Since our findings are mostly on the null side, it is important to consider the possibility that interaction effects confound the relationship between family characteristics and transmission patterns. Previous work suggests that affectivity and power relations in the family will be related to parent-child transmission primarily among highly politicized families. Only if politics is important to the parents will acceptance or rejection of parental values be affected by the parent-child relationship. In order to test this hypothesis, student-parent agreement was observed, controlling for family politicization and affectivity or power relations simultaneously. No strong interaction effects emerge from this analysis. The affectivity and power dimensions sometimes affect only the highly politicized, some-

---

[34] Nor was the intensity of parental feelings related in any consistent fashion to the amount of parent-student correspondence.

times the most unpoliticized, and at other times their effect is not at all dependent on the level of politicization.[35] The lack of impressive bivariate relationships between family characteristics and the transmission rate of political values is not due to the confounding influence of multiple effects within the family.

With hindsight, reasons for the failure of the hypothesized relationships bearing on family structure can be suggested. But to give a clear and thorough explanation and test alternative hypotheses will be difficult and time-consuming. One exploratory avenue, for example, brings in student perceptions of parental attitudes as an intervening variable. Another is concerned with the relative homogeneity of the environment for children of highly politicized backgrounds versus youngsters from unpoliticized families. A third possibility is the existence of differential patterns of political learning and, in particular, a differential impact of the various socializing agents on children from politically rich versus those from politically barren backgrounds.[36] It is also possible that knowledge about later political development of the students would help explicate these perplexing configurations.

IV. A CONCLUDING NOTE

In our opening remarks we noted the conflicting views regarding the importance of the family as an agent of political learning for the child. This paper has been primarily concerned with a fairly narrow aspect of this question. We sought evidence indicating that a variety of political values held by pre-adults were induced by the values of their parents. Thus our test has been rather stringent. It has not examined the relative impact of the family vis-à-vis other socializing agents, the interaction effects of the family and other agents, nor the other ways in which the family may shape political orientations.

Having said this, it is nevertheless clear that any model of socialization which rests on assumptions of pervasive currents of parent-to-child value transmissions of the types examined here is in serious need of modification. Attitude objects in the concrete, salient, reinforced terrain of party identification lend support to the model. But this is a prime exception. The data suggest that with respect to a range of other attitude objects the correspondences vary from, at most, moderate support to virtually no support. We have suggested that life cycle effects, the role of other socializing agents, and attitude instabilities help account for the very noticeable departures from the model positing high transmission. Building

---

[35] There is a moderate tendency for those children feeling most detached from their parents to exhibit greater fluctuation in agreement with their parents—at various levels of politicization—than is true of those feeling most attached to their parents.

[36] At another level, the explanation may be in the lack of validity of students' and parents' reports of family structure. See Niemi, "A Methodological Study of Political Socialization . . . ," Ch. 2 and pp. 184–85.

these forces into a model of political learning will further expose the family's role in the development of political values.

A derivative implication of our findings is that there is considerable slack in the value-acquisition process. If the eighteen-year old is no simple carbon copy of his parents—as the results clearly indicate—then it seems most likely that other socializing agents have ample opportunity to exert their impact. This happens, we believe, both during and after childhood. These opportunities are enhanced by the rapid socio-technical changes occurring in modern societies. Not the least of these are the transformations in the content and form of the mass media and communication channels, phenomena over which the family and the school have relatively little control. It is perhaps the intrusion of other and different stimuli lying outside the nexus of the family and school which has led to the seemingly different *Weltanschauung* of the post-World-War-II generation compared with its immediate predecessor.

The place of change factors or agents thus becomes crucial in understanding the dynamics at work within the political system. Such factors may be largely exogenous and unplanned in nature, as in the case of civil disturbances and unanticipated consequences of technical innovations. Or they may be much more premeditated, as with radical changes in school organization and curriculum and in enforced social and racial interaction. Or, finally, they may be exceedingly diffuse factors which result in numerous individual student-parent differences with no shift in the overall outlook of the two generations. Our point is that the absence of impressive parent-to-child transmission of political values heightens the likelihood that change factors can work their will on the rising generation. Shifting demands on the political system and shifting types of system support are natural outgrowths of these processes.

6

ATTITUDE DEVELOPMENT
AS A FUNCTION OF
REFERENCE GROUPS:
THE BENNINGTON STUDY

THEODORE M. NEWCOMB

Membership in established groups usually involves the taking on of whole patterns of interrelated behavior and attitudes. This was one of the hypotheses pursued in the study which is reported here in part. The group selected for study consisted of the entire student body at Bennington College—more than 600 individuals—between the years 1935 and 1939. One of the problems to be investigated was that of the manner in which the patterning of behavior and attitudes varied with different degrees of assimilation into the community.

Not all of the attitudes and behaviors that are likely to be taken on by new members, as they become absorbed into a community, can be investigated in a single study. A single, though rather inclusive, area of adaptation to the college community was therefore selected for special study, namely, *attitudes toward public affairs*. There were two reasons for this selection: (1) methods of attitude measurement were readily available; and (2) there was an unusually high degree of concern, in this community at this time, over a rather wide range of public issues. This latter fact resulted partly from the fact that the college opened its doors during the darkest days of the depression of the 1930s, and its formative period occurred in the period of social change characterized by the phrase "the New Deal." This was also the period of gathering war clouds in Europe. Underlying both of these circumstances, however, was the conviction on the part of the faculty that one of the foremost duties of the college was to acquaint its somewhat oversheltered students with the nature of their contemporary social world.

In a membership group in which certain attitudes are approved (i.e.,

From *Readings in Social Psychology,* Third Edition, edited by E. E. Maccoby, T. M. Newcomb, and E. L. Hartley. Copyright 1947, 1952, © 1958 by Holt, Rinehart & Winston, Inc.; reprinted by permission of the author and publisher, Holt, Rinehart & Winston, Inc.

held by majorities, and conspicuously so by leaders), individuals acquire the approved attitudes to the extent that the membership group (particularly as symbolized by leaders and dominant subgroups) serves as a positive point of reference. The findings of the Bennington study seem to be better understood in terms of this thesis than any other. The distinction between membership group and reference group is a crucial one, in fact, although the original report did not make explicit use of it.

The above statement does not imply that no reference groups other than the membership group are involved in attitude formation; as we shall see, this is distinctly not the case. Neither does it imply that the use of the membership group as reference group necessarily results in adoption of the approved attitudes. It may also result in their rejection; hence the word *positive* in the initial statement. It is precisely these variations in degree and manner of relationship between reference group and membership group which must be known in order to explain individual variations in attitude formation, as reported in this study.

The essential facts about the Bennington membership group are as follows:

(1) It was small enough (about 250 women students) so that data could be obtained from every member.

(2) It was in most respects self-sufficient; college facilities provided not only the necessities of living and studying, but also a cooperative store, post office and Western Union office, beauty parlor, gasoline station, and a wide range of recreational opportunities. The average student visited the four-mile-distant village once a week and spent one week end a month away from the college.

(3) It was self-conscious and enthusiastic, in large part because it was new (the study was begun during the first year in which there was a senior class) and because of the novelty and attractiveness of the college's educational plan.

(4) It was unusually active and concerned about public issues, largely because the faculty felt that its educational duties included the familiarizing of an oversheltered student body with the implications of a depression-torn America and a war-threatened world.

(5) It was relatively homogeneous in respect to home background; tuition was very high, and the large majority of students came from urban, economically privileged families whose social attitudes were conservative.

Most individuals in this total membership group went through rather marked changes in attitudes toward public issues, as noted below. In most cases the total membership group served as the reference group for the changing attitudes. But some individuals changed little or not at all in attitudes during the four years of the study; attitude persistence was in some of these cases a function of the membership group as reference group and in some cases it was not. Among those who did change, moreover, the total membership group sometimes served as reference group but sometimes it did not. An oversimple theory of "assimilation into the community" thus leaves out of account some of those whose attitudes did and some of those whose attitudes did not change; they remain unexplained exceptions. A theory which traces the impact of other reference groups as well as the effect of the membership group seems to account for all cases without exception.

The general trend of attitude change for the total group is from freshman conservatism to senior nonconservatism (as the term was commonly applied to the issues toward which attitudes were measured). During the 1936 presidential election, for example, 62 percent of the freshmen and only 14 percent of the juniors and seniors "voted" for the Republican candidate, 29 percent of freshmen and 54 percent of juniors and seniors for Roosevelt, and 9 percent of freshmen as compared with 30 percent of juniors and seniors for the Socialist or Communist candidates. Attitudes toward nine specific issues were measured during the four years of the study, and seniors were less conservative in all of them than freshmen; six of the nine differences are statistically reliable. These differences are best shown by a Likert-type scale labeled Political and Economic Progressivism (PEP) which dealt with such issues as unemployment, public relief, and the rights of organized labor, which were made prominent by the New Deal. Its odd-even reliability was about .9, and it was given once or more during each of the four years of the study to virtually all students. The critical ratios of the differences between freshmen and juniors-seniors in four successive years ranged between 3.9 and 6.5; the difference between the average freshman and senior scores of 44 individuals (the entire class that graduated in 1939) gives a critical ratio of 4.3.

As might be anticipated in such a community, *individual prestige was associated with nonconservatism*. Frequency of choice as one of five students "most worthy to represent the College" at an intercollegiate gathering was used as a measure of prestige. Nominations were submitted in sealed envelopes by 99 percent of all students in two successive years, with almost identical results. The nonconservatism of those with high prestige is not merely the result of the fact that juniors and seniors are characterized by both high prestige and nonconservatism; in each class those who have most prestige are least conservative. For example, ten freshmen receiving 2 to 4 choices had an average PEP score of 64.6 as compared with 72.8 for freshmen not chosen at all (high scores are conservative); eight sophomores chosen 12 or more times had an average score of 63.6 as compared with 71.3 for those not chosen; the mean PEP score of five juniors and seniors chosen 40 or more times was 50.4 and of the fifteen chosen 12 to 39 times, 57.6, as compared with 69.0 for those not chosen. In each class, those intermediate in prestige are also intermediate in average PEP score.

Such were the attitudinal characteristics of the total membership group, expressed in terms of average scores. Some individuals, however, showed these characteristics in heightened form and others failed to show them at all. An examination of the various reference groups in relation to which attitude change did or did not occur, and of the ways in which they were brought to bear, will account for a large part of such attitude variance.

Information concerning reference groups was obtained both directly, from the subjects themselves, and indirectly, from other students and from teachers. Chief among the indirect procedures was the obtaining of indexes of "community citizenship" by a guess-who technique. Each of twenty-four students, carefully selected to represent every cross section and grouping of importance within the community, named three individuals from each of three classes who were reputedly most extreme in each of twenty-eight characteristics related to community citizenship. The relationship between reputation for community identification and nonconservatism is a close one, in spite of the fact that no reference was made to the latter characteristic when the judges made their ratings. A reputation index was computed, based upon the frequency with which individuals were named in five items dealing with identification with the community, minus the number of times they were named in five other items dealing with negative community attitude. Examples of the former items are: "absorbed in college community affairs," and "influenced by community expectations regarding codes, standards, etc."; examples of the latter are: "indifferent to activities of student committees," and "resistant to community expectations regarding codes, standards, etc." The mean senior PEP score of fifteen individuals whose index was +15 or more was 54.4; of sixty-three whose index was +4 to −4, 65.3; and of ten whose index was −15 or less, 68.2.

To have the reputation of identifying oneself with the community is not the same thing, however, as to identify the community as a reference group for a specific purpose—e.g., in this case, as a point of reference for attitudes toward public issues. In short, the reputation index is informative as to degree and direction of tendency to use the total membership group as a *general* reference group, but not necessarily as a group to which social attitudes are referred. For this purpose information was obtained directly from students.

Informal investigation had shown that whereas most students were aware of the marked freshman-to-senior trend away from conservatism, a few (particularly among the conservatives) had little or no awareness of it. Obviously, those not aware of the dominant community trend could not be using the community as a reference group for an attitude. (It does not follow, of course, that all those who are aware of it are necessarily using the community as reference group.) A simple measure of awareness was therefore devised. Subjects were asked to respond in two ways to a number of attitude statements taken from the PEP scale: first, to indicate agreement or disagreement (for example, with the statement: "The budget should be balanced before the government spends any money on social security"); and second, to estimate what percentage of freshmen, juniors and seniors, and faculty would agree with the statement. From these responses was computed an index of divergence (of own attitude) from the estimated majority of juniors and seniors. Thus a positive index on the part of a senior indicates the degree to which her own responses are more conservative than those of her classmates, and a negative index the degree to which they are less conservative. Those seniors whose divergence index more or less faithfully reflects the true difference between own and class attitude may (or may not) be using the class as an attitude reference group; those whose divergence indexes represent an exaggerated or minimized version of the true relationship between own and class attitude are clearly not using the class as an attitude reference group, or if so, only in a fictitious sense. (For present purposes the junior-senior group may be taken as representative of the entire student body, since it is the group which "sets the tone" of the total membership group.)

These data were supplemented by direct information obtained in interviews with seniors in three consecutive classes, just prior to graduation. Questions were asked about resemblance between own attitudes and those of class majorities and leaders, about parents' attitudes and own resemblance to them, about any alleged "social pressure to become liberal," about probable reaction if the dominant college influence had been conservative instead of liberal, etc. Abundant information was also available from the college personnel office and from the college psychiatrist. It was not possible to combine all of these sources of information into intensive studies of each individual, but complete data were assembled for (roughly) the most conservative and least conservative sixths of three consecutive graduating classes. The twenty-four nonconservative and nineteen conservative seniors thus selected for intensive study were classified according to their indexes of conservative divergence and of community reputation. Thus eight sets of seniors were identified, all individuals within each set having in common similar attitude scores, similar reputations for community identification, and similar degrees of awareness (based upon divergence index) of own attitude position relative to classmates. The following descriptions of these eight sets of seniors will show that there was a characteristic pattern of relationship between membership group and reference group within each of the sets.

1. Conservatives, Reputedly Negativistic, Aware of Their Own Relative Conservatism

Four of the five are considered stubborn or resistant by teachers (all five, by student judges). Three have prestige scores of 0, scores of the other two being about average for their class. Four of the five are considered by teachers or psychiatrist, or by both, to be overdependent upon one or both parents. All of the four who were interviewed described *their major hopes,* on entering college, *in terms of social rather than academic prestige;* all four felt that they had been defeated in this aim. The following verbatim quotations are illustrative:

E2: "Probably the feeling that (my instructors) didn't accept me led me to reject their opinions." (She estimates classmates as being only moderately less conservative than herself, but faculty as much less so.)

G32: "I wouldn't care to be intimate with those so-called 'liberal' student leaders." (*She claims to be satisfied with a small group of friends.* She is chosen as friend, in a sociometric questionnaire responded to by all students, only twice, and reciprocates both choices; both are conservative students.)

F22: "I wanted to disagree with all the noisy liberals, but I was afraid and I couldn't. *So I built up a wall inside me against what they said. I found I couldn't compete, so I decided to stick to my father's ideas. For at least two years I've been insulated against all college influences.*" (She is chosen but once as a friend, and does not reciprocate that choice.)

Q10: (who rather early concluded that she had no chance of social success in college) "It hurt me at first, but now I don't give a damn. *The things I really care about are mostly outside the college.* I think radicalism symbolizes the college for me more than anything else." (Needless to say, she has no use for radicals.)

For these four individuals (and probably for the fifth also) the community serves as reference group in a *negative* sense, and the home-and-family group in a positive sense. Thus their conservatism is dually reinforced.

2. Conservatives, Reputedly Negativistic, Unaware of Their Own Relative Conservatism

All five are described by teachers, as well as by guess-who judges, to be stubborn or resistant. Four have prestige scores of 0, and the fifth a less than average score. Each reciprocated just one friendship choice. Four are considered insecure in social relationships, and all five are regarded as extremely dependent upon parents. In interviews four describe with considerable intensity, and the fifth with more moderation, precollege experiences of rebuff, ostracism, or isolation, and all describe their hopes, on entering college, in terms of making friends or avoiding rebuff rather than in terms of seeking prestige. All five felt that their (rather modest) aims had met with good success. Each of the five denies building up any resistance to the acceptance of liberal opinions (but two add that they would have resented any such pressure, if felt). Three believe that only small, special groups in the college have such opinions, while the other two describe themselves as just going their own way, *paying no attention to anything but their own little circles and their college work.* Typical quotations follow:

Q47: "I'm a perfect middle-of-the-roader, neither enthusiast nor critic. I'd accept anything if they just let me alone. . . I've made all the friends I want." (Only one of her friendship choices is reciprocated.)

Q19: *"In high school I was always thought of as my parents' daughter. I never felt really accepted for myself. . . . I wanted to make my own way here, socially, but independence from my family has never asserted itself in other ways."* (According to guess-who ratings, she is highly resistant to faculty authority.)

L12: "What I most wanted was to get over being a sacred bunny. . . . I always resent doing the respectable thing just because it's the thing to do, but I didn't realize I was so different, politically, from my classmates. At least I agree with the few people I ever talk to about such matters." (Sociometric responses place her in a small, conservative group.)

Q81: "I hated practically all my school life before coming here. I had the perfect inferiority complex, and I pulled out of school social life—out of fear. I didn't intend to repeat that mistake here. . . . I've just begun to be successful in winning friendships, and I've been blissfully happy here." (She is described by teachers as "pathologically belligerent"; she receives more than the average number of friendship choices, but reciprocates only one of them.)

For these five individuals, who are negativistic in the sense of being near-isolates rather than rebels, the community does not serve as reference group for public attitudes. To some extent, their small friendship groups serve in this capacity, but in the main they still refer such areas of their lives to the home-and-family group. They are too absorbed in their own pursuits to use the total membership group as a reference group for most other purposes, too.

3. Conservatives, Not Reputedly Negativistic, Aware of Their Own Relative Conservatism

Three of the five are described by teachers as "cooperative" and "eager," and none as stubborn or resistant. Four are above average in prestige. Four are considered by teachers or by guess-who raters, or both, to retain very close parental ties. All four who were interviewed had more or less definite ambitions for leadership on coming to college, and all felt that they had been relatively successful—though, in the words of one of them, none ever attained the "really top-notch positions." All four are aware of conflict between parents and college community in respect to public attitudes, and all quite consciously decided to "string along" with parents, feeling self-confident of holding their own in college in spite of being atypical in this respect. Sample quotations follow:

Q73: *"I'm all my mother has in the world. It's considered intellectually superior here to be liberal or radical. This puts me on the defensive,* as I refuse to consider my mother beneath me intellectually, as so many other students do. Apart from this, I have loved every aspect of college life." (A popular girl, many of whose friends are among the nonconservative college leaders.)

Q78: *"I've come to realize how much my mother's happiness depends on me, and the best way I can help her is to do things with her at home as often as I can.* This has resulted in my not getting the feel of the college in certain ways, and I know my general conservatism is one of those ways. But it has not been important enough to me to make me feel particularly left out. If you're genuine and inoffensive about your opinions, no one really minds here if you remain conservative." (Another popular girl, whose friends were found among many groups.)

F32: *"Family against faculty has been my struggle here.* As soon as I felt really secure here I decided not to let the college atmosphere affect me too much. Every time I've tried to rebel against my family I've found out how terribly wrong I am, and so I've naturally kept to my parents' attitudes." (While not particularly popular, she shows no bitterness and considerable satisfaction over her college experience.)

Q35: "I've been aware of a protective shell against radical ideas. When I found several of my best friends getting that way, I either had to go along or just shut out that area entirely. I couldn't respect myself if I had changed my opinions just for that reason, and so I almost deliberately lost interest—really, *it was out of fear of losing my friends."* (A very popular girl, with no trace of bitterness, who is not considered too dependent upon parents.)

For these five the total membership group does not serve as reference group in respect to public attitudes, but does so serve for most other purposes. At some stage in their college careers the conflict between college community and home and family as reference group for public attitudes was resolved in favor of the latter.

4. Conservatives, Not Reputedly Negativistic, Not Aware of Their Own Relative Conservatism

All four are consistently described by teachers as conscientious and co-operative; three are considered overdocile and uncritical of authority. All are characterized by feelings of inferiority. All are low in prestige, two receiving scores of 0; all are low in friendship choices, but reciprocate most of these few choices. Two are described as in conflict about parental authority, and two as dependent and contented. All four recall considerable anxiety as to whether they would fit into the college community; all feel that they have succeeded better than they had expected. Sample statements from interviews follow:

D22: "I'd like to think like the college leaders, but I'm not bold enough and I don't know enough. So the college trend means little to me; I didn't even realize how much more conservative I am than the others. *I guess my family influence has been strong enough to counterbalance the college influence.*" (This girl was given to severe emotional upsets, and according to personnel records, felt "alone and helpless except when with her parents.")

M12: "It isn't that I've been resisting any pressure to become liberal. The influences here didn't matter enough to resist, I guess. *All that's really important that has happened to me occurred outside of college,* and so I never became very susceptible to college influences." (*Following her engagement to be married, in her second year, she had "practically retired" from community life.*)

Q68: "If I'd had more time here I'd probably have caught on to the liberal drift here. But I've been horribly busy making money and trying to keep my college work up. *Politics and that sort of thing I've always associated with home instead of with the college.*" (A "town girl" of working-class parentage.)

Q70: "Most juniors and seniors, if they really *get excited about their work, forget about such community enthusiasms as sending telegrams to Congressmen.* It was so important to me to be accepted, I mean intellectually, *that I naturally came to identify myself in every way with the group which gave me this sort of intellectual satisfaction.*" (One of a small group of science majors, nearly all conservative, who professed no interests other than science and who were highly self-sufficient socially.)

For none of the four was the total membership group a reference group for public attitudes. Unlike the nonnegativistic conservatives who are aware of their relative conservatism, they refer to the total membership group for few if any other purposes. Like the negativistic conservatives who are unaware of their relative conservatism, their reference groups for public attitudes are almost exclusively those related to home and family.

5. Nonconservatives, Reputedly Community-identified, Aware of Their Relative Nonconservatism

Each of the seven is considered highly independent by teachers, particularly in intellectual activities; all but one are referred to as meticulous, perfectionist, or overconscientious. Four are very high in prestige, two high, and one average; all are "good group members," and all but one a "leader." None is considered overdependent upon parents. All have come to an understanding with parents concerning their "liberal" views; five have "agreed to differ," and the other two describe one or both parents as "very liberal." All take their public attitudes seriously, in most cases expressing the feeling that they have bled and died to achieve them. Interview excerpts follow:

B72: "*I bend in the direction of community expectation*—almost more than I want to. I constantly have to check myself to be sure it's real self-conviction and not just social respect." (An outstanding and deeply respected leader.)

M42: "My family has always been liberal, but the influences here made me go further, and for a while I was pretty far left. Now I'm pretty much in agreement with my family again, but it's my own and it means a lot. It wouldn't be easy for me to have friends who are very conservative." (Her friendship choices are exclusively given to nonconservatives.)

E72: "I had been allowed so much independence by my parents that I needed desperately to identify myself with an institution with which I could conform conscientiously. Bennington was perfect. I drank up everything the college had to offer, including social attitudes, though not uncritically. I've become active in radical groups and constructively critical of them." (Both during and after college she worked with C.I.O. unions.)

H32: "I accepted liberal attitudes here because *I had always secretly felt that my family was narrow and intolerant, and because such attitudes had prestige value.* It was all part of my generally expanding personality—*I had never really been part of anything before.* I don't accept things without examining things, however, and I was sure I meant it before I changed." (One of those who has "agreed to differ" with parents.)

Q43: "It didn't take me long to see that liberal attitudes had prestige value. But all the time I felt inwardly superior to persons who want public acclaim. Once I had arrived at a feeling of personal security, I could see that it wasn't important—it wasn't enough. *So many people have no security at all. I became liberal at first because of its prestige value.* I remain so because the problems around which my liberalism centers are important. What I want now is to be effective in solving the problems." (Another conspicuous leader, active in and out of college in liberal movements.)

The total membership clearly serves as reference group for these individuals' changing attitudes, but by no means as the only one. For those whose parents are conservative, parents represent a negative reference group, from whom emancipation was gained via liberal attitudes. And for several of them the college community served as a bridge to outside liberal groups as points of reference.

6. Nonconservative, Reputedly Community-identified, Not Aware of Their Own Relative Nonconservatism

The word *enthusiastic* appears constantly in the records of each of these six. All are considered eager, ambitious, hard-working, and anxious to please. Four are very high in prestige, the other two about average. None is considered overdependent upon parents, and only two are known to have suffered any particular conflict in achieving emancipation. Each one came to college with ambitions for leadership, and each professes extreme satisfaction with her college experience. Sample quotations follow:

Qx: "Every influence I felt tended to push me in the liberal direction: my underdog complex, *my need to be independent of my parents, and my anxiousness to be a leader here.*"

Q61: "I met a whole body of new information here; I took a deep breath and plunged. When I talked about it at home my family began to treat me as if I had an adult mind. *Then too, my new opinions gave me the reputation here of being open-minded and capable of change.* I think I could have got really radical but I found it wasn't the way to get prestige here." (She judges most of her classmates to be as nonconservative as herself.)

Q72: "I take everything hard, and so of course I reacted hard to all the attitudes I found here. I'm 100-percent enthusiastic about Bennington, and that includes liberalism (but not radicalism, though I used to think so). Now I know that you can't be an *extremist if you're really devoted to an institution,* whether it's a labor union or a college." (A conspicuous leader who, like most of the others in this set of six, *judges classmates to be only slightly more conservative than herself.*)

Q63: *"I came to college to get away from my family,* who never had any respect for my mind. Becoming a radical meant thinking for myself and, figuratively, thumbing my nose at my family. *It also meant intellectual identification with the faculty and students that I most wanted to be like."* (She has always felt oppressed by parental respectability and sibling achievements.)

Q57: "It's very simple. *I was so anxious to be accepted that I accepted the political complexion of the community here.* I just couldn't stand out against the crowd unless I had many friends and strong support." (Not a leader, but many close friends among leaders and nonconservatives.)

For these six, like the preceding seven, the membership group serves as reference group for public affairs. They differ from the preceding seven chiefly in that they are less sure of themselves and are careful "not to go too far." Hence they tend to repudiate "radicalism," and to judge classmates as only slightly less conservative than themselves.

7. Nonconservatives, Not Reputedly Community-identified, Aware of Own Relative Nonconservatism

Each of the six is described as highly independent and critical-minded. Four are consistently reported as intellectually outstanding, and the other two occasionally so. All describe their ambitions on coming to college in intellectual rather than in social terms. Four of the five who were interviewed stated that in a conservative college they would be "even more radical than here." Two are slightly above average in prestige, two below average, and two have 0 scores. Three have gone through rather severe battles in the process of casting off what they regard as parental shackles; none is considered overdependent upon parents. Sample interview excerpts follow:

Q7:   *"All my life I've resented the protection of governesses and parents.* What I most wanted here was the intellectual approval of teachers and the more advanced students. Then I found you can't be reactionary and be intellectually respectable." (Her traits of independence became more marked as she achieved academic distinction.)

Q21:   "I simply got filled with new ideas here, and the only possible formulation of all of them was to adopt a radical approach. *I can't see my own position in the world in any other terms. The easy superficiality with which so many prestige-hounds here get 'liberal' only forced me to think it out more intensely."* (A highly gifted girl, considered rather aloof.)

C32:   *"I started rebelling against my pretty stuffy family before I came to college.* I felt apart from freshmen here, because I was older. Then I caught on to faculty attempts to undermine prejudice. I took sides with the faculty immediately, against the immature freshmen. I crusaded about it. *It provided just what I needed by way of family rebellion,* and bolstered up my self-confidence, too." (A very bright girl, regarded as sharp tongued and a bit haughty.)

J24:   *"I'm easily influenced by people whom I respect,* and the people who rescued me when I was down and out, intellectually, gave me a radical intellectual approach; they included both teachers and advanced students. *I'm not rebelling against anything.* I'm just doing what I had to do to stand on my own feet intellectually." (Her academic work was poor as a freshman, but gradually became outstanding.)

For these six students it is not the total membership group, but dominant subgroups (faculty, advanced students) which at first served as positive reference groups, and for many of them the home group served as a negative point of reference. Later, they developed extracollege reference groups (left-wing writers, etc.). In a secondary sense, however, the total membership group served as a negative point of reference—i.e., they regarded their nonconservatism as a mark of personal superiority.

8. Nonconservatives, Not Reputedly Community-identified, Not Aware of Own Relative Nonconservatism

Each of the five is considered hard-working, eager, and enthusiastic but (especially during the first year or two) unsure of herself and too dependent upon instructors. They are "good citizens," but in a distinctly retiring way. Two are above average in prestige, and the other three much below average. None of the five is considered overdependent upon parents; two are known to have experienced a good deal of conflict in emancipating themselves. All regard themselves as "pretty average persons," with strong desire to conform; they describe their ambitions in terms of social acceptance instead of social or intellectual prestige. Sample excerpts follow:

E22: "*Social security is the focus of it all with me.* I became steadily less conservative as long as I was *needing to gain in personal security, both with students and with faculty.* I developed some resentment against a few extreme radicals who don't really represent the college viewpoint, and that's why I changed my attitudes so far and no further." (A girl with a small personal following, otherwise not especially popular.)

D52: "*Of course there's social pressure here to give up your conservatism.* I'm glad of it, because for me this became the *vehicle for achieving independence from my family.* So changing my attitudes has gone hand in hand with two *very important things: establishing my own independence and at the same time becoming a part of the college organism.*" (She attributes the fact that her social attitudes changed, while those of her younger sister, also at the college, did not, to the fact that she had greater need both of family independence and of group support.)

Q6: "I was ripe for developing liberal or even radical opinions because so many of my friends at home were doing the same thing. So it was really wonderful that I could agree with all the people I respected here and the same time move in the direction that my home friends were going." (A girl characterized by considerable personal instability at first, but showing marked improvement.)

Qy: "I think my change of opinions has given me *intellectual and social self-respect at the same time.* I used to be too timid for words, and I never had an idea of my own. As I gradually became more successful in my work and made more friends, I came to feel that it didn't matter so much whether I agreed with my parents. It's all part of the feeling that I really belong here." (Much other evidence confirms this; she was lonely and pathetic at first, but really belonged later.)

These five provide the example *par excellence* of individuals who came to identify themselves with "the community" and whose attitudes change *pari passu* with the growing sense of identity. Home-and-family groups served as supplementary points of reference, either positive or negative. To varying degrees, subgroups within the community served as focal points of reference. But, because of *their need to be accepted, it was primarily the membership group as such which served as reference group for these five.*

SUMMARY

In this community, as presumably in most others, all individuals belong to the total membership group, but such membership is not necessarily a point of reference for every form of social adaptation, e.g., for acquiring attitudes toward public issues. *Such attitudes, however, are not acquired in a social vacuum. Their acquisition is a function of relating oneself to some group or groups, positively or negatively.* In many cases (perhaps in all) the referring of social attitudes to one group negatively leads to referring them to another group positively, or vice versa, so that the attitudes are dually reinforced.

An individual is, of course, "typical" in respect to attitudes if the total membership group serves as a positive point of reference for that purpose, but "typicality" may also result from the use of other reference groups. It does not follow from the fact that an individual is "atypical" that the membership group does not serve for reference purposes; it may serve as negative reference group. Even if the membership group does not serve as reference group at all (as in the case of conservatives in this community who are unaware of the general freshman-to-senior trend), it cannot be concluded that attitude development is not a function of belonging to the total membership group. The unawareness of such individuals is itself a resultant adaptation of particular individuals to a particular membership group. The fact that such individuals continue to refer attitudes toward public issues primarily to home-and-family groups is, in part at least, a result of the kind of community in which they have membership.

In short, the Bennington findings seem to support the thesis that, in a community characterized by certain approved attitudes, the individual's attitude development is a function of the way in which he relates himself both to the total membership group and to one or more reference groups.

7

POLITICAL SOCIALIZATION
AND THE HIGH SCHOOL
CIVICS CURRICULUM
IN THE UNITED STATES

KENNETH P. LANGTON / M. KENT JENNINGS

Attempts to map the political development of individuals inevitably become involved with the relative contribution of different socialization agencies throughout the life cycle. Research has focused to a large extent on the family and to a much lesser degree on other agents such as the educational system. At the secondary school level very little has been done to examine systematically the selected aspects of the total school environment. To gain some insight into the role of the formal school environment, this paper will explore the relationship between the civics curriculum and political attitudes and behavior in American high schools.

A number of studies, recently fortified by data from Gabriel Almond and Sidney Verba's five-nation study, stress the crucial role played by formal education in the political socialization process.

> [None of the other variables] compares with the educational variable in the extent to which it seems to determine political attitudes. The uneducated man or the man with limited education is a different political actor from the man who has achieved a high level of education.[1]

Such conclusions would not have greatly surprised the founders of the American republic, for they stressed the importance of education to

From *American Political Science Review* 62, no. 3 (September 1968): 852-67; reprinted by permission of the authors and the American Political Science Association.

Financial support for the study reported here came from the Danforth Foundation and the National Science Foundation. Kenneth Langton also wishes to acknowledge the support of the National Institute of Mental Health. We express our appreciation to Philip Converse for his helpful comments.

[1] Gabriel Almond and Sidney Verba, *The Civic Culture* (Princeton, N.J.: Princeton University Press, 1963), pp. 135–36.

the success of democratic and republican government. Starting from its early days the educational system incorporated civic training. Textbooks exposing threats to the new republic were being used in American schools by the 1790s. By 1915, the term "civics" became associated with high school courses which emphasized the study of political institutions and citizenship training.[2]

Throughout this period to the present, however, there has been controversy over the objectives, content, and impact of government courses. While most educators can agree that the development of good citizenship is important, the "good citizen" is something of an ideal type whose attitudes and behavior vary with the values of those defining the construct. Yet when the literature on the development of civics is examined a few consistent themes appear. The civics course should increase the student's knowledge about political institutions and process, make him a more interested and loyal citizen, and increase his understanding of his own rights and the civil rights of others. The literature also implies that good citizenship does not exist *in vacuo;* it means active political participation as well as loyalty and interest.[3]

It is apparent that curriculum, teachers, school climate, and peer groups all may contribute to the political socialization process; but the relative contribution of each is unclear.[4] Attempts to assess the actual impact of the school in general, and the curriculum in particular, have produced controversial and inconsistent results. College studies which have examined general curriculum effects (for example, liberal arts vs. natural science programs) upon the political values and beliefs of students have generated differing results.[5] Because of the lack of comparative research

---

[2] For a short historical background and bibliography on the civics curriculum in American high schools, see, *inter alia:* I. James Quillen, "Government Oriented Courses in the Secondary School Curriculum," in *Political Science in the Social Studies,* ed. Donald H. Riddle and Robert S. Cleary (36 Yearbook, National Council for the Social Studies, 1966), pp. 245–72; and Franklin Patterson, "Citizenship and the High School: Representative Current Practices," in *The Adolescent Citizen,* ed. Patterson et al. (New York: Free Press, 1960), Ch. 5.

[3] See for example: Educational Policies Commission, *Learning the Ways of Democracy: A Case Book in Civic Education* (Washington: National Education Association of the United States, 1940), Ch. 1; and Henry W. Holmes, "The Civic Education Project of Cambridge," *Phi Delta Kappan* 33 (December 1951): 168–71.

[4] For related bibliography and a general discussion of this problem see: James S. Coleman, "Introduction" in *Education and Political Development,* ed. James S. Coleman (Princeton, N.J.: Princeton University Press, 1965), pp. 18–25.

[5] C. Robert Pace, "What Kind of Citizens Do College Graduates Become," *Journal of General Education* 3 (April 1949): 197–202; W. H. Holtzman, "Attitudes of College Men Toward Non-Segregation in Texas Schools," *Public Opinion Quarterly* 20 (1956): 559–69; Theodore Newcomb, *Personality and Social Change* (New York: Dryden, 1943); Rose Goldsen et al., *What College Students Think* (Princeton, N.J.: Van Nostrand, 1960); A. J. Drucker and H. H. Remmers, "Citizenship Attitudes of Graduated Seniors at Purdue University," *Journal of Educational Psychology* 42 (1951): 231–35; and Irvin Lehman, "Changes in Attitudes and Values Associated with College Attendance," *Journal of Educational Psychology* 57 (April 1966): 89–98.

designs and controls for pre-selection as well as the differences in institutional cultures being examined, the impact of college curricula is still an open question.[6]

Other inquiries have been more focused. Arthur Kornhauser [7] and Albert Somit,[8] among others, used student panel studies to measure attitude change resulting from exposure to one or more specific courses. While Kornhauser found significant change in attitudes toward liberal economic positions among students in an economics class, Somit concluded that introductory courses in political science which emphasized personal political participation had no significant impact on the students' own attitudes along that dimension.

At the high school level the outcome of research on the association between curriculum and political socialization has also been mixed. Moreover, the conclusions of these studies are often hampered by their lack of generalizing power to broader universes of students and by the rather restricted nature of the dimensions being studied.

In a quasi-experimental study of three Boston-area high schools, Edgar Litt found that while civics courses had little impact upon students' attitudes toward political participation, these courses did affect students' "political chauvinism" and "support of the democratic creed." [9] Experimental pedagogical methods have also resulted in some observable short term cognitive and affective changes.[10] However, other studies of the relationship between formal courses in social studies and politically relevant attitudes report either inconclusive or negative results. The early New York Regent's Inquiry on Citizenship Education, which found that the

---

6 Allen H. Barton, *Studying the Effects of College Education* (New Haven, Conn.: Edward Hazen Foundation, 1959), p. 76; Charles G. McClintock and Henry A. Turner, "The Impact of College upon Political Knowledge, Participation, and Values," *Human Relations* 15 (May 1962): 163–76; and Theodore M. Newcomb, "The General Nature of Peer Group Influence," in Theodore M. Newcomb and Everett K. Wilson, *College Peer Groups* (Chicago: Aldine, 1966), p. 2.

7 Arthur Kornhauser, "Changes in the Information and Attitudes of Students in an Economics Class," *Journal of Educational Research* 22 (1930): 288–308.

8 Albert Somit et al., "The Effect of the Introductory Political Science Course on Student Attitudes Toward Political Participation," *American Political Science Review* 52 (December 1958): 1129–32; Marvin Schick and Albert Somit, "The Failure to Teach Political Activity," *The American Behavioral Scientist* 6 (January 1963): 5–8; James A. Robinson et al., "Teaching with Inter-Nation Simulation and Case Studies," *American Political Science Review* 60 (March 1966): 53–65; and Charles Garrison, "The Introductory Political Science Course As An Agent of Political Socialization" (Ph.D. dissertation, University of Oregon, 1966).

9 Edgar Litt, "Civic Education Norms and Political Indoctrination," *American Sociological Review* 28 (February 1963): 69–75.

10 See, e.g., C. Benjamin Cox and Jack E. Cousins, "Teaching Social Studies in Secondary Schools and Colleges," in *New Challenges in the Social Studies,* ed. Byron Massialas and Frederick R. Smith (Belmont, Calif.: Wadsworth Publishing Company, 1965), Ch. 4; and Robert E. Mainer, "Attitude Change in Integroup Programs," in *Anti-Democratic Attitudes in American Schools,* ed. H. H. Remmers (Evanston, Ill.: Northwestern University Press, 1963), pp. 122–54.

quantity of work done in social studies was not reflected in changed "citizenship" attitudes, was later echoed by the Syracuse and Kansas studies of citizenship [11] and data from the Purdue Opinion Panel.[12]

Almond and Verba asked adult respondents in their comparative study to recall if any time was spent in their school teaching about politics and government. They compared the level of subjective political competence of individuals who reported that time was spent in their school teaching about politics with those who reported that it was not. The authors indicate that the data show "a relatively clear connection between manifest political teaching and political competence in the United States, Britain, and Mexico." [13] They conclude that manifest teaching about politics can increase an individual's sense of political competence, but this is less likely to happen in nations (like Germany and Italy) whose educational systems have been dominated for much of the life span of the respondents by anti-democratic philosophies.

In addition to the mixed findings of various studies, there is also some question as to the potential of the secondary school for political socialization. It is possible that by the time students reach high school many of their political orientations have crystallized or have reached a temporary plateau. Recent research [14] on the political socialization of American pre-adults argues that the elementary school years are the most important for the formation of basic political orientations.[15] It is also possible that the high school civics courses to which students are exposed offer little that is new to them, that they simply provide another layer of information which is essentially redundant.

Granting either or both of these points one should, perhaps, not expect dramatic movements simply on the basis of one or two courses. However, some incremental changes should be visible. One might also hypothesize differential incremental effects according to some central characteristics of the students, their families, the school, the curriculum, or the political orientations themselves. It is to an examination of such possibilities that we now turn.

---

[11] Franklin Patterson et al., *The Adolescent Citizen*, pp. 71–73; Roy A. Price, "Citizenship Studies in Syracuse," *Phi Delta Kappan* 33 (December 1951): 179–81; and Earl E. Edgar, "Kansas Study of Education for Citizenship," ibid., 175–78.

[12] H. H. Remmers and D. H. Radler, *The American Teenager* (New York: Charter, 1962), p. 195.

[13] Almond and Verba, *The Civic Culture*, p. 361.

[14] Robert D. Hess and David Easton, "The Role of the Elementary School in Political Socialization," *The School Review* 70 (1962): 257–65; David Easton and Robert Hess, "The Child's Political World," *Midwest Journal of Political Science* 6 (August 1962): 229–46; Robert Hess and Judith Torney, *The Development of Political Attitudes In Children* (Chicago: Aldine, 1967); and Fred Greenstein, *Children And Politics* (New Haven, Conn.: Yale University Press, 1965).

[15] On the other hand, Adelson and O'Neil find important political cognitive development taking place during the adolescent years. See Joseph Adelson and Robert O'Neil, "The Growth of Political Ideas in Adolescence: The Sense of Community," *Journal of Personality and Social Psychology* 4 (September 1966): 295–306.

I. STUDY DESIGN

The data to be employed come from a study conducted by the Survey Research Center of The University of Michigan in the spring of 1965. Interviews were held with a national probability sample of 1669 high school seniors distributed among 97 secondary schools (public and non-public). An important feature of the student sample is that it was drawn from a universe of 12th graders; school dropouts in that age cohort are therefore automatically eliminated. For all but 6 percent of the sample each student's mother or father, designated randomly, was interviewed. Additional interviews were conducted with 317 of the students' most relevant social studies teachers. Finally, in order to determine some general academic and structural characteristics of each school, interviews and questionnaires were administered to school officials.

The particular social studies courses taken by each student were determined in the following way. In each school a list was made of the social studies courses offered during grades 10–12. As each individual course offered in a school was read to the respondents, he indicated if and when he had taken it during the past three years—that is during the 10th, 11th and 12th grades.

We were particularly interested in those courses which are commonly referred to as high school government or civics courses. A broad array of courses were included under this rubric. They ranged from the usual American Government and Problems of Democracy courses, through Political Science, Americanism, Communism and Democracy, to International Relations, World Citizenship, and Comparative Politics. Contemporary History courses which were essentially studies of current events were also included in this dimension. Normally, however, we distinguished between history and civics courses. While both types of courses (as well as other social studies) may have an impact on students' political orientations, in this paper we shall generally limit our focus to the civics curriculum.

Each student in the sample was scored according to the number of government courses he had taken during his three years of high school. About one-third of the students had not taken such a course, and of those who had the great majority had taken no more than one (Table 1). Therefore in the following analysis when we talk about the direct impact of the civics curriculum upon political orientations it will mean for most students the difference between no civics course and one civics course. Since a civics course is usually taken by requirement, we may assume that there is little self-selection bias at work.[16]

---

[16] A regional pattern is present. Appreciably more students in the West and Midwest had taken such courses than was true in the South and, especially, in the Northeast. It appears that this variation did not influence the findings reported below. Other personal and school characteristics did not discriminate among takers and nontakers of civics courses.

TABLE 1.   Number and Type of Civics Courses Taken By
American High School Seniors in Grades 10-12

Number of Courses	Percent	Type of Course Among Those Taking A Course	Percent
0	32	American Government	67
1	59	American Problems	37
2+	9	Other	10
	100%		114%[a]
	N = (2060)[b]		N = (1401)

[a]Percentages exceed 100 because some students have taken more than one course.

[b]This is a weighted N resulting from a factor applied to correct for unavoidably imprecise estimates made at the time the sampling frame was constructed. All results reported here are based on weighted N's. In the case of multivariate analysis using data from the parents as well as students, the base weighted N will be 1927, a reduction occasioned by the fact that interviews were not held with 6% of the students' parents.

Table 1 also shows a breakdown of the *type* of course experienced. The division is between the more frequently-taken American Government course, the less popular American Problems course, and a sprinkling of more esoteric titles. The "Problems" course is commonly called Problems of Democracy, Contemporary Problems, Problems of American Life, and so forth. Schools typically offer either American Government or American Problems although they are occasionally found together, and infrequently—in nonpublic or especially small schools—neither course may be offered.[17] Whereas the American Government courses focus heavily on the forms, structures, backgrounds, and traditions of American political life, the Problems courses are more eclectic in terms of the disciplines utilized, emphasize a wider scope of socio-political activities, are more contemporary in nature, and are typically organized around major problems in American public life. Because of the different emphases and formats of the two types of courses, educators have suggested that they will have differential effects.

In selecting the dependent variables for this analysis, we attempted to touch on many of the consistent themes in the "civics" literature which are germane for political science. Rather than examine only one or two variables, we have elected to pursue a wide variety so that the possible variations in effects may be uncovered.

1. Political Knowledge and Sophistication

For better or worse, performance on factual examinations is a prime way in which the success of a course and teacher is evaluated. Students

---

[17] For a more detailed account of social studies curriculum offerings see M. Kent Jennings, "Correlates of the Social Studies Curriculum: Grades 10–12," in *Social Studies in the United States,* eds. Benjamin Cox and Byron Massialas (New York: Harcourt Brace Jovanovich, 1967).

were asked six questions dealing with recent and contemporary political events and personalities. The pattern of responses formed a Guttman-type political knowledge scale.[18] Another measure (explained below), touching more directly on political sophistication, ascertained the students' perception of ideological differences between political parties.

2. Political Interest

A hallmark of the "shoulds" of political education in the United States is the shaping of citizens to take an active interest in political affairs. Although numerous studies of adults suggest that the schools and other socializing agents fall short of the goals envisioned by the authors of civics textbooks, it is nevertheless possible that these achievements would be even less impressive in the absence of intensive inculcation in the civics courses. Among many alternative measures of interest available in the interview protocols, we shall rely on the answers to a straightforward inquiry.[19]

3. Spectator Politicization

A more direct measure of interest in political matters is the degree to which students consume political content in the mass media. If the civics curriculum spurs an interest in politics, it should be reflected in greater media consumption. Separate soundings were taken of the students' behavior *vis-a-vis* television, newspapers, and magazines.[20]

4. Political Discourse

Even more dramatic evidence of the success of the civics experience would be an upsurge in the pre-adult's level of politically-tinged dialogue. In view of the fact that there are relatively few ways in which the high school senior can (or does) assume active political roles, the frequency of political conversations is not an improbable surrogate for forms of

---

[18] Respondents were asked to identify (1) the number of years a U.S. Senator serves; (2) the country Marshall Tito leads; (3) the number of members on the U.S. Supreme Court; (4) the name of the Governor of their state; (5) the nation that during WWII "had a great many concentration camps for Jews"; and (6) whether President Franklin Roosevelt was a Republican or a Democrat.

The six items formed a Guttman scale with a coefficient of reproducibility (CR) of .92.

[19] "Some people seem to think about what's going on in government and public affairs most of the time, whether there's an election going on or not. Others aren't that interested. Would you say you follow what's going on in government and public affairs most of the time, some of the time, only now and then or hardly at all?"

[20] Students were asked how often they "read about public affairs and politics" in newspapers or magazines and how often they watched "any programs about public affairs, politics, and the news on television."

adult-level political activity. For present purposes the student's report of the frequency with which he discusses politics with his peers will be used.[21]

5. Political Efficacy

The belief that one can affect political outcomes is a vital element of political behavior, and Easton and Dennis have demonstrated the rising sense of efficacy as the child progresses through elementary school.[22] Much of civic education's thrust is toward developing a sense of civic competence. Efficacy was measured by the students' responses to two items.[23]

6. Political Cynicism

While trying to create interest in politics and a sense of efficacy, the civics curriculum almost inevitably tries to discourage feelings of mistrust and cynicism toward the government. Indeed, cynicism seems in part to be antithetical to a feeling of civic competence.[24] A six-item scale was used to arrange the students on a political cynicism dimension.[25]

7. Civic Tolerance

Considerable discussion exists in the citizenship literature on the necessity for inculcating norms of civic tolerance. Even though the curriculum materials and the teachers often fail to grapple with the complexities of

---

21 "Do you talk about public affairs and politics with your friends outside of classes?" (If yes) "How often would you say that is?"

22 David Easton and Jack Dennis, "The Child's Acquisition of Regime Norms: Political Efficacy," *American Political Science Review* 61 (March 1967): 25–38; Almond and Verba, *The Civic Culture*, Ch. 12; and Angus Campbell et al., *The American Voter* (New York: John Wiley, 1960), pp. 103–5, 480–81.

23 The following two items were used to construct a three point political efficacy scale with a CR of .94:

(1) Sometimes politics and government seem so complicated that a person like me can't really understand what's going on.

(2) Voting is the only way that people like my mother and father can have any say about how the government runs things.

24 Robert E. Agger, Marshall Goldstein, and Stanley Pearl, "Political Cynicism: Measurement and Meaning," *The Journal of Politics* 23 (August 1961): 477–506.

25 The following six items formed a political cynicism scale which had a CR of .92:

(1) Over the years, how much attention do you feel the government pays to what the people think when it decides what to do. . . . ?

(2) Do you think that quite a few of the people running the government are a little crooked, not very many are, or do you think hardly any of them are?

(3) Do you think that people in government waste a lot of money we pay in taxes, waste some of it, or don't waste very much of it?

(4) How much of the time do you think you can trust the government in Washington to do what is right?

(5) Do you feel that almost all of the people running the government are smart people who usually know what they are doing, or do you think that quite a few of them don't seem to know what they are doing?

(6) Would you say the government is pretty much run by a few big interests looking out for themselves or that it is run for the benefit of all the people?

these norms, a proper and necessary role of civics courses is seen as creating support for the "Bill of Rights," due process, freedom of speech, recognition of legitimate diversity, and so forth.[26] In order to probe the effect of exposure to civics courses on these types of beliefs, a three-item civic tolerance scale was devised.[27]

8. Participative Orientation

Instilling a propensity toward participation in public life becomes especially evident as a civic education goal as the adolescent approaches legal age. In particular, one might hypothesize that the participation ethic would displace a more basic and early-formed orientation such as loyalty to country. Responses to an open-ended question tapping the students' view of the "good citizen" form the basis of the participative-orientation measure.[28]

Before turning to the findings it will be instructive to consider some of the factors which could affect the relationship between exposure to civics and the dependent variables. For example, one could argue that a positive association between exposure and political knowledge may only be found among students from less educated and less politicized families. This "sponge" theory maintains that children from more culturally deprived families are less likely to be saturated with political knowledge and interest in the family environment; therefore they are more likely to be affected by the civics curriculum when they enter high school. Conversely, one might hypothesize that it is the child from the more highly educated family who is most likely to have developed the minimal learning skills and sensitivity to politics which would allow him to respond to civics instruction.

The academic quality of the high school could also affect the efficacy of the civics curriculum. A school that sends 75 percent of its seniors on to a four–year college might be presumed to have a significantly different and better academic program than a school that sends only 15 percent of its students.

Since we are focusing on civics courses rather than history courses— taken in moderate to heavy amounts by virtually all high school students —we also want to be sure that we are measuring the independent effect of the civics curriculum and not the interactive effect of the history courses. One can easily think of other possible predictor variables: grade average, sex, political interest, and so forth.

---

26 See Byron Massialas, "Teaching American Government in High School," in Cox and Massialas, *Social Studies in the U.S.,* pp. 167–95.

27 The following three agree-disagree questions formed a Guttman scale with a CR of .95:

(1) If a person wanted to make a speech in this community against religion, he should be allowed to speak.

(2) If a Communist were legally elected to some public office around here, the people should allow him to take office.

(3) The American system of government is one that all nations should have.

28 The question wording is found on page 27 of the questionnaire.

The problem of multiple predictors clearly calls for a form of multivariate analysis. We chose the Multiple Classification Analysis Program (MCA).[29] This program is useful for examining the relationship of each of several predictors to a dependent variable at a zero order level and while the other predictors are held constant. Eta coefficients and partial beta coefficients indicate the magnitudes of the relationships for zero order and partial correlations, respectively. The program assumes additive effects and combines some features of both multiple regression and analysis of variance techniques. Unlike conventional regression procedures the program allows predictor variables in the form of nominal as well as higher order scales and it does not require or assume linearity of regression.

In the subsequent multivariate analysis seven variables were held constant while the independent effect of the civics curriculum was examined: 1) quality of the school; [30] 2) grade average; 3) sex; 4) student's political interest; [31] 5) the number of history courses taken; 6) parental education; and 7) parental politicization (discussion of politics within the family). Information on the latter two variables was based on interviews held with the students' parents, not from students' reports, as is commonly the case.

II. FINDINGS FOR THE WHOLE SAMPLE

One of the first points to be established here is that scant differences emerge in the dependent variables as a consequence of whether the student had taken a more traditional American Government course or the more topically-oriented, wider ranging American Problems course. There is a consistent, though quite small tendency for students taking the former course to consume more political content in newspapers, magazines, and on television, and to discuss politics with peers more frequently. But compared with students taking the American Problems course they more often stress the loyalty (48 percent versus 37 percent) rather than the participation aspect of good citizenship behavior. Aside from these rather meager differences, students taking the two major types of courses are virtually indistinguishable in terms of their political orientations. Knowing this, we may proceed with some confidence to treat them (and those taking a sprinkling of other courses) together and to focus our analysis primarily on the amount of exposure, viz., none, one, or two courses during grades 10–12.

An overview of the results offers strikingly little support for the impact of the curriculum. It is true that the direction of the findings is generally consonant with the predictions advanced above. That is, the more civics

---

[29] Frank Andrews, James Morgan, and John Sonquist, *Multiple Classification Analysis* (Ann Arbor: Institute for Social Research, University of Michigan, 1967).

[30] School academic quality is based on the percent of seniors going on to four-year colleges or universities in each school. This information was obtained from school sources.

[31] When political interest was examined as a dependent variable in the MCA analysis it was, of course, dropped as a control variable.

courses the student has had the more likely he is to be knowledgeable, to be interested in politics, to expose himself to the political content of the mass media, to have more political discourse, to feel more efficacious, to espouse a participative (versus loyalty) orientation, and to show more civic tolerance. The possible exception to the pattern is the curvilinear relationship between course-taking and political cynicism. Thus, the claims made for the importance of the civic education courses in the senior high school are vindicated if one only considers the direction of the results.

However, it is perfectly obvious from the size of the correlations that the magnitude of the relationships are extremely weak, in most instances bordering on the trivial. The highest positive eta coefficient is .06, and the highest partial beta is but .11 (for political knowledge).[32] Our earlier anticipation that course-taking among older adolescents might result in only incremental changes is borne out with a vengeance. Indeed, the increments are so miniscule as to raise serious questions about the utility of investing in government courses in the senior high school, at least as these courses are presently constituted. Furthermore, when we tested the impact of the history curriculum under the same control conditions it was as low or lower than the civics curriculum.[33]

It could be argued that the inclusion of a key variable, viz., the quality and type of teaching, would produce differential effects among those students who have taken one or more courses. This may be true, and in another place this possibility will be examined in detail. However, given the meager zero-order correlations, it is doubtful if that impact will be particularly large.[34] Another factor which might elicit differential patterns among students taking such courses is the content of the materials

---

[32] For convenience partial beta coefficients will be referred to as betas or beta coefficients. The beta coefficient is directly analogous to the eta, but is based on the adjusted rather than the raw mean. It provides a measure of the ability of the predictor to explain variation in the dependent variable after adjusting for the effects of all other predictors. This is not in terms of percent of variance explained. The term beta is used because "the measure is analogous to the standardized regression coefficient, i.e., the regression coefficient multiplied by the standard deviation of the predictor and divided by the standard deviation of the dependent variable, so that the result is a measure of the number of standard deviation units the dependent variable moves when the explanatory variable changes by one standard deviation." Andrews, op. cit., p. 22.

As mentioned earlier, the MCA program assumes additive effects. While some interaction may be present, a close scrutiny of the statistical analysis makes it doubtful if the impact is particularly large.

[33] In a preliminary analysis the impact of taking social studies courses as a whole was examined. The number of social studies courses taken accounted for little difference in the students' orientations.

[34] We are interested in what effect the students' perceptions of the quality of their civics teachers and courses as well as the sex of the teacher might have on the relationships. Students were asked to rank each of the courses they had taken from extremely good to extremely poor. They also ranked the quality of their teachers in the same way. Prior to the MCA analysis the relationship between the civics curriculum and the dependent variables was examined within contingency tables controlled for course and teacher ratings. Course and teacher ratings had no consistent, significant effect upon the relationships. Controls for the sex of the student's teacher also produced no significant differences.

used and the nature of the classroom discourse. This contingency, too, will be dealt with elsewhere, but it faces in large part the same difficulty as does the teacher contingency. It also confronts the reality of considerable uniformity in curriculum materials and the domination of the textbook market by a few leading books.[35]

Do these findings mean that the political orientations of pre-adults are essentially refractory to change during the senior high school years? This possibility cannot be easily dismissed. Certainly the pre-high schooler has already undergone, especially in the American context, several years of intensive formal and informal political socialization. He may have developed, by the time he reaches secondary school, a resistance to further formal socialization at this stage in his life cycle. But there is also an alternative or additional explanation. If the course work represents information redundancy, there is little reason to expect even modest alterations. By redundancy we mean not only repetition of previous instruction, though there is surely a surfeit of that. We mean also redundancy in the sense of duplicating cues from other information sources, particularly the mass media, formal organizations, and primary groups. Students not taking civics courses are probably exposed to these other sources in approximately the same doses as those enrolled in the courses. Assuming that this is the case, and that the courses provide relatively few new inputs, the consequence would be lack of differentiation between course takers and non-course takers.

For these reasons it would be well to look at courses and teachers which do not generate information redundancy. That is the virtue of examining the finer grain of teacher performance and course content, as proposed above. Another strategy, and one to be adopted in the remainder of this paper, would be to look at subpopulations of pre-adults where redundancy might be less frequent than for pre-adults in general. Less redundancy could be occasioned either by infusion of new information where relatively little existed before, or by information which conflicts with information coming from other sources.

Among the universe of subpopulations one could utilize, perhaps none is as distinctive as that of the Negro minority. The unique situation of Negroes in American social and political life and the dynamics now at work have been well-documented.[36] Because of cultural differences be-

---

35 See James P. Shaver, "Reflective Thinking, Values, and Social Studies Textbooks," *School Review* 73 (1965): 226–57; Frederick R. Smith and John J. Patrick, "Civics: Relating Social Study to Social Reality," and Byron Massialas, "Teaching American Government in High School," both in Cox and Massialas, *Social Studies in the U.S.,* pp. 105–27, 167–95.

36 In addition to such classics as Gunnar Myrdal's *An American Dilemma* (New York: Harper & Bros., 1944), see more recent works: Thomas F. Pettigrew, *A Profile of the American Negro* (Princeton, N.J.: Van Nostrand, 1964); William Brink and Louis Harris, *The Negro Revolution in America* (New York: Simon & Schuster, 1964); Kenneth B. Clark, *Dark Ghetto* (New York: Harper & Row, 1965); Lewis Killian and Charles Grigg, *Racial Crises in America* (Englewood Cliffs, N.J.: Prentice-Hall, 1964); Donald R. Matthews and James W. Prothro, *Negroes and the New Southern Politics* (New York: Harcourt Brace Jovanovich, 1966); Dwaine Marvick, "The Political Sociali-

tween the White majority and the Negro minority, the frequent exclusion of Negroes from socio-political life, the contemporary civil rights ferment, and the less privileged position of Negroes in our society, it seems likely that information redundancy would occur less often among the Negro pre-adults. Therefore, the student sample was divided along racial lines.

III. FINDINGS FOR THE NEGRO SUBSAMPLE

Although the Negro portion of the sample is not as large as one might desire for extensive analysis (raw $N = 186$, weighted $N = 208$), it is sufficiently large to permit gross comparisons with White students of similar social characteristics and also permits some analysis within the Negro subpopulation. The subsample size and the fact that the dropout rate is appreciably higher among Negroes than Whites underscores the admonition that this subsample should not be extrapolated to the Negro age cohort in general. It should also be noted that the subsample contains twelve respondents classified as non-Whites other than Negro.

Demographically, the Negro students are located disproportionately in the South (55 percent versus 25 percent for Whites) and come from more disadvantaged backgrounds than do the Whites. The latter is true despite the fact that the backgrounds of Negro students who have persevered through high school are undoubtedly less deprived than are those of their cohort who dropped out. Social status differences between Negroes and Whites are more pronounced in the South than in the North.

Negro and White students have taken civics courses in approximately the same proportions (Negroes 63 percent, Whites 68 percent). When the association between the civics curriculum and the dependent variables discussed above was reexamined within both racial groups, some intriguing differences appeared. These caused us to reassess the place of the civics curriculum in the political socialization of American youth.

Political Knowledge

White students score more highly on the knowledge scale than do Negroes; and when parents' education is controlled the differences persist at all levels. Civics courses have little effect on the absolute political knowledge level of Whites (beta $= .08$). The number of courses taken by Negroes, on the other hand, is significantly associated with their political knowledge score (beta $= .30$). The civics curriculum is an important source of political knowledge for Negroes and, as we shall see later, appears in some cases to substitute for political information gathering in the media.

Although the complex multivariate analysis holds parental education

---

zation of the American Negro," *The Annals* 361 (September 1965): 112–27; and William C. Kvaraceus et al., *Negro Self Concept: Implication for School and Citizenship* (New York: McGraw-Hill, 1965).

constant, it does not allow us to observe easily the singular role of this crucial socialization factor upon the relationship between curriculum and political orientations. Therefore, contingency tables were constructed with parental education controlled for all relationships between the number of government courses taken on the one hand, and each political orientation on the other. All instances in which education makes a distinctive imprint are reported.[37] For the case at hand—political knowledge—controls for parental education did not alter the effects of the curriculum among either Whites or Negroes.

In another attempt to measure political knowledge as well as ideological sophistication, students were asked which political party they thought was most conservative or liberal. Each party has its "liberal" and "conservative" elements, but studies of roll call voting in Congress as well as the commentary of the politically aware places the Republican party somewhat to the right of the Democrats. Forty-five percent of the students said that the Republicans were more conservative than the Democrats. Thirty-eight percent confessed to not knowing the answer.

In answering this question the student was faced with a problem not of his own making. It can be presumed that some respondents made a random choice (i.e., guessed) to extricate themselves. One gauge of the frequency of guessing is how often the Democrats were assigned a conservative position (17 percent). If we make the reasonable assumption that this form of random guess is symmetric around the midpoint of the response dimension, we can say that an additional 17 percent of the students guessed "correctly" by putting the Republicans in the conservative column. Accordingly, we may deduct 17 percent from the 45 percent who said Republicans were more conservative, leaving 28 percent who are able to connect the conservative label to the Republican party.[38]

We are less interested in the absolute number of students who are able to connect symbol with party than with the role the civics curriculum plays in this process. Again we see that course work has little impact on White students while the percent of Negroes who "know" the parties' ideological position increases as they take more civics courses (Table 2).

These findings using both measures of political knowledge offer an excellent example of redundancy in operation. The clear inference as to why the Negro students' responses are "improved" by taking the courses is that new information is being added where relatively less existed before. White students enrolled in the courses appear to receive nothing beyond that to which their non-enrolled cohorts are being exposed. This, coupled with the great lead which Whites in general already have over the Negro students, makes for greater redundancy among Whites than Negroes.

---

37 Parental education was used as a summary control variable because we felt that it best captures the tone of the whole family environment as well as other sources of socialization.

38 We have borrowed this method of adjusting "correct" answers from Donald E. Stokes, "Ideological Competition of British Parties," paper presented at 1964 Annual Meeting of the American Political Science Association, Chicago.

TABLE 2.   The Relation Between the Civics Curriculum
and Knowing the Ideological Position of the
Republican and Democrat Parties Among
Negro and White Students

Number of Civics Courses	Adjusted Percentage of Correct Responses			
	Negro		White	
	%	N	%	N
0	0	(72)	29	(543)
1+	19	(122)	31	(1184)

One should not deduce from these results that the White students have a firm grasp on political knowledge; as Table 2 and other data indicate, they clearly do not. Rather, White students have reached a saturation or quota level which is impervious to change by the civics curriculum. From their relatively lower start the Negro students' knowledge level can be increased by exposure to the civics curriculum.

Political Efficacy and Political Cynicism

Almost twice as many Negro students as White scored low on the political efficacy scale. When the effect of parental education is partialed out the racial differences remain at each educational level, although they are somewhat diminished. Interestingly enough, the difference in the percentage of those who scored low is less between Negro and White students whose parents have had only an elementary school education (13 percent) than between Negro and White students whose parents have had a college education (24 percent).

The number of civics courses taken by White students has little perceptible effect on their sense of political efficacy (beta = .05). Among Negroes, though, course exposure is moderately related to a sense of efficacy (beta = .18). As can be seen in Table 3, this is particularly true for Negroes from less educated families. The strength of the relationship decreases significantly among higher status students. Course-taking among the lower-status Negroes acts to bring their scores into line with their higher-status cohorts. There is but a faint trace of this pattern among White students.

Although Negro students at all levels of parental education feel less efficacious than their White counterparts, it must be concluded that without the civics curriculum the gap would be even greater. As in the case of political knowledge, we have another illustration of less redundancy at work among the Negro subsample. For a variety of reasons the American political culture produces a lower sense of efficacy among Negro youths compared with Whites. But by heavily emphasizing the legitimacy, desirability, and feasibility of citizen participation and control, the civics course adds a new element in the socialization of low and middle-status Negro students. Since those from the less educated families are more likely

TABLE 3.   The Relation Between the Number of Civics Courses Taken and
Political Efficacy Among Negro Students, by Parental Education

Number of Civics Courses[a]	*Elementary Political Efficacy*				*Gamma*
	Low	*Medium*	*High*		
	%	%	%	N	
0	64	20	16	(18)	
1+	30	27	43	(39)	.56

	High School Political Efficacy				
	Low	*Medium*	*High*		
0	56	20	24	(41)	
1+	34	27	39	(62)	.36

	College Political Efficacy				
	Low	*Medium*	*High*		
0	32	32	36	(15)	
1+	37	19	44	(24)	.02

[a]Parental education was set by the highest level achieved by either parent. "Elementary" means neither parent exceeded an eighth grade education; "high school" that at least one parent had one or more years of high school training; and "college" that at least one parent had one or more years of collegiate experience.

to be surrounded by agents with generally low efficacy levels, the curriculum has considerably more effect on them than on their peers from higher-status environments. Leaving aside the possible later disappointments in testing the reality of their new-found efficacy, the Negro students from less privileged backgrounds are for the moment visibly moved by course exposure.

While Negroes as a whole are less politically efficacious than Whites, they are not at the same time more politically cynical. The proportion of twelfth graders falling into the three most cynical categories of a six-point political cynicism scale includes 21 percent of the White and 23 percent of the Negro students. This relatively low level of political cynicism among Negroes may seem ironic, but it is consistent with their view of the "good citizen" role (discussed later). The high school civics curriculum has only a slight effect upon the cynicism level of Whites (beta = .11) and none among Negroes (beta = .01). However, this difference suggests that the cynicism of the latter may be somewhat less moveable than that for Whites.

Civic Tolerance

One of the abiding goals of civic education is the encouragement and development of civic toleration. Negroes as a whole score lower on the civic tolerance scale than do Whites. When parental education is controlled the racial differences remain at each education level, although they are moderately attenuated. Again, as with political efficacy, the differences in the percentage of those scoring low is less between Negro and White students whose parents have had only an elementary school education (18 percent) than between Negro and White students whose parents have had a college education (28 percent). What we may be witnessing is the result of Negro compensation for the White bias in American society—a bias to which higher status Negroes may prove most sensitive.

The number of civics courses taken has little effect on White students' civic tolerance scores (beta = .06), with somewhat greater impact being observed on those from homes of lower parental education. There is, however, a moderate association between exposure and Negro students' sense of civic tolerance (beta = .22). The more courses they take, the higher their level of tolerance. Negroes are more intolerant even when educational controls are introduced, but the civics curriculum appears to overcome in part the environmental factors which may contribute to their relatively lower tolerance. The items on which the civic tolerance measure is based all have to do with the acceptance of diversity. Aggregate student and parent data suggest that these items tap a dimension of political sophistication less likely to be operative in the Negro subculture. To the extent that the civics courses preach more tolerance, the message is less likely to be redundant among the Negroes than the Whites. Unlike political knowledge and efficacy, though, course-taking exerts its main effect on Negro twelfth graders from better-educated families, thereby suggesting that a threshold of receptivity may be lacking among those from lower-status families.

Politicization—Interest, Discussion, and Media Usage

Students were asked about their interest in public affairs and how often they discussed politics with their friends outside class. There is little difference between racial groups among those who expressed high interest in politics or said they discussed politics weekly or more often with their friends. Nor did controls for parental education uncover aggregate racial distinctions. Moreover, the civics curriculum appears at first glance to have little impact upon these two indicators of politicization among Negroes (beta = .15 and − .07, respectively) or Whites (beta = .06 and .04). Yet an examination of Table 4 indicates that curriculum effect is differentially determined by the educational level of the Negro students' parents (in contrast to a lack of variation among Whites). The differential effect may account for the low beta coefficient in the multivariate analysis.

As Negroes from less educated families take more civics courses their political interest and frequency of political discussion with peers increases. Since less educated parents ordinarily evince lower states of politicization, one could explain this in terms of nonredundant information spurring an upsurge in student politicization. Students from higher status families, however, actually appear to undergo depoliticization as they move through the civics curriculum.

TABLE 4.   Gamma Correlation Between
Number of Civics Courses Taken
and Political Interest and
Discussion with Peers Among
Negro Students, by Parental
Education

Parental Education	Political Interest	Political Discussion
Elementary	+.31	+.20
High School	−.18	−.31
College	−.21	−.36

In their excellent social and psychological inquiry into the personality of the American Negro, Abram Kardiner and Lionel Ovesey observed that it is the higher status Negro who is most likely to identify and have contact with Whites and their culture.[39] But due to their race, the disappointments are more frequent and their aspirations more likely to founder on the rock of unattainable ideals.

Because of his parents' experiences, the higher-status Negro student may have received a more "realistic" appraisal of the institutional and social restrictions placed upon Negro participation in the United States. Upon enrolling in the civics course he finds at least two good-citizen roles being emphasized. The first stresses a politicized-participation dimension. The second emphasizes a more passive role: loyalty and obedience to authority and nation. If he has absorbed from his parents the probability of restrictions, the participation-politicization emphasis in the curriculum may have little impact upon the higher status Negro student. Redundancy is low because the information conflicts with previous learning. The "reality factor" causes him to select out of the curriculum only those role characteristics which appear to be more congruent with a preconceived notion of his political life chances. As we shall see later, higher status Negro students' perception of the good citizen role is compatible with the above interpretation.

Students were also asked how often they read articles in newspapers or magazines or watched programs on television that dealt with public affairs, news, or politics. In the aggregate, students from each racial grouping employ newspapers and magazines at about the same rates; but Negro students use television more often than do Whites, and at all levels of parental education. The civics curriculum has a different impact upon political media usage among Whites and Negroes. Table 5 shows that for White students there is a consistent—but very weak—association between taking civics courses and use of the media as an access point to political information. Among Negroes there is a consistently negative but somewhat stronger association between the civics curriculum and political media usage.

---

[39] Abram Kardiner and Lionel Ovesey, *The Mark of Oppression* (Cleveland: World Publishing, 1962).

TABLE 5.   Partial Beta Coefficients
Between Number of
Civics Courses Taken
and Political Media
Usage Among Negro
and White Students

Media	Negro	White
Newspapers	−.17	+.07
Television	−.21	+.04
Magazines	−.10	+.10

Observing the same relationship within contingency tables under less severe control conditions, the civics curriculum continues to have a negative—although fluctuating—impact upon political media usage among Negroes at *all* levels of parental education (Table 6).

Negative correlations among Negroes might be explained on at least two dimensions: substitution and depoliticization. A civics course may increase a student's political interest while at the same time acting as a substitute for political information gathering in the media. This is what appears to be happening among Negroes from less educated families. Negative associations between course work and media usage suggest that the former may be substituting for political information gathering in the media. But as we saw before, there is a significant increase in political interest among lower-status Negroes as they take more civics courses. The lack of depoliticization in this group was further confirmed by the positive correlation between the civics curriculum and discussing politics with one's school friends (Table 4).

The case of the higher-status Negro seems to be of a different order. Negative correlations between the civics curriculum and media usage may indicate substitution, but what is even more apparent is the general depoliticization of higher status Negroes as they move through the curriculum. The more courses they take the less likely are they to seek political information in newspapers, magazines, and television. In addition there is also a decrease in their political interest and propensity to discuss politics with their friends.

TABLE 6.   Gamma Correlations Between Number
of Civics Courses Taken and Political
Media Usage Among Negro Students,
by Parental Education

Media	Parental Education		
	Primary	Secondary	College
Newspapers	−.07	−.36	−.28
Television	−.39	−.42	−.17
Magazines	−.27	−.07	−.42

Interjecting race adds a special complexity to the relationship between the civics curriculum and the student's belief about the role of a good citizen in this country. Students were asked:

> People have different ideas about what being a good citizen means. We're interested in what you think. Tell me how you would describe a good citizen in this country—that is, what things about a person are most important in showing that he is a good citizen.

Taking only their first responses, 70 percent of the Whites and 63 percent of the Negroes fell along two general dimensions: loyalty and political participation. Within these two response dimensions there are distinct racial differences. Sixty-one percent of the Negro responses focus on loyalty rather than participation. Only 41 percent of the White students, on the other hand, see the "good citizen" role as being one of loyalty rather than political participation. When we probe the relationship between taking civics courses and citizenship orientation some interesting differences are revealed. More civics courses mean more loyalty and less participation orientation for Negroes. In Table 7 there is a 24 percent difference in loyalty orientation between those Negroes who have taken no civic courses and those who have taken one or more. Civics course work has a slightly opposite effect among White students.

In other words, while the civics curriculum has little impact upon the

TABLE 7.   The Relationship Between Civics Curriculum and Good Citizenship Attitudes Among Negro and White Students

Number of Civics Courses	Negros Stressing:		
	Loyalty	Participation	
	%	%	N^a
0	51	49	(41)
1+	75	25	(85)
	Whites Stressing:		
	Loyalty	Participation	
0	46	54	(395)
1+	39	61	(803)

[a]These Ns run lower than corresponding Ns in other tables because those respondents not mentioning either loyalty or participation in their first response are excluded from the base.

White student's view of the good citizen role, it appears to inculcate in Negroes the role expectation that a good citizen is above all a loyal citizen rather than an active one. Yet looking at this same relationship among Negroes under the more severe multivariate control conditions the size of the beta coefficient (−.10) is not large.[40] While it is predictably negative (i.e., loyalty orientation increases with course work), the magnitude of the coefficients reduces our confidence in the earlier contingency table.

The difference in findings may be the result of moving from a relatively simple bivariate analysis with no controls for other possible intervening variables to a more sophisticated mode of multivariate analysis under more rigorously controlled conditions. This undoubtedly accounts for part of the difference, but we also found, as before, that the civics curriculum has a differential effect upon Negroes depending on the educational level of their parents.

Negro students whose parents have some secondary school or college education increase their loyalty orientation by 36 percent and 28 percent, respectively, as they take more civics courses (Table 8). Negroes from less educated families, however, increase their participation orientation much like White students. Due to the small N for Negro students who have taken no courses and whose parents have an elementary school education or less this relationship should be treated quite cautiously. Although differences between Negroes from different levels of parental education have been mentioned before, the most one would want to say here is that the civics curriculum seems to increase the loyalty orientations of higher-status

TABLE 8.   The Relation Between Civics Curriculum and Citizenship Attitudes Among Negro Students, by Parental Education

Number of Civics Courses	Elementary		
	Loyalty	Participation	
	%	%	N
0	83	17	(6)
1+	63	37	(28)
	High School		
	Loyalty	Participation	
0	54	46	(24)
1+	90	10	(41)
	College		
	Loyalty	Participation	
0	32	68	(11)
1+	60	40	(17)

---

[40] The beta coefficient for White students is +.07.

Negroes while having a slightly opposite effect among lower-status Negro students.

A number of interpretations can be placed on these findings. Both loyalty and participation are emphasized in the civics curriculum, and for White and lower-status Negro students the dual emphasis has about equal effect. But as we noted earlier, the higher-status Negro may have received from his more active parents a "realistic" appraisal of the institutional and social restrictions placed upon Negro participation in American politics. Consequently, the participation emphasis in the curriculum has little impact. The reality factor may cause the higher-status Negro to select out of the curriculum only those role characteristics which appear to be most congruent with a preconceived notion of his political life chances.

Another rationale for the findings might be found in the relative fulfillment of White and Negro needs to belong, to be accepted in this society. If we assume that the Negro is cut off from many of the associational memberships and status advantages that most Whites take for granted, then his unfulfilled need to belong and to be accepted is probably greater than that of his White counterparts. This may be particularly true of the higher-status Negro and his parents. Because of their relatively higher education in the Negro community, they have had more contacts with Whites—contacts which, because of their race, have led to more frequent rebuffs. The one association not explicitly denied Negroes is that of being a loyal American. It is entirely possible that the psychic relief a higher-status Negro receives in "establishing" his American good-citizenship is greater than that of his White counterpart or his lower-status racial peer. As a consequence, the loyalty emphasis in the curriculum may have the most impact on the higher status Negro.[41]

Regional Effects

The Negro students are located disporportionately in the southern part of the United States. Because of possible cultural differences we thought it advisable to control for region as well as parental education. Therefore the Negro subsample was divided into South and non-South with controls for high and low parental education employed in each region.[42]

---

41 In 1942 Gunnar Myrdal completed a comprehensive codification of the Negro culture and circumstances in America. He maintained that Negroes in this country were "exaggerated Americans," who believed in the American Creed more strongly than Whites. Myrdal, *An American Dilemma.*

42 The Negro subsample was not large to begin with, and a regional control in addition to the control for parental education reduced cell frequencies even further. Because the differential effects of parental education were found primarily between students whose parents had only an elementary school education versus those with high school or college education, we combined students from the latter two categories into one category. This retained the substance of the original education break in the South, but it still left only a small number of students outside the South whose parents had

When controlled for region as well as parental education, the effects of the civics curriculum upon political knowledge, interest, discussion, television-newspaper-magazine usage, and loyalty-participation orientations were consistent with the results for the Negro subsample as a whole in all except two cases. Among the seven variables discussed above there are twenty-eight cases (two for each region because of the education control or four for each variable) in which a possible deviation from the Negro subsample as a whole could occur. Due to the small marginals and the fact that there were twenty-six consistent findings, we attach little conceptual significance to these two exceptions.

In both regions the civics curriculum continued to be negatively associated with political media usage at all educational levels except for newspaper reading among higher status students outside the South. The relationships are slightly stronger in the South than in the non-South. The differential consequences of parental education were remarkably consistent across both regions. As before, civics courses had a negative effect upon the political discussion (and political interest in the South) of higher-status Negroes while having a positive impact upon lower-status Negroes. Finally, in both regions the civics curriculum continued to have its greatest negative effect on the participatory orientations of Negro students from the more educated families.

There appeared to be different regional effects on only three of the dependent variables. The first of these was political cynicism. In the South course work increases cynicism slightly among high and low status Negroes while in the North political cynicism decreased as the student was exposed to the civics curriculum. However, in both regions the outcome of taking a civics course is to make the student from the higher educated family relatively more cynical than his lower-status peer. As with cynicism, exposure to civics means a slight decrease in civic tolerance among high and low status southern Negroes. This is also true of lower-status Negroes outside the South. For all three cases the magnitude of the relationships are quite small, the highest being a gamma of $-.14$. It is only among higher-status nonsouthern Negroes that a stronger, positive relationship develops— $+.39$.

The political efficacy of lower status students in the South was increased much more by the civics curriculum (.64) than was the efficacy of their higher-status peers (.32). This is consistent with the picture for the entire subsample. However, while there was a positive relationship between exposure and increased efficacy among higher-status students in the non-South there was a negative relationship among lower-status students. We

---

an elementary school education or less. In order to enlarge this latter group the parental education cutting point in the non-South was moved to a point between those parents who were at least high school graduates and those who had only some high school or less. If there are important regional differences in curriculum effect they should be apparent under these control conditions.

The respective raw and weighted N's for the four groupings are as follows: southern low educated—33, 44; southern high educated—48, 64; non-southern low educated—45, 42; non-southern high educated—53, 50.

are at a loss to explain this negative sign other than point to the small frequencies which may account for this departure.

IV. CONCLUSION

A number of studies in the United States and other countries have stressed the importance of education in determining political attitudes and behavior. The man with only a primary school education is a different political actor from the man who has gone to high school or college. Yet direct evidence demonstrating the effect of college and high school curriculum upon political beliefs and behavior of students is scarce and generally inconclusive.

Our findings certainly do not support the thinking of those who look to the civics curriculum in American high schools as even a minor source of political socialization. When we investigated the student sample as a whole we found not one single case out of the ten examined in which the civics curriculum was significantly associated with students' political orientations.

The lack of positive results raised many questions in our minds concerning the simple correlations between years of education and political orientations which are so prevalent in the literature, particularly the differences between people with high school versus college education. Of course, high schools and colleges are complex institutions. While the formal curriculum may have little effect, there is still the acquisition of conceptual skills, the social climate of the school, and the presence of peer groups, all of which may play a significant role in the political socialization process.[43] These caveats still overlook one of the chief difficulties in studying the influence of higher education: the danger of confounding the effect of selection with that of socialization. For example, do the highly educated feel more politically competent because of their college socialization experiences or were they significantly different in this respect from their non-college-bound peers before they ever entered college?

College-bound students do differ significantly from those who are not planning to obtain a higher education. They tend to come from families with above average income and education and have all the cultural benefits of their higher status.[44] We found among the high school seniors a strong positive correlation between parents' education and students' intention to attend a four-year college or university ($\gamma = .52$). Because there was also a strong correlation between high school grades ($\gamma = .53$) and college intentions, we feel confident that stated intention to attend college is a fairly good predictor of future attendance.

---

[43] See Almond and Verba, *The Civic Culture*, Ch. 12; Kenneth P. Langton, "Peer Group and School and the Political Socialization Process," *American Political Science Review* 61 (September 1967): 751–58; and M. L. Levin, "Social Climates and Political Socialization," *Public Opinion Quarterly* 25 (Winter 1961), 596–606.

[44] Ernest Haveman and Patricia West, *They Went to College* (New York: Harcourt Brace & World, 1952).

The fact that college-bound students enjoy higher social status than those not planning to pursue a higher education suggests that there also may be important political differences between the two groups. Indeed, students who plan to attend college are more likely to be knowledgeable about politics ($\gamma = .39$); to express greater political interest (.32) and efficacy (.37); to support religious dissenters' rights of free speech (.37) and an elected communist's right to take public office (.44); to read about politics in newspapers (.18) and magazines (.34); to discuss politics with their peers (.26); and they are three times as likely to place the correct liberal-conservative label on the Democratic and Republican parties as are those students who are not planning to pursue a college education.

To summarize, there is a lack of evidence that the civics curriculum has a significant effect on the political orientations of the great majority of American high school students. Moreover, those who are college bound already have different political orientations than those who do not plan to attend college. These two conclusions suggest that an important part of the difference in political orientations between those from different levels of education, which is frequently cited in the literature and is usually explicitly or implicitly ascribed to the "education process," may actually represent a serious confounding of the effect of selection with that of political socialization.

Although the overall findings are unambiguous, there is reason to believe that under special conditions exposure to government and politics courses does have an impact at the secondary school level. When White and Negro students were observed separately, it became clear that the curriculum exerted considerably more influence on the latter. On several measures the effect was to move the Negro youths—especially those from less-educated families—to a position more congruent with the White youths and more in consonance with the usual goals of civic education in the United States. Among White students from less educated families this pattern was barely visible. With respect to some quasi-participative measures, taking a civics course served to depress Negro performance, especially among those from better-educated families. In virtually all instances the Negro students were much more affected by taking such courses than were the Whites, regardless of whether the results were positive or negative.

We argued that one explanation of the singular consequence of the curriculum upon Negro students is that information redundancy is lower for them than for White students. Because of cultural and social status differences, the Negro students are more likely to encounter new or conflicting perspectives and content. The more usual case for Whites is a further layering of familiar materials which, by and large, repeat the message from other past and contemporary sources.

It is conceivable that other subpopulations of students are differentially affected by the curriculum; that variations in content and pedagogy lead to varying outcomes; or that there will be delayed consequences from course exposure. In the main, however, one is hard pressed to find evidence of any immediate course impact on the bulk of the students. The programmatic implications of this conclusion are forceful. If the educational system continues to invest sizable resources in government and civics courses at the secondary level—as seems most probable—there must be a radical restructuring of these courses in order for them to have any appreciable pay-off. Changes in goals, course content, pedagogical methods, timing of exposure, teacher training, and school environmental factors are all points of leverage. Until such changes come about, one must continue to expect little contribution from the formal civics curriculum in the political socialization of American pre-adults.

8

DETERMINANTS OF SUPPORT
FOR CIVIL LIBERTIES

HANAN C. SELVIN | WARREN O. HAGSTROM

THE INFLUENCE OF FAMILY BACKGROUND
ON LIBERTARIANISM

A student's preuniversity background affects his support for civil liberties in two ways. It determines the attitudes he brings with him to the campus, and it affects the ways in which these attitudes change while he is there. The best way to study these changes is to measure the students' attitudes before they enter the university and when they leave, as well as at intervals during their stay—in short, a longitudinal or panel study. No such studies have been done yet at major universities (Theodore M. Newcomb's *Personality and Social Change* [1] is a panel study, but the small New England women's college at which it was done in the 1930s is not representative of American institutions of higher education.) A good approximation to the changes that can be observed in a panel study is to compare students who are at different phases of their education at one particular time (thus implicitly assuming that the same kinds of students are recruited each year). In this study we compare the attitudes of students in each of the four undergraduate years, as well as a small group of postgraduate students.

In order to see how different social backgrounds affect a student's libertarianism, it is helpful to examine the 'changes' in libertarianism for the sample as a whole first. Table 1 presents the distribution of libertarianism for the four undergraduate years and for the graduate students who came into our sample.

Libertarianism increases steadily from year to year among the undergraduates. The proportion highly libertarian almost doubles, from 21 percent among the first year students to 40 percent in the last year, and the proportion only slightly libertarian drops from 32 percent to 14 percent in the same period. Although the table shows that the graduate

From *British Journal of Sociology* 11, no. 1 (March 1960): 58–61, 65–73; excerpts reprinted by permission of the authors.

[1] Theodore M. Newcomb, *Personality and Social Change* (New York: Dryden, 1943).

TABLE 1.   Libertarianism and Year in University

	Undergraduates				Graduate Students
	First year	Second year	Third year	Fourth year	
	%	%	%	%	%
Highly libertarian	21	29	34	40	54
Moderately libertarian	47	44	50	46	30
Slightly libertarian	32	27	16	14	16
Total	100	100	100	100	100
Number of cases	(131)	(226)	(216)	(266)	(50)

students are still more libertarian than the fourth-year undergraduates, this difference represents more than the simple transition from undergraduate to graduate status. The two groups of students differ in many ways, and these differences cannot be examined when our sample includes only fifty graduate students. We have therefore largely confined our discussion to undergraduates.

THE EFFECTS OF SOCIOECONOMIC STATUS

There is ample reason to expect the social position of a student's family to affect his libertarianism. Stouffer and others have shown that tolerance for political and religious nonconformists decreases as one goes down the scale of occupational prestige.[2] Our data in Table 2 show something very much like this, a moderate association between the occupational status of the student's family and his libertarianism. But there is one surprise here: the children of blue-collar workers (skilled, semi-skilled, and unskilled workers and foremen), instead of having the poorest showing on libertarianism, turn out to have the best.

TABLE 2.   Libertarianism and Father's Occupation

Father's Occupation	Percentage highly libertarian (Undergraduates only)	Number of cases
Blue collar workers	44	(135)
Free and salaried professionals	35	(170)
Upper-level managers and officials, and large-scale proprietors	31	(249)
Farm owners and operators	30	(47)
Small businessmen	27	(98)
Clerical, sales, and public-service workers	25	(116)

---

2 Samuel A. Stouffer, *Communism, Conformity, and Civil Liberties* (New York: Doubleday, 1955), pp. 138ff.; and Martin Trow, "Small Businessmen, Political Tolerance, and Support for McCarthy," *American Journal of Sociology* 54 (November 1958): 270–81.

The most plausible explanation rests on the relations between these students and their parents. Of all occupational groups in Table 2, blue-collar workers' children are most likely to report being more libertarian than their parents. This attitudinal independence in turn results from greater economic independence; this group is the only one in which those who earn more than half of all their university expenses outnumber those who are fully supported by their parents. Greater economic independence, in the sense of self-support, is strongly associated with having more libertarian attitudes than one's parents.[3]

Although initially large, the effects of socioeconomic status on libertarianism diminish markedly as students move through the four years of undergraduate education. To show this, we shall examine the relationship between father's occupation and libertarianism separately for students in the first two years and in the last two years.

The order of the occupational categories is roughly the same among upper-division as among lower-division students. In both cases children of blue-collar workers are most likely to be highly libertarian, and children of small businessmen are among those least likely to be highly libertarian. The important finding of this table, however, is not so much the order of the occupational groups as the size of the differences between them. The differences are much smaller in the last two years than in the first two years. The extreme categories in the lower division are separated by 41 percentage points, in the upper division by only 8 percentage points. This table also serves to support the finding that libertarianism increases as students go through the university. In four of the five comparisons that can be made the upper-division students are more likely to be highly libertarian than the lower-division students. This shows that the results in Table 1 cannot be attributed to differences in the occupational strata from which each year's class is recruited, and it also helps to reject the rather implausible hypothesis that these year-to-year differences could have arisen 'by chance'. However, the curious result that the children of blue-collar workers are less libertarian in the upper division than in the lower division probably does stem from such differences in recruitment—for example, the greater proportion of blue-collar workers' children who have transferred to the University of California after one or more years at a less libertarian community college or junior college.

Table 3 exemplifies one of the major processes that occur at a university—"homogenization." The university takes in students of varied social backgrounds and attitudes. The differences in attitudes are steadily reduced, so that the graduates are appreciably more homogeneous than is the general public. University education 'declassifies' students (and then usually reclassifies them). As long as they live with their parents and attend high school in their home communities, the students automatically assume the social position of their parents. But entering the university is

---

[3] This explanation was first suggested to us by Audrey Wipper, Faith Denitch, and Maurice Zeitlin, of the University of California, who made an intensive reanalysis of the original data.

TABLE 3.   Libertarianism by Father's Occupation and Year in University

	Proportion highly libertarian			
	First two years (Lower division)		Last two years (Upper division)	
Father's Occupation	Percentage	Number of cases	Percentage	Number of cases
Blue collar workers	52	(48)	40	(87)
Professionals	32	(82)	37	(88)
Managers and officials	22	(104)	37	(145)
Farm Owners and operators	*	(15)	38	(32)
Small businessmen	21	(48)	32	(50)
Clerical, sales, and public service	11	(53)	36	(63)

*Too few cases for stable percentages.

like moving to a new town, even for those who live at home and commute to the campus, and students become aware that they will ultimately acquire their own statuses. As with their parents, the main determinant of this status will be their occupations (for the women, their husbands' occupations). But this is largely in the future. Most students have only a general idea of what life will be like for them in their future occupations, even if they have already made definite occupational choices. In a very real sense their social statuses are more similar than they were before entering the university and than they will be after graduation. And what is important here, they have lost the support for the beliefs and attitudes they had before entrance. No longer surrounded primarily by people of the same social background, they take on some of the dominant values of their new environment if these were not present in their pre-university environment. Since both the faculty and the students are predominantly libertarian, the result is a marked lessening of the effects of father's occupation as students move through their four years.

THE EFFECTS OF UNIVERSITY EXPERIENCES ON LIBERTARIANISM

The experiences that change students' libertarianism are of three kinds. First, courses in fields like history, political science, and law are necessarily concerned with the individual freedoms and legal safeguards of the Bill of Rights; perhaps the greater libertarianism of some students results from this kind of experience. Second, the training that results from academic work not directly concerned with civil liberties—for example, exposure to the varied beliefs men have held in different times and places—often induces a greater tolerance for new and strange ideas, even when courses are not designed to produce such tolerance. Third, students are affected by experiences that occur outside the classroom—discussions with other students, exposure to college nonconformists, participation in the

TABLE 4. Libertarianism by College Year and Grade-point Average

| | Proportion highly libertarian | | | |
| | First Two Years (Lower division) | | Last Two Years (Upper division) | |
Grade-point average	Percentage	Number of cases	Percentage	Number of cases
High (A to B+)	27	(120)	54	(97)
Medium (B to C+)	27	(140)	37	(247)
Low (C and below)	21	(75)	25	(110)

activities of student groups, and so on. College year makes a much greater difference for the relatively successful than for the relatively unsuccessful students in Table 4. Among those with low grades there is only a 4 percentage-point difference (25 minus 21) between upper- and lower-division students; the difference increases to 10 points for those with moderately high grades, and to 27 points for those with the highest grades. The most successful student is the most likely to increase his libertarianism as he goes through college.

Looking at these results in another way, it may be that libertarian attitudes enhance learning; perhaps the nonlibertarian, intolerant student is incapable of success in most areas because he lacks the capacity to consider unusual ideas objectively. Table 4 suggests, however, that the effect of learning on libertarianism is more important; if nonlibertarianism resulted in less learning and lower grades, there should be an association between grade-point average and libertarianism in both lower and upper divisions. But grades make a much smaller difference in the libertarianism of students in their first two years, where only 6 percentage points separate the extreme grade-point classes, as against 29 percentage points in the third or fourth years. This reinforces the conclusion that the greater libertarianism of those with high grade point averages is the result of accumulated learning.

MAJOR SUBJECT

Academically, the most important academic fact that differentiates students from one another is their 'major subject' of study. Whatever their speciality, students in most American colleges take courses in a variety of subjects, but some fields of study—political science, history, and journalism, among others—necessarily deal with questions of public policy and civil rights, while others, such as the physical sciences and engineering, never consider such questions. Consequently, differences in libertarianism tend to develop between students specializing in various fields. This process, by which the university *differentiates* students, works in the opposite direction to the homogenization discussed above.

'Major subject' means different things to different students; this must be taken into account in considering the influence of major subject on libertarianism. Men and women obviously attach different meanings to their major subjects. For men, a major subject is usually a stepping stone to a career, and their choices are of crucial importance. Most women, on the other hand, expect to be housewives; in our sample, 31 percent anticipate being occupied only as housewives within five years of graduation, and another 35 percent expect to be housewives and hold down a job at the same time. Even when college-educated women practice the calling for which they are trained it is often a secondary interest in their lives.

The effect of major subject areas on libertarianism is best observed in the column for men in Table 5. In the social sciences and the humanities men are about twice as likely to be highly libertarian as in engineering, education, and business administration; the physical sciences and the life sciences fall between these extremes. Approximately the same order of categories exists among the women, but the differences in libertarianism are of course smaller. The libertarianism of women is less influenced by their choice of major than that of the men; however, as we shall demonstrate later, women are more affected by certain nonacademic aspects of university life, notably the place where they live.

The relatively low position of the students whose major subject is education—that is, who intend to become elementary and secondary school teachers—is important and puzzling. Their attitudes are important because many will occupy positions where they will affect the attitudes of a

TABLE 5.   Libertarianism by Major Subject Area and Sex

	Proportion highly libertarian			
	Men		*Women*	
Major Subject Area	Percentage	Number of cases	Percentage	Number of cases
Applied social sciences (social welfare, criminology, etc.)	–	(9)	45	(20)
Social sciences (political science, sociology, etc.)	63	(30)	34	(32)
Humanities (literature, philosophy, history, classics, etc.)	62	(45)	34	(112)
Life sciences (medical and biological sciences, pure and applied)	41	(37)	35	(60)
Physical sciences (and mathematics)	39	(31)	–	(17)
Engineering and other applied physical sciences*	30	(245)	–	(2)
Education†	29	(24)	23	(73)
Business administration	24	(33)	–	(10)

*This category is 93 percent engineers; it also includes a few architects, foresters, and agricultural technologists.

† Since the University of California does not permit undergraduates to major in 'education' by itself, this category is perhaps too small. It includes those students who identified themselves as education majors (even if the University regards them as other majors) and students in an upper division course in the education department required of those planning to become teachers.

generation of students. Their low degree of libertarianism is puzzling because it cannot be attributed to a lack of emphasis on liberty and freedom in education courses; these values are stressed more in the education curriculum than in business administration, engineering, or science courses. Two of our findings explain part, but not all, of the low libertarianism of students planning to go into education. The libertarianism of education students is particularly low among those dissatisfied with their choice of fields and among those with low grade-point averages, of whom education recruits a disproportionate number.

Although what students learn in their courses accounts in part for these differences in libertarianism, there is also a strong selective process operating. If accumulated learning were the only important factor, the differences between the majors would be much smaller for those just beginning their college education. In fact, there is a large association between major subject and libertarianism among lower-division students. For example, 35 percent of those in the social sciences are highly libertarian as against 25 percent in engineering and 10 percent in business administration. Furthermore, many students change their major fields of study in the first year or two. We do not have data on such changes, but Morris Rosenberg has shown that many students in America change to subjects whose emphases are consistent with their own values.[4]

TYPE OF RESIDENCE

The total university experience includes more than classes and books. Especially in matters of taste and social attitudes, informal contacts between students are of great importance. For many students a good part of this interaction takes place in organized residence groups. In these groups lasting personal attachments are formed, and strong social pressures often promote a uniformity of taste and opinions that distinguishes the members of different groups. As a result, residence groups provide one of the major channels by which American college students become differentiated in their ideas and in their behaviour.

There is a wide variety of living arrangements. Some students live with parents or relatives. Others, mostly men and older women students, live by themselves or with one or two friends in apartments. But most undergraduate students live in more highly organized groups. First, there are University facilities or "dormitories". Second, there are "fraternities" and "sororities". These groups largely recruit among the wealthiest students; they have elaborate social programmes, and they are controlled by their alumni more than by the University. Finally, there are housing "co-operatives", which provide low-cost room and board for students on a first-come, first-served basis; such groups recruit mostly among students from poorer families. There is considerable variation from group to group. The proportion who are highly libertarian ranges from a low of 11 per-

---

4 Morris Rosenberg et al., *Occupations and Values* (New York: Free Press, 1957).

cent in one sorority to a high of 43 percent in a co-operative house. To provide a more complete analysis of the effects of residence groups it is necessary to consider types of groups rather than individual houses; the percentage of highly libertarian students in each of several types is presented in Table 6 for men and women separately. Among the men there are only very small differences between types of residences. Differences are somewhat larger among the women; the most unusual group is the sorority women, of whom only 17 percent are highly libertarian. Sororities apparently attract and select women who are not highly libertarian. This is suggested by the fact that sorority women who are in their first two years of college are even more extreme; among seventy-seven of them, only 9 percent are highly libertarian—as against 33 percent of lower division co-op women and 39 percent of lower-division women living in dormitories. Upper-division sorority women are also less likely to be highly libertarian, although the differences between them and the other upper-division women are smaller.

Sororities exert more control over the private lives of their members than do other kinds of residence groups, especially in matters of dress, dating, and even studying. According to reports we have collected, in many sororities there are social and physical pressures *against* studying and other forms of intellectual activity—for example, members may have a *maximum* time allowed for study. Conditions are quite different among the most independent students, those who are unmarried and live in apartments. For a man, nothing except his own preferences, his money, and the availability of an apartment prevents him from living in one; the University has no rules about where men students must live. It does have such rules for women: an unmarried woman student under twenty-one must have the written permission of her parents to live anywhere else than in an approved, organized residence group. Thus the unmarried women who live in apartments are probably more mature—at least mature enough to have convinced their parents to let them depart from the protection of an organized group. And it is only these mature women who are more libertarian than the men in comparable situations; in fact, they have the highest rate of libertarianism in Table 6.

TABLE 6. Libertarianism by Type of Residence and Sex

| | *Proportion highly libertarian (Undergraduate students only)* | | | |
| | *Men* | | *Women* | |
Type of living arrangement	Percentage	Number of cases	Percentage	Number of cases
Apartment with spouse	41	(51)	—	(14)
Apartment (no spouse)	36	(74)	46	(35)
With parents or relatives	38	(37)	38	(39)
Co-operative	35	(65)	35	(62)
University dormitory	37	(86)	34	(59)
Fraternity	32	(104)	—	
Sorority	—		17	(175)

As noted earlier, the academic aspects of university life make a greater difference in the libertarianism of men, and here we have shown that an important nonacademic aspect makes a greater difference among women. This follows from the greater likelihood of men to see the university as a stepping-stone to a career and from the greater likelihood of women to see it as an introduction to a distinctive style of life. Where circumstances have selected a group of emotionally mature women and put them in a situation of social independence, as in the apartment dwellers, women are likely to be highly libertarian. But where they live in an intellectually narrow and socially homogeneous environment, women are often very low in libertarianism.

LEADERSHIP

In all sections of America and for all types of organizations—even the Daughters of the American Revolution and the American Legion, which have been noted for their frequent attacks on "liberals" and "radicals"— leaders of community organizations are more libertarian than are the rank-and-file.[5] These findings seem paradoxical. Common sense and the findings of small-group research suggest that leaders typically embody the values of their groups.[6] Why, then, should leaders of groups with anti-libertarian ideologies (in the sense in which "libertarianism" is used here) be more libertarian than their followers?

One possible explanation is that the leaders are more highly educated. If this were the major explanation, then we would expect little difference between leaders and nonleaders with the same amount of education. In our sample leaders and nonleaders do have roughly the same level of education, live in the same surroundings, and do much the same kind of work. Nevertheless, even under these conditions, leaders are more libertarian than nonleaders. Something more than formal education is needed to account for the greater libertarianism of leaders.

In our definition a leader is anyone who has held an elected position in a living group, honour society, campus publication, religious group, or any other campus or off-campus organization. The more leadership positions a student holds, or has held, the more likely he is to be highly libertarian, as reported in Table 7.

Leaders are more libertarian despite the fact that we have included a great diversity of positions, some of them trivial: we would have classified as leaders everyone from the president of the organized student body of the University to the corresponding secretary of the Chess Club, had these students been in our sample. Actually, the type of leadership position makes considerable difference. If elected presidents and chairmen are considered separately from other elected positions, as in Table 8, the former are more libertarian.

---

5 Stouffer, *Communism, Conformity, and Civil Liberties,* Ch. 2.

6 See Cecil A. Gibb, "Leadership," Ch. 24 in *Handbook of Social Psychology*, ed. Gardner Lindzey (Cambridge, Mass.: Addison-Wesley, 1954), vol. 2.

TABLE 7.   Libertarianism by Number of Elected
            Leadership Positions

Number of elected positions	Proportion highly libertarian	Number of cases
Three or more	67	(15)
Two	42	(57)
One	38	(213)
None	31	(598)

TABLE 8.   Libertarianism by Type of Elected Position

Highest position achieved	Proportion highly libertarian	Number of cases
President or chairman	51	(81)
Other elected positions	36	(208)
No elected positions	31	(598)

The leaders and nonleaders in our sample do not have exactly the same amount of education; students who have been in college longer are more likely to be elected to offices in student groups. But when only students in the same year are considered, leaders are still more likely to be highly libertarian than nonleaders, and the differences are not much smaller than those reported in the preceding two tables.

The greater libertarianism of leaders holds up in a wide variety of social contexts. Just as Stouffer found that leaders of veterans' organizations were more libertarian than nonleaders, so the leaders of our least libertarian groups, the sororities tend to be more libertarian than the other members of these groups. And even where many members of a group are highly libertarian, as in the co-operative houses, the leaders are even more so. The same is true among categories of students that do not represent organized groups: among men and among women, in all of the major subject areas we have studied, and among supporters of both major political parties, those who have held some kind of elected position are more libertarian than the rest.

All of this demonstrates the importance of distinguishing leaders from the general population. Herbert Blumer and other critics of public-opinion research have assailed the practice of treating everyone's opinions as equally important—that is, of not distinguishing between the mass and those in positions of power.[7] Both Stouffer's study and ours demonstrate that the failure to make this distinction leads to a serious underestimate of support for libertarianism, for people who are or have been leaders are more likely to be in positions that determine the behaviour of others in times of crisis. People with antilibertarian sentiments are less often in positions where these sentiments can lead to collective action.

---

7 Herbert Blumer, "Public Opinion and Public Opinion Polling," *American Sociological Review* 13 (October 1948): 542–49.

There are two main types of explanations for the greater libertarianism of leaders. First, the leader's role usually requires him to seek consensus among the group members on various questions. For the group to function effectively, he must frequently reconcile divergent views, and some measure of tolerance for dissent may be developed in this task. Furthermore, as his group's spokesman and representative to other organizations, a leader is exposed to a more diverse assortment of people than in his own group. Experience with people unlike those with whom one has previously associated is often a key factor in the acquisition of libertarian attitudes.

This explanation of the greater libertarianism of leaders has focused on what happens to them after they assume their positions. A second and complementary explanation stresses the process by which leaders are selected. Because he is intolerant of the rights and views of others, the antilibertarian person may well be less popular and therefore less likely to be honoured by election to a position of leadership, especially in groups where most members are libertarian.[8] Then, too, the members of groups may anticipate that an intolerant person will not be able to function effectively as a leader. In sum, libertarianism may be a factor in the selection of leaders as well as an outcome of the experience of being a leader.

THE UNIVERSITY AND THE LARGER SOCIETY

This paper explores the ways in which university education changes students' support for individual liberties and civil rights. Essentially the same processes take place beyond the campus, but much less is known about them. It would be important, for example, to see how the processes of selection and training are carried on after students graduate from the university, for changes in values do not stop with the end of formal education. And next to nothing is known about the processes by which young adults who do not go to universities develop and change their values. A satisfactory assessment of the effects of university training on the development of values must compare the changes produced in university students with the changes in those who do not attend institutions of higher education.[9]

For sociologists, however, the study of the university and its students has a special appeal, apart from accessibility: the university is a miniature society with many smaller social systems within it. It also has the great advantage over the community that its 'life cycle' takes only four years for most students. Such processes as socialization into the norms of the community, recruitment into organizations, and selection for positions of leadership can all be studied easily. And the individual life cycle in the university is so standardized that a panel study of change can be approxi-

---

[8] For evidence from small group research see Gibb, "Leadership," pp. 909–12

[9] Allan H. Barton, *Studying the Effects of College Education: A Methodological Examination of "Changing Values in College"* (New Haven, Conn.: Edward W. Hazen Foundation, 1959).

mated, as in the present case, by comparisons between students at different stages of their university education. Nothing comparable exists in the open community. Finally, comparative analyses of the same processes in different social contexts can be carried on more easily within and between universities than within and between other large organizations, communities, or entire societies. Sociologists are only now beginning to take advantage of these possibilities.[10]

---

[10] Some examples are the works of Lazarsfeld and Thielens; of Norman Miller, "Academic Climate and Student Values," paper presented at the Fifty-Fourth Annual Meeting of the American Sociological Association, Chicago, September 1959; and Robert K. Merton, George Reader, and Patricia L. Kendall, *The Student-Physician* (Cambridge, Mass.: Harvard University Press, 1957).

9

THE ORGANIZATIONAL CONTEXT

BURTON CLARK | MARTIN TROW

TYPES OF STUDENT CULTURE

Instead of working with the formal properties of informal associations among students, we will focus on their normative content. Let us consider some of the orientations toward a college education which are represented on American campuses and which may be in competition on any one campus. These orientations are defining elements of student subcultures, in which they appear as shared notions of what constitutes right attitude and action toward the range of issues and experiences confronted in college. We will first distinguish several leading types of subcultures, then discuss some of the forces, both internal and external to the college, that shape the strength and distribution of the subcultures on any particular campus.

In passing, we wish to caution that the following are types of subcultures and not types of students, despite the fact that we often describe these subcultures by characterizing their members. First, an individual student may well participate in several of the subcultures available on his campus, though in most cases one will embody his dominant orientation. Second, these types of subcultures are analytical categories; the actual subcultures that flourish on any given campus may well combine elements of more than one of these types. Third, as will be seen, the analytical types simply break dimensions in half and hence oversimplify. These dimensions could be divided into a greater number of more homogeneous categories and combined in blends not here discussed or anticipated. Finally, we would not like to encourage the game of naming subcultures and then pigeon-holing individuals, groups of students, or colleges. Rather, we think of this typology as a heuristic device for getting at the processes by which social structures shape student styles of life in different kinds of colleges.

Collegiate Culture

The most widely held stereotype of college life pictures the "collegiate culture," a world of football, fraternities and sororities, dates, cars, drink-

From *College Peer Groups*, ed. Theodore M. Newcomb and Everett K. Wilson (Chicago: Aldine Publishing Company, 1966), pp. 19–63. Copyright © 1966 by National Opinion Research Center; excerpts reprinted by permission of the authors and the publisher.

ing, and campus fun.[1] A good deal of student life on many campuses revolves around this culture; it both provides substance for the stereotypes of movies and cartoons and models itself on those stereotypes. Teachers and courses and grades are in this picture but somewhat dimly and in the background. The fraternities have to make their grade-point average, students have to hit the books periodically if they are to get their diplomas, some gestures have to be made to the adult world of courses and grades which provides the justification for the collegiate round.[2]

In content, this system of values and activities is not hostile to the college, to which in fact it generates strong loyalties and attachments. It is, however, indifferent and resistant to serious demands emanating from the faculty for an involvement with ideas and issues over and above that required to gain the diploma. This culture is characteristically middle- and upper-middle class, for it takes money and leisure to pursue the busy round of social activities, and it flourishes on, though it is by no means confined to, the resident campuses of big state universities.[3] At other institutions, part-time work, intense vocational interests, an urban location, commuter students, all work against the full flowering of a collegiate subculture, as do student aspirations for graduate or professional school or, more generally, serious intellectual or professional interests on the part of students and faculty.

Vocational Culture

The countervailing forces of student poverty and vocationalism, on the one hand, and serious intellectual or academic interests, on the other,

---

[1] For a description and analysis of campus subcultures, see R. C. Angell, *The Campus* (New York: D. Appleton and Company, 1928); B. Johnson, *Campus versus Classroom* (New York: I. Washburn, 1946); and M. McConn, *College or Kindergarten?* (New York: New Republic, Inc., 1928). For an early (1909) classic indictment, see W. Wilson, "The Spirit of Learning," in *Selected Literary and Political Papers and Addresses of Woodrow Wilson*, vol. 1 (New York: Grosset and Dunlap, 1925), pp. 244–65. For a recent sociological analysis of this student world, see R. Goldsen et al., *What College Students Think* (Princeton, N.J.: Van Nostrand, 1960).

[2] Goldsen et al., ibid., p. 73. The following are quotations from interviews with fraternity men in their sample:

> Lots of pledges come in with the idea that fraternity life means all fun and no studying. We quickly educate them. Not that we want grinds—no—we try to get them to maintain a respectable average. Nothing very glittering, of course, just respectable.

> We try to keep our house's grades up to standard. There's plenty of help for the brothers who fall behind. We have files of old examinations in almost every course that they can use in studying. We even assign certain men to tutor any brothers who need help. They don't have to get super grades. After all, when you get out of college nobody asks what your grades were. Just maintain a decent average.

[3] In eleven universities across the country, fraternity members were found on the average to come from considerably wealthier homes than do independent students. In 1952 only 24 percent of the fraternity men as compared with 46 percent of the independents reported their fathers earning under $5000. Computed from data of Goldsen et al., ibid., p. 71, Table 3.3.

are strong enough to make the collegiate culture relatively weak on many American campuses which otherwise differ greatly. In the urban colleges which recruit the ambitious, mobility-oriented sons and daughters of working- and lower-middle-class homes, there is simply not enough time or money to support the expensive play of the collegiate culture. To these students, many of them married, most of them working anywhere from twenty to forty hours a week, college is largely off-the-job training, an organization of courses and credits leading to a diploma and a better job than they could otherwise command. These students have little attachment to the college, where they buy their education somewhat as one buys groceries. But like participants in the collegiate culture, these students are also resistant to intellectual demands on them beyond what is required to pass the courses. To many of these hard-driven students, ideas and scholarship are as much a luxury and distraction as are sports and fraternities. If the symbol of the collegiate culture is the football and fraternity weekend, the symbol of this vocationally oriented culture is the student placement office.

Academic Culture

Present on every college campus, although dominant on some and marginal on others, is the subculture of serious academic effort. The essence of this system of values is its identification with the intellectual concerns of the serious faculty members. The students involved work hard, get the best grades, talk about their coursework outside of class, and let the world of ideas and knowledge reach them in ways that neither of the foregoing types does. While participants in the collegiate subculture pursue fun, and the job-oriented pursue skills and a diploma, these students pursue knowledge: their symbols are the library and laboratory and seminar. If the faculty members who embody these values also represent the college as a whole, then this academic subculture is identified with the college. For these students, the attachment to the college, often as strongly felt as that among the collegiate crowd, is to the institution which supports intellectual values and opportunities for learning; the emotional tie to the college is through the faculty and through campus friends of similar mind and temper. This is the climate encouraged at the colleges that are academically strongest, and when colleges aim to upgrade themselves, it is the students already oriented in this direction whom they seek to recruit.

The products of this culture are typically aiming at graduate and professional schools; it is not surprising that they identify so strongly with the faculty and internalize the scholarly and scientific habits of mind and work as part of their anticipatory adjustment to future professional roles. These students are often oriented toward vocations but not so directly or narrowly as are the lower- and lower-middle-class commuters who hold the consumer-vocational values described above; they choose "a basic general education and appreciation of ideas" more often than "provide vocational training" as the goal of education most important to them.[4] In any case, it is not necessary to decide whether they are concerned with their studies more for the sake of learning than because of their career ambitions. The distinctive qualities of this group are, first, that they are seriously involved in their coursework beyond the minimum required for passing and graduation and, second, that they identify themselves with their college and its faculty.

Nonconformist Culture

It is in this latter respect, identification with the college, that "nonconformist," "intellectual," "radical," "alienated," "bohemian" students differ from their serious academic classmates. Some kind of self-consciously nonconformist subculture exists in many of the best small liberal arts colleges and among the undergraduates in the leading universities. These students are often deeply involved with ideas, both the ideas they encounter in their classrooms and those that are current in the wider society of adult art, literature, and politics. To a much greater degree than their academically oriented classmates, these students use off-campus groups and currents of thought as points of reference, instead of the official college culture, in their strategy of independence and criticism.[5]

The distinctive quality of this student style is a rather aggressive nonconformism, a critical detachment from the college they attend and from its faculty (though this often conceals a strong ambivalence), and a generalized hostility to the college administration. The forms that this style takes vary from campus to campus, but where it exists it has a visibility and influence far beyond its usually tiny and fluid membership. Its chief significance is that it offers a genuine alternative, however temporary, to the rebellious student seeking a distinctive identity in keeping with his own temperament and experience. In a sense it provides some intellectual content and meaning to the idealism and rebelliousness generated in adolescence in some parts of American society. While the preceding three types of students pursue fun, a diploma, or knowledge, these students

---

4 Goldsen et al., ibid.

5 C. Jencks and D. Riesman, "Patterns of Residential Education: A Case Study of Harvard," in N. Sanford, ed., *The American College* (New York: John Wiley, 1962), pp. 735–36. The academic, in their usage, refers to the pursuit of knowledge within some scholarly or professional discipline by experts and specialists (or their apprentices), whereas intellectual inquiry is the pursuit of wisdom—answers to perennial problems of living—through the play of intelligence rather than through specialized learning. As they observe, the official view holds that "the intellectual and the academic are largely synonymous," and they are concerned with those student organizations at Harvard that "have emerged to defend intellectual concerns against overt or covert pressures from the curriculum." Our typology to some extent cuts across this distinction: the academic cultures we speak of include students with genuine intellectual interests as well as "grinds" submissive to the demands of the faculty. In our typology, the members of the academic subcultures tend to link their interests to the curriculum; the nonconformist pursue theirs outside it.

pursue an identity, not as a by-product, but as the primary and often self-conscious aim of their education. And their symbol is often a distinctive style—of dress, speech, attitude—that itself represents the identity they seek.[6]

The nonconformist subculture eludes easy characterization. It may, in fact, constitute a residual category, concealing within it quite different kinds of attitudes and orientations, some of which are on the rise, some of which are declining in their importance. Here, next to the fashionable bohemians and the compulsive rebels are those who already exhibit in college the radical cosmopolitanism and skepticism, the commitment to abstract ideas, and the alienation from merely "institutional" attachments that are marks of the intellectual.

The types of subcultures we have been describing emerge from the combination of two variables: the degree to which students are involved with ideas and the extent to which students identify with their college. If we dichotomize these variables, the above four types of student orientations, which provide the content of the most important and distinguishable student subcultures, emerge in the pattern shown in Chart 1.

		Involved with ideas	
		Much	Little
Identify with their college	Much	Academic	Collegiate
	Little	Noncomformist	Vocational

Chart 1

These subcultures are fluid systems of norms and values which overlap and flow into one another on any one campus in ways that challenge the effort to distinguish them analytically. Yet that effort, for all the violence it does to the complexity of social life, appears justified by the light it promises to shed on colleges and their effects on students.[7]

---

[6] Nonconformist subcultures may provide opportunity and support for some of the processes of identity play discussed by E. H. Erikson, "The Problem of Ego Identity," *Journal of American Psychoanalytical Association* 4 (1956): 56–121. The relatively little attention given to nonconformist cultures in this essay reflects our ignorance about them and not their relative importance for American life and education.

[7] This simple typology does not take into account other dimensions of student orientations which may be important for understanding the specific forms that student subcultures take. Research aimed at applying, extending, and refining this typology is currently under way at the Educational Testing Service, Princeton, and in Berkeley at the American College Testing Program as well. For a report of a study employing this typology, see D. Gottlieb and B. Hodgkins, "College Student Subcultures," *School Review* 71 (Autumn 1963): pp. 266–90.

We now turn to several major structural aspects of colleges, the first being the distribution of authority. Authority in academic organizations has been little explored, and we do not propose a general analysis; our limited purpose is to discuss briefly two ways in which the structure of authority shapes student culture. One is through the support given to different values and interests; the other, through the involvement of students in college affairs.

Support of values and interests. Authority takes many forms in academic communities—control by traditional constituency, lay trustee, autocratic or charismatic president, bureaucratic official, or academic colleague. The secularization of American higher education has been accompanied by a change from traditional and autocratic forms of authority, such as the church and the college president, to the bureaucratic and colleague types: the administration and the faculty as a whole. The latter two types now actively contend with one another; today the conflict appears principally to take the form of the administration and governing board on the one side appealing to a bureaucratic principle of a legally based hierarchy of authority, and the professors on the other holding to the principle of a self-governing body of academic colleagues. In the main, faculties have won some control over the content of the curriculum and are increasing their influence in the selection and retention of faculty personnel.[8] But colleges are exceedingly diverse in authority structure, ranging from complete control by trustee and president to a middle ground where the faculty has some important decision-making power, to an extreme where the faculty chooses personnel and sets the budget as well as determines the curriculum.

There is apparently no binding connection between types of authority and types of student culture. Strong play cultures are found on campuses where faculty control is strong as well as where it is weak. Dominating presidents may support vocational or academic or collegiate student interests. Even so, certain tendencies and typical connections may be observed.

1. The four-year state colleges that are characterized by student vocationalism tend to have strong presidential authority and a bureaucratic structure. This often stems, in part, from the state colleges having been in the past a normal school and then a teachers college, earlier stages when the faculty was exceedingly weak. It is also related to close supervision by the state legislature or department of education, and to conceptions of efficient utilization of teachers in which scholarship and research are viewed as luxuries. But as the state college attempts to move beyond a narrow vocationalism to the status of a comprehensive college with some

---

[8] B. R. Clark, "Faculty Authority," *Bulletin of the American Association of University Professors* 47 (Winter 1961).

commitment to the liberal arts, the faculty tends to challenge the hierarchy of control. The faculty begins to compare its privileges and responsibilities to those of the faculties at the state university and leading private colleges. It wants an academic senate and control over the curriculum, and soon some faculty members are even proclaiming that administrators are incompetent to judge professors. The administrators also come to learn that able scholars will not remain in a barony, and in the push to become a liberal arts college and then a university they accommodate to some faculty authority. Broadly, vocationalism and size urge "efficient," hence bureaucratic, organization, but liberal education and the push for academic status and quality press for a "community of scholars."

2. The private liberal arts colleges that are characterized by academic student cultures and high status tend to have strong faculty control. Many such colleges have been pulled from a traditional localism to national prominence by vigorous, even charismatic, presidents, undergoing a transformation in character under a benevolent dictator. This is transitional authority. After the revolution comes consolidation; succeeding presidents are expected to preserve and administer the successful experiment. The faculty recruited by the charismatic leader, or attracted by the changes he made, takes over after he leaves. Their self-appointed role is to insure the continuity of the new character of the college, and their authority takes on this conserving function. Often a faculty council, or some other representative body of the faculty, becomes the key policy-making unit. In other cases, authority becomes lodged formally and informally in the hands of department heads and senior department members.

In either case, strong faculty control henceforth plays a role in attracting and binding faculty. Some men come because they are impressed by the college's combination of high status, distinctive name, strong faculty government and correlated freedom from administrative and lay control; they remain, in part, because the running of the college becomes "their" business. In a sense, a faculty that captures control is also captured in return, committed by involvement in policy-making—after a half-dozen years, a man has often invested too much of himself to leave. These tendencies can be of enormous advantage to a college in attracting and retaining a good teaching faculty despite a poor salary scale. This binding effect of faculty control appears to work in the direction of supporting vigorous academic subcultures in the student body by holding on a campus faculty members with serious intellectual interests.

3. The universities that are characterized by enormous size and a marked bifurcation of faculty and student interests are also the systems in which authority has the least consistent relationship to student culture. In some state universities the faculty has strong control while in others they have only weak authority and afford little protection for the individual. As noted above, the extent of faculty authority affects the quality of staff recruitment. But the locus of authority in the university does not

matter to the same degree for the attraction of students and the nature of their undergraduate life. Weak or strong colleague control, for example, may coexist with a collegiate student culture. As we previously remarked, the undergraduate student and the professor largely go their separate ways in the university; the distribution of authority among trustees, administration, and faculty little affects this underlying divergence of interest.

Faculty authority is most likely to be reflected in the student world when faculty influence encourages a tougher selection and retention policy; but faculties and administrations perhaps do not diverge so greatly in their wish for a general upgrading, and strong faculty authority probably changes the pressure in this direction only in modest degree on the large, comprehensive campus. In any case, changes made under the authority of the administration or the faculty will generally work around the edges of student life, changing selection slightly or establishing an honors program for a small segment. Such moves may eventually have large consequences, but in the university, with its impersonal relations and its wide divergence in faculty and student interests, the strength of the various student subworlds—academic, collegiate, vocational, nonconformist—is more dependent on basic commitments and general social trends than on who has power within.

Involvement of students. A second important aspect of academic control is the extent to which authority becomes lodged in the hands of students. Again, the variation on the American scene is great, extending from student governments that are no more than playful mockery to ones in which students have a dominant voice in a wide range of affairs and serve on committees of the faculty and the administration. The modal type is one in which student government is given the appearance of authority but in fact has little control, the college being either unable or unwilling to stand the costs of error and controversy. As suggested earlier, colleges and universities that have long accommodated to collegiate play have not found it equally rewarding to suffer strong student government. Weak student government supports the tendency for student involvement in the running of campus affairs to be minor. American students, little disposed by background and orientation to enter campus politics, turn further away when student government is seen as superficial. Weak student authority, we suggest, thus closes a main avenue of involvement— a road that encourages identification with the college and involvement with ideas, hence supports academic subcultures.

The effect of involving students actively in the formation of policy at the high and middle as well as the lowest levels of administration may be observed in such a college as Antioch, which has had a "community government" in operation for over a quarter of a century. Here student government is ideologically and structurally linked to the running of the whole enterprise, supporting and partly redeeming a definition of the college as community. According to doctrine, students, faculty members, and administrators participate as equals in the community government.

Although this is not fully realized in practice—the faculty being more equal than the students—the students have the majority vote on the community council and in the committees of the community government. Their minority membership on faculty committees also insures, at the least, that they are informed on affairs of the official college and that their views are heard. The elaborate system of committees found in the college's several overlapping governments has the function of involving students and providing avenues of participation for interest groups. Political militants can find their way to a civil-rights committee, for example, and there badger the faculty about their excluding students from the faculty lounge as well as to mobilize concern about segregation in the South. The joint student-faculty membership on committees insures that some students relate closely to some of the faculty outside the classroom and, at least part of the time, on meaningful issues. By offering actual participation in campus decision-making to some students and the symbols of that participation to all, Antioch's political structure becomes a dragnet of involvement, encouraging civic interest and helping to commit students deeply to the college. With a bright, liberal student body, it is also not unrelated to their involvement with serious ideas.

The colleges of strong student vocationalism appear generally to be at the other extreme in the character of their student government. The working, commuting student at the state college has no time for interest in campus matters, social or political, especially if he is supporting a family as well. Also, control over all important matters tends to remain in the hands of such distant authorities as the state board of education and with the top members of the administrative staff who are held accountable by the higher state officials. Thus one of the principal means of involvement is largely shut off, with little likelihood that identification with the college will be generated by civic participation or that interest in ideas will be excited by contact with genuine issues of social and political action.

Size and Complexity

We turn now to a quite different matter, the effect of organizational scale. The trend in western society toward increasing size and complexity in formal organization is nowhere more apparent than in American higher education: a large college before the Civil War had 600 students, and most were much smaller, while today central campuses of state universities run to 30,000. Large scale in college organization is permanently with us. Campuses of several thousand students or more will soon accommodate the overwhelming majority of college students. For the form and content of student life, nothing appears to be of greater consequence.

In any large organization that works on people rather than on products, thousands of individuals must be admitted, classified, treated, and ejected. This is generally done by routinizing procedures and processing people in batches. In the large university, impersonal batching is reflected in the registration line, the objective test, and the mass graduation. With increasing size, there is also a tendency for the faculty member to face more students in the classroom than ever before and to interact less with the individual student outside the classroom. With the TV camera and taped lecture, students may need a special appointment in order to meet the man. This mass processing does not seem to encourage a serious concern with ideas on the part of most students. Routinized classwork, for example, can be completed without serious thought. Increasing scale, it would appear, is most appropriate for a consumer orientation toward college and primarily promotes vocational subcultures. The tendency for increasing size to weaken social ties, turning groups into aggregations, leads toward the atomized vocational subcultures.

Conversely, vocationalism encourages growth in size and complexity. Business associations, professional bodies, and other interest groups that see the college as a training center encourage colleges to proliferate occupational curricula. Students mindful of upward mobility seek occupational preparation in a host of fields. Occupational training in a complex society is indeed efficiently handled by large enterprises tooled to train large numbers in diverse fields.

If increasing scale primarily promotes vocational subcultures in the student body, it secondarily supports the continuation of the collegiate life, principally through a weakened connection between the academic life and leisure. Large scale tends to separate work from nonwork, teaching and learning from what goes on outside the lecture hall. In a society where intellectual values have a marginal existence, it is not to be expected that the interests of the majority of entering students are intellectual; and many of those so inclined seek the small schools that have a liberal arts image. Those finding their way to the large institutions have predominantly a vocational interest, but some are also inclined to have fun, college-style, before work and marriage. Also the faculty members typically do little in these large places to determine the shape of the student's social life for, as previously pointed out, it is not in their realm of interest or authority. The collegiate world, in its less rah-rah forms, will continue to receive some administrative support in the very large places if for no other reason than that it helps the administration to handle the overwhelming problems of student housing and social life. The collegiate life also helps to soften the harsh contours of vocationalism, offering some leisurely play around the edges of the campus, and making the large college or university appear more like its smaller, historical antecedents.

Small size in college organization usually inhibits impersonal processing, for participation in small systems is more likely to have community qualities. Size and residence, the latter to be discussed later, appear to be the most important determinants of where colleges fall along a continuum from community to bureaucracy. At the extreme of community, approached principally through small size and residential facilities, the interaction of students, faculty, and administration is intense and informal, and judgments are particularistic, as faculty and students respond to one another as personalities ("she's bright but erratic and would profit from work with . . ."). The individual is known across the system; e.g., death is a campus event. Importantly, social and academic activity are integrated. Here the faculty has some chance to shape student culture and educate liberally through personal influence and example. But for occupational training in a complex society, such colleges are expensive, inappropriately oriented, and relatively unspecialized.

The bureaucratic end of the continuum is reached chiefly through large size and off-campus living. Here interaction is formal and segmented, universalistic criteria are used throughout the system, and academic activity is separated from the social. Teaching and studying are jobs, the personality of the student is little involved, and death is an announcement in the newspaper. Here the conditions are favorable not for liberal education but for occupational training, for such a college can offer expert instruction and service in a large number of fields.

The absolute size of colleges and universities may be a seriously misleading factor, however, because its effect on interpersonal relations and student cultures changes markedly with the nature of the organization substructure. Harvard's house system clearly "reduces" its size, and some state universities are psychologically and socially smaller than others of similar size because of the way that campus subunits ("colleges," "houses") substructure an otherwise loose aggregation. An effective substructure provides groups small enough to encourage networks of face-to-face relationships and to prevent the "we-they" dichotomy between the students and the faculty that inheres in large scale. It offers systems of action that are within the human scale of observation and comprehension, especially the limited scale of the adolescent and inexperienced adult. At the same time, when the smaller systems are part of a large college or university, the larger setting may also offer a cosmopolitan environment in which students can explore a wide range of experiences.[9]

Important to the psychological and social effectiveness of organization substructure are the criteria on which it is based; most important may be the homogeneity or heterogeneity of interest. The diversity of interests and orientations found in the total college may be reproduced in the subunits by random assignment of students. Then the large is writ small, no small change in itself. Alternatively, the substructure may be formed along broad lines of shared interests, causing subgroups to be different from the whole. We suspect that the interest substructures, rather than those that mirror the whole, provide the more meaningful centers of interaction and identification, since the subunits can then acquire a distinctive character. Certainly, diversity in a student group or residence hall may contribute to the liberal education of its members, and may break down the parochial ties of class, field of study, or the like; this apparently is one function of the Harvard houses, as Jencks and Riesman describe them.[10] On the other hand, without the tutorial system and the other

9 D. Riesman, "College Subcultures and College Outcomes," in *Selection and Educational Differentiation* (Berkeley, Calif.: University of California Field Service Center and Center for the Study of Higher Education, 1960).

10 Jencks and Riesman, "Patterns of Residential Education . . ."

mechanisms through which Harvard's houses link leisure to learning, the "diversity" resulting from random assignments to residence halls may lead to a common culture rooted in the lowest common denominator of student interests, and so prevent the development of intellectual communities among the students. Groupings based on natural common interests appear to be viable bases for intense interaction and interpersonal commitment; drama and art students illustrate this point on a number of campuses. The problem is to hook the substructure into natural interests (engage motivation institutionally), while at the same time leaving participation sufficiently voluntary and open so that the subunits do not encapsulate the student.

In the main, the universities whose size threatens the viability of student subsystems, especially the academic, have attempted little substructuring along these or other lines. Faculties have not been markedly interested, and college managements and outside supporters have held to logics of economy and efficiency that favor standardized procedure. College comptrollers, for example, do not like to work with diversely organized subunits.

At the same time, many small colleges worry about the consequences of large size every time they contemplate expanding by one or two hundred students, concerned that the character of the campus, especially the closeness of personal relations, will be changed. One answer now being offered to the problem of how to grow and yet stay small is a federation of colleges—essentially a multiplication of small, distinct units rather than the continued growth of one. The five colleges of the Pomona-Claremont complex are one such example, Wesleyan University's "College Plan" is another.[11] Wesleyan is attempting a reorganization that will allow the enterprise as a whole to grow larger, while newly established "colleges" involve the student in smaller systems of activity focused on a set of related disciplines. Of course, all universities have units called colleges, but in most cases these are largely paper assignments for students. Substructuring makes a difference when it actually changes the nature of involvement. A set of subcolleges on a comprehensive campus may enable students and faculty to keep one another in view and share some academic interests, important conditions for an academic student culture in a society in which collegiate fun and vocationalism come naturally.

Another aspect of college scale is rate of growth, one specially important as the public colleges of the nation move into a period of rapid expansion. Slow growth permits the assimilation of the new to the old: for example, new faculty members may be enculturated slowly and spontaneously to the special values and customs of a college. Rapid growth, on the other hand, reduces this possibility. New faculty come along so fast that there is neither time nor energy for the old staff to orient the new, and the student cultures are likely to be similarly overwhelmed. Administrative time and energy is also pre-empted by the operational problems

---

[11] The most impressive effort in this direction is being made on the new campus of the University of California at Santa Cruz.

of growth, e.g., recruiting personnel and expanding facilities to accommodate an annual increase in enrollment of 500 to 1,000 or more. The student cultures that are disrupted may have been primarily academic or primarily collegiate, but the outcome of rapid growth is predictably an increase in the vocational-consumer use of college, centering on the means of career achievement in the general society.

Requirements of Membership

The demands made by colleges on their client-participants also shape the strength of the several subcultures. What does it take to get in, survive, and get out in good standing? Selectivity in American colleges varies from none to severe; length of time in the system, for students in good standing, varies from a semester to four years or longer; and the standards of performance for retention range from subliminal to savage.

Relatively high selectivity seems a necessary but not sufficient condition for the dominance of academic subculture. Selectivity brings a clientele that has the potential ability for difficult study and vigorous intellectual life; the college may also select for seriousness. By contrast, the unselective college will contain a large number of students whose limited ability restricts serious attention to complicated issues and ideas and who have not been encouraged by the rewards of high performance to take on academic values.

The extremes of selection are now found in the public junior college, where open-door admission permits students of all levels of ability and achievement to enter and in the several dozen elite private colleges and universities where applicants outnumber vacancies over four to one and virtually all students are in the upper 20 percent of college students in ability.[12] The possibility of sharp selection adds greatly to the power of the official staff in shaping student cultures so that they embody academic values. Restraint by recruitment is perhaps the most important means of control by college officials over the values and practices of students.

The length of time that students in good standing spend in college systems also varies enormously. In the elite private colleges, typically 75 to 90 percent of the students graduate in four years. In state universities, 30 to 60 percent generally survive. Then there are some state colleges, e.g., in California, that lose over 80 percent of their students in the first *two* years, and the typical length of stay for students in public junior colleges is from one to one and one-half years. The length of uninterrupted time on campus undoubtedly affects the content of student subcultures as well as their viability. Where students remain in the same college for four years, relationships can grow and ripen. If this is combined with certain other conditions, especially small scale and faculty involvement, it means four years of community-like participation. At the other extreme, relationships are fleeting and are further attenuated by the realization that

---

[12] B. R. Clark, *Educating the Expert Society* (San Francisco: Chandler Publishing Co., 1962).

oneself and one's friends are here today and gone tomorrow to another college, marriage, or a job. Colleges of short duration and heavy dropout take on some of the atmosphere of a distribution center; they resemble the army's replacement depots in which people are classified and sorted.[13] The brief span of time students spend in these colleges virtually precludes the possibility of strong academic subcultures.

Performance standards work similarly. As discussed earlier, low standards of work allow heavy participation in collegiate life. High standards of performance, conversely, make hard work a condition of remaining in the system.[14] Perhaps this simple, obvious fact of academic life should not be obscured by elaborate sociological analysis of student subsystems. Faculties have the means, in the quality and amount of work they require, to weaken seriously the competition of the sidelines and the side shows. The danger here, of course, is that very heavy academic demands can crush the intellectual and cultural play and pursuits that students sustain outside the official structure, alone or in nonconformist subcultures. This is what seems to happen in the best engineering and professional schools.

Autonomy of the System

Academic systems vary enormously in their integration with the environment. Some colleges are almost of another world in their immediate surroundings, geographically detached, intellectually alien, and committed to a distinctive style of life; for example, Antioch in conservative southern Ohio, Bennington in small-town Vermont. In contrast, some municipal colleges are continuous with the sidewalk and at one with the environing city, and students in some junior colleges and state colleges have never left high school and home.

A central feature of the campuses that are closely fused with the general society is the considerable extent to which the student is a role, not a personality. This state is most likely to come about where the student does not sleep or play or work, for the most part, at the college. The student living at home, working, and commuting generally attends classes in the role of student-visitor.[15] At San Francisco State College, a typical

---

[13] Characteristically, the army replacement depots in World War II destroyed prior institutional loyalties, freeing the soldier for new attachments to his next regular outfit. But no loyalties were generated within or to these organizational decompression chambers, R. K. Merton and A. S. Rossi, "Contributions to the Theory of Reference Group Behavior," in R. K. Merton, ed., *Social Theory and Social Structure* (Glencoe, Ill.: Free Press, 1957), pp. 225–80. This "degrouping process" makes sense for colleges which are pre-employment training centers, and which are attempting to socialize students in the special values and perspectives of liberal education. As we might expect, student attachments to San Francisco State are much weaker than comparable ties of students at Reed, Antioch, or Swarthmore.

[14] For a case in which the demands of the curriculum generally predominate over student output norms, see L. Sussman, *Freshman Morale at M.I.T.* (Cambridge: Massachusetts Institute of Technology, 1960).

[15] See the study of Columbia University's School of General Studies reported by H. L. Zetterberg, *An American College for Adults* (New York: Columbia University Bureau of Applied Social Research, mimeo., 1958).

urban nonresidential college, 60 percent of the students live more than fifteen minutes away from campus, with 30 percent spending over an hour a day traveling to and from the campus. Only 8 percent walk or ride a bicycle, while 26 percent come by bus or trolley and 68 percent by automobile.

With his life lived off campus and his time and attention caught up in off-campus roles, neither the campus nor the classroom has much chance to engage the student's personality, other than in the special cases in which institutional purpose is unusually striking or student motivation unusually strong.

Physical location plays a role in the autonomy of some colleges, but by no means is the essential condition. Reed in the suburbs of Portland, Harvard in industrial Cambridge, and City College of New York in metropolitan New York are cases of physical contiguity in which bright students, able faculty, and an aura of distinction and challenge have combined to hold the environment at arm's length. In extreme cases of autonomous colleges, much seems to flow from the sense of holding to values quite different from those dominant in the bordering community and the larger society, even to the point of an ideology that divides mankind into the two worlds of "them" and "us."

The concept of intellectual autonomy sums up many impressions we have of the optimum conditions of academic impact. Colleges in this country are most likely to move students toward the ideal of the liberally educated man when (*a*) they self-consciously hold to values different from those of society at large and (*b*) the campus constitutes a community. In the first respect, the ideal of liberal education is a marginal rather than a central value of modern society and is strongly held by colleges only at the price of being different in a number of related ways, such as believing that knowledge is a value in its own right, that a life of study is meaningful, that amateur sports are for amateurs, that seventeen-year-olds should be defined as adults. In the second respect, men are shaped in college toward this ideal when they are so encompassed by the campus social system that they are made aware of the norms that define the ideal and participate in activities in which the ideal is, in fact, lived out. The most potent instrument of value change in education is the quasi-total institution, where members sleep, play, and work in the same place.[16] Intellectual autonomy and academic impact are thus generally dependent on the autonomy of ends, i.e., the purposes of the institution, and the autonomy of means, i.e., the internal conditions making for the involvement of the student.

The extent to which colleges in the United States have accepted the custodial role has greatly reduced their autonomy, for a college that stands in *loco parentis* to students deals with children rather than adults and is expected to guide unformed minds along conventionally approved paths. Where students are defined as adults, the college is freer to en-

---

16 E. Goffman, "On the Characteristics of Total Institutions," in Walter Reed Army Research Institute of Research, *Symposium on Preventive and Social Psychiatry* (Washington, D.C.: Government Printing Office, 1958), pp. 43–84.

courage independence and skepticism, qualities which are subversive of received truth at the same time as they are aspects of the ideal outcome of liberal education.

Residential colleges are commonly expected to assume the parental functions of nurture and guidance, and the freshman girls at coed residential colleges exert a pressure, both as fact and symbol, against intellectual boldness and innovation on many campuses. But the commuter colleges that are free of this expectation do not, by and large, translate that freedom into serious commitments to liberal education. For reasons we have discussed, they are vocational in orientation; they stand less as the specialized surrogate of the family and more as the pre-employment training arm of industry and government. The exchange, however, does not necessarily increase the autonomy of the college to pursue educational purposes which are different from, and sometimes at variance with, the socialization of children or the training of employees.

Despite the dominant philosophy of service which minimizes the autonomy of many public non-residential colleges, however, in some cases the relative freedom from the custodial function has permitted the emergence of adult liberal undergraduate education. At a few commuter colleges, especially those in large cities which recruit able and sophisticated students and faculty members who have independent connections with local intellectual and artistic circles, the larger worlds of politics, literature, and art find an institutional home in some segments of the college. These groups of faculty and students create their own nonconformist cultures around shared interests, sometimes in the institutional nooks and crannies of what are predominantly vocational enterprises. The art and drama departments at San Francisco State are an illustration of this phenomenon: these departments are in some ways more closely connected to the cultural life of San Francisco, and thus to larger cultural movements, than they are to the college itself. Within them, there is a good deal of direct relationship of faculty to student and the creation of a genuine cultural community with strong involvements, at variance with the impersonal and fleeting relationships typical of much of mass higher education. Although the non-residential character of much of the public section of higher education makes the development of institutional autonomy more difficult and tends to reduce the degree to which the majority of students are encompassed and affected by their formal education, the same factor may free parts of such colleges from their custodial responsibilities and thus allow them to develop pockets of adult undergraduate education which have impact on a minority of their students. The rapid growth of public commuter colleges increases the need for additional study of such developments. In 1958 only 30 percent of all college students lived in college housing. A third lived with parents or relatives while over a quarter made their own living arrangements.

part IV

STRATIFICATION AND SOCIALIZATION

Socialization is inherently a conservative process. What one knows, thinks and does largely is a result of what has been transmitted to him from existing institutions and agencies. Socialization also serves to perpetuate and reinforce inequality in society, thus lending support to the oft-repeated idea that "the rich get richer while the poor get poorer."

Both themes are illustrated in the first selection on social class differences in political learning by Fred Greenstein. Greenstein finds that middle-class children are apt to have greater amounts of political information, to experience more autonomy with regard to political choices, and to possess a greater predisposition to be politically active than their lower- or working-class counterparts. He also finds that these differences emerge fairly soon in life and, thus, may not be readily amenable to change either by schools or other agencies.

Life in the black ghettoes of America substantially differs from that in other places. Where many people might live in pleasant surroundings, with relatively few worries and cares, life for ghetto residents, in the words of Eugene Green, is a "fight for survival." Reactions to this struggle are evident in the results of Green's study of political socialization among black inner-city school children. Among other things he finds a marked degree of hostility towards the American political system.

Some of the most illuminating results about the impact of stratification dimensions on the political transmission process are to be found in the last article in this section. The authors, Dean Jaros, Herbert Hirsch and Frederic Fleron, collaborated on a study of political socialization among children in Appalachia. Comparing their results on a variety of issues with those of Hess and Torney's nationwide study, they found an unexpectedly high level of cynicism among the children. Upon further analysis, they also found that the level of cynicism was not a product of authority relations in the home, but rather seemed to be transmitted to the children as one of several ingredients of the larger subculture to which they belonged.

The cynicism observed among these white Appalachian children as well as the black children in Chicago is very much the stuff of which political activism is made. The next section deals with the roots of political activism among youth in America and identifies such subcultural pockets of cynicism as one of the chief sources.

10

SOCIAL CLASS DIFFERENCES
IN POLITICAL LEARNING

FRED I. GREENSTEIN

CLASS DIFFERENCES IN CHILD TRAINING
AND DEVELOPMENT

Lane summarizes his brief examination of the political significance of class differences in socialization by commenting that, "in general, the middle-class child seems to receive, at the same time, greater encouragement to explore and be ambitious and greater capacity for internal regulation and purposive action." [1] As he points out, much of the literature comparing social classes in their child-training practices is of questionable political relevance. Research has concentrated on a limited range of early socialization practices—on, in Sewell's words, "such aspects of infant discipline as manner of nursing, weaning, scheduling, bowel and bladder training." [2] Later research has failed to demonstrate that differences in these practices are unambiguously related to personality formation.[3]

In spite of the preoccupation with "infant discipline," there gradually has emerged a broader configuration of findings on class differences in

---

From *Children and Politics* (New Haven, Conn.: Yale University Press, 1965), pp. 89–106. Copyright © 1965 by Yale University; excerpt reprinted by permission of the author and publisher.

---

[1] Robert E. Lane, *Political Life* (Glencoe, Ill.: Free Press, 1959), p. 228.

[2] William H. Sewell, "Social Class and Childhood Personality," *Sociometry* 24 (1961): 350.

[3] See Sewell, ibid., for a valuable history of research on class and socialization. Much of the early literature was at pains to suggest that the more relaxed weaning-cleaning practices of lower-class families contributed to sounder psychological development than the rigidity of middle-class child-rearing practice. However, the effect of such practices on later development was never established. Later research indicated that lower-class child-training practices were not more easygoing. For an ingenious trend analysis of the child-training studies, suggesting that the seeming contradictions between the earlier and later studies are in fact indications of changing infant care practices but that class differences in the overall climate of child-rearing have remained consistent, see Urie Bronfenbrenner, "Socialization and Social Class Through Time and Space," in *Readings in Social Psychology*, 3d ed., ed. Eleanor E. Maccoby et al. (New York: Holt, 1958), pp. 400–425.

socialization—findings which enable us to characterize the nature and consequences of childhood experiences in different socioeconomic settings in the United States. These support and amplify Lane's conclusions.

Two somewhat related clusters of observations in the child development literature help us to understand class differences in the political involvement of New Haven children. These relate to (1) the superior verbal and scholastic capacity of higher-status children, and (2) their markedly greater intellectual and psychic autonomy—their willingness and ability to express feelings and ideas.

1. The higher his social status the more likely a child is to receive superior school grades, to show satisfactory adjustment to the classroom, and to score high on the various tests designed to measure intelligence. In New Haven, for example, 73 percent of the upper socioeconomic status children in the present sample, and only 41 percent of the lower socioeconomic status children, received school grades in the A–B range during the 1956–57 school year. Eighty-seven percent of the upper-status children and only 59 percent of the lower-status children received A or B grades for what once was called "deportment." The educational psychology literature amply demonstrates that these are typical findings. And, in spite of heroic efforts to develop intelligence tests which are free of class bias, measures of basic ability also consistently differentiate between socioeconomic groups.[4]

2. If lower-status children are equipped with fewer intellectual skills, they also are equipped with a weaker desire to use such skills. This seems in part to be a function of the general tone of parent–child relationships as they vary by class. There is some evidence that lower-class children enjoy more physical freedom than upper-class children. The former tend to stay up later at night, to be freer in their physical movements in the community, to be less controlled in their peer group activities.[5] But they are granted substantially less "psychological freedom." Upper-status parents take the child's opinions seriously, explain the reasons for parental requirements, and discuss family problems with the child.[6] In general, parent–child relationships are more open, less punitive, and more accommodating to the child's individuality. Maas comments that:

---

[4] Useful summary discussions of this literature are: Harold Jones, "The Environment and Mental Development," in *Manual of Child Psychology*, ed. Leonard Carmichael (New York: John Wiley, 1954), pp. 631–96; W. B. Brookover and David Gottlieb, "Social Class and Education," in *Readings in the Social Psychology of Education*, ed. W. W. Charters, Jr. and N. L. Gage (Boston: Allyn and Bacon, 1963), pp. 3–11; W. W. Charters, Jr., "Social Class and Intelligence Tests," ibid., pp. 12–21.

[5] George Psathas, "Ethnicity, Social Class, and Adolescent Independence from Parental Control," *American Sociological Review* 22 (1957): 415–23. Cf. Robert J. Havighurst and Allison Davis, "A Comparison of the Chicago and Harvard Studies of Social Class Differences in Child Rearing," *American Sociological Review* 20 (1955): 438–42, for instances in which lower-status children seem to enjoy less physical freedom than upper-status children.

[6] Psathas, "Ethnicity, Social Class"; Margherita MacDonald et al., "Leisure Activities and the Socio-Economic Status of Children," *American Journal of Sociology* 54 (1949): 505–19.

Lower-class parents are . . . closed or inaccessible to the child's communications, especially of the milder types of disapproval or refusal of parental
expectation or demand. Relationships between the parents being hierarchical
. . . the child is once removed . . . from direct communication with one
parent or the other. Fear of parental authority and its explosive anger
mutes the child, until he explodes in a similar manner or redirects his hostile
aggressions, as well as his tender feelings, toward siblings or other contemporaries. With them, he may become either a prototype of the bully—
status and power seeking—or an ever-submissive follower.

Upper-status parents are more receptive to their children's desires,

or so the children *feel*. Father and mother, being relatively equal powers in
the child's eyes, are equally accessible to him. Socially, they invite him to
share their activities . . . Psychologically he seems free to express both positive and negative feelings toward his . . . parents; they . . . modify decisions when the children . . . [seek] extensions of parental limitation.[7]

Kohn, in a recent summary of his own research and earlier studies, ob-
serves that

working-class parents value obedience, neatness, and cleanliness more highly
than do middle-class parents, and that middle-class parents in turn value
curiosity, happiness, consideration, and—most importantly—self-control more
highly than do working-class parents . . . there are characteristic clusters
of value choice in the two social classes: working-class parental values center
on conformity to external proscriptions, middle-class parental values on
self-direction. To working-class parents, it is the overt act that matters: the
child should not transgress externally imposed rules; to middle-class parents,
it is the child's motives and feelings that matter: the child should govern
himself.[8]

Related to the tendency of higher-status parents to encourage an internalized sense of responsibility in their children is the finding in a
number of studies that upper-status children are more likely than lower-
status children to think and plan in terms of the future; to be able to
defer immediate gratifications in order to obtain long-range goals. The
differences in "future orientation" extend even to such seemingly trivial
realms as whether the child is given music lessons.[9]

Class differences in child training, as Kohn suggests, are understand-

---

7 Henry S. Maas, "Some Social Class Differences in the Family Systems and Group
Relations of Pre- and Early Adolescents," *Child Development* 22 (1951): 146–52.

8 Melvin L. Kohn, "Social Class and Parent-Child Relationships: An Interpretation," *American Journal of Sociology* 68 (1963): 475.

9 MacDonald, "Leisure Activities." In the New Haven sample, 54 percent of the
upper-status children and only 21 percent of the lower-status children reported that
they received some sort of lessons (music, dancing, Sunday school, etc.) in addition to
their normal school work.

able in terms of the differences in life styles and requirements of blue-
and white-collar existence. Although

> there is substantial truth in the characterization of the middle-class way of
> life as one of great conformity . . . *relative* to the working class, middle-
> class conditions of life require a more substantial degree of independence of
> action. Furthermore, the higher levels of education enjoyed by the middle
> class make possible a degree of internal scrutiny difficult to achieve without
> the skills in dealing with the abstract that college training sometimes pro-
> vides. Finally, the economic security of most middle-class occupations, the
> level of income they provide, the status they confer, allow one to focus his
> attention on the subjective and the ideational. Middle-class conditions of life
> both allow and demand a greater degree of self-direction than do those of
> the working class.[10]

All of this is certainly relevant to the capacity and desire to raise children who are able to perform the rather intricate manipulations of symbols involved in effective political participation.

CLASS DIFFERENCES IN CHILDREN'S POLITICAL ORIENTATIONS

Some of the items in the New Haven questionnaire did not elicit different responses from children of upper- and lower-status backgrounds.
But wherever consistent class differences appeared they showed that
upper-status children exceed lower-status children in capacity and motivation for political participation. More important than the mere fact of
class differences in political involvement was the *pattern* of these differences. This pattern, as we shall see, is quite consistent with findings in
the general literature on class differences in socialization. Considered together, the general socialization literature and the New Haven political
socialization findings provide us with some rather precise indications of
the ways in which being socialized within a socioeconomic status group
affects the individual's later political behavior.

We may note in passing that clear-cut class differences emerged in the
New Haven findings even though two aspects of the analytic procedure
tend to depress the association between class and political involvement.
First, the technique of analyzing findings by school year rather than by
chronological age sets up comparisons between groups of slightly unequal
ages, since lower-status children are somewhat older (by three to six
months) than upper-status children at the same school year level. Analysis
by age would presumably have further sharpened the findings pointing
to lack of political involvement among lower-status children. Secondly, a
necessarily crude technique for measuring class was used: because school
records and children's reports proved to be unreliable indicators of parental occupation, social status was measured by drawing upon a block-

---

[10] Kohn, "Social Class and Parent-Child Relationships . . . ," p. 477.

by-block evaluation of the social level of New Haven neighborhoods based on a then seven-year-old sample of New Haven families. The findings are presented in terms of a rough division between children of blue- and white-collar occupational backgrounds.[11] Neighborhood is not a perfect indicator of class and undoubtedly there had been some changes in the interim between the neighborhood evaluation and the present study. As a consequence, some children probably were in the wrong status group, thus further diminishing the clarity of class differences in the findings.[12] The persistence of these differences in spite of the foregoing analytic deficiencies is evidence of the importance of class as a determinant of political socialization.

Class and Orientation Toward Issue and Party

. . . . Grade school children are not conspicuously issue oriented. Nevertheless, by seventh grade, 32 percent of the upper-SES children referred at least vaguely to issues in their attempts to distinguish between the parties; by eighth grade, 42 percent did. Only five percent of the lower-status seventh graders and 20 percent of the eighth graders referred to issues.[13] In addition, at every age level, the upper-SES children more frequently respond in political terms when asked how they would "change the world." Such responses, as we noted, increase rather sharply between fourth and fifth grade for upper-status children; there is a similar increase among lower-SES children, but it does not appear until a year later.

Children of upper- and lower-status backgrounds also differ in their developing orientations to political parties. . . . There are no significant differences between the status groups in the mere tendency to possess a party identification[14] but the party preferences of upper-status children are better grounded in information. They are more likely to be able to respond to the question asking how the parties differ and they are better able to name leaders of the parties.

One would expect the greater partisan information of upper-status children to augment their capacity to *use* party as an effective tool for making political discriminations and choices. And this seems to be the

---

[11] For further discussion of the index of social class used here and the class characteristics of the sample see Appendix B.

[12] Dichotomizing the class groups also reduces the impression of differences by concealing the responses of children at the very lowest and highest status levels.

[13] Significance levels are indicated in footnotes to the appropriate tables in Chapter 4. As indicated elsewhere, the data do not meet the requirements of statistical inference and tests have been performed simply to sort out findings for discussion. In this selection, differences are computed by combining chi-square values for each age level and computing an overall probability; this makes it possible to avoid discussing occasional inconsistent differences which emerge in specific school-year groups, but which do not appear elsewhere in the data. I have not avoided discussing consistent trends in the data (e.g. differences at the .10 level) which do not reach statistical significance.

[14] Nor do adults differ in this characteristic. An analysis of the frequency of party identification by various demographic characteristics is presented in Alfred DeGrazia, *The American Way of Government* (New York: John Wiley, 1957), pp. 208–9.

case. We noted [elsewhere] that Democratic children tended to evaluate Democratic politicians more favorably than did Republican children and vice versa. This association between party preference and assessment of public officials is stronger for upper- than for lower-status children. In the upper-status subsample, 80 percent of the children who identified themselves as Republicans rated Eisenhower in the highest category ("very good") and only 37 percent of the Democrats did so. In the lower-status group, 82 percent of the Republicans stated that Eisenhower had been doing a "very good job," but so did 68 percent of the Democrats. Eighty-two percent of the upper-status Democrats and 42 percent of the Republicans in this group gave "very good" ratings to New Haven's Democratic mayor; 75 percent of the lower-status Democrats, but also 60 percent of the lower-status Republicans rated Mayor Lee "very good." This squares with findings on the capacity of adults of different status levels to use their party preferences as a basis for political choice; upper-status adults are more consistently Republican in their voting than are lower-status adults Democratic.

. . . . At the seventh-and eighth-grade levels we also begin to find upper-status children volunteering the self-designation of "independent" when asked about their party preference. This at first seems paradoxical in view of the keener partisanship of upper-status children. However, the use of the language of nonpartisanship probably does *not* constitute withdrawal from politics by children in this social group. Rather, it fits a pattern which we shall return to later—the tendency for older upper-status children to begin to conceive of politics as a sphere in which it is legitimate and possible to exercise autonomous choice.

Class and Information about Formal Governmental Institutions

Another set of responses discussed [elsewhere]—information about formal government institutions—fails to vary by socioeconomic status. . . [Comparisons of] the status groups at each of the five school-year levels in awareness of the names of three executives (the incumbent mayor, governor, and president) and in two levels of familiarity ("reasonably accurate," "aware") with the duties of both the executives and the legislatures [reveal] no consistent differences . . . ; the few statistically significant differences do not regularly favor one group or the other.[15]

Since, as we have seen, there *are* substantial differences in information about a key *informal* aspect of politics—political parties—the possibility arises that classroom instruction may have something to do with equalizing the awareness of formal governmental information. Lessons about

---

15 The absence of class differences in formal political information also is indicated when these data are combined with a nine-point index of political information (based on "reasonably accurate" descriptions of the six institutions and awareness of the names of the three executives).

"How a Bill Becomes a Law," or "What the Mayor Does," are accepted parts of the grade school curriculum; discussions of partisan politics are less likely to be. Some aspects of partisanship, for example, the nature of differences between the parties, are probably considered too controversial and "subjective" to be dealt with in the classroom.[16] Therefore, if this information is not learned in the home and neighborhood, it probably is not learned at all early in childhood.

A comparison of political information scores by the various classrooms from which members of the sample were drawn generally supports the thesis that classroom teaching tends to equalize the information about formal aspects of government among upper- and lower-status children. For, although government information did not vary by SES, there *were* variations between classrooms which were generally consistent with impressions gained from my classroom discussions with children and their teachers after administering the questionnaire and with reports of school supervisors as to the teacher's assiduity in teaching current events and social studies.[17]

Further Class Differences in Political Learning

Table 1 reports several additional comparisons between the socioeconomic groups. The first two rows deal with items on children's exemplars: questions about what "famous person you want, or do not want, to be like. . . ." Both questions evoke a startling number of references to the heroes of popular culture—actors, actresses, singers, etc. They also bring forth references to public figures past and present, ranging from the incumbent president to the occupants of the gallery of American patriotic heroes and heroines. Upper-status children are more likely to select such public figures as their exemplars. Except in the fourth-grade subsample,

---

[16] As I have noted, civic instruction is not mandatory before eighth grade in Connecticut and in New Haven is first suggested as a *possible* topic in the sixth grade. Teachers vary in their attention to this subject matter. Even discussion of partisanship is not totally absent from the classroom . . . It may be that partisan information is not presented didactically and therefore that less of it is remembered.

[17] Several items about media information and attention were included in the study and these, under more satisfactory testing conditions, would probably have differentiated between upper- and lower-status children. Media items of the sort used in New Haven, mainly questions about which recent news events children found interesting, pleasing, and displeasing, and markedly influenced by temporal events—by the previous day's or week's news. Shortly before questionnaires were administered in one of the four schools from which respondents were drawn, a school which is heavily lower class, the United States succeeded in launching its first successful space satellite. A large proportion of the children referred to this event, demonstrating that aspects of politics (in this case international politics) can occasionally arouse great enthusiasm among children, but also invalidating socioeconomic status comparisons in the media items. . . . Class differences in attention to the political content of the media probably would have appeared if the questionnaires had been administered simultaneously to the entire sample, and at a time when the headlines were not filled with events of such overwhelming interest to *all* childern.

TABLE 1.   SES Differences and Similarities in Political Response by School Year[a]

			School Year		
	4	5	6	7	8
Names someone from public life			*Upper SES*		
as "famous person you want to	39%	22%	29%	13%	22%
be like"			*Lower SES*		
	16	21	16	6	12
Names someone from public life			*Upper SES*		
	18	32	35	36	32
as "famous person you *don't*			*Lower SES*		
want to be like"	10	8	15	13	22
			Upper SES		
Will vote when 21	76	82	70	87	86
			Lower SES		
	77	76	79	85	84
			Upper SES		
Believes "elections are	63	79	71	69	84
important"			*Lower SES*		
	76	66	68	66	75
			Upper SES		
Total cases	49	56	46	38	37
			Lower SES		
	62	62	69	97	143

[a]SES differences in choice of a public figure as someone "you *don't* want to be like" are significant (p > .01 < .05). Differences in positive reference to public figures approach significance (p > .05 < .10). On the procedure used for significance testing, see Table 4.1 (p. 58) and Appendix B.

the class differences are even more clear-cut in the choice of public figures as *negative* exemplars—"people you don't want to be like."

It is interesting to note that the socioeconomic groups do not differ in the two remaining observations in Table 1, which involve explicit statements about personal willingness to participate in politics and the "importance" of politics. Both groups are quite likely to say that they will vote when they are of age (almost no children deny that they will vote; the remaining responses are largely "don't know's") and to say that elections are important. These (or their adult equivalents) are items which we expect will vary by socioeconomic status in the general population.[18] Thus although we have evidence in the New Haven data of the class differences in political involvement and awareness present in the adult population, *the explicit rationalizations which go with low political involvement do not seem to be present by eighth grade.*

So far, we have seen a number of responses which are more often made by upper- than by lower-status children. Tables 2 and 3 report responses which are more common in the *lower*-status subsample, but which nevertheless reinforce our impression that lower-status children are less politicized than upper-status children.

Table 2 compares the status groups in their evaluations of the presi-

18 Gerhard H. Saenger, "Social Status and Political Behavior," in *Class, Status, and Power,* ed. Reinhard Bendix and Seymour Martin Lipset (Glencoe, Ill.: Free Press, 1953), p. 379.

TABLE 2. Class Differences in Evaluations of Political
Leaders by School Year: Leader Rated "Very
Good"[a]

	School Year				
	4	5	6	7	8
President			*Upper SES*		
	79%	68%	54%	51%	53%
			Lower SES		
	82	80	75	77	68
Governor			*Upper SES*		
	31	37	33	11	36
			Lower SES		
	56	46	40	47	44
Mayor			*Upper SES*		
	53	59	51	58	64
			Lower SES		
	77	75	66	56	61
Total cases[b]			*Upper SES*		
	48-49	53-56	44-45	37-38	36
			Lower SES		
	61-62	61	68-69	93-97	139-43

[a]SES differences in "very good" evaluations of the governor and
president are significant at the .01 level. Differences in "very good"
evaluation of the mayor approach significance ($p < .10 > .05$).
[b]Total cases vary due to invalid responses.

dent, governor, and mayor at the five school-year levels. In thirteen of the
fifteen evaluations (all but the seventh- and eighth-grade evaluation of the
Mayor), lower-status children are more likely to say that the executive
has been doing a "very good" job, the highest of the evaluative categories.
In Table 3, the evaluations by the two oldest age groups of a pair of com-

TABLE 3. Class Differences in Comparisons of Eisenhower
and Stevenson: Seventh and Eighth Grade
Subsample [a]

	Upper SES	*Lower SES*
	25%	36%
Both men rated "high" ("very good" and/or "good")		
Both rated "very good"	5	12
Polar: One "very good," one "bad"	10	7
Both rated the same	13	20
No answer	19	27
Total cases[b]	75	243

[a]SES differences are not significant when tested by the techniques
used here of testing each category of response, combining chi square values
(corrected for continuity) for each school year group (in this case, seventh
and eighth grades).
[b]Percentages in the various categories are neither exhaustive nor
mutually exclusive and therefore do not add up to 100 per cent.

peting politicians—Eisenhower and Stevenson—are presented. Lower-status children show a generally more favorable disposition toward *both* men; they are more likely to evaluate both men favorably and less likely to make polar ("very good" or "bad") distinctions between them. These findings are reminiscent of two observations we have already discussed—the reluctance of lower-status children to name politicians as negative exemplars, and the low correlation of their party preferences with their evaluations of leaders.

[Elsewhere], I argued that idealization of leaders is an "immature" pattern of political response. Here we see (and the Chicago data also reveal class differences in idealization) [19] that the lower-SES child is in effect more deferential toward leaders than the higher-status child, another indication of less fully developed capacities for political participation.

Before I attempt to recapitulate and interpret these observations about class differences in political learning, let us consider one further set of findings. The New Haven children were asked

> If you could vote, who would be best to ask for voting advice? (*Check one*)
> A friend your own age ....
> Brother or sister ....
> Father ....
> Mother ....
> Teacher ....
> Someone else ....
>
> *(Write in whether this person is
> a neighbor, relative, or what.)*

Table 4 compares the status groups on three categories of response to this item. As might be expected, the bulk of the references were to parents. (Many children did not distinguish between their parents, in spite of instructions to do so.) References to parents diminish with age and two classes of response become more common. The older upper-status children begin to volunteer the statement, which is in no way suggested in the questionnaire, that they would make their *own* choices. Lower-status children, however, virtually never make this statement; instead they refer to the school teacher.

The teacher is probably the one emissary of middle-class subculture with whom many lower-status children are acquainted. One suspects that, since by sixth, seventh, and eighth grades children are well aware of status differences,[20] the lower-class child has begun to develop a sense of his own

---

[19] Judith V. Torney, "The Child's Idealization of Authority" (M.A. thesis, University of Chicago Library, 1962). Mrs. Torney argues the interesting thesis that lower-class children, in their idealization of remote authority figures, are responding in a compensatory fashion to threatening experiences with family authority.

[20] On awareness of social class by children see Bernice L. Neugarten, "Social Class and Friendship among School Children," *American Journal of Sociology* 51 (1946): 305–13; Frank J. Estvan, "The Relationship of Social Status, Intelligence and Sex of Ten and Twelve Year-Old Children to an Awareness of Poverty," *Genetic Psychology Monographs* 46 (1952): 3–60; Benjamin Pope, "Socio-Economic Contrasts in Children's

TABLE 4.   Children's Preferred Sources of Voting Advice by
School Year and Socioeconomic Status[a]

| | School Year | | | | |
	4	5	6	7	8
One or both parents			*Upper SES*		
	86%	88%	70%	76%	57%
			Lower SES		
	81	74	71	70	63
"Would decide myself"			*Upper SES*		
(written in)	2	4	11	10	11
			Lower SES		
	0	0	1	3	2
Ask teacher			*Upper SES*		
	4	2	0	0	11
			Lower SES		
	8	8	16	14	15
Total cases			*Upper SES*		
	49	56	46	38	37
			Lower SES		
	62	62	69	97	143

[a]SES differences in choice of teacher are significant ($p > .01 < .05$).
Differences in "decide myself" approach significance ($p < .10 > .05$).

(and his parents') inadequacy in coping with the abstract, the verbal, and
the remote—including the symbols of the world of politics. References to
the teacher as a preferred source of advice may be the first harbinger of
later attitudes which explicitly deny the desirability, appropriateness, and
effectiveness of personal political participation.

CAUSES AND CONSEQUENCES OF CLASS
DIFFERENCES IN POLITICAL DEVELOPMENT

In general the New Haven findings mesh convincingly with the existing
literatures dealing with class differences in adult political participation
and children's socialization, providing us with something of a bridge between the two bodies of research.

We find that there are clearly evident preadult precursors to the class
differences in the political behavior of adults. Lower and upper socioeconomic status children differ in the same ways as do their elders on a
good number of the indicators of political awareness and involvement
used in New Haven—this in spite of the crudeness of the procedure used
for comparing the status groups.

Explanations of the lower political participation of lower-status people
vary in the degree to which they emphasize *situational* restraints operating in the individual's adult environment, or *psychological* restraints

Peer Culture Prestige Values," *Genetic Psychology Monographs* 48 (1953): 157–220;
Hans Schneckenburger, "Das sociale Verständnis des Arbeiterkindes," *Zeitschrift für
Pädagogische Psychologie* 34 (1933): 274–85.

which he, in effect, brings with him to his adult setting. A situational explanation of lower-class political apathy is suggested by Hyman and Sheatsley. They refer to "families who are weighed down by a pressing burden of personal problems . . . women who wear themselves out daily with the care of large families in substandard living quarters . . . abject poverty, crushing illness." [21] If the main factors are situational, the solution, as Hyman and Sheatsley point out, is change in the adult's environment: "Sometimes the task is only to free people from their pressing concern with personal problems so that they may have occasional opportunities to look out to broader horizons." [22] But when we find that differences in political involvement already are present in the grade school years, it becomes clear that nonsituational factors—predispositions acquired before the age of formal entrance into citizenship—also are relevant.

Explanations of class differences in participation also may vary in the *depth* of the psychological factors which are said to affect participation. Emphasis may be placed on "surface" factors, of a sort which could be (relatively) easily remedied by increasing an individual's education (educational levels *are* rising quite rapidly in the United States), or encourging him to change consciously held attitudes—such as "voting is a waste of time," or "votes don't really have much of an effect on what politicians do." On the other hand, one may suspect that more fundamental, less readily changed psychological processes are at work—for example, strongly felt beliefs in one's personal inadequacy, deferential tendencies, constricted imagination.

The New Haven data certainly indicate that differences in educational accomplishment and the related differences in intellectual skill make up part of the childhood heritage of the different classes and in this way contribute to political participation differences. But taken with the broader literature on social class and socialization, the New Haven findings also suggest that there are even more deeply imbedded psychological impediments to the participation in politics of lower-status groups. These barriers to participation seem to result from lack of self-direction and self-confidence and from inability and unwillingness to express personal feelings and ideas. It is especially notable that lower socioeconomic status children do not share the explicit unwillingness to participate in politics found among adults of the same background. But they *do* show a greater deference toward political leadership; unlike upper-status children they do not begin to display in sixth, seventh, and eighth grades a sense that political choices are theirs to make—that *their* judgments are worth acting upon. And this seems part of a much larger pattern in the socialization practices of American status groups.

---

[21] Herbert H. Hyman and Paul B. Sheatsley, "The Current Status of American Public Opinion," *National Council for Social Studies Yearbook* 21 (1950): 11–34, reprinted in *Public Opinion and Propaganda*, ed. Daniel Katz et al. (New York: Holt, Rinehart and Winston, 1962).

[22] Ibid.

Again we have found that socialization helps to explain the persistence of existing political practices. The findings suggest that participation patterns are rooted in complex social and psychological aspects of the subcultures of the classes. These differences are not likely to yield to simple, straightforward programs of education and reform; instead, fundamental and inevitably slow changes of life styles and values will probably be necessary if differential participation is to disappear.

11

THE POLITICAL SOCIALIZATION OF BLACK INNER-CITY CHILDREN

EUGENE GREEN

Political socialization is an interdisciplinary field that employs the techniques of the behavioral sciences. Emerging only in the last decade as a distinct field of political inquiry, the concept of political socialization is still very ill-defined. Research and theory have been limited, but the number of studies concerned with political socialization, broadly defined, has grown rapidly in the past five years.

The St. Cecilia political socialization study, which is the subject of this paper, deals with childhood political socialization. There are several significant conceptualizations of childhood political socialization, of which one of the more widely discussed is that of Robert D. Hess and Judith V. Torney.[1] They view political socialization as a child's progression toward adult political thought processes, and believe that the most important forces guiding the growth of political behavior are the character, quality, and amount of adult political participation, as well as the images of government, citizen, and role of the citizen that are prevalent in the adult population.[2] This view of socialization is based on two assumptions: (a) there is a consensus in the population about many of the basic ideals of citizen behavior, and (b) children are moving toward the political concepts, attitudes, and expectations of the adults.[3] Hess and Torney view political socialization as a lifelong process with reference groups either acting to reinforce or diminish the strength of attitudes and orientations developed in school.

Hess and Torney also look at childhood political socialization in terms of three phases, involving (1) an awareness of political objects, (2) the direction of affective and cognitive states, and (3) a phase in which the

---

An original contribution, based on a Master's thesis, Roosevelt University, June 1969.

---

[1] Robert D. Hess and Judith V. Torney, *The Development of Political Attitudes in Children* (Chicago: Aldine, 1967).

[2] Robert D. Hess, "Models of Political Socialization" (a paper prepared for the Lincoln Filene Center for Citizenship and Public Affairs, Tufts University, Medford, Massachusetts, 1965), p. 2.

[3] Ibid., p. 3.

child begins to involve himself in political activity by talking to friends about political matters, and the like.[4] These phases are seen as a developing set of relationships in which the relative roles played by the citizen and the government depend on the assumption of reciprocity. Thus, Hess and Torney regard political socialization as the process by which reciprocal role relationships are developed.[5] Their view of the process of political socialization is not one which heavily stresses psychological traits, but rather one which emphasizes the development of relationships between individuals and institutions. In this process, the individual acquires images of persons and institutions and complementary attitudes about himself and how he should behave.

Though there is no single "school" of political socialization, none of the widely discussed conceptualizations are very dissimilar. For, in general, all are concerned with the processes in which political socialization takes place, and the agents which do the socializing.

THE PURPOSE OF THIS STUDY

The St. Cecilia study was undertaken as a first step in discerning if there are any differences between black children and white children in childhood political learning. In this study, political socialization will simply be defined as the acquisition and maturation of political knowledge, values, and attitudes. Specifically, this study deals with the political socialization of black inner-city children. Two significant works on childhood political socialization which are used as bases for comparisons with this study are *Children and Politics* by Fred I. Greenstein (all references to Greenstein refer to this work), and *The Development of Political Attitudes in Children* by Robert D. Hess and Judith V. Torney (all references to Hess and Torney refer to this work).[6]

The decision to concentrate on black inner-city children was made for two reasons. First, neither of the two major works cited above provide data on black children. Greenstein's sample was almost totally lacking in black children, while the Hess and Torney study lacked any consideration of race as a variable. Considering the attention currently focused on improving the education of black children and the proliferation in the past decade of youthful black organizations which work outside the normal political channels to achieve political change, especially in the inner-city areas of our large cities, it appeared that a significant proportion of our urban school-age children were being neglected in political socialization studies. (For example, over 50 percent of Chicago's public school students are black, with the vast majority of these students attending school in areas referred to as "inner-city.")

---

4 Ibid., p. 5.

5 Ibid., p. 7.

6 Fred I. Greenstein, *Children and Politics* (New Haven and London: Yale University Press, 1964), p. 12; Hess and Torney, *The Development of Political Attitudes in Children.*

Second, the decision to concentrate on black inner-city children evolved from serious doubts about the validity of generalizations arising out of studies consisting almost totally of white children or studies which included black children, but failed to separate their responses. For example, is it valid to say that children "seem to be more sympathetic to individual political leaders than are adults," "the widespread adult cynicism and distrust do not seem to have developed by the eighth grade," or "the young child perceives . . . government as benign and trusts it to offer him protection and help," when referring to black children? [7] Very little information about this is available. Therefore, in part, this study was undertaken to provide some indication of the applicability of the generalizations just noted.

SAMPLE AND DATA

The findings presented in this study consist of the responses of 148 Chicago, Illinois, fourth- through eighth-grade children to a pencil and paper questionnaire. The questionnaire was adapted from those used by Greenstein and Hess and Torney to facilitate comparisons.

Except for two children of Oriental ancestry, the sample consisted entirely of black children. At least 90 percent of these children could be considered "low" in socio-economic status. Approximately 40 percent of the children reside in the Robert Taylor Homes, a high-rise public housing project placed in an environment of railroad tracks and a twelve-lane expressway. Ill-run, ill-lit, and ill-policed, the Robert Taylor homes are far from an ideal place in which to raise children. The great majority of the other children live nearby in small, old, but generally well-kept homes and apartments. Approximately 10 percent of the sample live with their biological father, although close to 50 percent have a "father" in the home. And roughly one third of these children are Catholic. Further aspects of the methodology are noted in the last sections of this paper.

FEELINGS ABOUT POLITICAL AUTHORITY

Many students of political socialization devote their attention to the processes by which loyalty toward the nation is inculcated among the young people of a society. Specifically, they are concerned with the orientations toward the political system and political authority figures. Although the classifications vary from scholar to scholar, these political orientations may be roughly classified as knowledge (cognitions), attitudes or feelings (affects), and values (evaluations). In a summary of a number of studies of the development of political orientations, Richard E. Dawson states that,

---

[7] Greenstein, *Children and Politics,* p. 42; Hess and Torney, *The Development of Political Attitudes in Children,* p. 213.

Children develop feelings or attitudes toward political objects (affective orientations prior to the acquisition of information or knowledge (cognitive orientations) about the objects.[8]

Favorable attitudes of elementary school children toward political figures have been found by Greenstein and Hess and Torney. They found an almost complete absence of unfavorable attitudes toward politics. In other words, elementary school children tend to idealize political authority. In this light, let us now look at the St. Cecilia findings.

The St. Cecilia findings concerning such feelings may be summarized as follows: (1) the black inner-city children are as likely to perceive the importance of political roles as are white middle-class children; (2) they seem to be less sympathetic to individual political leaders than adults; (3) they place little emphasis on the benevolence of political leaders; and, (4) in sharp contrast to the other samples, they have developed a marked degree of malevolence and distrust toward political leaders as early as the fourth grade. A number of possible reasons for the existence of these racially identifiable differences will be considered.

Greenstein believes that the most important source of children's conceptions of authority is:

> . . . the civic instruction which goes on incidental to the normal activities in the family. Children overhear parental conversation; they sense, or are informally told of, their parents' stance toward political authority in general and partisan politics in particular.[9]

This is probably true with respect to the St. Cecilia children, for formal civic instruction is not introduced at their school until the seventh grade. Greenstein offers a number of hypotheses about his sample's idealization of political authority figures, one of which is that the parents, when talking about politics, "unconsciously sugarcoat the political explanations they pass on to children." [10] In other words, parents tend to shield their children from the "dirty" aspects of politics. However, it is doubtful that this "sugarcoating" exists in black inner-city families. Charles Hamilton, a black political scientist and urbanologist, believes that "Tell it like it is," is a way of life for black inner-city people.[11] Inner-city life for black people is a fight for survival. The parents of the St. Cecilia children are unlikely to distort reality, political or otherwise, as much as white middle-class parents.

A second hypothesis put forward by Greenstein derives from psychoanalytic theory. He suggests that:

> . . . authority figures in the immediate environment may effect responses to authority in the wider political world. Figures in the latter setting, for

---

[8] Richard E. Dawson, "Political Socialization," *Political Science Annual* (1966), p. 24.
[9] Greenstein, *Children and Politics*, p. 43.
[10] Ibid., p. 45.
[11] Charles Hamilton, Lecture in Political Modernization, Roosevelt University, Fall 1968.

instance the president, are unconsciously (i.e., in a way not accessible to the conscious awareness) perceived as the analogues of . . . immediate environment authorities.[12]

The *Report of the National Advisory Commission on Civil Disorders,* better known as the *Kerner Report,* states that blacks believe that police brutality and harassment are common occurrences in black neighborhoods, and that this belief is one of the major causes of black resentment against the police.[13] As we shall see in the section dealing with the law, the police are not viewed as exemplars by the St. Cecilia children. Harassment by the police of black inner-city children, especially in Chicago, is no secret. These children may tend to displace their negative feelings toward the police onto other authority figures such as the President and the Mayor whom many of the children in Chicago associated with the rioting by black people shortly after Dr. Martin Luther King's death.

There is another possible explanation as well. Hess and Torney argue that:

> . . . the young child's highly positive image of the President exists because of feelings of powerlessness and vulnerability in the presence of powerful authority . . . the child compensates by seeing the President as benign and nurturant.[14]

The section dealing with the children's sense of political efficacy will indicate that the St. Cecilia children do feel powerless in relation to the government. However, they do not appear to have compensated for this powerlessness by seeing either the President or Mayor as a benevolent authority figure. Hamilton believes that inner-city black people are collectivity prone, seeing unified action and group rights (e.g., black principals and teachers for black schools).[15] It may be that the St. Cecilia children have compensated for their sense of powerlessness by identifying themselves with ideals such as "black pride" and "black power" rather than idealizing political authority figures. This proposition is lent support by similar findings of Edward S. Greenberg:

> Of additional interest is the clustering of disaffection for government and political officials among black lower-class children (ghetto residents in our sample), primarily males who have accurate perceptions of the nature of race relations. This describes a population remarkably similar to the participants in urban disorders. There is a relationship between deprivation and political orientation. It is precisely the most deprived (the black and poor) yet aware children who are least likely to maintain their positive evaluations of the political system.[16]

---

[12] Greenstein, *Children and Politics,* p. 46.

[13] *Report of the National Advisory Commission on Civil Disorders,* Otto Kerner, Chairman (Washington, D.C.: Government Printing Office, March, 1968), p. 302.

[14] Hess and Torney, *The Development of Political Attitudes in Children,* p. 135.

[15] Hamilton, Lecture in Political Modernization.

[16] Edward S. Greenberg, "Black Children and the Political System," *Public Opinion Quarterly,* 34, no. 3 (Fall 1970): 344.

POLITICAL INFORMATION

This section deals with political information or the cognitive dimension of childhood political learning. Specifically, we will concentrate on the development of the St. Cecilia children in terms of their knowledge of three political executives (president, mayor, and governor), three legislatures (Congress, Chicago City Council, and Illinois General Assembly), and the children's participation in political discussion.

The Development of Political Information

As mentioned earlier, children develop affective orientations toward political objects before they acquire cognitive orientations about these objects. This proposition holds true for the present black inner-city sample. In general, there is an even development from the fourth through eighth grades of the St. Cecilia children's awareness of "who is" the President of the United States, Governor of Illinois, and Mayor of Chicago. In each of the five grades the President received the most correct answers and the Governor received the least correct responses. In response to questions asking them if they had "heard of" Congress, the Illinois General Assembly and the Chicago City Council, two-thirds of the St. Cecilia fourth-grade children had "heard of" Congress and one-third had "heard of" the other two legislatures. By the seventh and eighth grades, almost everyone had "heard of" Congress and two-thirds of the children had "heard of" the Illinois General Assembly and the Chicago City Council. In general, the St. Cecilia children compared quite favorably with Greenstein's "lower" socioeconomic status (SES) subsample.

The St. Cecilia children were asked to respond to three open-ended questions asking them what the President of the United States, Governor of Illinois, and the Mayor of Chicago do. Greenstein's sample gave more reasonably accurate (referring to the strictly executive) responses than the St. Cecilia sample. However, a greater percentage of the St. Cecilia sample was aware of the public nature of the three political executives.

Concerning the Congress, Illinois General Assembly, and Chicago City Council, the St. Cecilia children, like Greenstein's group, were much less aware of the roles of these legislatures than the roles of the previously discussed executives. Nevertheless, it appears that the St. Cecilia children compare quite favorably with Greenstein's group as to awareness and knowledge of the roles of the legislatures at three levels of government.

Participation in Political Discussion

At the end of elementary school, most of the St. Cecilia children had developed some knowledge and feelings about political executives and legislatures. Many of the students of political socialization stress that the acquisition and maturation of political orientations (knowledge, feelings, and values) occur in informal situations, such as in discussions with one's parents or in informal conversations with one's peers. Therefore, three questions were asked of the St. Cecilia children in order to receive an indication of their experience in discussing political matters with their parents and friends. The sample was asked to respond to the following statements with a "yes" or "no":

> I have talked with my mother or father about our country's problems.
> I have talked with my friends about a candidate.
> I have talked with my mother or father about a candidate.

It was quite surprising to have found a substantial decrease from the sixth through eighth grades in the children's concern with political matters. This was not the case with Hess and Torney's sample, which showed a rapid increase with age in reports of discussions with friends and family about political matters.[17] Other political socialization studies have shown that as children grow and develop knowledge, attitudes, and values about political things, as well as the ability to think in abstract terms, there is a parallel growth in children's concern with political matters. Possibly, by the seventh and eighth grades, the St. Cecilia children may realize that there is a large gap between reality and what they are taught in the classroom, and lose interest in political matters. This hypothesis will be discussed in the section, "If They Could Change the World."

PARTISAN MOTIVATION

In his study of a number of significant works on childhood political socialization, Dawson proposed that political party identification in America is a basic political orientation and ". . . is acquired early and serves as an important reference point around which later orientations and socializing experiences are based." [18] In this light, let us examine the St. Cecilia findings.

Party Differences

The St. Cecilia study sought to discover if its black inner-city sample developed an awareness of party differences as early as the almost totally white sample used by Greenstein. The children were asked to write in a difference between the Democratic and Republican parties. The percentage of children who responded to the party difference question was far greater than Greenstein's sample or even his "upper" SES subsample. In reference to the party difference item, the St. Cecilia children offered more correct differences than Greenstein's sample in the fourth, fifth, and sixth grades. However, Greenstein's sample offered more correct differences (e.g., "one party is on the business side of things, the Republicans) by the seventh grade. The great majority of the St. Cecilia children's re-

---

[17] Hess and Torney, *The Development of Political Attitudes in Children,* p. 68.
[18] Dawson, "Political Socialization," p. 28.
findings.

sponses dealt with the belief that Democrats are for black people and spend money for poor people, and that Republicans are rich and care only about white people.

Party Affiliation

In response to the question "If you were 21 now, whom would you vote for most of the time?", 65 percent of the sample would vote for Democrats, 24 percent did not know, and only 11 percent would vote for Republicans. The percentage of children who would vote for Democrats increased with each grade. In the eighth grade, not one child responded that he would vote for a Republican. The strong partisan motivation for the Democratic party is evident even in the fourth grade, where 62 percent of the sample would vote for Democrats and only 19 percent would vote for Republicans. These findings seem to contradict the observation of Hess and Torney that ". . . the image of political parties develops late and differences between the parties are not celarly defined . . ." for the St. Cecilia children very much believe that the Democratic party is more responsive to the welfare of black people and other minority groups.[19]

INFLUENCING GOVERNMENT POLICY

Much has been written lately about the factors accounting for stability in democracies. In *The Civic Culture*, a five-nation (United States, United Kingdom, Germany, Italy, and Mexico) study of the political culture of democracy and of the social processes and structures that maintain it, Gabriel Almond and Sidney Verba argue that one factor accounting for the stability of a political system is the existence of a large number of people who do not try to exert influence over government policy, but who think they could exert influence if they wished. They feel that this is extremely important because

> Before the norm that one ought to participate can be translated into the act itself, the individual will probably have to perceive that he is able to act. One can believe that he ought to participate, but . . . perceive himself unable to do so. . . . Certainly a great source of discontent is the acceptance of the norms of participation coupled with the belief that one cannot in fact participate. This, it has been suggested, is the danger of overselling the norms of political democracy in the schools. When the myth of democracy comes into serious conflict with the realities of politics, the results are cynicism.[20]

---

[19] Hess and Torney, *The Development of Political Attitudes in Children,* p. 80. It was noted in the *Introduction* that the St. Cecilia sample is approximately 30 to 40 percent Catholic. A number of studies have shown that there is a strong affiliation between Catholic children and the Democratic party (Hess and Torney, op. cit., p. 116). Because voting studies indicate that the great majority of black people vote for Democrats, the fact that a large minority of these children are Catholic probably has little or no influence on this study's party affiliation findings.

[20] Gabriel A. Almond and Sidney Verba, *The Civic Culture: Political Attitudes and Democracy in Five Nations* (Boston and Toronto: Little, Brown, 1965), p. 135.

Sense of Political Efficacy

In view of Almond and Verba's argument, this study sought to find out to what extent the St. Cecilia children felt a sense of political efficacy, which is defined here as

> The feeling that the individual political action does have, or can have, an impact upon the political process, i.e., that it is worthwhile to perform one's civic duties. It is the feeling that the individual citizen can play a part in bringing about this change.[21]

The St. Cecilia children were asked to respond to the following five statements:

(1) What happens in the government will happen no matter what people do. It is like the weather, there is nothing people can do about it.

(2) There are some big, powerful men in the government who are running the whole thing and they do not care about us ordinary people.

(3) My family doesn't have anything to say about what government does.

(4) I don't think people in the government care much what people like my family think.

(5) Citizens don't have a chance to say what they think about running the government.[22]

The alternatives were "yes," "no," and "don't know." These statements were originally adapted by Hess and Torney from those designed by Campbell et al., to measure feelings of political efficacy in adults.

The St. Cecilia findings lend no support to the conclusion by Hess and Torney that the "Children's sense of efficacy of citizen action increases with age." [23] Instead, we found a steady increase in the percentage of children answering "yes" (low efficacy), especially from the sixth through eighth grades. In other words, the St. Cecilia children's sense of political efficacy declines with age. Edward Greenberg reports similar findings:

> Black children . . . are less likely to see government leaders as responsive to the demands of people. Controlling for social class does not wash out this generalization. Black middle-class children are no more likely to see the impact of ordinary people than lower-class children, and they trail far behind white students of equal social status.[24]

---

[21] A. Campbell, G. Gurin, and W. E. Miller, *The Voter Decides* (Evanston, Ill.: Row, Peterson, 1954), p. 190.

[22] Ibid., p. 187.

[23] Hess and Torney, *The Development of Political Attitudes in Children*, p. 68.

[24] Edward S. Greenberg, "Children and Government: A Comparison Across Racial Lines," *Midwest Journal of Political Science* 14, no. 2 (May 1970): p. 273.

Today, much is being said, but little is being done about black people's beliefs that they have too small an influence over the government. Few public programs have been enacted to alleviate this situation since the National Advisory Commission on Civil Disorders concluded that "Our nation is moving toward two societies, one black, one white—separate and unequal." [25] Currently, many organizations are being formed by black people, especially youths, to enable them to work "outside" of the political system in order to influence government policy. The St. Cecilia findings tend to support the arguments of a number of political scientists who believe that one reason for the proliferation of "grass-root" organizations working outside of the political system in the inner-city areas of our large cities is the black people's belief that electoral politics is too slow and not very responsive to black people's needs. It is hard to refute this claim in view of the lack of a sense of efficacy among this study's sample as late as the eighth grade.

IF THEY COULD CHANGE THE WORLD

The St. Cecilia children were asked to respond to the open-ended question "If you could change the world in any way you wanted, what change would you make?" The researcher sought to discover if the St. Cecilia children would make any politically relevant changes and if so, what the changes would be.

The responses fell into four broad categories: (1) war and peace; (2) civil rights; (3) police and law enforcement; and (4) improvements in living conditions. The serious tone of the comments was impressive. The percentage of responses which could be considered political in nature was about the same for each grade as Greenstein's sample. This seemed surprising considering the present sample's low sense of political efficacy and drop in political discussion in the later grades.

The St. Cecilia children were quite concerned about equality and brotherhood between whites and blacks. Of interest is the fact that there was an increase in responses dealing with civil rights from the fourth through the eighth grades. Of special interest is the fact that there was a large jump from the sixth grade, where only 15 percent of the children referred to civil rights, to the seventh and eighth grades where an average of 43 percent of the children referred to civil rights. This may be of great significance inasmuch as we also found declines in the seventh and eighth grades in both political discussion and sense of political efficacy. It seems that the St. Cecilia children's concern for their civil rights coincides with the appearance of the decline in their sense of political efficacy and their discussion of political matters. In other words, the decreases in political interest may take place when the St. Cecilia children realize to what an extent they (black people) are treated as "second-class" citizens in the

---

[25] *Report of the National Advisory Commission on Civil Disorders*, p. 1.

United States. This proposition is lent support by similar findings by Greenberg:

> While the young black child expresses great affection for the national political community, this affective attachment becomes seriously undermined with maturation. This would suggest that as the black child more directly confronts the reality of his life in America, he comes increasingly to reject America. Indeed, the lowest affect is displayed by the most perceptive children, those aware of the unequal treatment of black people in general. Thus the growth of perception and awareness seems to undermine affective attachments.[26]

REGARD FOR LAW

In order to function adequately, a government must inculcate among its subjects a respect for its laws and law enforcing powers. Hess and Torney state that:

> Benevolent qualities, attributed to both authority figures and to the system of laws, offer a basis of positive regard which justifies and encourages compliance . . . A child trusts the system of laws, believing that all laws are fair and that those who do enforce them do so in order to protect citizens.[27]

In this light, let us now look at the present sample's responses.

The Fairness of Laws

Concerning the fairness of laws, this study's findings are quite contrary to those of Hess and Torney, especially when their above-mentioned quote is taken into consideration. The St. Cecilia children were asked to respond to the question "Are all laws fair?" An index scale of "1" for "Strongly agree" to "4" for "Strongly disagree" was used. The fourth-grade children averaged "1.85" and the eighth-grade children averaged "3.1." However, in Hess and Torney's sample the fourth grade averaged "1.4" and the eighth grade averaged "2.4." In other words, the St. Cecilia sample tends to view laws in a less favorable light than Hess and Torney's sample.

In the last section we saw that the St. Cecilia children believed that the government was not responsive to their wishes. Their great concern for civil rights in the later grades was also noted. It seems reasonable that they should view laws as being much more unfair than Hess and Torney's group.

---

[26] Edward S. Greenberg, "The Political Socialization of Black Children," in *Political Socialization,* ed. Edward Greenberg (New York: Atherton Press, 1970), p. 181.

[27] Hess and Torney, *The Development of Political Attitudes in Children,* p. 50.

Views about Policemen

The St. Cecilia children were asked to respond to the statement "Policemen give equal treatment to everyone." What was found was a steady decline from the fourth through eighth grades in the belief that policemen give equal treatment to everyone. As early as the fourth grade 50 percent of the children felt that policemen did not give equal treatment. Of special interest, is the fact that not one child in the eighth grade felt that policemen treated everyone equally. It would not be an exaggeration to say that policemen are much more a part of the lives of black inner-city children than of those children who live closer to the city's periphery. With the constant presence of police and their not infrequent harassment of black people, it is easy to see how the St. Cecilia children's image of the police develops in this way.[28] Greenberg comes to the same conclusion:

> Black lower-class children show a rather precipitous decline with respect to police, a phenomenon that is not too surprising. It is lower-class black children, to be sure, who are most likely to become members of a street, peer culture and to "get in trouble" with the agents of social control. Their contact with the police is not likely to be pleasant.[29]

As was the case with President Nixon, and more so with Mayor Daley, although the St. Cecilia children show more unfavorable attitudes toward the police than white middle-class children, they still felt that policemen were important. For the St. Cecilia children mentioned Police Chief as the fourth most important adult role out of eight (behind President, Mayor, and Doctor, in that order). It may be a sign of their political realism that these children view authority roles as being important, even though they do not look favorably on the people who are playing those roles.

SUMMARY OF THE FINDINGS

We have taken note of a small number (148) of black inner-city children's views toward political authority, political information, partisan motivation, sense of political efficacy, and regard for law, and have compared their knowledge, feelings, and evaluations with Greenstein's sample, which consisted of children from New Haven, Connecticut, over 90 percent of whom were white and Hess and Torney's sample, which was nationwide in character, but whose responses were not categorized on the basis of racial identification. Without attempting to be exhaustive, let us review this study's main findings.

---

[28] *Report of the National Advisory Commission on Civil Disorders,* p. 304.

[29] Edward S. Greenberg, "Orientations of Black and White Children to Political Authority Figures," *Social Science Quarterly* 51, no. 3 (December 1970).

First, it was noted that black inner-city children, in contrast to white middle-class children, are at least as likely to perceive political roles as being important, and place little emphasis on the benevolence of political leaders, having developed by the fourth grade a marked degree of distrust of political authority figures. Two major hypotheses were offered to partially explain these differences: (1) black inner-city parents probably do not "sugarcoat" the political explanations they pass on to children; and (2) black inner-city children may realize quite early that there is a gap between reality and what is taught in school, and therefore cynicism may develop as a result of this.

Second, we saw that this sample's knowledge of certain political executives and institutions was equal to the knowledge of white middle-class children. However, in the seventh and eighth grades, the black inner-city children's incidence of political discussion fell far below that of Hess and Torney's sample. It was suggested that some political orientations acquired by the seventh and eighth grades serve to lessen their interest in political matters.

Third, it was noted that the St. Cecilia children are extremely partisan toward the Democratic party, believing that Republicans do not help black or poor people. It was also seen that these children could correctly identify party differences at a much earlier age than Hess and Torney's sample.

Fourth, in sharp contrast to nationwide samples, the St. Cecilia children have little sense of political efficacy, and also believe that government is not responsive to their wishes. We also noted that in the seventh and eighth grades the black inner-city sample evidenced a strong concern for civil rights. We also saw that in the same grades the St. Cecilia children showed a large decline in the discussion of political matters. It was suggested that black inner-city children lose interest in political matters when they realize that they are treated as "second-class" citizens in this country.

Concerning our final area of investigation, it was brought to light that in contrast to Hess and Torney's nationwide sample, the St. Cecilia children believe that all laws are not fair and that policemen do not give equal treatment to everyone. It was suggested that these differences were possibly due to the fact that policemen are more an immediate part of these children's lives and that discriminatory practices by the police are not uncommon in black inner-city neighborhoods. Also of interest is the fact that although the St. Cecilia children had acquired these views, they still felt that policemen were important.

METHODOLOGICAL CONSIDERATIONS

A number of methodological difficulties in this study should be noted: (1) the sample was small, consisting of 148 children; (2) although the sample consisted almost entirely of black inner-city children, these children may not be representative of all black children in the area, for they attend a private school where tuition (though small) is charged. Therefore, to some extent, the parents are willing to sacrifice financially to send their children to a private school. This may be evidence of a middle-class "aspirations" group; (3) little is known about black Catholics as a group, and approximately 30 to 40 percent of the sample was Catholic (this is probably a much lower percentage than many of Chicago's public schools). However, Hess and Torney state that a number of studies have shown that "Denomination of religious affiliation has relatively little effect on basic attachment to the country and government in the elementary school years." [30] (Points two and three appear to become unimportant because the findings were quite the opposite of what one would expect knowing the school was Catholic and the children were privileged); and (4) the possibility that the differences between the St. Cecilia findings and those of Hess and Torney, and Greenstein were historical rather than ethnic-class types.

Despite the above limitations, we believe that the St. Cecilia findings cast enough of a shadow of doubt over generalizations about childhood political socialization, evolving from studies which have used almost totally white samples or have failed to use racial identification as a variable, that further childhood political socialization studies involving black children and other subgroups are warranted. In his study of black school children, Greenberg comes to basically the same conclusion:

> Many of the extant definitions assume that political socialization is the acquisition of attitudes and behaviors "acceptable to the ongoing political system" . . . Many scholars see the role of political socialization as basically a stabilizing one of maintaining the current political system and political culture . . . The data generated in this study surely questions the utility of those definitions . . . which stress conformity to the ongoing political culture. The study suggests that black children are socialized to political orientation different from those of the members of the majority culture.[31]

THE IMPLICATIONS OF THE ST. CECILIA STUDY

One of the basic propositions of political socialization is that political orientations learned early in life tend to endure and influence what is learned in adult life. Therefore, it may be that today's young breed of black political activists who use techniques of non-negotiable demands, confrontation politics, and the like, are manifestations of the malevolent political orientations they have acquired while in elementary school. These activists are working outside of normal political channels to make their country's government respond to their needs and wishes. This study indicates what might be a three-pronged attack to get youthful black

---

[30] Hess and Torney, *The Development of Political Attitudes in Children,* p. 116.
[31] Greenberg, "Black Children and the Political System," pp. 344–45.

activists to work within this country's political framework. First, educators must be much more realistic in what they teach black children about our political system. Prejudice against blacks makes their socialization into society tough enough, without their having the extra burden of being told the equivalent of fairy tales about our political system. Second, institutionalized discrimination by the police against blacks must be eliminated. It is no secret that young blacks are searched, arrested, and convicted for many "crimes" that the police do not consider violations when committed by white youths. Finally, those with political power must give black people a greater voice in the many decisions that affect black people's lives. For example, in many instances when youthful blacks have tried to set up community health centers, city administrations have closed them up for not meeting certain minimum standards which even many of the health centers in the more affluent parts of the cities do not meet. Instead of coming to the youths' aid, city administrations only look for obstacles to place in their way. Examples of this type of discrimination are not uncommon.

Unless the above recommendations are implemented, political cynicism and the working for political goals outside the political system probably will continue to be characteristics of future youthful black political movements. It is of some interest to note that in reference to the "If you could change the world . . ." question not one child spoke of "revenge" against white people. Brotherhood, equality, and peace is for what the black inner-city children hoped. Are these children asking for too much?

12

THE MALEVOLENT LEADER: POLITICAL SOCIALIZATION IN AN AMERICAN SUBCULTURE

DEAN JAROS | **HERBERT HIRSCH** | **FREDERIC J. FLERON, JR.**

Perhaps the most dramatic finding of recent research on the political socialization of children is that youngsters appear to be overwhelmingly favorably disposed toward political objects which cross their vision. Officers and institutions of government are regarded as benevolent, worthy, competent, serving and powerful.[1] The implications of such findings are striking indeed. Childhood political dispositions may represent the roots of later patriotism; we may be observing the building of basic regime-level supportive values at a very young age.[2]

These findings are by no means new; in fact, they might be classified as part of the conventional wisdom of the discipline. Moreover, they are extremely well documented, and the study of childhood political socialization has advanced to consider far more than basic regime-level norms. Despite all this, however, there are still many empirical questions to be asked about such norms. Perhaps the recent assertion that the political scientist's model of socialization is "static and homogeneous"[3] is particu-

From *American Political Science Review* 62, no. 2 (June 1968): 564–75; reprinted by permission of the authors and the American Political Science Association.

The data on which this paper is based were collected under Contract #693 between the University of Kentucky Research Foundation and the Office of Economic Opportunity.

[1] Robert D. Hess and David Easton, "The Child's Changing Image of the President," *Public Opinion Quaretrly* 14 (Winter 1960): 632–42; Fred I. Greenstein, *Children and Politics* (New Haven, Conn.: Yale University Press, 1965), pp. 27–54; Robert D. Hess and Judith V. Torney, "The Development of Basic Attitudes Toward Government and Citizenship During the Elementary School Years: Part I" (Cooperative Research Project No. 1078; University of Chicago, 1965), pp. 102–5; Dean Jaros, "Children's Orientations Toward the President: Some Additional Theoretical Considerations and Data," *Journal of Politics* 29 (May 1967): 368–87.

[2] David Easton and Robert D. Hess, "The Child's Political World," *Midwest Journal of Political Science* 6 (August 1962): 243; Greenstein, *Children and Politics,* p. 53.

[3] Roberta S. Sigel, "Political Socialization: Some Reactions on Current Approaches and Conceptualizations" (Paper presented at the 1966 Annual Meeting of the American Political Science Association, New York, 6–10 September 1966), p. 14.

larly apropos here. Consider two closely related charatceristics of the appropriate literature: 1) the "positive image" which children have about politics and political figures has been synthesized from data gathered largely in the United States and to some extent in urban, industrialized communities within the United States; [4] and 2) empirical explanation of the favorable disposition which children manifest has not progressed very far. Though there may be hypotheses about how children get this way, there has been little systematic testing of the relationships between variables.

There is some danger that the major findings may be essentially "culture bound." There are few data on the political values of children in other countries or even in rural, racial, or ethnic subcultures within the United States. Moreover, what evidence there is hints at important cross-cultural variations in political learning; [5] less positive images may characterize other cultures. Political socialization is the process by which the child learns about the political culture in which he lives.[6] The content of what is socialized may well differ from culture to culture or from subculture to subculture.

The failure to explain children's positive orientations toward politics may be a function of the cultural problem. If the great majority of children in one culture manifest a glowing image, variance in disposition is not prominent, and empirical explanation in terms of accounting for variance may not suggest itself as a crucial task; also it may be quite difficult. In order to explain children's political images, one has to have a distribution of affect; there have to be some relatively negative images to come by. Research into children's political views in other cultures or sub-cultures may provide us with such negative images. But even if it does not generate the necessary data to conduct explanatory analysis, it would lessen the culture-bound nature of findings in political socialization.[7]

This paper attempts to realize these desiderata through a study of childhood socialization in the Appalachian region of eastern Kentucky. Appalachia may be classified as a subculture within the United States for at least two reasons. First, the poverty and isolation of the region impose characteristics that differentiate it from most other areas in the country. Secondly and relatedly, many cultural norms of Appalachia differ radically from those considered to be standard middle-class imperatives.[8]

---

[4] The Chicago area, New Haven, and Detroit provided the research environments for some of the studies cited in Note 1.

[5] Robert D. Hess, "The Socialization of Attitudes Toward Political Authority: Some Cross-National Comparisons," *International Social Science Journal* 14, no. 4 (1963): 542–59.

[6] Gabriel A. Almond and G. Bingham Powell, Jr., *Comparative Politics: A Developmental Approach* (Boston: Little, Brown, 1966), pp. 23–24.

[7] Michael Argyle and Peter Delin, "Non-Universal Laws of Socialization," *Human Relations* 18 (February 1965): 77–86.

[8] Several analyses contributory to this assertion are: Virgil C. Jones, *The Hatfields and the McCoys* (Chapel Hill: University of North Carolina Press, 1948); Jack E. Weller, *Yesterday's People* (Lexington: University of Kentucky Press, 1965); Harry M. Caudill, *Night Comes to the Cumberlands* (Boston: Little, Brown, 1963).

I. TWO EXPLANATIONS OF CHILDREN'S
POLITICAL AUTHORITY ORIENTATIONS

There are several relatively untested hypotheses about the sources of the positive notions children are observed to hold toward the political. Many of them prominently involve the family as a socializing agent. Because of the intriguing nature of family-related variables in Appalachia, the region provides an excellent context in which to investigate these assertions.

Among these explanations is the view that the family directly transmits positive values about government and politics to the child while shielding him from stimuli which have negative connotations, such as stories of political corruption, expedient bargaining, etc.[9] In short, the family directly indoctrinates the child as to the beneveolent nature of political authority, to view the political world in essentially the same terms as characterize the parents' generally supportive outlook on the political regime.[10] In Appalachia, in contrast to most of the rest of the United States, there is a great deal of overt, antigovernment sentiment in the adult population. Rejection of and hostility toward political authority, especially federal authority, has long characterized the region.[11] It is very difficult to believe that here parents could transmit positive images of regime symbols to their children. In fact, ". . . the civic instruction which goes on incidental to normal activities in the family," [12] suggested as a likely cause of children's favorable affect, would in Appalachia be a source of political cynicism.

Secondly, we might take the thesis that the family is an important socializing agent because the child's experiences with his immediate authority figures (parents) are somehow projected to include more remote agencies, including the political. The father, perceived as providing and benevolent, supposedly becomes the prototypical authority figure.[13] For the child, the regime becomes "the family writ large," [14] especially sacred

---

[9] Greenstein, *Children and Politics*, pp. 45–46; Easton and Hess, *Midwest Journal of Political Science* 6 (November 1962): 229–35.

[10] Herbert Hyman, *Political Socialization* (Glencoe, Ill.: Free Press, 1959), Chap. 4; Leonard W. Doob, *Patriotism and Nationalism* (New Haven, Conn.: Yale University Press, 1964), pp. 119–26.

[11] Weller, *Yesterday's People*, pp. 33–56, 163; also Thomas R. Ford, ed., *The Southern Appalachian Region: A Survey* (Lexington: University of Kentucky Press, 1960), pp. 12–15. These may characterize the entire American South. Indeed, some basic socialization data from the South could be most interestingly compared with that gathered elsewhere. But apart from South-wide considerations, there are historical reasons why one would expect such values to be especially strong in Appalachia.

[12] Greenstein, *Children and Politics*, p. 44.

[13] Harold D. Lasswell, *Power and Personality* (New York: Viking Press, 1962), pp. 156–59; Sebastian DeGrazia, *The Political Community* (Chicago: University of Chicago Press, 1948), pp. 11–21; James C. Davies, "The Family's Role in Political Socialization," *Annals* 361 (September 1965): 10–19.

[14] Easton and Hess, *Midwest Journal of Political Science* 6 (November 1962): 242–43.

as its image benefits from the emotional kind of bond that exists between parent and child. In Appalachia, there is a high degree of family disruption. The father may well not live at home. Far from providing a glowing prototype of authority, he may be a pitifully inadequate figure, unemployed or absent, not providing for his family, deserving of (and receiving) scorn.[15] If the Appalachian child generalizes the father figure or the family authority structure to the political, he is not very likely to be generalizing a positive configuration.[16]

II. METHOD

Data were gathered from a nearly complete enumeration (N = 2,432) of rural public school children in grades 5–12 in Knox County, Kentucky during March, 1967. Paper-and-pencil questionnaires were administered in classrooms in connection with an evaluation of a Community Action Program of the Office of Economic Opportunity. This paper is based on the responses of a random sample of 305 of these subjects.[17]

Affect toward political authority was measured in two ways: through

---

[15] The effects of widespread unemployment in the coal industry and other economic malaises are well known. Because they are unable to provide, men reportedly invent physical disabilities or contrive "abandonments" of their dependents in order to qualify their families for public assistance. Such men become ciphers: Weller, *Yesterday's People,* pp. 76–78; Ford, *The Southern Appalachian Region,* pp. 245–56. In addition to anecdotal accounts of such situations, there are some hard data which are consistent with these assertions. The great proportion of Appalachian men who are not in the labor force (23 percent in Knox County, site of the present study, as opposed to 11 percent in the U.S. as a whole) plus a high unemployment rate (11 percent in Knox County) suggests a large number of non-providing fathers (Source: U.S. Census of Population, 1960). A high incidence of incomplete families can also be confirmed. Fully 22 percent of the Appalachian children sampled for the present study reported father-absence, while only 12 percent of the Survey Research Center's national sample of high-school seniors are from fatherless homes. The authors wish to thank Richard Niemi for the last datum.

[16] At this point, it should be noted that these two general hypotheses do not exhaust the list of suggested socialization processes. In fact, some observers stress the efficacy of altogether different agencies, for example the public school: Hess and Torney, "The Development of Basic Attitudes . . . ," pp. 193–200. But even with this emphasis, such observers believe that some political values are implanted in youth by their parents, namely, those which "insure the stability of basic institutions" (p. 191). This is a reference to what we have called "regime level" values, which are the sole topic of this paper. At least for socialization to this kind of political affect, testing of family-related hypotheses is of undoubted importance. See M. Kent Jennings and Richard Niemi, "Family Structure and the Transmisson of Political Values" (Paper presented at the 1966 annual meeting of the American Political Science Association, New York, Sept. 6–10, 1966).

[17] A few schools, not accessible by road, did not participate in the study. The cost of including them would have been very high and the returns realized very small. These schools had a total enrollment of less than fifty and a somewhat smaller number than this in grades five through eight. The questionnaire was administered by regular classroom teachers who had been instructed in its use. Every attempt was made, however, to convince the subjects that despite the context, they were not being tested. Teachers were asked explicitly to communicate this notion. This mode of administration prob-

reports of images of the President,[18] and through "political cynicism" scale scores.[19] Images of the President were used because this figure apparently occupies a key position in the development of both cognitions of and affect toward the regime.[20] The Presidency provides an introduction; notions first held toward this role are probably subsequently generalized to other political institutions and to the entity of government itself.[21] The specific instrumentation is that developed by Hess and Easton.[22]

By contrast, political cynicism, "rather than referring to specific political issues and actors . . . is a basic orientation toward political actors and activity. It presumably pervades all encounters with political objects.[23] In short, political cynicism relates to a basic, general evaluative posture toward politics. Though perhaps a developmental descendant of images of the President, this variable represents far less specifically focussed regime-level affect. The specific instrumentation is the political cynicism scale developed by Jennings and Niemi.[24]

In addition to desiring variables important in the introduction of children to politics and ones which seem to encapsulate a more generalized and developed kind of regime-level affect, we chose these measures because of the fact that they have generated reliable data. We wished to take advantage of direct replicative possibilities.

Unfortunately, no direct information about the political values of the parents of our sample is presently available.[25] Though the aggregate view of political institutions and personalities held by Appalachian adults is reportedly less positive than those of other Americans, the only personal level data available are child-reported. Our indicators of parental affect toward political authority consist of two family-related items from

---

ably produced fewer invalid responses than exposing the subjects to a nonindigenous investigator who would have aroused suspicion.

Knox County was chosen as the site for this study because it to some extent typifies Appalachia. That is, it is isolated, rural, and poor. No air or rail passenger transportation is available and only one U.S. highway crosses the county. Knox County has an annual per capita income of $501 as compared with $2223 for the U.S. as a whole. It is 84 percent rural while the nation is only 30 percent. (Source: U.S. Census of Population, 1960.)

[18] For commentary on images of the President, see Fred I. Greenstein, "More on Children's Images of the President," *Public Opinion Quarterly* 25 (Winter 1961): 648–54.

[19] For remarks on political cynicism, see Robert E. Agger, Marshall N. Goldstein, and Stanley A. Pearl, "Political Cynicism: Measurements and Meaning," *Journal of Politics* 23 (August 1961): 477–506.

[20] Fred I. Greenstein, "The Benevolent Leader: Children's Images of Political Authority," *American Political Science Review* 54 (December 1960): 936; Easton and Hess, *Midwest Journal of Political Science* 6: 241.

[21] Greenstein, *Children and Politics,* p. 54.

[22] Hess and Easton, *Public Opinion Quarterly* 14, p. 639.

[23] Jennings and Niemi, "A Family Structure . . .", p. 13.

[24] Ibid., footnote 30.

[25] The evaluation of the Community Action Program in Knox County involved the solicitation of data from a sample of adults. These data can be arranged with those on youngsters to form parent-child pairs. These data are being exploited by Herbert Hirsch.

Easton and Dennis's scale of political efficacy.[26] Two problems arise in using these items as indicators of parental values. First, the index in question was designed to measure a variable in children, not adults. However, the items "inquire about the relationship between government and the child's family. . . ." The index is not regarded as a direct reflector of children's efficacy per se. In fact, it shows how a child has come to "view expected relationships between adult members of the system and the authorities" as well as tapping a "nascent attitude" of the child himself.[27] Youngsters tend to evaluate political objects in child-related terms.[28] Clearly this index does not measure that kind of dynamic. The items can be interpreted as a report on family (adult) orientations to political authorities. Indeed, such a report, involving the perception of children, may be a more significant independent variable than the actual values of the parents. A person's values, of course, can have no direct impact on the behavior of another individual. Any effect must be mediated through the influences cognitive and evaluative processes.

Secondly, given this, can items which tap efficacy be said to reveal anything about "positive" or supportive regime-level attitudes among adults? Though it is easy to imagine people highly enthusiastic about their political authority without possessing "citizen competence," [29] it is probable that in democratic societies sense of efficacy is in fact related to general affect toward political authority. Inefficacious feelings are related to alienation and what has been called "political negativism." [30] These are the very antithesis of supportive dispositions. Moreover, recent scholarship has specifically considered efficacy to be a crucial variable in regime-level supports.[31]

The nature of the family authority structure is measured by 1) "father image" items analogous to Hess and Easton's Presidential image items [32] and 2) noting whether the father in fact lives at home.[33]

III. THE APPALACHIAN CHILD'S AFFECT TOWARD THE POLITICAL

Our subjects' evaluations of political authority have a very prominent feature: they are dramatically less positive than those rendered by children in previously reported research.

26 David Easton and Jack Dennis, "The Child's Acquisition of Regime Norms: Political Efficacy," *American Political Science Review* 61 (March 1967): 25–38.

27 Ibid., p. 32.

28 Greenstein, *American Political Science Review,* 54, 938–39.

29 Gabriel A. Almond and Sidney Verba, *The Civic Culture* (Princeton, N.J.: Princeton University Press, 1963), Chapter 6.

30 John E. Horton and Wayne Thompson, "Powerlessness and Political Negativism," *American Journal of Sociology* 67 (March 1962): 435–93.

31 Easton and Dennis, "The Child's Acquisition of Regime Norms . . ."

32 Hess and Easton, *Public Opinion Quarterly* 14: 635–42.

33 On father-absence see: David B. Lynn and William L. Sawrey, "The Effects of Father-Absence on Norwegian Boys and Girls," *Journal of Abnormal and Social Psychology* 59 (September 1959): 258–62; George R. Bach, "Father-Fantasies and Father-Typing in Father-Separated Children," *Child Development* 17 (March 1946): 63–80.

Table 1 describes the affective responses of the Appalachian children to the President and directly compares them to Hess and Easton's findings on Chicago-area children. Though our sample includes children from fifth through twelfth grades and Hess and Easton's from second through eighth, it is possible to make comparisons using only the fifth through eighth grade portions of both. It is clear that for all five President-evaluation items, the distribution of responses of the Knox County youngsters is significantly less favorable than that of the Hess and Easton sample. In fact, when compared against "most men," the President does

TABLE 1. Fifth-eighth Grade Children's Evaluations of the President

	Response	*Knox County data*	*Chicago area data*	*Smirnov two-sample test*
1) View of how hard the President works compared with most men.	harder as hard less hard	35% 24 41	77% 21 3	$D = .42, p < .001$
	Total	100% ($N = 128$)	101% ($N = 214$)	
2) View of the honesty of the President compared with most men.	more honest as honest less honest	23% 50 27	57% 42 1	$D = .34, p < .001$
	Total	100% ($N = 133$)	100% ($N = 214$)	
3. View of the President's liking for people as compared with most men.	like most everybody likes as many as most doesn't like as many	50% 28 22	61% 37 2	$D = .20, p < .01$
	Total	100% ($N = 125$)	100% ($N = 214$	
4) View of the President's knowledge compared with most men.	knows more knows about the same knows less	45% 33 22	82% 16 2	$D = .37, p < .001$
	Total	100% ($N = 124$)	100% ($N = 212$	
5) View of the President as a person.	best in world a good person not a good person	6% 68 26	11% 82 8	$D = .19, p < .01$
	Total	100% ($N = 139$)	101% ($N = 211$)	

not do particularly well. In aggregate, he is not a paramount figure, and there are a fair number of youngsters (about a fourth) that express overtly unfavorable reactions to him.

Hess and Easton, it will be recalled, note that age greatly affects the nature of their sample's responses. Generally, they showed that the very favorable view that the very young have of the President's personal qualities (Items 2, 3, and 5) declines with increasing age, while high regard for his performance capabilities is maintained or even increased as the child grows older.[34] The diminution of "personal" portions of the image is not interpreted as a disillusionment with authority, but as increasing realism. The maintenance of the role-filling portions is regarded as most relevant to future adult behavior, translating into respect for political institutions.[35] In short, the changes of children's images of the President with age present a very fortunate configuration considered from the standpoint of loyalty and support for the regime. The Knox County data, bleak to begin with, show few such encouraging tendencies when controls are imposed for age. Even extending the analysis to the older portions of the sample does little to effect change. To be sure, the personal portions of the image appear slightly less positive than those of younger children. Only 31 percent of the high-school seniors think the President likes almost everybody, while 31 percent think he likes fewer people than most men; no twelfth graders think the President is the best person in the world, while 31 percent think he is not a good person. But overall, the picture is static. *Tau* correlations between age and positive responses to the three personal image items range between .02 and .04 and are not significant.

In those portions of the image supposedly more crucial to adult regime-level behavior, there is no increase in favorable response to the President. However, a decline in the proportion of overtly unfavorable reactions does produce a significant relationship between age and positiveness on the item dealing with how hard the President works ($\tau_c = .14$, $p < .05$) and a perceptible though not significant relationship between age and positiveness on the item dealing with the President's knowledge ($\tau_c = .09$, $p > .05$). At best, these are modest trends. There is relatively little ground for saying, "The President is increasingly seen as a person whose abilities are appropriate to the demands of his office. . . ."[36]

Furthermore, the very high incidence of "don't knows" does not decline significantly with age (see note to Table 1). Such a high rate was to be expected of a deprived, unsophisticated population. But the fact that it remains high even among high-school seniors (mean non-response rate is 27 percent) provides further evidence that, politically speaking, nothing is happening to these Appalachian youth as they mature. They certainly do not appear to be developing into adults devoted to symbols of extant political authority.

---

[34] Hess and Easton, *Public Opinion Quarterly* 14, 635–42.
[35] Ibid.
[36] Ibid., p. 639.

Finally, the stark contrast of these data to those on other American children is heightened when the consideration of social class is introduced. It has often been observed that lower-class children have a greater propensity to idealize political figures.[37] This may well be due to the fact that such children are less politicized than their middle-class counterparts. Being less developed and less knowledgeable, they have developed fewer critical faculties and continue to exhibit the "immature" response of excessive deference. It is impossible to determine whether the same class phenomenon operates within Appalachia, for the sample as a whole is overwhelmingly lower-class.[38] But because of their lower-class position relative to the rest of the country, Knox County youngsters generally should be highly idealizing. The data, of course, reveal the diametric opposite. It is clear that Appalachia constitutes a distinct subculture, one in which there are operative variables sufficiently powerful to prevent the occurrence of what is by now expected as a matter of course.

Table 2 describes the more generalized affect manifested in political cynicism. The scores of the Knox County youngsters are compared to

TABLE 2.   Political Cynicism Scores*

		Knox County data (whole sample)	Knox County data (high school only)	SRC national sample	Smirnov two sample test
most cynical	6	8%	26%	5%	Knox County data
	5	11	22	3	(whole sample)
	4	19	11	13	and SRC national
	3	19	20	37	sample, $D = .16$,
	2	23	15	25	$p < .001$
least cynical	1	21	6	17	Knox County data (High school only) and SRC national sample, $D = .40, p < .001$
Total		101% $N = 305$	100% $N = 54$	100% $N = 1869$	

*It has been assumed that the Political Cynicism Scale generated Guttman scalar patterns in the Knox County Data as it did in the SRC National Sample. To compensate for the possible invalidity of this assumption, the items were conservatively dichotomized and conservatively scored. Only choice of the most cynical available alternative was considered a cynical response. Failure of a respondent to choose the most cynical alternative *for whatever reason*, including nonresponse, resulted in the recording of a noncynical item score.

37 See for example, Greenstein, *Children and Politics*, Ch. 5.

38 No reliable information on social class could be secured from the children themselves. Information on occupation or estimated family income simply was not given by these youngsters. Assigning class on the basis of the neighborhood in which individuals live, as Greenstein did, requires that virtually every subject be placed in the lowest social stratum. These rural residents are universally poor. Only 9 percent of the country's families have incomes over $6,000, and these are almost entirely to be found in the "urban" county seat, which was not sampled. (Source: U.S. Census of Population 1960.)

those of the Survey Research Center's nationwide sample of high school seniors.[39]

The greater cynicism of the subculture sample is evident. Since the Survey Research Center deals only with high-school students, perhaps comparisons should be made only with the high-school portion (grades 10–12) of the Knox County sample. Though this portion is significantly more cynical, the small number of subjects in it perhaps recommends use of the entire sample. One might think that the introduction of younger respondents would depress cynicism scores (age and cynicism are reportedly positively related in children),[40] but this does not happen to any great degree. In any event, even the entire 5–12 grade Knox County sample is significantly more cynical than the SRC twelfth graders. The implication of this, of course, is that in Appalachia, unlike the rest of the United States, there is relatively little change in cynicism with maturation. That this is the case is revealed by the nonsignificant $\tau_c = -.02$ between school grade and political cynicism score. Early in life these children appear to become relatively cynical and they stay that way.

Thus, though at this point it remains unexplained, there is no doubt that Appalachian children manifest far less favorable political affect than do their counterparts elsewhere in the United States. Regardless of the index in question, the responses of our sample stand in sharp contrast to other research. Just as supportive dispositions in citizens have been asserted to have early roots, so may the Appalachians' often-noted rejection of political authority germinate during early years. Moreover, also in some contrast to findings of other research, the affective orientations of these subjects does not change greatly with increasing age. These negative images are relatively static. This nonvariant affect suggests the operation of a pervasive socialization agent early in the lives of these children.[41] This in turn suggests the desirability of examining the causal efficacy of variables related to an early agent frequently assumed to be an important socializer: the family. It is to this task that we now turn.

IV. THE FAMILY AS TRANSMITTER OF SPECIFIC POLITICAL VALUES

What kinds of general explanatory propositions about the socialization process are consistent with these data? If parents typically transmit the

---

39 Jennings and Niemi, "Family Structure . . . ," p. 15.

40 Greenstein, *Children and Politics,* pp. 39–40.

41 This nonvariance, a preliminary look at our data suggests, may be due to the homogeneity and isolation of the area. Family, peer groups, schools, and other possible agents of socialization indigenous to the region probably manifest substantially the same configuration of values. Thus if families transmit an initial set of political notions to children, subsequent exposure to school, peers, etc., is likely to reinforce rather than change values. The remote location of the county probably insulates it from electronic or printed media and other external stimuli. Any value implications at variance with indigenous norms which such sources might transmit are thus prevented from having a widespread effect on maturing children.

substantive content of their values about government to their children, then the very negative political affect observed among Appalachian youngsters should be related to similar assessments on the part of their mothers and fathers.[42] Evidence on this can be gained by examining the nature of the relationship between our family political orientation items and children's political affect (Table 3).

TABLE 3. Relationship Between Family Political Orientation and Child's Political Affect

Family political orientation item	Child's political affect measure	τ_c	Significance
"I don't think people in the government care much what people like my family think"*	view of how hard President works	.23	$p < .001$
	view of the honesty of the President	.06	$p > .05$
	view of the President's liking for people	.18	$p < .001$
	view of the President's knowledge	.01	$p > .05$
	view of the President as a person	.05	$p > .05$
	political cynicism scale	−.20	$p < .001$
"My family doesn't have any say about what the government does."*	view of how hard President works	.10	$p > .05$
	view of the honesty of the President	.06	$p > .05$
	view of the President's liking for people	.07	$p > .05$
	view of the President's knowledge	.13	$p < .01$
	view of the President as a person	.06	$p > .05$
	political cynicism scale	−.13	$p < .01$

*Disagreement scored as positive value.

---

42 In the absence of additional data, it is difficult to show empirically that the parents of this sample have negative dispositions toward political authority. However, responses to the family political value items, when the distribution is dichotomized, reveal about equal number of agreements (negative dispositions) and disagreements (positive dispositions). Following each item is the percentage of respondents expressing agreement:

"I don't think people in the government care much about what people like my family think," 58 percent;

"My family doesn't have any say about what the government does," 43 percent.

The authors are fully aware of the precarious nature of the family value measures. Their proxy nature makes them somewhat suspect. The data they generate are displayed, however, because they are suggestive and because they indicate the kind of research which, in the authors' opinions, should be performed more often. In subsequent publications based on the Appalachian data, direct information on parental values and children's perceptions thereof will be available (See note 25).

Since responses to family political orientation items were recorded in terms of degree of agreement (from disagree very much to agree very much), they constitute ordinal variables as do the Presidential image and cynicism measures. The evidence on the amount of impact they have on these child political affect variables, however, is mixed. Some fairly substantial *taus* are accompanied by others approaching zero. But it is interesting to note where the significant relationships occur. Primarily, they involve Presidential competence items and the cynicism scale. These may be the most important dependent variables. Several scholars have observed that childhood evaluations of the personal qualities of the President, which here do not relate to family political orientation, are "less functionally relevant" to future adult behavior than are assessments of role-filling capabilities. As stated above, these observers express no alarm at the decline with age of evaluations of Presidential benevolence. Similarly, the fact that parental values do not seem to influence them may not be great evidence about the inefficacy of familial values in conditioning important childhood orientations.

If political cynicism represents a more developed kind of evaluation, it is significant that it appears to depend upon these parental variables. Regarded as an important encapsulator of youthful political affect, this construct may be a crucial indicator whose antecedents should be known.

Family political values, then, appear to have some effect on children's political affect. Especially given the fact that the affective variables in question appear to be among the most significant, the direct transmission hypothesis takes on some credibility. This suggests the desirability of more detailed investigations of the content of intrafamilial political communication.

V. THE FAMILY AS PROTOTYPICAL
AUTHORITY STRUCTURE

A totally different kind of dynamic is implied in the notion of relations with the family as a model for political affect. It is not, however, incompatible with the notion that the family transmits specific value content to the young. It is entirely possible that both processes operate simultaneously. Moreover, since the relationships are relatively small, our data on value transmission fairly demand that additional explanatory tacks be taken. Table 4 demonstrates the effects of father-image and integrity of the family on Appalachian children's political orientations. Again, evidence is somewhat mixed. Three father-image items [43] are placed against their Presidential-image parallels and against cynicism. There is almost a complete lack of relationship. Not only does the "great overlap

---

[43] The father-image items are analogous to the Presidential-image items used by Hess and Easton. Though there are five Presidential-image items, only three father-image analogues are used because of objection to asking respondents to evaluate their fathers' honesty or diligence at work.

TABLE 4. Relationship Between Family Authority Characteristics and Child's Political Affect

Family authority characteristics	Child's political affect	τ_c	Significance
View of father's liking for people	view of President's liking for people	.05	$p > .05$
	political cynicism	−.07	$p > .05$
View of father's knowledge	view of President's knowledge	.02	$p > .05$
	political cynicism	.02	$p > .05$
View of father as a person	view of President as a person	.05	$p > .05$
	political cynicism	−.03	$p > .05$
	view of how hard President works	−.08	$p < .05$
	view of President's honesty	−.09	$p < .05$
Father living with family*	view of President's liking of people	−.12	$p < .05$
	view of President's knowledge	−.23	$p < .001$
	view of President as a person	.00	$p > .05$
	political cynicism	.05	$p > .05$

*This is a dichotomous variable − either the father lives at home or he does not. However, since father's living at home constitutes a less disrupted family authority structure, we continue to apply ordinal statistics.

of the images of father and President" [44] fail to appear among these children, but the more generalized political affect measured by cynicism does not depend on how they see their fathers. In short, there is no evidence at all to support the hypothesis that evaluations of family authority figures are directly projected to remote, political ones.

If the father-image hypothesis thus suffers, another dynamic by which the family might serve as a model for regime affect fares even worse. The presence or absence of the father might be thought to have political consequences for children. A fatherless home is disrupted and generally thought to have negative implications. Children might project their negative evaluations of such homes onto the political authority.[45] If this

[44] Hess and Easton, *Public Opinion Quarterly* 14: 640.
[45] Davies, "The Family's Role in Political Socialization," 13–15.

were the case, children from fatherless homes should have less positive views. Table 4 reveals exactly the opposite. There are generally low to moderate, but significant, negative relationships between having a father at home and evaluating the President in a favorable light. Fatherless children are more positive toward the political. How can this remarkable result be interpreted? One could argue that there is a cathartic process at work; that there is some sort of psychic necessity (possibly anxiety-related) to regard authority as benign. Perhaps unfortunate home life heightens this need which is then manifested in positive evaluations of the political.[46] This does not seem likely, for as we have just seen, specific negative evaluations of their fathers are not related to childrens' positive political orientations.

Rather than resulting in negative authority orientations, father-absence could interfere with the transfer of specific political value content from family to child. A major agent in the transfer process may be absent. Though mixed, there is some evidence in previous research of "male political dominance" in the family. Fathers may be particularly important communicators of political values.[47] Children from fatherless homes become more dependent upon their mothers. But mothers are not typically strong political cue-givers. Hence, the typical adult political values of Appalachia will not be so effectively transmitted in the father-less home. These adult values supposedly involve relatively unfavorable assessments of political authority. The fatherless child escapes close contacts with these values and emerges more positively disposed toward political authority. When this agent is absent, perhaps the media, or other agents bearing more favorable cues, assume a more prominent role in the socialization process.

This interpretation, which of course returns us to the transmission-of-specific-values hypothesis, is strongly supported by additional analysis of the data. First, it is clear that there is no unknown process operating to produce more positive adult political values in fatherless families. Father-less and two-parent families are identical in this regard (*tau*'s between father at home and family political value items are $-.03$ and $.00$). Though the starting point is the same, it is also clear that the transmission process is greatly attenuated in fatherless homes. This can be seen by imposing a control for father-presence on the relationship between family political orientation and child's political affect (Table 5). The data for father-present children are very similar to the collapsed data shown in Table 3, except that the relationship between family value and

[46] Judith V. Torney, *The Child's Idealization of Authority* (Master's thesis, University of Chicago, 1962).

[47] Greenstein, *Children and Politics*, p. 119; Kenneth P. Langton, *The Political Socialization Process: The Case of Secondary School Students in Jamaica* (Ph.D. dissertation, University of Oregon, 1965), p. 119. On the other hand, male dominance in the political learning of the young fails to appear in some research: Hyman, *Political Socialization*, pp. 83–89; Eleanor E. Maccoby, Richard E. Matthews, and Anton S. Morton, "Youth and Political Change," *Public Opinion Quarterly* 18 (Spring 1954): 23–39.

TABLE 5. Relationship Between Family Political Orientation and Child's Political Affect, with Father-presence Controlled

Family political orientation item	Child's political affect measure	Father-present children τ_c	Father-absent children τ_c	Significance of the difference
I don't think people in the government care much what people like my family think*	view of how hard the President works	.25	.12	$p < .001$
	view of honesty of the President	.12	−.10	$p < .001$
	view of President's liking for people	.23	.04	$p < .001$
	view of President's knowledge	.00	.06	$p < .01$†
	view of President as a person	.10	−.11	$p < .001$
	political cynicism scale	−.18	−.26	$p < .01$†
My family doesn't have any say about what the government does*	view of how hard the President works	.17	−.15	$p < .001$
	view of honesty of the President	.10	−.06	$p < .001$
	view of President's liking for people	.17	−.23	$p < .001$
	view of President's knowledge	.17	.03	$p < .001$
	view of President as a person	−.06	.08	$p < .001$†
	political cynicism	−.13	−.16	$p < .05$†

* Disagreement scored as positive value.
† Relationship not in predicted direction.

child affect is generally somewhat stronger. But for father-absent children, the relationship generally declines and in several cases is actually reversed. Not only can the fatherless family not promulgate its political values, but it seems to leave its children very vulnerable to the socialization of other agents, agents with rather different (more positive) values. To be sure, child political cynicism, which is related to family political values, does not appear to be governed by these considerations. Other family-related roots may affect this variable—perhaps those which relate to generalized cynicism.

VI. CONCLUSION

Children in the relatively poor, rural Appalachian region of the United States are dramatically less favorably inclined toward political objects than are their counterparts in other portions of the nation. Moreover, the image which these children have does not appear to develop with age in the fashion observed for others; there is no indication that a process conducive to the development of political support is operative in Appalachia. Here, children's views appear to be relatively static. These findings have two implications. First, they point to the possibility that the often-emphasized highly positive character of children's views of politics may be a culturally bound phenomenon. One should exercise much caution in accepting such views as a universal norm. Secondly, the occurrence of such divergent findings underscores the desirability of *explaining* children's political orientations.

Since, at the subcultural level, these atypical findings are paralleled by 1) atypical adult (parent) political values, and 2) atypical family structure, two broad hypotheses involving the effect of family-related variables on children's political affect were tested. Examination of the hypothesis that parents directly transmit the content of their political values to their children produced some confirming evidence. Reported parental values showed moderate relationship to certain aspects of children's political affect. This was especially true of the competence items in Presidential images (supposedly the most important for subsequent behavior) and of political cynicism, a more generalized kind of system affect.

The thesis which posits the family as prototypical authority structure fares less well, however. There is no support at all for the notion that affect toward the father is extended to remote, political authority. Relationships between specific aspects of children's father images and parallel components of Presidential images are not significant. Nor is there evidence that disrupted family structure, measured by father-absence, contributes to negative political evaluations. In fact, father-absence is associated with more favorable political valuations in Appalachian children! This remarkable result is interpreted as supporting the first hypothesis regarding the direct transfer of value-content from family to child. Where the father is absent, an agent communicating the predominantly negative adult political values to youngsters is lost. This notion seems the more plausible when it is observed that there is a marked relationship between family political values and child political affect among father-present families, but no such relationship—if anything a slight negative gradient—among father-absent families.

Thus, of the two broad hypotheses posited at the outset, our data support the notion of direct value transfer, while leading us to doubt that the family is an effective authority prototype. Though these findings are offered as significant in and of themselves—they certainly suggest the importance of closer examination of parent-child political communication processes in the understanding of regime-level values—there are other implications. The explanatory relationships presented here are of relatively modest magnitudes. The small amount of variance in children's political affect which is explained here by the family suggests that we should search for other agents of socialization, or for other dynamics which may operate within the family. A preliminary view of other of the Knox County data suggests that there may be conditions under which other, less personal agents assume a great role. Fortunately, the move toward cross-cultural and explanatory analysis of childhood socialization will proceed and these and related questions will be joined.[48]

---

[48] The forthcoming doctoral dissertation by Herbert Hirsch explores other socialization agents at greater length.

part V

THE DEVELOPMENT
OF ACTIVISM

The attentive reader must now find himself in something of a quandary. For it is evident that, prior to the 1960s and more recently, both the historical foundations and social psychological bases of political activism were missing in the case of American young people. How, then, did the contemporary activism develop at all?

There are, I believe, four sources of this activism. The first, subcultural pockets of cynicism, was partly discussed in the preceding section. Aside from Appalachia, there are other such pockets, including the black middle classes and certain segments of the white middle class in America. These contributed disproportionate shares of political activists during recent years as the articles by David Westby and Richard Braungart, and by Richard Flacks among others, suggest in this section.

Of equal significance to the emergence of political activism among young people in America in the 1960s were certain *socialization mechanisms*. Some observers, in fact, claim that a defective brand of political socialization was almost wholly responsible for the activism in the 1960s. Bearing on such assertions is the initial selection. The authors distinguish among the possible political responses found among youth and suggest the specific socialization practices and psychological characteristics corresponding to each type of response. On the basis of their analyses, they conclude that the political activist of today seems to have been raised by parents who respected him and encouraged his independent thinking. This respect and admiration was reciprocated by the child, quite in contrast to the typical image painted of contemporary political activists.

A third major source of contemporary political activism comprises the characteristics of *educational settings*. As we saw earlier, in articles by Hanan Selvin and Warren Hagstrom, and by Burton Clark and Martin Trow, the university can play an important part in shaping the general political orientations of students. Thus, it should not be surprising to find that it also can play a part in encouraging the development of activism. John Orbell's article reveals some of the dimensions of this phenomenon in the case of black student protest in the early 1960s. He finds, for instance, that protest among black youngsters tended to be more extensive in private, high quality colleges and universities. Other research into white student activism also has revealed the potency of such variables.

Some people, including a few who, themselves, are young activists, assign a major role in the unfolding of political activism to the fourth and final source: large-scale social changes and specific historical events occurring in America during the past couple of decades. These are considered in the selection by Jacob Fishman and Fredric Solomon (Reading 15) in which the authors argue, in part, that the rapidity of social change may serve as one impetus to activism, and illustrate their contention with data from Germany and Japan as well as America.

The last three articles in this section deal with the varieties of political activism by youth in America in the 1960s and 1970s and, in some respects, supplement Fishman and Solomon's analysis of the impact of social change and historical events on young peoples' political activism. The first of these, by David Westby and Richard Braungart (Reading 16), examines the social bases of both the leftwing Students for a Democratic Society (SDS) and the rightwing Young Americans for Freedom (YAF). They conclude that the SDS members are apt to be from upper middle-class origins while the YAF members are the products of working-class backgrounds.

Richard Flacks's article is an intensive examination of the development of leftwing political activism among youth in America in the 1960s. Flacks, perhaps the most sympathetic and insightful analyst of contemporary youth activism in America, presents an illuminating picture of this development as well as some concrete suggestions for sustaining the movement in the future.

The last article, written by me, traces the transformation of black youth protest in America during the decade of the 1960s and the early part of the 1970s. Among other things, I attempt to forecast the future of this movement, suggesting that revolution is impossible in the short run, but substantial change is likely in the long run, through the resocialization programs of such groups as the Black Panthers.

13

SOCIALIZATION CORRELATES
OF STUDENT ACTIVISM

JEANNE H. BLOCK | NORMA HAAN | M. BREWSTER SMITH

Studies assessing the intellectual dispositions, academic careers, value systems, and personality characteristics of student activists are amassing. In the studies completed to date, activist students have been defined variously as members of the Students for a Democratic Society [1] marchers in peace parades,[2] protestors against university compliance with ranking students for the draft,[3] dissenters against university cooperation with the House un-American Activities Committee,[4] organizers of the Vietnam Summer Project [5] and participants in the Berkeley Free Speech Movement (FSM).[6] Despite these differing selective criteria for student activ-

From *Journal of Social Issues* 25, no. 4 (Autumn 1969): 143–48, 160–65, 169–77; reprinted and abridged by permission of the authors and the Society for the Psychological Study of Social Issues.

The research on which this paper draws was supported by grants from the Rosenberg Foundation and the Foundations' Fund for Research in Psychiatry which we gratefully acknowledge. The preparation of this paper was supported additionally by a National Institute of Mental Health Research Development Award to the first author. The authors wish to express their appreciation to the many students and administrations at both the University of California and San Francisco State College and to the Peace Corps volunteers and officials who cooperated with us in this research.

[1] R. G. Braungart, "SDS and YAF: Backgrounds of Student Political Activists," paper presented at the annual meeting of the American Sociological Association, Miami, Fla., August, 1966.

[2] F. Solomon and J. R. Fishman, "Youth and Peace: A Psychological Study of Student Peace Demonstrators in Washington, D. C.," *Journal of Social Issues* 20, no. 4 (1964): 54–73.

[3] R. Flacks, "The Liberated Generation: An Exploration of the Roots of Student Protest," *Journal of Social Issues* 23, no. 3 (1967): 52–75.

[4] Z. F. Gamson, J. Goodman, and G. Gurin, "Radicals, Moderates and Bystanders During a University Protest," paper presented at the annual meeting of the American Sociological Association, San Francisco, August, 1967.

[5] K. Keniston, *Young Radicals: Notes on Committed Youth* (New York: Harcourt Brace Jovanovich, 1968).

[6] W. A. Watts and D. N. E. Whittaker, "Free Speech Advocates at Berkeley," *Journal of Applied Behavioral Science* 2, no. 1 (1966): 41–62; P. Heist, "The Dynamics of Student Discontent and Protest," paper presented at the SPSSI Symposium of the annual

ism, the results across studies have been remarkably coherent. Activists are found to be intellectually gifted, academically superior, and politically radical young people from advantaged homes in which the parents are successful in their careers, comfortable in their economic position, and liberal in their political orientations.

The positions taken by youth vis-a-vis contemporary issues provide a social laboratory in which commitment, rebellion, apathy, and disengagement can be studied. The present paper is concerned with (a) extending our understanding of the antecedents of activism as they may be inferred from students' retrospective descriptions of the child-rearing orientations and values of their parents, and (b) identifying socialization practices differentially associated with diverging orientations toward political-social activism that could be identified in 1965–1966.

The assessment of socialization practices and their relationship to student activism gains importance in the present social climate. The recent change in the character of student activism has tried society's patience and increased its hostility toward activists, resulting in demands for repressive action on the part of societal institutions to control student behavior. Furthermore, the child-rearing doctrines of the recent past, based on differentiated responsiveness to the legitimate needs of the child, are being repudiated in the popular press, perhaps in reaction to the indictment of Dr. Benjamin Spock who provided the blueprint for contemporary child-rearing practices. Parents are being implicated for their "permissiveness" and their failure to establish limits for their children. Fundamental to the arguments for "law and order" and restoration of "respect for authority" is the assumption that contemporary youth are lacking in internal controls because they were not disciplined sufficiently in their malleable years. Our data speak directly to these questions.

Additionally, this paper seeks to demonstrate that, despite the constancies noted among studies of student activists, a more articulated definition of activism conjoined with more differentiated analyses reveals important differences among activists heretofore obscured by the broad criteria used in studies to date.

Two dimensions seem helpful to us in considering activism in young

meeting of the American Psychological Association, New York, Sept., 1966; G. Lyonns, "The Police Car Demonstration: A Survey of Participants," in *The Berkeley Student Revolt: Facts and Interpretations,* ed. S. M. Lipset and S. S. Wolin (Garden City, N.Y.: Anchor Books, 1965); R. H. Somers, "The Mainsprings of the Rebellion: A Survey of Berkeley Students in November, 1964," in *The Berkeley Student Revolt,* ed. Lipset and Wolin; J. H. Block, N. Haan and M. B. Smith, "Activism and Apathy in Contemporary Adolescents," in *Understanding Adolescence: Current Developments in Adolescent Psychology,* ed. J. F. Adams (Boston: Allyn & Bacon, 1968); Hahn, Smith, and Block, "The Moral Reasoning of Young Adults: Political-Social Behavior, Family Background and Personality Correlates," *Journal of Personality and Social Psychology* 10 (1968): 183–201; and Smith, Haan, and Block, "Social-Psychological Aspects of Student Activism," paper presented to the annual meeting of the American Sociological Association, San Francisco, August 28–31, 1967.

adults.[7] First is the *degree of involvement* with contemporary political-social issues. At one extreme of this dimension are the uninvolved or apathetic youth unconcerned with political or social matters; at the opposite pole are the active, politically and socially involved young people, who feel a sense of instrumentality lacking in apathetic youth.

The quality of activism is determined in large part by a second dimension relating to the *acceptance or rejection of institutional authority and traditional societal values*. At one end of this continuum we find the conforming young person who accepts the prevailing values of society, while the opposite pole is defined by young people who categorically reject traditional societal values and repudiate both personal and institutional authority.

In accruing samples of young people to participate in this research, we attempted to recruit subjects representing different degrees of commitment, varying attitudes about institutional authority, and divergent ideological positions. Approaching activism in this more differentiated way, we studied the nature, scope, and patterns of political-social activity, moral orientations, and socialization antecedents in samples of students recruited during 1965–66 from the University of California at Berkeley and from San Francisco State College, plus several groups of Peace Corps trainees.[8]

THE CONTACT SAMPLES

Sampling strategies were designed (*a*) to identify activist students by virtue of criterion behaviors (arrest in the FSM sit-in, tutoring in the ghetto, participation in demonstrations, joining the Peace Corps) rather than solely by organizational affiliations, (*b*) to include activists varying in the degree to which their activities involve overt rejection of institutional authority (those arrested in sit-ins vs. those working in the ghetto or joining the Peace Corps), and (*c*) to replicate findings and extend the generalizations possible by conducting the study on two campuses differing in academic selectivity and in the prevalent socioeconomic levels from which their students are drawn.

Student activists were recruited from those arrested in the 1964 Free Speech Movement sit-in at Berkeley and from participants in the Experimental College, Tutorial Project, and Community Development Program at San Francisco State College. Three political groups from Berkeley representing different ideological positions (members of the campus Democratic and Republican groups as well as the California Conservatives for Political Action) were included to extend the definition of activism to include explicitly political behaviors. Both at Berkeley and at San

---

[7] Block et al., "Activism and Apathy in Contemporary Adolescent Psychology."

[8] Ibid.; Haan et al., "The Moral Reasoning of Young Adults"; and Smith et al., "Social-Psychological Aspects of Student Activism."

Francisco State College, students were selected randomly from the registration files to constitute contrast samples against which the activist samples could be compared. All student samples were restricted to sophomores, juniors, and seniors. Finally, a sample of Peace Corps volunteers was included, anticipating that their commitments did not involve a challenge of institutional authority. In all, 1033 young people participated in this research. Demographic description of the various contact samples can be found in Smith et al.[9]

THE ACTIVISM SAMPLES

From the total pool of subjects, relatively homogeneous subgroups were identified to permit a more differentiated analysis of activism. It was apparent that neither formal membership, informal commitment to an ad hoc movement, or even arrest in the FSM sit-in provided an unambiguous indication of a student's characteristic orientation to political-social action. The Berkeley random sample, for example, included a number of students who had sat in at Sproul Hall, but who left before arrests were made. Larger numbers had been active in the FSM crisis—picketing, attending FSM rallies, raising money for bail and other purposes. Also, among the FSM participants differences existed in their previous involvements with political-social issues. Accordingly, using the information available about the political-social *behaviors* of our participants, we defined five subgroups according to the following criteria:

Inactives: young people who reported no participation in political or social organizations or activities. They may be either socially isolated or career-oriented young people who have not involved themselves with campus organizations or ad hoc movements.

Conventionalists: young people who were fraternity or sorority members but who fell below the mean in their participation in protest activities (sit-ins, picketing, demonstrating, etc.) and in social service activities (tutoring, social agency or hospital volunteer work, helping the handicapped, etc.). The Conventionalists tend in these respects to follow the traditional college student stereotype, more concerned with social functions than with social action.

Constructivists: young people whose scores on social service were above the mean of the total sample but whose scores on protest activities fell below the mean. The Constructivists tend to commit themselves to restitutive work aimed at relieving social ills and are infrequently involved in organized protest.

Dissenters: young people whose scores on protest activities were above the mean but whose scores on social service activities were below the mean of the total sample. The Dissenters tend to devote

---

9 Smith et al., ibid.

their energies to protesting the policies of Establishment-oriented institutions.

Activists: young people whose scores on both social action and protest action fell above the means of the total sample. Note that we make a distinction between the Activist and the Dissenter. The Activist, according to our definition, is concerned about the plight of his fellow human beings and works to alleviate pain and poverty and injustice. At the same time, he is disillusioned with the status quo and involves himself in protest against policies and institutions that do not accord with his image of a just society.

RESEARCH PROCEDURES

Students were contacted by letter describing the intent of the research and requesting their cooperation. Materials were mailed to those agreeing to participate. The extent of participation, as evidenced by the return of completed materials was, overall, approximately 50 percent of the total sample. Obviously, results based on voluntary participation and representing only half the initial group must be interpreted with circumspection.

The Child-rearing Practices Report (CRPR) [10] was included in the assessment battery. The CRPR is composed of ninety-one items descriptive of child-rearing attitudes, behaviors, and values; it is administered in Q-sort format with a rectangular seven-step distribution. The CRPR was administered in third person form with appropriate introductory stems: "My mother . . ." and "My father . . ." Each subject completed Q-sorts for both parents unless death, divorce, or separation of the parents early in life made it an inappropriate task.

Since our study did not include the parents themselves but was based on students' perceptions of their parents' values and attitudes, the causal relationships between different patterns of socialization and different political-social orientations are more tenuous. These perceptions of parents, however, are important data in their own right in that they represent the child's interpretation of his parents' child-rearing intentions and values. We need not rely only on this assertion of relevance, however, since the first author has conducted subsequently a study of both student and parental responses to the CRPR.[11] For a sample similar to that of the

---

10 J. H. Block, "The Child-Rearing Practices Report." Institute of Human Development, University of California, 1965 (mimeo).

11 In collaboration with Professor Robert Somers of the Sociology Department at the University of California, Berkeley, the first author collected child rearing data, in the Spring 1968, using the Child Rearing Practices Report, from 190 mothers and 161 fathers of students who had been extensively interviewed by Professor Somer's research teams and classified on the basis of their political-social activities into activism groupings using the definitions established in the present study. In addition, CRPR data were obtained from 140 students whose parents had contributed their own CRPR responses.

present research, average correlations, corrected for attenuation, were obtained between parent-child Q-sort for mother-child that ranged between .50 and .57, depending upon the reliability estimate used (.40 uncorrected), and that ranged between .46 and .53 for the father-child descriptions (.37 uncorrected). The baseline correlation for random pairings of parent and child ranged between .27 and .31, corrected for attenuation (.22 uncorrected). Although the magnitude of the correlations is modest, cross validation at the level of the item content itself lends further justification to our attempt to relate perceptions of parental socialization practices to political-social orientations. . . .

The Inactives

Overall, the Inactives characterized their parents rather neutrally with respect to the affective quality of the parent-child relationship. The parents were seen as being both most worried about the health of their children and, relative to the other groups, least emotionally involved. Inactives' parents tended to suppress sex, emphasize self-control, and inhibit self-expressiveness, according to the CRPR descriptions by their young. These parents were adjudged relatively high in their concerns about conformity but were only moderate in their emphasis on achievement and independence. They were described as using anxiety arousal to control the behavior of their children; and this psychological mechanism, coupled with intrusive supervision, augmented other techniques of discipline in the socialization of the Inactives. The parents of Inactives appeared to be somewhat anxious, suppressive, and concerned with obedience and conformity to parental demands. They seemed to value docility and to discourage steps toward individuation in their children.

The suppressive control attributed to the parents of Inactives appears to be more true for males where the mothers emphasized early training and self-control for their sons and tended to discourage both self-assertiveness and independence. Fathers of the male Inactives were oriented toward punishments and discipline and concerned about conformity, according to the CRPR descriptions by their sons. These fathers were also most anxious about the health status of their sons.

In summary, the parents of Inactives were depicted as being concerned about conformity, obedience, and docility. Their demands were primarily for "good" behavior rather than for achievement or independence as shown by the rank ordering or the standardized factor scores in terms of their salience for the Inactives. The five factors ranked highest in terms of the overall means are: *Worry about Child's Health, Emphasis on Conformity, Control by Anxiety Induction, Prohibition of Self-expression,* and *Suppression of Sex.* The five factors ranked lowest in terms of their overall means are: *Prohibition of Teasing, Emotional Involvement, Emphasis on Early Achievement of Physiological Controls, Encouragement of Independence,* and *Emphasis on Achievement.*

The Conventionalists

The Conventionalists described relationships with their parents most positively and felt their parents were emotionally involved in their parental roles. The child-rearing orientation of Conventionalists' parents emphasizes (according to their young) socially-appropriate behavior, independence, achievement, and obedience. These parental demands were invoked with clarity (see scores on *Structuring of Responsibilities*) and enforced with a variety of disciplinary techniques, ranging from physical punishment to psychological mechanisms of control. The Conventionalists' parents scored highest on *Punishment Orientation, Intrusive Control, Guilt Induction* as well as the selective use of rewards and punishments (although the last factor was not significant). The parents of Conventionalists were described as suppressing sex but were more tolerant of aggression—physical aggression in males and verbal aggression in both sexes. Despite the circumscription of behavior in many areas, the parents of Conventionalists were seen as moderately accepting of self-assertiveness, and as recognizing the needs of their children for privacy. More than any other group, these parents were described as demanding—both in terms of insistence on socially-appropriate behavior and in their emphasis on achievement and assumption of responsibility.

The pattern of factor scores for the two sexes suggests that the child-rearing orientations of Conventionalists' parents may be most differentiated in terms of sex role. For male Conventionalists, parental socialization seems most focused upon the development of assertive masculinity. Males were encouraged to be independent; self-expression and aggression were accepted more often than was true of female Conventionalists. Both mothers and fathers of the Conventionalist males scored highest on the dimension of *Suppression of Sex* and the various factors reflecting disciplinary practices were somewhat more salient for males than for females in the Conventionalist group.

The parents of female Conventionalists appear to emphasize sex-typed behavior in their daughters as reflected in their highest scores on the dimensions of *Suppression of Aggression* and *Prohibition of Self-expression*. The parents also emphasize achievement and encourage competition in their daughters, an unexpected departure from the traditional definition of the feminine role but explainable, perhaps, if one recalls the sorority affiliations of these young women, possibly an expression of social ambition in these families.

In summary, the conventional orientation of students in this group seems to have been achieved through identification with parents who themselves adhere to traditional societal values. The socialization of the Conventionalists emphasizes classical Protestant virtues—responsibility, conformity, achievement, obedience as shown by the five factors ranked highest in terms of salience by the Conventionalists: *Control by Guilt Induction, Punishment Orientation, Emphasis on Achievement, Suppres-*

sion of Sex, and *Emphasis on Sex-appropriate Behavior*. The factors with the lowest mean scores for the Conventionalists are: *Prohibition of Teasing, Opposition to Child's Secrecy Needs, Worry about Child's Health, Control by Anxiety Induction*, and *Emphasis on Self-control*. The child training of the Conventionalists appears to have been accomplished more by precept than by percept within a learning context that was described as caring and consistent.

The Constructivists

The Constructivists—like the Conventionalists—evaluated the parent-child relationship positively, but differed from the Conventionalists in that they described their parents as somewhat lower in their emotional involvement in their parental roles. They also appeared to share with the Conventionalists a coherent child-rearing philosophy that values obedience and inhibits self-expression. The parents of Constructivists, like the Conventionalists, were perceived as emphasizing discipline, but diverged in their greater (although not significantly so) use of nonphysical punishments. Prohibition of self-expression was characteristic of both Constructivists' and Conventionalists' parents, but the former differed in that they tended to place less emphasis on achievement and competition.

Constructivists' parents were seen as controlling the child by the use of anxiety induction; however, they were low on the dimension of guilt induction relative to the other groups.

Parental restrictions of spontaneity seemed to be related more to self-assertive behaviors than to physical aggression where Conventionalists' parents were rated as least suppressive. Again, the results are most readily summarized by listing the five factors ranked in terms of salience for the Constructivists: *Punishment Orientation, Positive Evaluation of the Parent-Child Relationship, Prohibition of Self-expression, Control by Anxiety Induction*, and *Emphasis on Conformity*. The five factors which the Constructivists placed lowest are: *Control by Guilt Induction, Emphasis on Achievement, Worry about Child's Health, Suppression of Aggression*, and *Naive Faith in Child's Dependability*. The relatively high positive evaluation of the parental relationships despite the restrictiveness noted in parental practices indicates that little overt rebellion has been directed against these parents, at least not at this time in the life histories of the Constructivist young people. The altruistic volunteer activities in which the Constructivists engage seem to be consistent with the parental values according to which they have been raised.

The Activists

Affectively, the Activists are not reliably distinguished from the other groups: they describe the parent-child relationship in somewhat negative terms, admitting to conflict with parents and feeling that they may have disappointed their parents. At the same time, however, they describe their parents as moderately involved in their parental roles.

In their maturity demands, the Activists' parents are similar to the Conventionalists' in that both tend to emphasize independence, responsibility, and early maturity. However, the parents of Activists diverged from the Conventionalists (and were more like the Constructivists) in their deemphasis of achievement and competition. As might be expected, the parents of Activists were low in their demands for conformity, tending rather to encourage the individuation and independent judgment of the child.

The parents of Activists were described as most suppressing of aggression and as most prohibiting of teasing, although differences in teasing behavior did not reliably distinguish among the groups. Activists' parents were seen as accepting of sexual curiosity and encouraging of self-expressiveness. They were perceived as most tolerant of the child's secrecy and privacy needs.

In terms of discipline, the Activists' parents were portrayed as low on Punishment Orientation with its emphasis on obedience, docility, and use of physical punishments. Psychological mechanisms of control, *Anxiety Induction* and *Intrusive Control,* were also significantly less often relied upon. Rather, there is a tendency, although not significant, for Activists' parents to be more oriented to nonphysical punishments (isolation, withdrawal of privileges, etc.) for enforcing their demands.

Differential training emphases ascribed to parents by male and female Activists indicate that less pressure is characteristic of the upbringing of girls. Activist women described the parent-child relationship as less emotionally involved, less oriented to discipline, less concerned with achievement and competition, and less inhibiting of self-assertiveness than did the males. Parents of women were seen, however, as more suppressive of sex, and opposed to secrecy and privacy needs. For male Activists, the parents appeared to be relatively more oriented to the suppression of aggressive behaviors.

In summary, the parents of Activists encourage their children to be independent and responsible, qualities shared to some degree with parents of Conventionalists. Diverging from the Conventionalists, the parents of Activists were described as encouraging the child's differentiation and self-expressiveness, with discipline per se being less critical. Activists' parents tended to be unaccepting of aggression. The factors accorded most salience in the socialization of Activists are: *Suppression of Aggression, Encouragement of Independence, Emphasis on Early Achievement of Physiological Controls, Emotional Involvement, Prohibition of Teasing.* The factor scores with the lowest ranked means are: *Punishment Orientation, Intrusive Control, Suppression of Sex, Control by Anxiety Induction,* and *Opposition to Child's Secrecy Needs.* Like the parents of Conventionalists, the Activists' parents appear to be preparing their young to lead responsible, autonomous lives, but in accordance with inner-directed goals and values rather than externally defined roles.

Dissenters evaluate their parents most negatively in terms of the affective quality of the parent-child relationship. This factor includes items dealing with admitted conflict, anger, expressions of criticism and disappointment, authoritarianism, tension, lack of respect for the child, absence of intimacy, warmth, and appreciation. The negative evaluation given by Dissenters may relate to the inconsistency attributed to these parents by their young. The pattern of factor scores shows Dissenters' parents to be permissive, even laissez-faire, in many areas of child training, but controlling in others. Although not significant, Dissenters' parents are described as placing the least emphasis on independence and early maturity relative to the other groups, while pressing at the same time for achievement and encouraging competition. They appear to stress self-expression and individuation of the young, while opposing the secrecy and privacy needs of their children. Dissenters described their parents as low in their emphasis on discipline and punishment, and neither were they said to control the child by invoking anxiety.

The Dissenters' parents diverge most markedly from the parents of Activists in their opposition to the child's secrecy and privacy needs. Although not significant, the means of the two groups were at opposite extremes on *Encouraging Independence* and *Emphasis on the Early Achievement of Physiological Controls,* with Dissenters' parents de-emphasizing these dimensions. The descriptions of Activist and Dissenter parents converged on the dimensions of conformity where both are low relative to other subgroups, in their encouragement of self-expression, in their lesser use of psychological mechanisms to control the child, and in the negative evaluation ascribed to parent-child relationships, particularly by the Dissenters.

Male and female Dissenters characterized their parents' child-rearing attitudes in rather similar ways. Dissenting women said their fathers were more involved emotionally in the parent-child relationship, and indicated that self-expression was more acceptable than for the males. Male Dissenters were most negative in their affective evaluations of the parent-child relationship, and saw their mothers as more permissive relative to punishments and self-control while also being most opposed to secrecy in their sons.

In summary, the child-rearing of the Dissenters' parents appeared somewhat lacking in coherence. The most salient child-rearing dimensions for the Dissenters, judged by the rank ordering of the factors are: *Opposition to Child's Secrecy Needs, Prohibition of Teasing, Emphasis on Achievement, Suppression of Aggression,* and *Emotional Involvement.* The least salient factors for the Dissenters are: *Positive Parent-child Relationship, Control by Anxiety Induction, Punishment Orientation, Emphasis on Self-control,* and *Worry about Child's Health.* It is perhaps not surprising that this pattern of indulgence and permissiveness—conjoined with an interest in achievement, encouragement of competition, and opposition to the child's privacy needs—results in the conflicted, unsatisfying parental relationship described by the Dissenting young.

COMPARISON WITH OTHER STUDIES

The results of this study, based on the perceptions of parental childrearing practices by their young, are consistent with those gained from studies of parents themselves.[12] Flacks found that parents of student activists "place greater stress . . . on opportunity for self-expression, and tend to deemphasize or positively disvalue personal achievement, conventional morality and conventional religiosity." Parents of nonactivists expressed "conventional orientations toward achievement, material success, sexual morality, and religion," according to Flacks. Schedler found activists' parents to be significantly more tolerant of unconventional behavior and more permissive, as defined by allowing the child autonomy in decision making, than were parents of nonactivists. Mothers of activists were less strict while fathers of activists were not differentiated by strictness in Schedler's study.

In the study of parents of Berkeley students recently completed and cited earlier, Block has replicated many of the essential findings reported here: Parents of Activists described greater parent-child conflict while a more positive evaluation was given by Constructivists. Suppression of aggression, a rational (rather than punitive) approach to discipline, deemphasis of conformity and competition, encouragement of independence and expectations for responsible, mature behavior were found to characterize the child-rearing orientations of the parents of Activist students. In addition, the parents of Activists described their child-rearing in ways that differed from the descriptions offered by parents of Dissenters and that paralleled results reported here: Dissenters' parents were more inconsistent in their demands, were less rational in their disciplinary practices, were less restrictive of the child, and placed less emphasis on independence and maturity.

Methodologically, the confluence of findings from direct studies of parents with those reported here based on student appraisals of parental child-rearing practices offers justification for using this approach when parent samples cannot be assessed directly. The obtained replication for the several activism groups of salient distinguishing features derived from the student perceptions to the results obtained from samples of parents argues for the validity of young adults' evaluations of parental socialization practices.

PSYCHOLOGICAL VS. SOCIOLOGICAL ANTECEDENTS

Reassured by the convergence of the findings, we can now confront issues regarding the interpretation of the relationships found between constel-

---

[12] Flacks, "The Liberated Generation . . ."; and P. Schedler, "Parental Attitudes and Political Activism of College Students," Master's thesis, University of Chicago, 1966.

lations of socialization practices and political-social protest. The sociologist Lipset has suggested that the attempts by psychologists to relate activism and parental child-rearing practices are unconvincing because

> the extant studies do not hold constant the sociological and politically relevant factors in the backgrounds of the students. For example, they report that leftist activists tend to be the offspring of permissive families characterized by a strong mother who dominates family life and decisions. Conversely, conservative activists tend to come from families with more strict relationships between parents and children, and in which the father plays a dominant controlling role. But to a considerable extent these differences correspond to little more than the variations reported in studies of Jewish and Protestant families. Childhood rearing practices tend to be linked to social-cultural-political outlooks. To prove that such factors play an independent **role in** determining the political choices of students, it will first be necessary to compare students *within* similar ethnic, religious, and political-cultural environments. This has not yet been done.[13]

Lipset is, of course, correct in reminding us of a confounding of psychological and sociological sources of explanation in much previous research. What is necessary in order to clarify matters is to disentangle the competing explanatory variables.

If Lipset's contentions are correct, the differences found between activist and nonactivist groups should wash out when these samples are matched on relevant demographic variables. In the present study, separating particular demographic variables from activism is possible because of the relatively large sample size and the articulated definitions used to compose activist and nonactivist subgroups.

The "unconfounding" analysis to be reported used only the nonactivist Conventionalist and the Activist subgroups since analyses of variance had demonstrated that these two groups were not significantly different with respect either to occupational or educational levels of the parents. There was, however, a disproportionately higher number of Jews in the Activist group. In order to match these two subgroups as closely as possible, *all* Jews were excluded from the analyses in order to evaluate Lipset's assertions that the permissive, maternally-dominated environment found to characterize the homes of protest-oriented students was a manifestation of child-rearing practices that are basically and uniquely Jewish.

The non-Jewish students in the Conventionalist and Activist subgroups were compared with respect to the child-rearing attitudes attributed to parents, using t-tests to evaluate the reliability of differences. The results of this analysis are presented in Table 1.

These results in which religious, educational, and occupational differences between the Conventionalists and Activists have been controlled reproduce the essential findings reported earlier characterizing the differ-

---

[13] S. M. Lipset, "The Activists: A Profile," *The Public Interest* (Fall 1968): 39–51.

TABLE 1. Comparison of Non-Jewish Conventionalists and Activist Groups on CRPR Factors

	Conventionalists	Activists	Level of Significance
Males' Mothers Descriptions	(N = 38)	(N = 35)	
Suppression of child's sexual impulses	54.2	46.5	.01
Suppression of aggression	47.6	52.6	.05
Firm discipline	54.3	48.0	.01
Emphasis on achievement	51.2	46.7	.10
Psychological manipulation of child	46.5	50.9	.10
Males' Fathers Descriptions	(N = 35)	(N = 32)	
Firm discipline	51.4	46.7	.05
Emphasis on achievement	53.3	46.5	.01
Suppression of child's sexual impulses	54.8	48.6	.05
Intrusive control	52.1	46.9	.05
Control of guilt induction	53.8	49.3	.10
Emphasis on early physiological controls	48.4	53.2	.10
Emphasis on self control	53.6	47.4	.05
Prohibition of teasing	47.3	52.1	.10
Females' Mothers Descriptions	(N = 26)	(N = 37)	
Negative evaluation of parent-child relationship	45.1	50.6	.05
Prohibition vs. encouragement of self-expression	53.1	48.3	.05
Emphasis on achievement	52.7	47.9	.05
Intrusive control	52.3	46.2	.01
Emphasis on early physiological control	54.0	49.5	.10
Suppression of aggression	54.5	50.6	.05
Females' Fathers Descriptions	(N = 34)	(N = 36)	
Firm discipline	46.1	52.0	.01
Orientation to non-physical punishments	47.8	51.8	.10
Encouragement of competition	55.5	48.9	.01
Over-conscientious parenthood	52.7	47.4	.05

ences between these two groups as a whole.[14] The parents of the Conventionalists are portrayed as more concerned with achievement, competition, docility, and obedience. The parents of non-Jewish Activists are revealed as less controlling, less punishing (with the exception of the fathers of females who are more punishing), and less concerned with

[14] After excluding students with Jewish backgrounds from the two samples, t-tests of socio-economic status and educational achievement were completed to determine if the samples remained comparable after being redefined. For the female sample, no differences were found; for the male sample, the only significant finding was that the mothers of Activists tended to be better educated (p < .05) than were the mothers of Conventionalists.

achievement. They are more suppressive of both verbal and physical aggression, and they emphasize early maturity.

It is instructive, also, to examine the dimensions on which the parents were described similarly by the Activist and Conventional students. The factors on which no differences were found—despite respectable N's (35 and 38, respectively)—in any of the four analyses of the two matched groups include: *Encouragement of Independence and Responsibility; Emotional Involvement with Child; Socialization via Explicit Rewards and Punishments; Control by Anxiety Induction; Naive Faith in Child's Dependability;* and *Subservience to Spouse*. In addition, no differences were found on the following factors in three of the four analyses: *Emphasis on Self-control, Emphasis on Sex-appropriate Behavior, Emphasis on Conformity vs. Differentiation,* and *Opposition to Child's Secrecy Needs*. Clearly, both the Conventionalists and the Activists see their parents as emphasizing maturity, dependability, and the need for behavioral limits.

These results based on samples that are comparable with respect to educational, occupational, and religious variables undermine Lipset's contentions about the explanatory power of ethnic and other demographic variables. A second line of evidence against the causal significance of demographic variables *per se* (granted as we do not, that demographic variables can *ever* have direct, theoretically interpretable causal significance) is provided by the results of the within-activism group comparisons presented earlier. Although differences in child-rearing orientations were found to exist, the Activists and Dissenters did *not* differ significantly with respect to socioeconomic or educational levels. The religious backgrounds of students in the two protest-prone categories were not significantly different, and the average ratings of parents' radicalism-conservatism were also similar. Despite these similarities on the usual demographic indices, significant differences on the CRPR were found between the Activist and Dissenter groups. Again, it follows that differences in religion, education, socioeconomic status, or political ideology *cannot* be invoked to explain the divergences in child-rearing orientations that were found to discriminate the two activist subgroups.

These results suggest that demographic characteristics may not be as potent as Lipset (together with other sociologists) has assumed in determining the differences in socialization practices found to distinguish activists' parents. Certainly socioeconomic and educational levels, religious orientations, together with ecological variables, personality dispositions, and parental value orientations conjoin to pattern the parental socialization practices and so to define the learning matrix in which the child develops and matures. Alone, however, these indices cannot be considered determinative.

DIFFERENTIATING AMONG ACTIVISTS

The classification of the sample into subgroups representing different political-social orientations has not only helped to demonstrate the independent role of socialization variables, as shown above, but has resulted, also, in more discriminating descriptions of students with different political-social orientations. The divergence between the Activist and Dissenter subgroups is perhaps the most interesting, not only because this distinction has not been made previously in the literature but also because the change in the character of student protest in the years since the inception of this study stresses the outer limits of dissent as measured here. The present study may be only tangentially relevant for an understanding of the new student generation. The differences between the Activists and Dissenters presented here may, however, provide a basis for extrapolation to the new "Confrontationist" generation. Developing such extrapolations is beyond the scope of the present paper but the adventurous reader so inclined may find some help for his predictions in some additional comparisons of the two activist subgroups with respect to family background variables.

REBELLION VS. CONCORDANCE WITH PARENTS

Perhaps not surprisingly, the Dissenters were found to be more frequently in rebellion against the political-social ideologies of their parents than were the Activists. Table 2 compares the political preferences of the parents of Activists and Dissenters. Significantly more mothers ($p < .05$) and fathers ($p < .10$) of the Dissenters were rated as conservative in their political ideologies. Block [15] found that, within the political spectrum

TABLE 2. **Comparison of Parental Political Preferences for Activist and Dissenter Groups**

	Political Preference of Father (N = 235)		
	Conservative	Moderate	Liberal-Radical
Activist	8	42	37
Dissenter	30	65	53

Chi-square = 5.04

$p < .10$

	Political Preference of Mother (N = 235)		
Activist	4	46	37
Dissenter	22	57	69

Chi-square = 7.99

$p < .05$

[15] J. H. Block, "Rebellion Re-examined: The Role of Identification and Alienation," (Paper presented at the Foundations' Fund for Research in Psychiatry Conference on Adaptation to Change, Puerto Rico, June 1968).

of the Left, gross disjunction between the political-social attitudes of young people and those of their parents is associated with less integrated personality functioning, particularly for women. Among the Dissenting women, 20 percent of their fathers and 15 percent of their mothers were rated in the conservative category whereas the comparable figures for Activist women are 9 and 4 percent, respectively. This divergence in political attitudes between Dissenter and parents is not an isolated finding since the Dissenters were found to score uniformly lowest on the dimensions reflecting overall agreement with mother and with father on six contemporary political-social issues.[16]

This set of findings suggests that Dissenters are in greater rebellion against parental attitudes than Activists who exhibit concordance across generational boundaries. It might be anticipated that studies of today's student demonstrators, more extreme now on the dimension of protest, would reveal even greater disjunction between parent and student attitudes than was found here.

PARENTAL PERMISSIVENESS

The second distinction to be made between the Activists and Dissenters involves the notion of permissiveness and its applicability to the parental child-rearing orientations of activists. When the descriptions of student protesters' parents are compared with the stereotype of permissiveness ascribed to these parents by the lay press, it is apparent that the newspaper interpretation is reasonably correct in regard to the *Dissenters'* origins but is quite wrong regarding the *Activists*.

The data from this study indicate that permissiveness, with its corollary laissez-faire attitudes, is more characteristic of the parents of Dissenters. Dissenters' parents were described as making relatively minimal demands upon the child for independent mature behavior, being laissez-faire with respect to limits and discipline, being tolerant of self-assertiveness, and de-emphasizing self-control. These parental practices have been subsumed under the permissive label as it has been popularly understood and, accordingly, permissiveness does seem an appropriate description of the socialization practices experienced by the Dissenters. The departures from permissiveness for these parents are in the areas of aggression, opposition to secrecy, and concern with competition and achievement.

In contrast, the parents of Activists make more demands upon their children, particularly for independence, for responsible and mature behaviors. They are unaccepting of aggression, both physical and verbal. Although low in punishment orientation, Activists' parents tend to respond to misbehaviors—but with nonphysical rather than physical punishments. These perceived parental behaviors are not consistent with permissiveness. Rather these parents seem to have imparted to their young a reasonably coherent set of expectations, consistent with parental values, in a manner that maintains parental dignity. Activists' parents may be

---

[16] Smith et al., "Social-Psychological Aspects of Student Activism."

considered permissive in the sense that they encourage the individuation and self-expression of the child, are more accepting of sexuality, and reject harsh punitive disciplinary methods. Although these latter parental practices and policies embody the concept of permissiveness in the circumscribed definition (and redefinition) provided by Benjamin Spock, they diverge importantly from the concept as more generally, loosely, and incriminatingly used today. The Activists, like the nonactivist Conventionalists, see their parents as attempting to prepare them to lead responsible, independent lives. This coherent set of expectations seems lacking in the Dissenters' perceptions of their parents.

These aggregated results, conjoined with the differences in ego functioning of Activist and Dissenter parents noted in the previous section, offer rather convincing evidence that parents of Activists (using the restricted definition of Activist given here) are seen as more differentiated with respect to ego functioning than are parents of Dissenting (and Nonactivist) students. Their relatively more mature ego functioning appears to be manifested in a more coherent child-rearing philosophy that is involved with respect for both self and child. The learning context established by Activists' parents appears to rely on rational, cognitive principles of learning, and the perceived goals of socialization appear to be an independent, mature, self-knowing child. Were it not for the independent confirmation of these results found in Block's study of parents themselves, it might be argued that the less charitable picture of parents portrayed by the Dissenters might be an attempt to retrospectively justify their own rebellion. This interpretation does not appear to be warranted on the basis of the external validation of these results that has been offered.

These findings taken *in toto* imply that generalizations about activists are not valid for all student demonstrators. Participants in student protests have been shown to be heterogeneous, and distinctions of consequence have been found between Activists and Dissenters. Similarly, heterogeneities have been found to characterize non-active students as documented by the differences between the Inactives and the Conventionalists. Respect for these diversities should result in better understanding and more articulated predictions. . . .

14

PROTEST PARTICIPATION AMONG SOUTHERN NEGRO COLLEGE STUDENTS

JOHN M. ORBELL

A recent article in this journal has drawn attention to the inadequacies in our knowledge of how great social movements arise.[1] On the Negro protest movement there are many hypotheses but few attempts to relate them to differences in individual behavior. Considerable confusion also exists in the variety of explanatory terms involved. James A. Geschwender lists five hypotheses that focus variously on economic conditions and the psychological meaning given them. They are the *Vulgar Marxist* hypothesis—that Negro dissatisfaction results from a progressive deterioration in the social and economic position of the race; the *Rising Expectations* hypothesis—that Negro expectations are rising more rapidly than their fulfillment; the *Sophisticated Marxist* hypothesis or the *Relative Deprivation* hypothesis—that Negro perceptions of white life have led to dissatisfaction with their own rate of improvement; the *Rise and Drop* hypothesis —that improvement in conditions followed by a sharp drop is responsible; and the *Status Inconsistency* hypothesis—that a group possessing status attributes ranked differently on various status hierarchies of a society will be dissatisfied and prone to rebellion.[2]

This paper will suggest that theory based on variations in the structure of intergroup relations can go some way toward integrating the different kinds of explanation that have been advanced. A more general aspiration is to draw attention to one set of terms that might be useful in the long overdue development of a genuinely comparative study of social movements such as the Negro movement. The broad hypothesis arising from —but by no means fully tested by—an examination of several individual and contextual variables is that *proximity to the dominant white culture*

From *American Political Science Review* 61 (June 1967): 446–52, 454–56; reprinted and abridged by permission of the author and the American Political Science Association.

[1] See Jack Walker, "A Critique of the Elitist Theory of Democracy," *American Political Science Review* 60 (June 1966): 293–95.

[2] James A. Geschwender, "Social Structure and the Negro Revolt: An Examination of Some Hypotheses," *Social Forces* 43 (December 1964): 248–49.

increases the likelihood of protest involvement. The analysis will give a priority to structural considerations, but will also suggest something about intervening psychological variables.

Most of the existing knowledge about this and other social movements comes from case studies of one, or at best very few, cities or districts.[3] Consequently, we know little about the variation in participation *among* such areas. The data on which the present study is based are drawn from a survey of Negro college students conducted in 1962, about two years after the sit-in movement began, by Professors Donald R. Matthews and James W. Prothro as part of their wider study of Southern attitudes and behavior.[4] Included were 264 Negro students who attended, in all, thirty colleges of various kinds in all eleven former Confederate states. Although there were never enough students interviewed in any one college to treat them as a separate sample, the breadth of the survey lets us test a variety of ecological and institutional variables as well as many individual variables.

The dependent variable of this study is participation in the Negro college student protest movement. Presumably this should be conceptualized, in the manner of more general political participation, as stretching on a continuum of related activities.[5] A number of different kinds of behavior suggest themselves. Students belonged to protest organizations, marched, picketed, took part in sit-ins and freedom rides. Simply giving support to the protest movement was nearly universal among the students and of little use in differentiating them. In this case, however, the various kinds of protest behaviors reported by the students could not be related acceptably as a Guttman scale [6] and instead a simple index was adopted. In what follows, the term "participants" refers to those students who had either taken part in a sit-in or a freedom ride or belonged to one of several kinds of protest organizations.[7] Although these two variables are strongly

---

3 See for example, Lewis Killian and Charles Grigg, *Racial Crisis in America* (Englewood Cliffs, N.J.: Prentice-Hall, 1964); Daniel C. Thompson, *The Negro Leadership Class* (Englewood Cliffs, N.J.: Prentice-Hall, 1963); Jack Walker, "Protest and Negotiation: A Case Study of Negro Leadership in Atlanta, Georgia," *Midwest Journal of Political Science* 7 (May 1963): 99–124.

4 See Donald R. Matthews and James W. Prothro, *Negroes and the New Southern Politics* (New York: Harcourt Brace Jovanovich, 1966). The present survey was made in addition to their surveys of the adult Negro and white populations in the South. The author is most grateful for their permission to use these data and their helpful suggestions at several stages of the research.

5 See, for example, Campbell et al., *The American Voter* (New York: John Wiley, 1960), p. 92; and Matthews and Prothro, op. cit., 53–58. The latter uses a cumulative scale of political participation stretching from talking politics, voting, taking part in campaigns, belonging to political organizations and holding party or public office, and demonstrates that these factors ". . . are not only related to one another but are, in fact, different forms of the same phenomenon" (p. 53).

6 See R. N. Ford, "A Rapid Scoring Procedure for Scaling Attitude Questions," *Public Opinion Quarterly* 14 (Fall 1950): 507.

7 The protest organizations included were: The National Association for the Advancement of Colored People (NAACP), The Congress of Racial Equality (CORE), The Student Non-Violent Coordinating Committee (SNCC), the Southern Christian Leadership Conference (SCLC), The Urban League and any other Negro Voters' League. No students claimed membership in the black Muslims.

TABLE 1.   The Dimensions of Protest Participation

| | | Participation in Freedom Rides or Sit-ins | | |
		Yes	No	Totals
Membership in Protest Organizations	yes	42	41	83
	no	23	158	181
Totals		65	199	264

associated, in several instances it will be appropriate to examine them separately. Table 1 gives the distribution of students according to these categories.

I. COLLEGE VARIABLES

Not all protest activities that Negro college students get involved in have their origin in the colleges they attend, but the data suggest that at least two college variables have a significant impact on protest, independent of all other factors.[8] These are the manner in which the college is supported—by state or private finance—and its quality.

Control of the College

The reasons for believing that college control may have an impact on protest are straightforward: state-run institutions are open to many kinds of pressures from which private colleges are free. Undoubtedly the willingness and ability of college administrators to resist such pressures vary from college to college and state to state, but there is ample evidence that they can be most compelling. At Southern University, Baton Rouge, students became involved in demonstrations shortly after the sit-in movement began in North Carolina. On March 29, 1960, a large number of Southern's students were arrested following sit-ins at S. H. Kress and Co. and the Greyhound Bus Station. As had already happened elsewhere, the all-white State Board of Education immediately warned that "stern disciplinary action" would be taken against any future demonstrators. The president of the University, Dr. Felton Clark, was reported as saying he had "no alternatives," and further demonstrations resulted in eighteen students being expelled from the University.[9] In a speech to the students

---

8 In *Organizational Measurement and Its Bearing on the Study of College Environments* (New York: Collge Entrance Examination Board, 1961), Alan H. Barton gives useful guidance to the dimensions of colleges that may be measured and may have an impact on the behavior of individuals in them.

9 *The New York Times,* 11 April, 1960, p. 25.

he said, "Like Lincoln who sought to preserve the Union, my dominant concern is to save Southern University." [10]

Colleges not run by state governments can be divided according to whether their administration is formally secular or denominational. Participation was about equally likely among students attending these two kinds of colleges: 55 percent in the former and 53 percent in the latter participated. However, only 33 percent of the students attending state colleges were participants. Table 2 shows that both organizational membership and participation in demonstrations were less probable among state college students—although it also suggests that the difference between the two modes of participation at state colleges was less than at either of the two kinds of private colleges. All plausible situational or individual control variables failed to eliminate this relationship.

Some further data support the conclusion that more restrictive circumstances do exist at the state colleges and also suggest something about subculture tensions accompanying the development of protest. Louis Lomax has commented on such tensions between Negro teachers and their students:

"Intellectual Uncle Tom!" That's the phrase one hears through the South nowadays. It is uttered by college students and their supporters, and it is used in the open, at public meetings and rallies. It is the students' way of talking about the "failure" of Southern Negro intellectuals—school teachers, for the most part—to support the revolt in clear, open terms.

This is excruciatingly painful.[11]

TABLE 2.   **Percent of Students Participating in Different Forms of Protest by College Control**[a]

	Type of Participation	
Control of College:	*Sitting-in*	*Membership*
State	19% (169)	23% (169)
Denominational, private	37% (62)	57% (62)
Secular, private	30% (33)	55% (33)

[a]The entry in each cell is the percent of respondents in colleges of a given kind who reported participation of the type indicated. In this table and those following, the figures in parentheses are the base from which the percentages were calculated.

---

[10] Quoted in Louis E. Lomax, *The Negro Revolt* (New York: Harper & Row, 1962), p. 209.

[11] Ibid., p. 207.

The interview schedule included two questions asking sit-inners for their perceptions of what their college administrators and professors thought about what they were doing. Although such perceptual data should not necessarily be taken as recording an *actual* state of affairs, the responses were different between state and private colleges. For each sit-inner who perceived neutrality from a given group, a score of zero was recorded; "strong approval" and "strong disapproval" were scored +2 and −2 respectively; while "approval" and "disapproval" were scored +1 and −1 respectively. The resulting figures were then normalized in percentage terms. The final scores, shown in Table 3, suggest plenty of scope for the development of the hostilities Lomax writes about: no matter where the students attended college, their perceived support from both professors and college administrators fell far below the possible 100 percent. On the other hand, the striking thing about these data is the similarity of all the scores except that recording the attitudes of state college administrators. Private college sit-inners saw little difference in the attitudes of their professors and administrators; but at state colleges, while support from professors is seen at about the same level as at private colleges, support from administrators is seen far less frequently than from their private counterparts. Perhaps evidence can also be found in these perceptual data that points to differences of opinion between professors and administrators at state colleges. At any rate, the conclusion seems justified that sub-culture tension arising from the student movement is most acute in state colleges, and that it centers on those roles which mediate between the sub-culture and the dominant white culture.

Quality of the College

College quality was measured in essentially the manner developed by Lazarsfeld and Thielens in *The Academic Mind*.[12] Five indicators of quality were selected, the appropriate data on the thirty colleges included in the sample were collected from a number of standard sources, and an

TABLE 3. Sit-inners' Perceptions of Support from Professors and Administrators in State and Private Colleges

Perceived Attitudes	Type of College	
	Private	*State*
of Professors	46%	50%
of Administrators	46%	15%

12 P. F. Lazarsfeld and Wagner Thielens, Jr., *The Academic Mind* (Glencoe, Ill.: The Free Press, 1958), p. 412.

acceptable Guttman scale was developed.[13] Four categories of quality were used. The resulting data show quite clearly that protest participation—both organizational membership and participation in demonstrations—increased as the quality of the college increased. Only 22 percent of the students in the lowest category colleges claimed participation, 41 percent did so in the second lowest, while in the highest two participation was nearly equal—around 54 percent. In each category of colleges organiza-

---

[13] Lazarsfeld and Thielens developed an index rather than a scale. In this case the scale was preferred because it gave the added assumption of uni-dimensionality in the indicators selected. The index, however, did have some advantages. It was not necessary for Lazarsfeld and Thielens to dichotomize their indicators, and as a result the index could take into account disproportionate "contributions" of quality by one of the indicators. An index was also developed in the present case and findings based on it were found to compare closely with those derived from the scale method. As it resulted, the scale findings were the more conservative of the two in terms of fulfilling expectations of an association between college quality and protest participation.

Obviously no single indicator of quality would do justice to variations in such a heterogeneous collection of colleges; agriculture and technical colleges, teachers' colleges, and some of the most outstanding of southern Negro colleges concentrating on the humanities were all included. The indicators adopted were as follows:

The number of books in the college library
The ratio of books in the library to students
The proportion of Ph.D.'s on the faculty
Dollars in the college budget per student
The faculty-student ratio

The last mentioned indicator was not used by Lazarsfeld and Thielens, despite the fact that it is one of the most frequently used "rules of thumb" about the quality of the education a college offers. Two indicators used by them were not used in the present case. They were tuition fees paid and the Knapp and Greenblaum index of scholar productivity. Lazarsfeld and Thielens argued that higher tuition fees gave a college greater financial resources with which to provide education, and also that "tuition to some extent indicates the demand for a college educational 'product'" (p. 412). However appropriate this indicator might have been for the population of colleges they studied, for the present state and private colleges it does not seem likely to make valid distinctions of quality. The Knapp and Greenblaum index of scholar productivity, used by Lazarsfeld and Thielens, was not used here for the very good reason that the data on which it was based were not available for the colleges under consideration. It is also true that scholar productivity might not be a particularly good indicator of quality in a mechanical or agricultural college.

The variables were dichotomized in the following ways:

Student-faculty ratio: better than 1:11.8
Ph.D.'s on faculty: better than 22.5%
Books in library: better than 38,000
Books per student: better than 25
Dollars per student: better than $800.00

The decision was made by inspection in each case. The coefficient of reproducibility for the scale was .889.

The sources from which the college data were collected were: *The College Blue Book*, 1962 (10th ed.; New York: The College Blue Book, 1962); *American Universities and Colleges* (8th ed.; Washington: American Council on Education, 1960); *American Junior Colleges* (5th ed.; Washington: American Council on Education, 1960); *The World Almanac 1961*. In addition, use was made of G. W. Jones, "Negro Colleges in Alabama," *Journal of Negro Education* 31 (Summer 1962), 354–61.

tional membership was more frequent than activism, but both increased as the quality of college increased.

Several explanations are available for this association between college quality and protest participation. On the one hand, high-quality colleges may selectively recruit students whose participation can adequately be accounted for by certain individual variables; on the other hand, high quality in Negro colleges may be associated with some other situational factor which itself explains the levels of protest. Perhaps the distribution reflects the spatial spread of protest throughout the South; perhaps protest spread first to the comparatively few high quality colleges in the South, and only later to the poorer institutions. Without a panel design surveys are poorly suited to treat such longitudinal processes as the spread of a social movement through time, but even if this spread were systematically associated with college quality we would still be left with the original question unanswered.[14]

As might be expected, the data leave no doubt that the higher quality colleges recruit from the higher status part of the Negro population, but they also show that such high status is strongly associated with protest participation. Only 35 percent of students from households where the head was classed as semi-skilled or unskilled were participants, while 53 percent of the skilled or professional group could be similarly classed. There is a nearly linear association between participation and family income from the under-$2,000 bracket in which only 13 percent were participants to the above-$6,000 bracket in which 53 percent participated.

However, the data given in Table 4 show that quality of college has an

TABLE 4.   Percent of Students Participating by Quality of College and Income of Student's Family

Quality of College:	Income of Student's Family[a]	
	High	*Low*
High	57% (44)	50% (34)
Low	46% (63)	25% (102)
Difference:	11%	25%

[a]The cut-off point between the "high" and "low" income categories was $4999.

14 Newspaper reports of student demonstrations give reasonably good grounds for believing that geographic patterns were well established by the time the survey was taken in the early months of 1962. Examination of *The New York Times* for the two years between that date and February 1960, when the movement started in Greensboro, N. C., suggests that it took only a matter of two or three months for sit-ins to spread to other states outside the Deep South and then to penetrate the Deep South itself. It would be extremely hard to demonstrate from historical data that protest had still to reach the large number of low-quality colleges scattered throughout the whole South two years after the movement had begun, although the possibility must be admitted.

effect even when family income is held constant, although the *strength* of the quality-participation relationship varies between income categories. There are signs here of what Hubert M. Blalock and others have called a "multiplicative effect." In one kind of situation—called "additive"— there is no evidence that independent variables X_1, X_2 . . . X_n interact with each other in their impact on the dependent variable Y; their effect remains the same regardless of empirical juxtapositions with each other. In a multiplicative situation the combined impact of two or more independent variables is greater than expectations based on knowledge of each acting in isolation from the others. "In a fairly common kind of theoretical situation," says Blalock, "one assumes that a given phenomenon is most likely when two (or more) factors are *both* present, but that it is unlikely whenever either of these factors is absent." [15]

This crude dichotomization of income and quality modifies the conclusions that can be drawn from examination of both variables acting in isolation from each other, while failing to eliminate the original association in either case. Adopting the method used by Blalock to infer interaction, we can observe a 14 percentage point difference between the two difference scores in Table 4. If low family income and low college quality are both present the depressing effect on participation is substantially greater than additive expectations.

The data also confirm the suspicion that most high-quality Negro colleges in the South are private and that most low-quality ones are state-run. But again that fact is not sufficient to eliminate the original association between college quality and participation. Holding control of college constant and varying quality produces an 8 percentage point difference in participation among state college students—31 and 39 percent at the high and low quality state colleges respectively—and a 20 percentage point difference among private college students—41 and 61 percent respectively. As in the previous case, the relation between the three variables appears to be multiplicative. When quality and control are acting together to boost participation, their impact is greater than the sum of each acting in isolation.

II. SOCIAL CHARACTERISTICS
OF THE COUNTY

County-level social variables have been shown to relate importantly to many aspects of Southern politics. Two in particular should be tested in the present case: the urban-rural character of the county and the Negro proportion of the population.

Urbanism

Matthews and Prothro find that urbanism and industrialization ". . . are vastly overrated as facilitators of Negro registration. Urbanization and

---

[15] Hubert M. Blalock, "Theory Building and the Statistical Concept of Interaction," *American Sociological Review* 30 (June 1965): 375.

industrialization may provide necessary conditions for high levels of Negro participation but, by themselves, they are not sufficient to ensure them." [16] Protest participation is markedly different from Negro voter registration in this respect, but the relation is a threshold rather than a linear one. Variation in the proportion of the population that is rural-farm in the county where the college is situated makes very little difference in protest until the least rural category is reached. At that point (0–4.9 percent rural-farm), there is a jump of 23 percentage points—from 29 percent participating to 52 percent. Student protest, unlike other forms of Negro political activity, is characteristically an urban phenomenon.

The addition of further variables to the analysis elaborates on this association. Table 5 shows percent rural-farm and quality of college have an independent impact on participation, but it also suggests that when they are acting together their impact goes considerably beyond simple additive expectations. The difference between the differences in this case is 14 percentage points. Interestingly, a comparable finding does not appear when control of colleges and percent rural-farm are considered together; the data confirm that each variable has an impact independent of the other, but the difference-of-differences score is almost zero. When income and percent rural-farm are considered together in relation to participation, however, there is once again evidence of interaction. The data are given in Table 6.

The presence of two interaction effects such as these raises the possibility of what Blalock calls a "second-order" interaction—that all three variables may interact to produce levels of participation beyond additive expectations for the three individually.[17] Unfortunately, testing this pos-

TABLE 5.   Percent of Students Participating By Percent of County Population Rural-Farm and Quality of College

Quality of College:	Percent of County Population Rural-farm[a]	
	Low	High
High	71% (44)	38% (45)
Low	43% (84)	24% (91)
Difference:	28%	14%

[a]The cut-off point between the "high" and "low" categories was 4.9% rural-farm.

---

[16] Donald R. Matthews and James W. Prothro, "Social and Economic Factors and Negro Voter Registration in the South," *American Political Science Review* 52 (March 1963): 28.

[17] Blalock, "Theory Building and the Statistical Concept of Interaction."

TABLE 6. Percent of Students Participating
by Percent of County Rural-Farm
and Income of Family[a]

	Percent of County Population Rural-farm	
Income of Family:	*Low*	*High*
High	54% (62)	44% (45)
Low	46% (55)	20% (81)
Difference:	8	24

[a]The cut-off point between "high" and "low" categories of income was $4,999.

sibility involves frequencies too small to use with any confidence. The data do suggest, however, that such a higher level of interaction also exists.[18] When urban living, high college quality and high income all occur together, participation is boosted beyond what would be the case if all three variables were acting independently. In other words, although the generalization does not include variations in the control of colleges, adding successive favorable conditions to attending college in an urban county produces an accelerating curve of participation.

Percent Negro in the College County

The power of the percent Negro in a Southern county to predict many aspects of its social and political life has been repeatedly documented.[19]

---

[18] Testing for such a second-order interaction involves relating college quality and percent rural-farm to participation with income held constant. It is thus possible to arrive at a difference between the two difference-of-differences scores. In this case the difference of difference-of-differences scores was 11 percentage points. The data are as follows:

	High Income			*Low Income*	
Quality:	*Percent rural-farm* *Low*	*High*	*Quality:*	*Percent rural-farm* *Low*	*High*
High	67% (24)	45% (20)	High	67% (15)	37% (19)
Low	47% (38)	44% (25)	Low	38% (40)	16% (62)
Difference:	20	1	Difference:	29	21

$(20-1) - (29-21) = 11$

[19] For example, see V. O. Key, *Southern Politics* (New York: Alfred A. Knopf, 1949); John H. Fenton and K. N. Vines, "Negro Registration in Louisiana," *American Political Science Review* 51 (September 1957): 704–13, and H. D. Price, *The Negro in Southern Politics* (New York: New York University Press, 1957).

Matthews and Prothro conclude that the variable is "more strongly associated with the county's rate of Negro registration than any other social and economic attribute on which we have data." [20] There are, however, good reasons for expecting its impact on student protest participation to be somewhat muted. H. D. Price has argued that the percent Negro should not be seen as working in some mechanical way on the behavior in question, but as representing in a summary way the history and cultural traditions of race relations in the area.[21] Thus, where Negroes are a large part of the population there is also likely to be a history of a particular kind of race relations often dating to slavery times. A student population, however, is often a distinct community with its own mores and traditions that may run quite counter to those of the locality. Even in colleges where no such community exists—possibly a majority of those included in this study—the population is distinct in age, socio-economic status, education, and usually the frequency of social roots outside the area itself. The history and cultural traditions of the area seem likely to have less impact on participation in the student protest movement than on other kinds of political participation among the general Negro population in the county.

Despite these expectations student protest participation seems to be inversely related to percent Negro, in line with other kinds of behavior. Participation increases in a linear fashion from about 22 percent among those students attending college in areas with more than 40 percent Negroes to about 62 percent among those where there is less than 20 percent Negroes. The association is maintained when all other individual and contextual factors are held constant, and there is little evidence of interaction between percent Negro and any of the other variables tested. The data also show only a very slight and probably insignificant association between the percent Negro in the students' home counties and protest participation of any kind.

Matthews and Prothro have demonstrated that areas where Negroes are a high proportion of the population have whites with considerably less permissive attitudes toward Negro political participation,[22] and James W. Vander Zanden has pointed out the general role that resistance to social movements can have in shaping the course of a movement.[23] Perhaps this opposition is an important factor in explaining the varying rates of student protest participation by percent Negro, just as the opposition of state college administrators seems to be important in explaining the power of variations in college control.

But the question of motivation is also relevant here. Matthews and Prothro have demonstrated that "Negro commitment to voting declines

---

[20] Matthews and Prothro, "Social and Economic Factors . . ."

[21] H. D. Price, "The Negro and Florida Politics, 1944–1954," *The Journal of Politics* 17 (May 1955): 198–200.

[22] Matthews and Prothro, *Negroes and the New Southern Politics*, p. 118.

[23] James W. Vander Zanden, "Resistance and Social Movements," *Social Forces* 37 (May 1959): 312–315.

as white disapproval of Negro voting increases. Not only are fewer Negroes registered where white attitudes are less permissive, but fewer Negroes express a desire to vote." This lack of desire, they suggest, represents in part, "a realistic adjustment to the environment and in part the psychological mechanism of rationalization. Some Negroes will realistically calculate that they do not want to vote if the costs in terms of possible social, economic, or physical reprisals are too great." [24] Quite possibly such a lowering of motivation extends across the barriers that separate the college from the population at large and is responsible, in turn, for lowering rates of student protest participation.

If overt pressures are involved, however, there is no sign of it in the reports from demonstrators of the white hostility they encountered as a consequence of their participation. There was no difference in the number or character of the incidents reported by students in areas with a high proportion of Negroes and those with only few—although the n's involved are admittedly very small. While it seems quite likely that differences in Negro assertiveness are associated with differences in the percent Negro in the area, how much of this is a "mechanical" result of white attitudes in the area and how much is due to other properties of social structure must remain an open question. . . .

IV. PROTEST AND THE SOCIAL STRUCTURE

A full explanation of the variance in protest would require consideration of such things as the role of initiators and accidents of leadership in certain places, underlying economic conditions, the role of resistance from groups opposing the movement, geographic spread and many other factors. Nothing so ambitious has been attempted here. Rather, the suggestion is made that by focusing on one factor—the structure of intergroup relations—some advance can be made toward integrating various theoretical propositions about the origin of the Negro protest movement. In a nutshell, the argument runs as follows: Certain structural positions in Negro society are characterized by higher awareness of the wider society and, as a consequence, individuals occupying these positions are more prone to develop the particular set of attitudes and perceptions that lead to protest. Resistance from the white community, particularly as it is channeled through state college administrators and, possibly, as it occurs in certain kinds of areas, plays a role in modifying and shaping the particular patterns of protest that arise.

Unfortunately, it is necessary to rely on a rather small amount of data and a rather large amount of inference in arguing that such structural factors as high quality in colleges, high socioeconomic background, and urban residence all involve high levels of interaction with the wider society. The inferences, however, are not too strained. All the respondents in the survey were students and therefore more likly to have higher levels

---

[24] Matthews and Prothro, "Social and Economic Factors."

of general awareness than the rest of the Negro population; high quality colleges might not unreasonably be expected to increase that awareness. In fact the data show that students attending these colleges were more able to answer correctly a series of factual questions about politics than were the others.

In his large study of intergroup relations in several communities, Robin Williams finds support for the basic proposition that

> exposure to intergroup situations available in a community depends to a large extent upon the individual's daily living patterns—which in turn are strongly influenced by his position and function (or status and role) in the community.[25]

He also shows that in these communities, ". . . the more educated Negro has more opportunity for contact with whites than the less well-educated," and that higher occupational status works the same way.[26] Data from the present study show that students attending high-quality colleges do have considerably higher levels of social interaction across the race barrier—particularly with white students and teachers, although the generalization extends to a wide variety of contacts. The same applies to students from high socioeconomic backgrounds.

Attending college in an urban county is likewise associated with a higher frequency of intergroup contact than doing so in a rural county. The presence of such contact seems to make the urban environment a particularly fertile ground for protest. When urban living is considered in conjunction with several indicators of intergroup contact, a marked multiplicative effect appears. Matthews and Prothro comment that urban living appears to provide the necessary conditions for high levels of Negro voter registration.

> The urban-industrial life is more rational, impersonal and less tradition-bound; both Negroes and whites enjoy more wealth and education; the Negroes benefit from a concentration of potential leaders and politically relevant organizations in the cities. The urban ghetto may provide social reinforcement to individual motivations for political action.[27]

When intergroup social fluidity is added to these conditions, the data suggest that such individual motivations are particularly high.

Intergroup communication is, of course, a most difficult concept to operationalize; social contact across the race barrier is only one indicator of a complex process that can go on in a great variety of informal and formal ways. There are, nevertheless, several reasons why it is congenial to focus theory building in the present case on such communication and the structural conditions that promote it. First, it provides a firm basis

---

25 Williams, *Strangers Next Door*, p. 146.
26 Ibid.
27 Matthews and Prothro, "Social and Economic Factors . . . ," p. 34.

for what Sherif and Sherif call a "clear functional picture" of the factors that lead to protest participation.

> . . . Social psychological theories of intergroup relations which base the whole edifice primarily on a universal instinct (e.g., aggression), on displacements of aggressions always as the product of frustrations in personal life history, on a leadership principle, on situational factors, on culture, on national character, or, in a direct and mechanical way, on economic considerations result in one-sided pictures. . . . Compilations of these factors side by side in the form of a syllabus have not led to a clear functional picture.[28]

Economic and psychological variables are, from this perspective, placed in a theoretical context from which their importance in the whole structure of explanation can be assessed. Data have been given indicating that feelings of discontent about *personal* prospects in a biracial world are not associated with particularly high levels of protest. On the other hand, there is a marked association between protest and feelings about the general position of the *whole Negro race:* among students who recorded "high" on a measure of satisfaction with the present racial situation 28 percent were participants; among those recording "low" 52 percent were participants.[29] Evidently, explanation that focuses on feelings of personal relative deprivation must be modified to emphasize perceived deprivation of the *group* with which the individual identifies.[30] The present data do not detail just what objective social and economic conditions might lead to such feelings, but it is clear that such feelings would be particularly likely to develop in situations that constantly emphasize the differences between the races. The objective conditions are there for the whole group; but only some individuals are constantly exposed to the fact that they are differences. It is among this population that protest is most likely to develop.

A further advantage is that such a theoretical position also provokes useful speculation about why the Negro protest developed at this particular point in American history and about its likely future course. Arguing that protest can be explained adequately in terms of the economic fortunes of the Negro group as a whole fails to explain why the movement did not develop when—as seems quite possible—comparable conditions existed in the past. By emphasizing that other structural changes have a priority over purely economic ones, we are led to search for factors that can increase the visibility of whatever objective situations may lead a

---

28 M. Sherif and C. W. Sherif, *Groups in Harmony and Tension* (New York: Harper & Row, 1953), p. 136.

29 The students were given a self-anchoring scale and asked to indicate where on a continuum between the "very worst" and the "very best" possible race situations they would place the South at the present time.

30 For example, see Ruth Searles and J. A. Williams, "Negro College Students' Participation in Sit-Ins," *Social Forces* 40 (March 1962): 215–20. The authors argue that reference groups have changed for a large part of the Negro middle class that now identifies with the middle-class standards of the wider society. The result is feelings of relative deprivation that have led to the protest movement.

group to revolt. They are readily available in the increased mobility of all groups in Unted States society, the development of modern mass communications, and major wars that have at once increased mobility and brought different groups into close proximity with each other. So long as the objective conditions exist, we can expect that increased communication between the races will bring a furtherance of protest, not a quieting. Conservative Southern claims that the progress of integration will only bring an increase of Negro assertiveness seem quite plausible from the present theoretical position.

Much significant contemporary history concerns massive demands from various groups for large-scale adjustments in their social, economic and political positions, but there has been little systematic theory-building about such phenomena. Existing knowledge about the conditions that give rise to various kinds of social movements is generally couched in terms unique to the movement being considered and meaningless to the analysis of others. The structural perspective on the Negro movement suggested here does point to one direction in which research might be fruitful. If analysis were to concentrate, first, on the objective economic, social and political differences between groups, and then on the processes by which such differences are communicated and given meaning to the individuals concerned, major advances might be made. A large literature on the relation between communication and national integration has appeared in recent years. Analysis of the structure of communication between groups might lead to a better understanding of why some groups —such as the American Negroes—produce integrative movements, while others—such as the French Canadians—produce disintegrative ones. It would at least cast the analysis of broadly comparable phenomena in comparable terms.

15

YOUTH AND SOCIAL ACTION:
AN INTRODUCTION

JACOB R. FISHMAN / FREDRIC SOLOMON

The past few years have witnessed what appears to be a significant increase in social and political interest and action on the part of youth in various parts of the world.[1] This is not a new phenomenon in Europe where the traditions of the youth movement as an important force on the political scene go as far back as the late nineteenth century *Wandervogel*.[2] The youth movement is, however, an important new factor in the

From *Journal of Social Issues* 20, no. 1 (Winter 1964): 1–2, 7–8, 20–23; reprinted and abridged by permission of the authors and the Society for the Psychological Study of Social Problems.

[1] Charles Chin, "100 Korean Students Arrested After Rioting," *Washington Post*, 6 June 1962; Todd Gitlin, "The Student Political Scene, 1960–63," paper presented at the Howard University Conference on Youth and Social Action, October, 1963; Russell Howe, "Era of Violent Politics Predicted in Nigeria," *Washington Post*, 28 May 1962; R. S. Mowrer, "Student Tension Grows in Madrid," *Washington Post*, paper presented at Howard University Conference on Youth and Social Action, October, 1963; Fred Powledge, "Eastern College Students Adopt a 'Bill of Rights' Scoring Administrators," *New York Times*, 29 March 1965, p. 17; Powledge, "The Student Left: Spurring Reform/The New Student-Left: Movement Represents Serious Activities in Drive for Changes," *New York Times*, 15 March 1965, p. 1, col. 7 passim; Martin Tolchin, "200 Students Quit Gideonse Lecture, Say Brooklyn College Lacks Academic Freedom," *New York Times*, 30 March 1965; Andrew Wilson, "Moscow Kenya Students Clash with Red Officials," *Washington Post*, 14 April 1962; Howard Zinn, "Argentine Youth in Nazi Group 'Tacuara' Fights 'Zionism,' 'Capitalism,' 'Communism,'" *New York Times*, 16 September 1962, p. 29; Zinn, "Era of Protests Opened by Sit-Ins," *New York Times*, 14 May 1962, p. 1; Zinn, "Portugal Arrests 987 in Student Crackdown," *Washington Post*, 11 May 1962; Zinn, "Quito (Venezuela) Captures 40 More Rebels," *Washington Post*, 8 April 1962, p. 25; Zinn, "Students Battle Police in Japan," *Washington Post*, 14 May 1963; Zinn, "Students Clash in Athens," *Washington Post*, 11 April 1963; Zinn, "Students Riot as French Feelings Erupt," *Washington Post*, 13 December 1962; and Zinn, "Campus '65," *Newsweek*, 22 March 1965.

[2] Walter Z. Laquer, *Young Germany* (New York: Basic Books, 1962).

developing and newly independent nations of Asia and Africa. Further-more, such modern states as Israel, Egypt, Ghana and Turkey are, in large measure, products of youth movement revolutions.[3] Widespread social action by youth also appears to represent a relatively recent social development in the United States, including not only widespread campus demonstrations and student political movements, but also the vanguard of the civil rights revolution.[4] These activities in the contemporary world have ranged the entire spectrum from armed revolution and guerrilla warfare, to election campaigning, peace marches, freedom rides, violent and nonviolent public demonstrations and volunteer service for a variety of social causes—including mental health, the anti-poverty program and the Peace Corps.

The unique intersection of adolescence [5] and social change raises many questions of interest to social and behavioral scientists as well as to the formulators of government and community policy. For example, what forces and influences—psychological, social, political, historical—turn ado-lescents into a dedicated, significant and often volatile force for social change? As pointed out by a number of investigators, the process of social change itself may be a potent enzyme in the development of social action groups among youth.[6] What is not usually as obvious is the fact that the directions and pace of social change may be heavily influenced if not instigated by the activities of these young people. As may be seen in daily headlines, these actions may become a destructive social force or may turn to constructive and creative channels. The movements may be totalitarian or in the best traditions of the democratic process. What kinds of youth become involved in social action? What are the factors which influence ideology, commitment, choice of action and risk-taking? What is the in-fluence of social change and, conversely, what effect do these youth have on the process of change itself? . . .

---

3 D. Ben Gurion (Selection). Labor Zionist Organization (New York, 1948); Howard University. Interagency Conference on Youth and Developing Nations. Sponsored jointly by the U.S. State Department and the Center for Youth and Community Studies, May 1964; Homer Jack, ed., *The Gandhi Reader* (New York: Grove Press, 1961); Hella Pick, "Nkrumah Molds Ghana in His Image," *Manchester Guardian*, 15 April 1962; and United States Department of State: External Research Staff Paper "Research on Youth Groups and Young Leaders in the Developing Countries 1957–64," June 1964.

4 F. Solomon and J. R. Fishman, "Youth and Social Action: II. Action and Identity Formation in the First Student Sit-In Demonstration," *Journal of Social Issues* 20, no. 2 (April 1964): 36–45; Howard Zinn, *SNCC: The New Abolitionists* (Boston: Beacon Press, 1964); and Zinn, "Era of Protests Opened by Sit-Ins," *New York Times,* 14 May 1962, p. 1.

5 "Adolescence" and "youth" are used interchangeably in this paper. Chronologically, we mean the period from approximately 12 to 21 years of age. Conceptually, we mean the psychosocial stages of adolescence and late adolescence.

6 Erik Erikson, ed., *Youth—Change and Challenge* (New York: Basic Books, 1963); and J. R. Fishman and F. Solomon, "Youth and Social Action: I. Perspectives on the Student Sit-In Movement," *American Journal of Orthopsychiatry* 33, no. 5 (October 1963): 872–82.

SOCIAL CHANGE AND DISCONTENT

The unique susceptibility and responsiveness of youth to social change is a well documented phenomenon. Adolescence and late adolescence in the contemporary world is a time of transition, preparation, uncertainty and exploration. The transition from childhood to adulthood is heavily influenced not only by tradition and family, but also by the opportunities, restrictions, and uncertainties of the social and economic world. For the child, the changing social world is not yet relevant. The adult, already "established," must adapt as best he can to social change within the framework of established individual patterns. But the adolescent has a lowered threshold to all things affecting the verification of the past, the events of the present, and the possibilities of the future. Erikson describes this phenomenon as the unique intersection of life history with history.[7] In another context, one might describe it as a congruence of the unique needs of the adolescent and the changes of value and circumstance during social upheaval.

The life histories of contemporary Japanese and Negro youth [8] are quite relevant in this sense. The adolescence of both groups took place during a time of radical social change and resultant discontent. For the Japanese, the Second World War was followed by the overthrow of old traditions and patterns and the opening of society to concepts of social freedom, relativity of values, and new forms of social and economic competition. For the Negro youth, early adolescence included the period of the Supreme Court Decision of 1954, followed by an increasing momentum of political and social change in which the long-standing patterns of social, political and economic segregation which had characterized their childhood were undermined and questioned. At the same time dark-skinned "underdogs" in other parts of the world found it possible to rebel and assert their nationhood and adulthood. In this sense, historical dislocation may play a major role in the development of adolescent social action. This dislocation brings uncertainty and discontent, undermines the authority of the older generation, and leaves the adolescent with a need as well as a justification for finding new norms to supplant the old.

It is apparent in this that *change* may involve combinations of new challenges (mental hospital), new threats (nuclear war) or dangers to old values (the conservative movement), and the bubbling over of long-standing discontent (segregation and civil rights). One repeated image in youth movements is the representation of history as a continual dialectic struggle

---

[7] Erikson, *Youth—Change and Challenge.*

[8] Robert Coles, "Social Struggle and Weariness," *Psychiatry* 12, no. 4 (November 1964): 305–15; Erikson, op. cit.; Fishman and Solomon, "Youth and Social Action: I. Perspectives on the Student Sit-In Movement"; Solomon and Fishman, "The Psychosocial Meaning of Nonviolence in Student Civil Rights Activities," *Psychiatry* 27, no. 2 (May 1964): 91–99; and Solomon and Fishman, "Youth and Social Action: II. Action and Identity Formation."

between the uncertainties and hopes of youth on the one hand and the fears and rigidities of age on the other. Does this "conflict of generations" become most intense during times of social dislocation when old values and powers are weakened or deprived of what theretofore held unquestioned validity? How do parents and families reflect the impact of social change and thus somehow transmit the "license" for discontent to some youth? Which psychosocial variables in the youth make them most responsive? . . .

SOCIAL AND EDUCATIONAL DISLOCATION

Rapid social change may disarticulate youth from the social, educational, and economic structure and make the knowledge, skills, and the values of the past seem irrelevant to the present (and future). Perhaps this is the reason why the breaking away of youth into movements of rebellion and discontent began among the middle-class students of late nineteenth century Germany who found themselves with an increasing wealth of knowledge but locked out of the rigid social and political system. At the same time, this system and its values were being undermined by a developing economic and industrial society. These youth found themselves with an irrelevant past but with none of the instruments or pathways which might provide a meaningful, secure, and potent future for themselves. The forces of industrialization, modern commerce, and liberalism ushered in a period of social change and turmoil in the countries of Europe which is still in process. Students not only learned about the spirit of the new age and of possible alternatives to current practices but this awareness coincided with a more personalized awareness of the problems implicit in their own role—caught between the new and the old without position or power in either. Youth movements became the vanguard of the new revolutionary parties springing up in all parts of Europe. The movements themselves ranged widely over the spectrum of ideology and social action including the romantic folk nostalgia of the peasant movements (Tolstoian and Social Revolutionary, Iron Guard and German Free Youth); the democratic and Socialist Moderates (Bund, Christian Socialists); the extreme left wing (which became the socialist left and Communists) with their emphasis on the "scientific" view of history and social structure; and the variety of anarchist fringe groups.[9]

The fact that students in the vanguard have traditionally come from the upwardly mobile middle class suggests the possibility that they had already experienced, through their families, many of the pressures of social change and discontinuity. Other students have traditionally come from minority groups or repressed lower classes where access to social and economic opportunity was cut off more severely through prejudice, class structure, or repressive laws. Thus the Jews of Europe were heavily rep-

---

[9] A small group of high school students has recently appeared in New York and Chicago inexplicably dedicated to anarcho-syndicalism and the writings of Bakunin.

resented in the ranks of revolutionary youth movements, particularly those movements radically rejecting the present and recent past (Zionist, Socialist, Communist). The Nationalist and Facist movements had similar origins but tended to project the reasons for many of their grievances on to scapegoats—particularly minority groups who were seen as parasites and alien contaminants. These movements extolled the simple folk traditions of the past with a strong emphasis on membership in a pure and unified nation with a single direction. Interestingly enough, a number of minority groups developed their own brand of reactive intolerant nationalism (these were generally separatist movements not unlike the contemporary Black Muslims. A striking example was the Zionist-Revisionist Movement in Europe which, in a number of ways, emulated the methods and trappings of the Fascists). These groups exhibit a significant element of identification with the aggressor. The reaction of minority or lower class youth to economic and social blockage may also be seen in the occasional appearance among these groups of more spiritual movements whose attention is turned towards mysticism, moral revival and away from the unpleasantness of social reality.

Disarticulation and the exclusion of students and middle-class youth in the face of social upheaval are probably crucial factors in the student riots and rebellions in many countries today. These factors may well be affecting the American civil rights workers (white and Negro alike) and other student demonstrators in our own country. In the United States the increase in opportunities for education and prosperity for many has left an increasingly obvious gap between ideal possibilities and social realities for American youth, particularly Negroes.[10] One may note in listening to students involved in civil rights demonstrations, peace demonstrations and university "crises" an increasing sense of discontent. They take issue with what they see to be the irrelevancies of much of present-day education. To them it appears to be lacking in its ability to prepare them for "the real world." Instead education seems geared simply to preparing them for traditional careers and self-seeking advancement. They are upset about what they see as the alienation of government and university from serious concern about social problems. They want a voice in the formulation of social and educational policy, and they desire experiential, first-hand practical knowledge of social issues. What started as a movement to redress the problems and achieve the rights of Negro students is rapidly becoming a movement for *all* students.

We should be particularly concerned with the kind of socialization process and conditions which gear youth to social action within the framework of an open democratic society on the one hand and that which predisposes or forces youth into an extremist position, leading to violent revolution or totalitarianism, quite opposite from the interests and ideals of our own society, on the other. Perhaps this is related to the extent to which the social system tends to lock certain young people out, and the degree to which secondary and higher education which the young person

---

[10] Paul Goodman, *Growing Up Absurd* (New York: Random House, 1960).

is receiving seems inappropriate for the system which he has to enter. In the youth movement the adolescent may find a "substitute for society" not only in its function of providing a framework for the process of self-definition and indentity development but also because the movement provides access to a social stream.

In the context of a rapidly changing world, as youth look upward and see opportunities closed off with a considerable gap between themselves and those with power, wealth, or influence they become ripe for "revolution." This is one of the dilemmas of American foreign policy. In hypothetical African country X, independence has come suddenly. Money is provided for economic development. However, without adequate vocational training and planning for job opportunity this may not substantially increase the opportunity for employment for youth. Thus again we have the not uncommon situation of money for the few and no jobs for the many. Or the United States may invest a lot of money in traditional secondary school education for country X and the results may be youth who have education which is quite inappropriate for available jobs and employment realities which are far beneath the new social and economic horizons for which these youth have been educated. . . .

16

CLASS AND POLITICS
IN THE FAMILY BACKGROUNDS
OF STUDENT POLITICAL ACTIVISTS

DAVID L. WESTBY / RICHARD G. BRAUNGART

Recent years have seen the growth and projection of student groups into national politics with an intensity and impact never before experienced in American history. This abrupt turn from the often-criticized juvenile college culture of earlier years has provided sociologists with opportunities to study social movements without leaving their own bailiwick.

Much of the research on student youth movements has found its theoretical point of departure in socialization theory in that it attempts to explain political beliefs and action in terms of family-based experience and family structure.[1] Thus, Maccoby, Mathews, and Morton, in a study of 339 first-time voters, explain the "political conformity" exhibited by some members of their sample in terms of the degree to which their parents exercised control over their youthful activities.[2] In somewhat similar fashion, Middleton and Putney, in a study of 1440 college youths, endeavored to demonstrate that those "rebelling" against the political positions of their fathers were more estranged from their fathers, especially if the fathers were interested in politics.[3] Generally, the focus of research in this area, with its concentration on socialization patterns in the family, seems to neglect the older class-based model of political beliefs

From *American Sociological Review* 31, no. 5 (October 1966): 690–92; reprinted by permission of the authors.

Revised version of a paper read at the meetings of the Eastern Sociological Society in Philadelphia, Penn., April, 1966.

[1] The general importance of the family in the continuity of party and voting traditions is, of course, a well-established generalization in political sociology.

[2] Eleanor Maccoby, Richard Mathews, and Anton Morton, "Youth and Political Change," *Public Opinion Quarterly* 18 (Spring 1954): 23–39.

[3] Russell Middleton and Snell Putney, "Student Rebellion Against Parental Political Beliefs," *Social Forces* 41 (May 1963): 377–83.

which assumes that the latter are primarily a function of the stratification system.[4]

The present study, based on a relatively small number of student activists, suggests that the class and party of the student's family of orientation may be significant factors in understanding at least certain features of the student movement. It should be clear that we regard the findings presented here as suggestive for further research and definitely not sufficient to establish valid generalizations.

METHOD

Our study focused on "left" and "right" activists in a large public institution in the eastern United States, and was conducted during the spring of 1965. The data reported here deal with class and party backgrounds of the membership bodies of two campus activist organizations, SENSE (Students for Peace) and the Young Americans for Freedom (Y.A.F.), which may be taken to represent the extremes of political opinion on the "left" and "right" respectively. There are other activist groups at the institution in question, especially on the left, but their membership is heavily overlapping with that of SENSE.[5]

A questionnaire was administered *en masse* to each of the two groups. The first part of the questionnaire consisted of items tapping class backgrounds and related variables, while the second part was composed of a 22-item Likert-type attitude scale dealing with attitudes toward the present war in Viet Nam.[6] The questionnaire was administered to twenty-nine students at a SENSE meeting, to nineteen students at two Y.A.F. meetings, and to 105 students in an introductory sociology class. A few members were absent from these meetings and there is reason to believe that those missing were less extreme and less active.

FINDINGS

Tables 1 through 3 present the origins of SENSE and Y.A.F. members. Table 1 shows a significant difference in median income for the two

[4] See, for instance, Paul Lazarsfeld, Bernard Berelson, Hazel Gaudet, *The People's Choice* (New York: Duell, Sloan & Pearce, 1944); Phillip Converse, "The Shifting Role of Class in Political Attitudes and Behavior," in Eleanor Maccoby et al., *Readings in Social Psychology* (New York: Holt, Rinehart & Winston, 1947); Richard Centers, *The Psychology of Social Class* (New York: Russell & Russell, 1961); and Herbert Hyman, *Political Socialization* (New York: Free Press, 1959). Of course, practically everything in the Marxist tradition takes this view.

[5] That these two groups represent the extremes of political opinion was demonstrated in a series of attitude items dealing with the present administration policy in Viet Nam. The groups took overwhelmingly opposed positions on this controversial political issue, while a control group composed of a class of Sociology I students, roughly representative of the student body, fell in between the two, although somewhat closer to Y.A.F. than to SENSE. Mean scores on the attitude scale items, which ranged from 22 (most liberal) to 110 (most conservative), were: SENSE, 37; Sociology I, 72; Y.A.F., 85.

[6] An example of how a typical attitude scale item distributed itself over our three groups may be seen below (opposite page):

TABLE 1. Distribution of Student Activists by Annual Family Income

Family Income	SENSE		Y.A.F.	
	N	%	N	%
Above median	19	68	4	24
Below median	9	32	13	76
Total	28	100	17	100

$\chi^2 = 8.36$, d.f. = 1, p < .005.
Median income: SENSE, \$12,232; Y.A.F., \$6,625.

TABLE 2. Distribution of Student Activists by Hollingshead's Two-Factor Index of Social Class

Social Class	SENSE		Y.A.F.	
	N	%	N	%
I, II	15	52	5	26
III	10	35	7	37
IV, V	4	13	7	37
Total	29	100	19	100

$\chi^2 = 4.60$, d.f. = 2, p < .10.

QUESTION 9: Viet Nam is historically and geographically an Asian country and should therefore be allowed to develop autonomously within the Asian sphere of influence and power.

Response	SENSE		Soc. I		Y.A.F.	
	N	%	N	%	N	%
Agree	24	83	24	23	2	11
Uncertain	5	17	22	21	5	26
Disagree	..	..	59	56	12	63
Total	29	100	105	100	19	100

$\chi^2 = 47.18$, d.f. = 4, p < .001.

Twenty-one of the 22 attitude questions were significant at the .001 level. The remaining attitudinal comparison was significant at the .02 level. The composite political attitude scale developed for this study had an internal consistency of .92 as determined by a Pearson product-moment correlation coefficient using a Spearman-Brown correction.

TABLE 3.   Distribution of Student Activists
by Political Affiliation of Parents

Political Affiliation of Parents	SENSE		Y.A.F.	
	N	%	N	%
Democrat, Socialist	17	68	5	29
Republican	8	32	12	71
Total	25	100	17	100

$\chi^2 = 6.03$, d.f. = 1, p $<.01$.
Note: A few parents could not be classified by political affiliation because they had none or were independent.

groups, while Table 2 gives the social class distribution for the two groups, utilizing the Hollingshead Two-Factor Index. The predominantly upper-middle-class high-income origins of SENSE members contrast sharply with the generally low-income and lower-middle- or working-class backgrounds of Y.A.F. members. We shall briefly consider these findings in the light of current stratification theory.

That "revolutionary reactionaries," to use Clinton Rossiter's term, or adherents to the "radical right," should be drawn from the lower-middle and working classes is not surprising if one accepts the "status politics" theory of Hofstadter and others.[7] The "status politics" theory suggests that extreme "right" activists, or "pseudoconservatives" as Hofstadter prefers to call them, are generally found within status-threatened groups. It is precisely the lower-middle and working classes that are least secure and tend to feel threatened by the upward thrust of new minorities. As Hofstadter wrote in his seminal discussion, "conformity is a way of guaranteeing and manifesting respectability among those who are not sure that they are respectable enough." [8]

Upper-middle-class status, on the other hand, typically provides the social and economic security that is lacking in the lower-middle and upper-working classes. These latter strata provide a kind of protective belt insulating the upper-middle classes from any immediate challenge on the part of militant lower-status groups. As members of a fully "arrived" stratum, upper-middle-class individuals can afford the luxury of "deviance" from straight-line conformist politics, especially if their position is relatively well-established, and their mobility not too recent.[9]

---

[7] Richard Hofstadter, "The Pseudo-Conservative Revolt—1955," in *The Radical Right,* ed. Daniel Bell (New York: Doubleday, 1962), pp. 63–80. In the same volume, see also S. M. Lipset, "The Sources of the 'Radical Right'," and "Three Decades of the Radical Right: Coughlinites, McCarthyites, and Birchers," pp. 259–377.

[8] Hofstadter, ibid., pp. 76–77. Our data on the marital status of parents also seem to support the insecurity—conformity relation. Eight Y.A.F. students (46 percent) came from homes with divorced or widowed parents, while this was true of only 2 (6 percent) of SENSE members.

[9] We should note that whenever such insulation is absent, as in certain Northern suburban areas and in the South generally, the upper-middle class is as susceptible to right-wing extremist forms of politics as any other group.

While this interpretation may seem plausible, it casts a very wide net for a few small fish. Classes are enormous aggregates, while student activists are a small segment of the student body at any university or college. It is important to try to demonstrate which factors *within strata* are decisive in their influence on political action at the extremes of the political spectrum. Table 3 gives the political affiliations of the students' parents and shows a pronounced relationship between left activism and Democratic or Socialist background on the one hand, and Republican background and right activism on the other. In other words, families of SENSE members are predominantly high-status Democrats while Y.A.F. members come mainly from low-status Republican families. Within each stratum, it seems, it is party identification and presumably the accompanying ideological orientation that are the more particular factors that predispose students toward political extremism.

Finally, despite their opposed ideological stances, these two groups are similar in one respect—they both exhibit a kind of inconsistency or absence of crystallization. Lenski and others have presented evidence that such types are more insistent upon or receptive to change, more radical as it were, than the highly crystallized.[10] Both the far left and far right press for policies and actions representing considerable departures from those current today.

Generally, student activists seem to be expressing ideological positions that, though extreme, are in the main consistent with the political orientations of their families. It may be that activists are rebelling against their parents, but, if so, it seems to be in a highly selective way in which the intersection of the class structure and the political system is a powerful predisposing force. We think that researchers of the student movement would do well to consider the class and political backgrounds of their subjects.

---

10 Gerhard Lenski, "Status Crystallization: A Non-Vertical Dimension of Social Status," *American Sociological Review* 19 (August 1954): 405–13. "Crystallization" is defined as the degree to which positions within two or more ranking systems are congruent. Thus, a white Anglo-Saxon, Protestant doctor making $30,000 a year could be said to be highly crystallized, whereas a Negro doctor making $4,000 would be uncrystallized.

17

YOUNG INTELLIGENTSIA IN REVOLT

RICHARD FLACKS

COMING TOGETHER

In the decade since 1960, the offspring of the intelligentsia have become politicized and increasingly radicalized, despite the fact that, having been born to relatively high privilege and social advantage, they saw society opening ever wider vistas for personal success and enrichment. Why have they, in large numbers, refused to follow their fathers and mothers—adopting a stance of slightly uneasy acceptance of the prevailing social order while trying to establish a personal life on a somewhat different cultural basis?

In part, the disaffection of these youth is a direct consequence of the values and impulses their parents transmitted to them. The new generation had been raised in an atmosphere that encouraged personal autonomy and individuality. Implicitly and explicitly it had been taught to be skeptical about the intrinsic value of money-making and status and to be skeptical about the claims of established authority. It incorporated new definitions of sex roles. Having seen their parents share authority and functions more or less equally in the family, and having been taught to value aesthetic and intellectual activity, these were boys who did not understand masculinity to mean physical toughness and dominance, and girls who did not understand femininity to mean passivity and domesticity. Moreover, they were young people—young people for whom the established means of social control were bound to be relatively ineffective (and here they were particularly different from the older generation). Growing up with economic security in families of fairly secure status, the normal incentives of the system—status and income—were of relatively minor importance, and indeed many of their parents encouraged them to feel that such incentives ought to be disdained.

In retrospect, it seems inevitable that young people of this kind should

From *TRANS-action* 7, no. 8 (June 1970): 49–55. Copyright © June 1970 by TRANS-action, Inc., New Brunswick, New Jersey; excerpts reprinted by permission of the author and publisher.

come into some conflict with the established order. Because of their central values, they, like the earlier generations of intellectuals, would necessarily be social critics. Because of their material security, they, like earlier generations of high status youth, were likely to be experimental, risk-taking, open to immediate experience, relatively unrepressed. Because of their character structure, they would very likely come into conflict with arbitrary authority in school and other situations of imposed restriction. Because of their values and sex role identifications, they would find themselves out of harmony with the conventional youth culture with its frivolity, anti-intellectualism and stereotypic distinctions between the sexes.

Furthermore, their impulses to autonomy and individuality, their relative freedom from economic anxiety and their own parents' ambivalence toward the occupational structure would make it difficult for them to decide easily on a fixed vocational goal or life style, would make them aspire to construct their lives outside conventional career lines, would make them deeply critical of the compromise, corruption and unfreedom inherent in the occupations of their fathers—the very occupations for which they were being trained.

Much of this had happened before, but the situation of the young intelligentsia of the sixties differed radically from that of their precursors. First, their numbers were enormously greater than ever before. Second, they faced, not a scarcity of jobs, but an abundance of careers—yet the careers for which they were being trained no longer held the promise of social melioration and personal fulfillment that their parents had anticipated. Third, these youth sensed not only the narrowness and irrationality of the prevailing culture but the deeper fact that the dominant values of bourgeois society, appropriate in an age of scarcity and entrepreneurial activity, had become irrelevant to a society which was moving beyond scarcity and competitive capitalism. Thus, by the late fifties, more youth were feeling more intensely than ever before a sense of estrangement from capitalist culture—an estrangement which could not be assuaged by the promise of material security the system offered.

The cultural crisis these youth experienced provided the ground for their coming together. But the transformation of cultural alienation into political protest, and eventually into revolutionary action, was due to more immediate and concrete pressures. It was the emergence of the southern civil rights movement which, more than any other single event, led the young intelligentsia in the early sixties to see the relevance of political opposition and social change to their own problems. The non-violent movement showed, for one thing, how small groups of committed youth could undertake action that could have major historical impact. It demonstrated how such action could flow directly from humanistic values. But above all, it confronted these white students with the fact that all of their opportunities for personal fulfillment were based on white upper-middle-class privilege and that continued passivity in the face of racism meant that one was in fact part of the oppressive apparatus of society, no matter what one's private attitudes might be.

Participation in the civil rights struggle seemed, however, to offer a way out of this dilemma, and civil rights protest helped to open the consciousness of many students to other political issues. It made them aware that there was more to their problems than the fact that the culture offered little support for their personal aspirations; it also threatened their existence. But at the same time numbers of students became rapidly sensitive to the fact that the nuclear arms race, the cold war and the militarization of society were not simply facts of life but deliberate, therefore reversible, policies. It was not long before the protest tactics acquired in the civil rights movement began to be applied to the demand for peace.

When one reads today the Port Huron Statement (June 1962) and other documents of the early Students for a Democratic Society (SDS) and the New Left, one is struck by the degree to which the early New Left conceived of itself largely as a political reform movement rather than in clearly revolutionary terms. While it's true, as Todd Gitlin has suggested, that the early new radicals of the sixties were filled with "radical disappointment" with the American way of life, it is also the case that they retained a good deal of optimism about the possibilities for change in the context of American politics. In particular, it was hoped that the labor movement, the religious community, the liberal organizations, the intellectual community, the civil rights movement all could eventually unite around a broad-based program of radical reform.

The role of the student movement was seen by the early SDS leaders as providing the intellectual skills needed for such a new movement and, somewhat later, as important for producing people who would help to catalyze grass root activities in a variety of places. Direct action such as the sit-ins, freedom rides and other forms of protest and civil disobedience was seen, on the one hand, as a vital tactic for the winning of reform and, on the other hand, as a method by which the more established institutions such as the labor movement could be induced to move in the direction of more vigorous action. In this early phase of the student movement, SDS and other New Left leaders were little aware of the possibility that a mass movement of students on the campus could be created and engaged in collective struggles against university authority. Rather the New Left's role on the campus was seen primarily as one of breaking through the atmosphere of apathy, educating students about political issues, so that they could begin to take a role off the campus in whatever struggles were going on.

But the early reformism of the New Left was soon abandoned. The failure of the established agencies of reform to create a political opposition and to mobilize mass support for political alternatives was most decisive in preventing the new movement of the young intelligentsia from becoming absorbed by conventional politics, thereby following in the footsteps of previous movements of American intellectuals. This collapse of the so-called liberal establishment thus marked a new stage in the consciousness of the American intelligentsia—beyond cultural alienation, beyond social reform, beyond protest—toward active resistance and revolution.

The emergence of the student movement in the sixties, then, signifies a more fundamental social change and is not simply a species of "generational conflict." The convergence of certain social structural and cultural trends has produced a new class, the intelligentsia, and, despite the apparent material security of many in this class, its trajectory is toward revolutionary opposition to capitalism. This is because, first, capitalism cannot readily absorb the cultural aspirations of this group—aspirations that fundamentally have to do with the abolition of alienated labor and the achievement of democratic community. Second, the incorporation of this group is made more difficult by the concrete fact of racism and imperialism—facts which turn the vocations of the intelligentsia into cogs in the machinery of repression rather than means for self-fulfillment and general enlightenment. Third, the numerical size of this group and the concentration of much of it in universities make concerted oppositional political action extremely feasible. Finally, the liberal default has hastened the self-consciousness of students and other members of this class, exacerbated their alienation from the political system and made autonomous oppositional politics a more immediate imperative for them. Thus, a stratum, which under certain conditions might have accepted a modernizing role within the system, has instead responded to the events of this past decade by adopting an increasingly revolutionary posture.

In part, this development grows out of the antiauthoritarian impulses in the fundamental character structure of the individual members which provide much of the motivation and emotional fuel for the movement. But, as the history of the movement shows, there was an early readiness to consider whether established political alternatives were in fact viable. That such readiness has virtually disappeared is almost entirely due to the failure of the political system itself—a failure most manifest in the crises of race, poverty and urban life on the one hand and the international posture of the United States on the other.

Over the last decade the American government has consistently failed to enforce new or existing legislation guaranteeing civil rights. It has consistently failed to implement promised reforms leading to social and economic equality. It has demonstrated a stubborn unwillingness and/or incompetence in dealing with the deepening crises of urban life, and it has supported essentially repressive, rather than ameliorative, policies with respect to the black revolt.

Even more crucial in undermining the legitimacy of the system for young people was, of course, the war in Vietnam—the fact that the United States was unable to win the war; the fact that it dragged on endlessly to become the longest war in American history; the fact that the United States in Vietnam was involved in an effort to suppress a popular uprising; the fact that the United States in Vietnam committed an interminable series of atrocities and war crimes, especially involving the destruction of civilian life; the fact that the war was accompanied by a military draft and that alongside the draft a system involving the social tracking of all young males in America had grown up; the fact that the war in Vietnam was not simply an accident of policy but an essential ingredient of what became increasingly identified as a worldwide imperialist policy involving the suppression of popular revolution and the maintenance and extension of American political and corporate power throughout the Third World.

Moreover, alongside the growth of conventional and nuclear military power and the penetration of American institutions, including especially the universities, by military priorities, there grew up a paramilitary establishment which had attempted to control and manipulate organizations and events throughout the world and also at home. This development was perhaps best symbolized for students by the fact that the Central Intelligence Agency had subsidized the National Student Association and had extensive ties with American academics. Finally, the war continued and escalated despite vast expressions of popular discontent.

This, more than anything else, reinforced the New Left's disbelief in the efficacy of conventional political means of affecting policy. By the time of the Democratic Convention in 1968, a very large number of young people were convinced that only extreme action of a disruptive sort could have any substantial effect on major policy and that "working through the system" was a trap, rather than a means to effect change.

Obviously, many young people, fearing the consequences of a full-scale delegitimation of authority, continue to search for a more responsive political alternative within the system. But the stagnation of liberalism in these years along with the astonishing series of assassinations of spokesmen for its revitalization have made such hopes appear increasingly unrealistic. Thus the growth of revolutionary sentiment among the students proceeds apace. As the legitimacy of national authority declines, a process of delegitimation occurs for all in authoritative positions—for instance, university officials—and proposals for melioration and compromise are viewed with deepening suspicion. Political polarization intensifies, and those in the opposition feel, on the one hand, the imperative of confrontation as a means of further clarifying the situation and, on the other hand, that the entire structure of social control is being organized for the purpose of outright repression. And for American students confrontation is made more urgent by the moral pressure of the black liberation movement, which continuously tests the seriousness of their proclaimed revolutionary commitment.

NEW FRONT LINE

The early New Left frequently criticized university life as well as the larger society, but it was also quite ambivalent toward the university as an institution. University authority was seen as paternalistic and as subservient to dominant interests in the society. University education was regarded as a contributor to student indifference towards social questions. At the same time, the Port Huron Statement and other early New Left writing viewed the university as a potential resource for movements for change, university intellectuals as potentially useful to such movements and the university as a relatively free place where political controversy could flourish provided it was catalyzed.

Prior to the fall of 1964, SDS leaders ignored the campus as a base of operation, persuading a considerable number of students to either leave school or to work off the campus in the efforts to organize the urban poor. In large measure, university reform campaigns were felt by the most committed activists to be both irrelevant and, in a certain sense, immoral, when people in the South were putting their bodies on the line. The Berkeley free speech movement of 1964 helped to change this perception of the campus. The police action at Berkeley, the first of numerous large-scale busts of student protestors, suggested that a campus struggle could be the front line. And the political impact of Berkeley in California, and indeed internationally, suggested that there was nothing parochial or irrelevant about an on-campus struggle. Moreover, these events coincided with the turning away of portions of the civil rights movement, especially the Student Nonviolent Coordinating Committee, from efforts to work with white students. Further, Berkeley coincided with the escalation of the war in Vietnam and with the discovery, only dimly realized before, that the universities were major resources in the development of the military potential of the United States.

Beginning in the fall of 1966 attacks on military research installations, on ROTC, on connections between the university and military agencies, on military recruitment and recruitment by defense corporations became the prime activity of SDS and other student groups for a number of months. Every major confrontation mobilized hundreds of students for highly committed direct action and many thousands more for supportive action. Typically the issues raised by the student movement on a campus were supported by as many as two-thirds of the student body, even though large numbers of students were unwilling to participate in disruptive actions as such. And as previously uncommitted students joined these actions, many were radicalized by the experience of participation in a community of struggle, by the intransigence and obtuseness of university administrators and by the violence of police repression of the protests. Institutional resistance was fostering student "class consciousness."

By the late sixties, the movement was no longer the exclusive property of those I've been calling the young intelligentsia. It was having a widening impact on students at nonelite campuses, in junior colleges and high schools, and on nonstudent youth in the streets and in the Armed Forces. To a great extent, the availability of larger numbers of young people for insurgent ideas and actions is rooted in the cultural crisis we alluded to at the outset of this paper. For all youth experience the breakdown of traditional culture, the irrelevance of ideologies based on scarcity. Vast numbers of youth in America today are in search of a less repressed, more human, more spontaneous life style.

The radicalization of youth is enhanced by the peculiar social position of high school and college students, who have achieved some degree of independence from family authority but are not yet subject to the discipline of work institutions. The high school and college situation is, on the one hand, extremely authoritarian but, on the other hand, functions to segregate young people, maintaining them in a peculiar limbo combining dependency with irresponsibility. The impact of the cultural crisis on the school situation is to make really vast numbers of young people ready for new and more liberating ideas, while they have the freedom and energy to spend time in examination and criticism of prevailing values and ideologies.

In addition, the situation of youth is exacerbated by the demands of the imperialist system for manpower and by the increasing bureaucratization of both education and vocation. More concretely, the draft is the reality that undermines the endless promises made to American youth. What the draft means is that one is not really free to pursue self-fulfillment, even though one has been taught that self-fulfillment is the highest goal and purpose of the system. Not only is that promise undermined by the necessity to serve in the army and die in the mud of some distant jungle, a fate reserved for relatively few young men, but the draft serves to facilitate control over the careers of all young men by serving explicitly as a means for tracking youth into occupations believed to be in the interest of the state. The result for school youth is postponement or avoidance of the military but subjugation to an educational system that reproduces many of the worst features of the larger society in terms of authoritarianism, competitiveness, individualism and dehumanization. The growth of a mass youth movement depended on the emergence of a group of young intelligentsia whose own socialization was particularly at odds with the dominant culture, but once such a circle of youth emerged, their expressions, both cultural and political, spread like wildfire.

Thus, the story of the student movement in the United States over the past decade has been one of continued self-transformation. Once student activism was characteristic of tiny groups of campus rebels, the offspring, as we have suggested, of the educated middle class, who faced severe value and vocational crisis, could find no moral way to assimilate into American society and so searched for a new basis for living in cultural avant-gardism and moralistic dedication to social reform. In the past decade, obviously, the movement has spread well beyond this original group. It has transformed itself from a nonideological movement for vague principles of social justice into a new radical movement in quest of a new social vision and a new framework for social criticism, and finally into a movement spearheaded by revolutionaries tending, more and more, to look to classical revolutionary doctrine as a guiding principle and to embody, more and more, classical models of revolutionary action as their own.

It is a movement that rejects and is at the same time entangled by its roots in what I have called the intelligentsia. Yet it has expressed most clearly the fundamental aspirations of the rising generation of that class for a new social order in which men can achieve autonomy and full participation in determining the conditions of their lives, in which hierarchy and domination are replaced by community and love, in which war, militarism and imperialism are obsolete and in which class and racial distinctions are abolished. It is a movement of surprising strength. It has touched the minds of millions and changed the lives of thousands of young people, both here and abroad. It has severely shaken the stability of the American empire and challenged the basic assumptions of its culture. But its most sensitive adherents have become increasingly despairing, as the movement has reached the limit of its possibilities. This despair is rooted first in the unresponsiveness of the political system to pressure for reform; second, in the narrow class base of the movement; third, in the seemingly overwhelming capacity of the authorities to manage social control. Out of this despair arises the sense that revolution is an urgent, if impossible, necessity, that the movement must transcend its social base, that it must make common cause with other enemies of the empire around the world.

CO-OPTATION

Given this new consciousness, what can be said about the future of the movement? It seems to me that one can envision several possibilities. First, any student and youth movement has the potential of becoming a relatively insulated expression of generational revolt. This is not the explicit intention of very many spokesmen for the New Left, but it certainly appears to be the implicit expectation of many agencies of social control. A generational movement may be understood as a movement of cultural and social innovation whose impact has been contained within the framework of existing society. For agencies of social control, the ideal circumstance would be the opportunity to eliminate those elements in the movement that are most disruptive and destructive, while putting into effect some of the cultural, social and political innovations and reforms the movement advocates.

Accordingly, you put Yippies in jail but work out some means to legalize the use of marijuana. You put draft-resisters in jail or into exile while abolishing conscription. You expel SDS from the campus while admitting student representatives to the board of trustees. You deride and derogate the women's liberation movement while liberalizing abortion laws. You break up and harass hippie urban communities while providing fame and fortune to some rock music groups. This is all done with the aid of ideological perspectives that emphasize that what is going on is a generational revolt, that there is a generation gap, that the big problem is one of communication between the old and the young. The hope is that if reforms can be made that will liberalize the cultural and social atmosphere, particularly in relation to sex, drug use, art, music, censorship and so forth, the mass of youth will not become tempted by the message of the radical vanguard.

If the new political and cultural radicalism were to become channeled more fully in the direction of generational revolt, it would then be serving stabilizing and modernizing functions for the going system, and it would not be the first time that a radical movement in the United States ended up functioning this way. But from the point of view of New Left activists, such an outcome for the movement would represent profound failure, particularly if it meant, as it does now seem to mean, that the most active and militant of the participants of the movement would suffer, rather than benefit, from any social change that might be forthcoming.

There is a substantial likelihood, however, that the student movement and the New Left of the sixties will move in the direction we have just outlined. The most important fact supporting this outcome is that the movement has, in the ten years of its existence, failed very largely to break out of its isolation as a movement of the young, and particularly of the relatively advantaged young. There are reasons to think that this isolation could be broken in the near future, and we shall suggest some of these shortly, but it is important to recognize that most of the public understanding of what is happening has revolved around the generational problem, rather than the substantive political and social questions that the movement has raised. Most of the expressed sympathy for the movement on the part of the elders has been couched in terms of solving the problems of youth and liberalizing the cultural atmosphere, rather than in joining in the making of a social revolution.

At the same time, however, despite the very large-scale public discussion of the need for reform and innovation, the prevailing tendencies of the state and other dominant institutions do not seem to be primarily in this direction. Even such apparently unthreatening changes as liberalization of laws governing drug use, the 18-year-old vote, the involvement of students in direct participation in university government or the abolition of the draft meet very strong resistance and do not now seem to be on the agenda. Instead, what is in prospect is further tightening of drug laws, further restrictions and harassment of the communal outcroppings of the youth culture, further efforts at censorship, a continuation of the draft and a generally more hostile climate with respect to even the modest aspirations for change of most young people today. All of this, of course, could change in a relatively short period of time as those who are now young move into full citizenship and have the opportunity directly to influence public and institutional policies. But what happens in the intervening years is likely to be crucial.

Another reason for believing that the New Left has considerable capacity for resisting this kind of incorporation into the culture is that the movement is profoundly suspicious of and sensitive to the dangers of cooptation. Most movement participants are aware at one level or another that the classic American pattern for controlling revolutionary and quasi-revolutionary movements is to destroy or isolate the most militant sections while implementing, at least on paper, the programmatic thrust of the movement. This is what happened in the labor movement. It is what is happening in the black liberation movement, and it is certainly what is being advocated for the student movement. In this way the American political system has served to contain the revolutionary thrust of movements that develop within it, while keeping these movements fragmented, preventing their outreach into sectors of the population beyond those that form the original constituency of the movement. . . .

As I say, new leftists wish to avoid at all costs the buying off of the movement through piecemeal reform. This is one reason why the movement is so hesitant to propose concrete reforms and to proclaim its interest in short-range goals. A greater danger, however, is that the movement has been unable to offset pressures, both internal and external, that maintain it as a movement of youth.

The future of the New Left depends now on its ability to break out of its isolation and to persuade the majority of Americans that their interests depend on the dismantling of imperialism and the replacement of capitalism with a fully democratized social order. The movement cannot afford to be encapsulated as a generational revolt. It cannot wait until the present young "take over." It cannot survive in a climate of repression and polarization unless large numbers of people are moving in a similar political direction. It cannot survive and ought not survive if it conceives itself to be an elite band of professional revolutionaries, aiming to "seize power" in the midst of social chaos and breakdown.

What are the structural conditions that might open up the possibility of the New Left transcending its present age and class base? Here are at least some:

- The class base of the movement is rapidly changing as the "youth culture" spreads to the high schools and junior colleges, to army bases and young workers. Along with this cultural diffusion, the mood of resistance spreads—protest is now endemic in high schools, it is evident in the armed forces, it is growing in the junior colleges.

- Inflation and high taxes have led to a decline in real wages. Current fiscal policies generate rising unemployment. A new period of labor militance may have already begun. This situation converges with the influx of postwar youth into the labor force, with the militant organization of black caucuses in unions, with intensifying organization and militance among public employees and with the first efforts by former student radicals to "reach" workers. It may be that in spite of the Wallace phenomenon, racism and the alleged conservatism of the American working class a new radicalism is about to become visible among factory, government and other workers.

- The impoverishment and disintegration of public services, the systematic destruction of the natural environment, urban squalor, the tax burden—all are deeply felt troubles which are directly traceable to the profit system and the military priority. The sense of crisis and frustration that these problems generate throughout society offers the ground for the formulation and promulgation of radical program, action and organization.

- Political repression, although obviously dangerous for the survival of radicalism, can have the effect of intensifying rather than weakening insurgency. This would be particularly true if repression is seen as an assault on whole categories of persons, rather than on handfuls of "outside agitators." So, for instance, many participants in the youth culture now connect their own harassment by the police with the Chicago Conspiracy trial and other government attacks on radicals. Repression at this writing seems more likely to stiffen the mood of resistance among young people than it is to end attacks on "law and order."

- By 1975 there will be well over 50 million adults born since 1940. Most of these will have achieved political consciousness in the past decade. This fact alone suggests a major transformation of the political landscape by the second half of the seventies.

- In the next five years the proportion of the labor force definable as "intelligentsia" will have substantially increased. Current Bureau of Labor Statistics manpower projections for "professional, technical and kindred workers" are for a 40 percent increase in this category between 1966 and 1975, reaching a total of about 13 million in 1975. If my analysis in this essay is correct, this group should be a major source of radicalism in the coming period. The situation of these workers is now dramatically changing from one of high opportunity to relative job scarcity due to current federal and state budgetary policies. Thus one can expect that the radicalization of the intelligentsia will continue to intensify in the years ahead.

One might suggest that these conditions provide the opportunity for a large-scale and successful "new politics" of liberal reform to assert itself. But the current exhaustion of political liberalism may well mean that a new "center-Left" coalition cannot be formed—that we have finally arrived in this country at the point where reformism is no longer viable.

An alternative possibility would be the emergence of a popular socialist party oriented to both "parliamentary" and "extraparliamentary" activity. Although this would certainly facilitate the transcendence of the New Left, there are as yet no signs that such a development is even incipient. In any case, the most important insight of the New Left is that political organization is not enough—the heart of revolution is the reconstruction of civil society and culture.

"THE LONG MARCH"

It may well be that the singular mission of the new mass intelligentsia is to catalyze just such a transformation—to undertake what Rudi Dutschke called "the long march through the institutions of society." This march began in the universities. In coming years it may well continue through all significant cultural, educational, public service and professional institutions. It would have a double aim: to force these institutions to serve the people rather than the corporate system and the state and to engage cultural workers and professionals in struggles to control their work and govern the institutions that coordinate it and determine its use.

It is possible that such struggle by the intelligentsia could stimulate similar struggles in the primary economic institutions—to build a basis for workers' control and for the abolition of technologically unnecessary labor.

In addition to such institutional struggle, the reconstruction of civil society and culture requires the further development of self-organization of communities and especially of exploited and oppressed minorities. Such self-organization—of racial and ethnic minorities and of women—is necessary for any general cultural transformation. Struggle by communities for control of their own development and services prepares the basis for a decentralized and democratized civil society. It is obvious that all such developments have profound need for the services of professional, intellectual, cultural and scientific workers.

It is natural to assume that the development of political, civil and cultural struggle requires central, disciplined organization. My own feeling is that it requires something prior to, and perhaps instead of, the classical revolutionary party. What is really crucial is the organization of local "collectives," "affinity groups," "communes," "cells" of people who share a revolutionary perspective, a common locale of activity, a sense of fraternity, a willingness to bind their fates together. Each such group can be free to work out its priorities, projects and work style. What is necessary is that these groups generally conceive of themselves as catalysts of mass action rather than as utopian communities or elite terrorists. Most of the dramatic movements of the sixties occurred because small groups of friends undertook action that was catalytic or exemplary to larger masses. Most of the exciting cultural development in this period occurred in a similar way. Many of the problems the party is supposed to exist to solve can be coped with without centralization. Problems of communication can be handled by the underground media—which up to now have been the expression of a host of small collectives. National action projects can be coordinated by ad hoc coalitions and umbrella organizations. The generation of resources can be managed through movement banks and quasi foundations. There is no reason why collectives in different or similar milieus cannot meet together to exchange experience. If the purpose of a revolutionary movement is not to seize power but to educate the people to take it for themselves, then a maximally decentralized mode of work is appropriate. And in a period of tightening repression, a cellular rather than centralized mode of organization is obviously advantageous.

The revolution in advanced capitalist society is not a single insurrection. It is not a civil war of pitched battles fought by opposing armies. It is a long, continuing struggle—with political, social and cultural aspects inextricably intertwined. It is already underway. It is not simply a socialist revolution—if by that one means the establishment of a new form of state power that will introduce social planning and redistribute income. It is more than that. For it must be a revolution in which the power to make key decisions is placed in the hands of those whose lives are determined by those decisions. It is not, in short, a revolution aimed at seizing power but a revolution aimed at its dispersal.

It is possible that the New Left's current return to Old Left styles and models signifies that the kind of revolution of which I speak is premature, that the classes and groups that would be most active in producing it have not achieved full consciousness. We are not yet in an age of "post-scarcity," and consequently the revolutionary visions appropriate to that age will have a difficult time establishing their reality. Perhaps, then, the New Left of the sixties is not destined to be the catalyst of the new revolution. I am personally convinced, however, that whatever the immediate destiny of the movement might be, the social and cultural changes that produced it and were accelerated by it are irreversible and cannot be contained within a capitalist framework. Once the material basis for human liberation exists, men will struggle against the institutions that stand in its way. The rise of the student movement in the United States and other industrial societies is a crucial demonstration of the truth of this proposition. For it is a sign that a revolutionary class consciousness appropriate to the era of monopoly capital, advanced technology and dying imperialism is in existence.

18

PATTERNS OF PROTEST:
THE POLITICS OF
BLACK YOUTH IN THE 1960s

ANTHONY M. ORUM

It seems highly improbable that American political life in the decade of the 1970s will be quite as full of political unrest as it was in the decade of the 1960s. This was a time which began with a young president urging a united America to step forward into the future, and ended with a nation divided in many new and fundamental ways. It was a period when large numbers of young people placed themselves in opposition to established authority and values. It was an era in which the material ambitions bred among many people in the depression years were fulfilled and their attainment was found to be unsatisfying; and when the lives of countless others were discovered to be wretched because they lacked the minimum possessions necessary for survival. And it was a time when the "melting pot" revealed itself to be a myth, and the "boiling pot" showed itself to be the true reality of American politics.

At the center of this political maelstrom were distinct portions of the American public. Black Americans were the most vigorous advocates of a substantial reorganization of American politics and, as a consequence, polarized the sentiments of large blocs of other Americans. Small but highly articulate groups of white youths on college campuses also took up the cudgel of protest and by the end of the decade had assumed the twin roles of America's political gadfly and her moral conscience. Black college students especially seemed to have inherited the discontent that came from being both black and young in the America of the sixties. Indeed, when future historians look back upon this decade in American history in a search for its prime movers they may see in the sit-in demonstrations begun by black students in a small North Carolina town in 1960 the portent of things to come in the period.

In this paper, we shall consider some of the developments that took

---

This is an expanded version of the "Epilogue" in Orum's *Black Students in Protest: A Study of the Origins of the Black Student Movement,* Arnold and Caroline Rose Monograph Series (Washington, D.C.: American Sociological Association, 1972).

place in the politics of black youths during the decade of the sixties. We also shall look at some of the conditions which shaped these activities as well as the implications of protest by black young people for American political life in the seventies.

TRANSFORMATION OF THE POLITICS OF BLACK YOUTHS

It was during the decade of the sixties that black college students first emerged as a group to be seriously reckoned with in American politics. Moreover, the mood and dynamics of the movement with which they began the era had fundamentally changed by the end of the era. Their politics had been transformed from a *parochial* to a *mass* phenomenon; from the use of *expressive* strategies of protest to *instrumental* ones; from *integrationist* goals to *separatist* goals; and from being held together by a *religious* ideology to being crystallized about a *political* ideology.

The protests of black youths at the beginning of the sixties were *parochial* in several different respects. First of all, they occupied only a single region of the United States. The thrust of those first black student efforts took place in the South, were directed primarily at Southern institutions, and remained in the South for a period of about four to five years. In addition, the original sit-in movement of black students was *parochial* in that its constituency consisted solely of black students. Although there were groups of white students in the North and the South who engaged in sympathy marches and picketing, these students did not become an active part of the black student movement until about 1964.

The constituency of the early demonstrations by black students was *parochial* in another respect as well. At the start of the decade, the membership of the black student movement was confined not only to black youths, but to those black youths who were from middle-class upbringings. Most of the black young people who became involved in the initial demonstrations were from colleges and, among the college youths who did become active in the protests, one was more apt to find that their parents were comparatively affluent. Moreover, the reference group of the original black student movement, that group whose style of life and goals the black students seemed to emulate, consisted of white middle-class students. In fact, some social scientists saw in the comparisons that the black college young people drew between themselves and this group of white youths sufficient motive for the outbreak of the protest movement.

Finally, the political demonstrations of black college students at the beginning of the decade were *parochial* in so far as their objectives were limited and specific. Particular stores, or chains of stores, were the targets of the student sit-in demonstrations, picketing, and boycotts. And even though such businesses may have been selected in some instances as part of a larger plan, that plan itself called simply for establishing equal access to public facilities. Only later in the decade did the objectives of the student protestors proliferate and become more general.

By the middle of the sixties, the politics of black young people had lost many of its *parochial* characteristics. In a word, the movement begun by the black college students turned into a *mass* phenomenon. The changes were evident in the above dimensions. The political efforts of young black Americans spread from a single region to diverse locations. Not only did they branch out into the far West, Midwest, and Northeast, but the student demonstrations also moved from predominantly black college campuses to white college campuses, and even to sites where there were no campuses at all. In addition, the membership of the black student movement was no longer made up only of black students, but comprised white students as well. Beginning perhaps in 1963, but certainly by 1964, the constituency of the black student movement changed from being composed primarily of black young people to a mixture of black and white. Indeed, so many white youths entered the activities that they eventually became a source of resentment among the young black Americans and a visible reason for altering the movement's objectives. In addition, as early as 1964, a new sort of young black American—one from a lower, rather than a middle-class background—had begun to participate in the movement. And by the end of the decade the black youth movement, though now lacking the active support of previously sympathetic white students, widened to encompass numbers of young blacks who lived in the urban ghettoes of America.

Partly as a result of the enlarged and diversified black membership of the movement, the reference group of the politically active black youths also became transformed. Black young people at the end of the decade had chosen to identify only with black people and sought to pattern their political aspirations and objectives in America after those of black people in other nations, particularly Africa.

A last way in which the political movement of young black Americans changed from a *parochial* to a *mass* phenomenon during the decade of the sixties was in terms of its political objectives. By the latter half of this period, the activities of black young people had come to include work for voting rights and black political candidates, demands for changes in the educational system and curriculum revisions to include courses such as Afro-American history in American colleges, and demands for black ownership of businesses in the black ghettoes. In short, the political goals of black youngsters over the course of the decade became more diverse and numerous, paralleling the increased diversity and numbers of the black student movement's constituency.

Besides the transformation from a *parochial* to a *mass* movement, by the end of the decade one could observe other differences in the politics of young black Americans. The style of the protest marches and other demonstrations changed in several respects. First of all, the strategy of the participants was transformed from an *expressive* to an *instrumental* one. In the first few years of the black student movement, sit-ins, wade-ins, jail-ins and related protests were undertaken as much to manifest a general dissatisfaction with the "system" as to attain particular ends. To have been jailed was as worthy of respect among black student participants in the movement as to have attained the desegregation of a particular place of business. In contrast, at the end of the decade and the beginning of the seventies, there was greater emphasis placed on the negotiable character of student demands, symbolized in the shift of the confrontation between black youths and authorities from the sidewalks to the conference room.

Among the more dramatic and potentially more influential alterations in the politics of young black Americans during the sixties was the change from a *religious* to a *political* ideology. *The Student Nonviolent Coordinating Committee,* founded in 1961 as a means of coordinating the political efforts of black students, was notable for a religious spirit which pervaded the organization and the lives of its members. The founding charter read, in part:

> We affirm the philosophical ideal of nonviolence as the foundation of our purpose, the pre-supposition of our faith, and the manner of our action. Nonviolence as it grows from Judaic-Christian traditions seeks a social order of justice permeated by love.[1]

Yet, by about 1966, after experiences in places like Mississippi and Alabama, individual leaders in the black student movement and the civil rights movement as a whole began to question the ability of a religious faith in nonviolence to effect enduring change between whites and blacks in America. Increasingly, the energies of young black Americans became directed toward acquiring power, both as an end in itself and as a way of making sure that black Americans got their fair share in the American system. Finally, by the very end of the era, *SNCC* was virtually nonexistent and the star of more militant groups like the Black Panthers shone far brighter on the political horizon.

Another development of black youths' politics during the sixties was the change from *integrationist* to *separatist* goals. The objectives of those young Afro-Americans who involved themselves in demonstrations in the early sixties were to attain equal benefits and privileges for blacks by integrating with whites in restaurants, bus stations and similar places. Black students in the early sixties believed that integration meant equality, and vice-versa. And once the protest brought about eating, traveling and even voting together among blacks and whites, students then felt that they had achieved their ends. But in the latter part of the era, *integrationist* ideals surrendered to *separatist* ones. Black young people cared little for integration in any form. The structure of the joint ventures between white and black youths in things like the Mississippi

---

[1] James Lawson, Draft of *SNCC* Statement of Purpose, 14 May 1960; reprinted in Joanne Grant, ed., *Black Protest: History, Documents and Analyses* (New York: Fawcett World Library, 1968), pp. 289–90.

Summer Project of 1964 proved to many black youngsters that integration in American society inevitably meant blacks taking orders from whites. Black youths came to believe that equality could only be achieved if blacks and whites worked separately, and began to emphasize the intrinsic advantages in being a member of the black population and having a black heritage. By 1968 and 1969, many black students on white and black college campuses were urging the establishment of residence halls just for black people, and the adoption of a wide range of courses about the contribution of black Americans to American life.

These developments in the politics of black youths during the sixties were substantial and profound ones. What took place in this era to bring about these changes? Let us turn to examine some possible answers to this question.

SOURCES OF TRANSFORMATION

Some of the seeds of the black youth protest and its transformation over the decade of the sixties were found in America long before the actual outbreak of the sit-ins, marches and picketing in 1960. Outstanding among these was the tension that enveloped the lives of many black persons in America because of the distinction between their legal rights and actual opportunities. Those things to which black Americans were entitled by law were nowhere to be found in everyday life. The "dilemma," as Gunnar Myrdal called it, became especially visible to black young people after the Supreme Court in 1954 required the desegregation of schools "with all deliberate speed." By the beginning of the sixties, most colleges and universities in America—and all of them in the South—still had not permitted the enrollment of any black students. Black young people were forced to attend the poorly equipped and staffed black institutions and faced the prospects of far poorer educational training than the law prescribed for them. The situation, many observers felt, was appropriately ripe for protest by black students.

Coupled with this fact was the tension that resulted from the enormous disparity between the aspirations and opportunities of black young people in America. The occupational and economic prospects for black youths after college were far dimmer than those of their white peers, yet the black students possessed many of the same goals and aspirations. As one social scientist remarked about the problem: "We might speak of the motivation provided the civil rights movement by the discovery on the part of thousands of young Negroes that their coveted education wasn't worth much on the open market." [2]

Were these two sources of tension for young black Americans—the gaps between their legal rights and actual opportunities, and between their aspirations and opportunities—to have diminished appreciably in

---

[2] Paul M. Siegel, "On the Cost of Being a Negro," *Sociological Inquiry* 35 (Winter 1965): 57.

the sixties, then their protest movement might have kept its same form and certainly would have declined in intensity. But in the eyes of many black youngsters the disparities were not reduced. The rate of employment, the kinds of positions open in industry, the financial rewards offered by the system, all continued to greatly favor the educated white American. Thus, black young people had to face the fact that the spirit, strategy and goals of their protests at the beginning of the period seemed to have had very little effect in altering the system so as to accommodate their desires and the desires of other black Americans.

It was quite natural, then, that black young people would not only increase the intensity of their protests during the sixties, but also act to alter the nature of these activities. The change from a religiously-inspired, nonviolent protest to a politically-inspired, militant action would almost seem to be an inevitable consequence of black students' continuing inability to achieve equality with white youths. So, too, the replacement of a *religious* ideology with a *political Weltanschauung* would seem to require the substitution of instrumental tactics for primarily *expressive* ones. Moreover, the discovery by many Americans in the early sixties that the discrepancies between rights and opportunities, and between aspirations and opportunities existed for blacks in the North as well as the South helped to make possible the transition of the black student movement from a *parochial* to a *mass* effort, especially insofar as it prompted the spread of the movement northward and encouraged white students to participate.

A related factor that acted to transform the political movement of young black Americans was the intransigent attitude of many individual white citizens to the demands of their fellow black citizens. Curiously enough, the earliest and some of the most vigorous demonstrations by black college youths arose in areas of the South where the resistance by whites seemed to be weakest. But as the decade unfolded, and as the demonstrations by black students and other black Americans persisted, the charitable feelings of white Americans toward black people declined to their lowest point in many years.

Scholars who reflect on these events will probably note distinct times and places when the attitude of white Americans measurably affected the nature of the black youth movement. Among such incidents, one may count the experiences in Alabama and Mississippi in 1963 and 1964. The great influx of white youths into the black student movement came about because of the virtual inability of young black people and other black Americans to get the white citizens of these states to provide them with equal rights in education and politics. Political overtones to the spirit of the protests by black youths—in contrast to the religious ones— emerged as a result of the experiences in Mississippi during the summer of 1964 and were exemplified in the establishment of the Mississippi Freedom Democratic Party in that same year. Young black leaders such as Stokely Carmichael seemed to grow convinced after the frustrations in Alabama and Mississippi that the success of black people in America could only be secured through the acquisition and use of force. There were additional episodes in the sixties which symbolized the heightened intransigence of white Americans and proved to be turning points in the transformation of black student protest, among them the assassinations of such political figures as Medgar Evers in 1963 and Martin Luther King, Jr. in 1968.

Another key role in transforming certain aspects of the politics of black youths during the sixties was played by the mass media. Like the forces already mentioned, television and newspapers were not sufficient by themselves to bring about modifications of the black youth political phenomenon. But without their existence and influence the black youth protest would probably have remained a *parochial* type of movement. Not only did the media's coverage of demonstrations help to spread these demonstrations throughout the South, but it provided national exposure to the protests by black youngsters and laid the groundwork for the development of these activities throughout America. An enlarged and more heterogeneous constituency of the black student movement was a further consequence of the information about marches and picketing black students reported in newspapers and on television. Moreover, the changes in the protest movement involving the shifts from identification with a white reference group to a black reference group, and from *integrationist* to *separatist* ideals, were made possible by the news in the media about nationalist movements developing among black people in Africa.

None of the changes in the fabric of protest by black youths would have been possible in the sixties, however, without the appearance of three outstanding black leaders: Malcolm X, Stokely Carmichael and Eldridge Cleaver. At the start of the era, Martin Luther King, Jr. had furnished the inspiration for the nonviolent and religious character of the demonstrations, but by the middle of the decade his influence on young black Americans had been eclipsed. In part, the emergence of these three as spokesmen for black youngsters and many other black Americans was a response to the kinds of tensions in the period we have already talked about. Yet, these men were more than mere reflections of their times. They were creators as well and seemed to provide a special shape and direction to the unarticulated hopes of many black young people.

The membership of the black youth movement as well as of the overall efforts on behalf of black people in America was enlarged appreciably by the work of Malcolm X, Carmichael and Cleaver. The first of these men, for example, seemed to have an uncommon gift for voicing the thoughts of residents of the black ghettoes. His own upbringing in a lower-class slum and years spent in jails demonstrated that politics was a suitable vocation for lower-class black youths. Cleaver, as Minister of Information for the Black Panther Party, was successful in many of the same ways and yet he appealed equally to the idealism of white young people.

The growth of the identification with blacks throughout the world and the separatist ideals of black youngsters were fostered by these three individuals as well, particularly by Malcolm X. He believed that black people in America would only be effective in their drive to attain equal status and power with white people if they established a unity with black people in other nations. During the early sixties, he argued that:

> Today, power is international. . . . Real power is not local. . . . When you see that the African nations at the international level comprise the largest representative body and the largest force of any continent, why, you and I would be out of our minds not to identify with that power bloc.[3]

The organization which he founded after his split with the Black Muslims and Elijah Muhammed in 1964, the Organization for Afro-American Unity, became a vehicle for implementing these ideas. Towards the end of the decade, Carmichael picked up these same themes and made them popular among many of the black youths throughout the country.

Malcolm X, Carmichael and Cleaver also were partly responsible for effecting the changes in the black student movement from an ideology relying upon *religious* motives to one that relied upon *political* motives, and from an overriding concern with *expressive* goals to a similar emphasis upon *instrumental* ends. Malcolm X's departure from the Black Muslims revealed his own feelings about the futility of a movement devoted to improving the life of black Americans solely through religious stoicism. And at the same time, he believed that the black community had to turn to political actions to break the grip of the white community in America. "A ballot," he once claimed, "is like a bullet. You don't throw your ballots until you see a target, and if that target is not within your reach, keep your ballots in your pocket." [4]

In conclusion, the differences between the style and strategy of the politics of black youths at the beginning and end of the sixties can be traced to several major forces in America: the continuing discrepancies between the rights and opportunities of black young people, on the one hand, and their aspirations and opportunities, on the other hand; the growing reluctance of white people to permit black people to share the resources of America; the nationwide exposure in the news media of the demonstrations by black young people; and the ideas and ideologies of particular black leaders. Let us turn now to examine how some of these changes in black youth protest may affect the future of this phenomenon in America.

THE FUTURE OF PROTEST BY BLACK YOUTHS

Many people wonder whether the new form of black student political action can be any more effective in achieving an equitable distribution of wealth and power among all Americans than its predecessor was in the

---

[3] Malcolm X, *Malcolm X Speaks* (New York: Merit Publishers, 1965), pp. 137–38. Copyright © 1965 by Merit Publishers and Betty Shabazz; reprinted by permission.
[4] Ibid., pp. 38–39.

early sixties. Can a *mass* phenomenon succeed where a *parochial* one failed? Or can *separatist* goals and *instrumental* tactics prompt a fairer distribution of social, economic and political resources than *integrationist* ideals and *expressive* strategies of protest?

To begin with, there are some scholars who argue that the transformation of protest by black young people into a *mass* phenomenon will not simply bring about the reallocation of benefits in American society, but will result in a destruction of all her foundations as well. We do not agree that the *mass* features of the new political efforts will be nearly so potent. Protests on a mass scale by black young people could only radically alter the structure of American society if they were guided and directed by a single organization. But there is no such organization now and its development in the future appears unlikely. Many of the concerns of black youths in the urban ghettoes are quite literally worlds apart from the interest of their counterparts on college campuses. Moreover, the numbers of politically active black young people as well as their widespread dispersion throughout America almost render a single master plan for their dissent virtually unattainable.

Besides this, the fact that the constituency of the black youth political phenomenon has become so diverse has also meant that its audience can no longer be easily identified. It was quite evident that the audience of the earliest of black student protests in the sixties was the same as the constituency, and that it consisted primarily of middle-class black students. But as the membership of the movement began to envelop different kinds of groups, such as lower-class black youths and middle-class white youths, it became more and more difficult for leaders to agree upon whom they should address. Should their appeals be directed at white liberals, for instance? Or, at the white conservatives in America? Or, at the black poor people in places like Harlem? As a result of this diminishing sense of coherence in the membership and audience of the movement, the effectiveness of the movement began to suffer a similar fate.

Moreover, the protests of black youths are beginning to demonstrate that a *mass* political phenomenon in contemporary American society is as likely to be destroyed as to be produced by the news media. The media have assiduously reported the activities of the young black leaders, minor as well as major ones. They have gone to great lengths to present to the public many of the trivial details about the political actions by black young people. But so extensive has the news been that it has produced a tremendous sense of boredom about the concerns of black youths among their followers and detractors alike. The thrust and excitement which once was part of the political demonstrations by black young people have been eroded by overexposure in the press.

The ability of the new political movement by black young people to fashion a reorganization of American society depends not only on its characteristics as a *mass* movement, but on its other features, too—that is, its *political* ideology, its *separatist* goals, and its *instrumental* tactics. However, even these features of the protests by black youths, represented in the activities of such groups as the Black Panthers in urban ghettoes, seem unlikely to bring about a larger share of wealth and power for black Americans, at least in the immediate future. As the protests by these young people have become more militant, they have elicited an ever increasing hostile response from white groups and organizations which could have helped them to achieve their goals. The white urban liberals who once could be counted among the strongest supporters of the campaign for equal rights by black Americans have become some of the most vociferous opponents of these efforts. The only chance that the new form of politics by black youths in urban America can succeed despite white hostility is one which lies in the distant future and with the very youngest of black Americans who now are being trained in large numbers in the spirit of black self-consciousness by young black political activists.

The prospects of immediate success of the new protests by black youths appear to be greatest on the campuses of many predominantly white colleges and universities throughout America. Already it has been shown at particular schools, such as Cornell University, that the new *instrumental* tactics and *separatist* goals of the black students could effect a change in the living conditions and educational curricula. But such success is not always guaranteed for the protest by black students and seems to be contingent on different characteristics of the college itself.

There is the question, first of all, of who runs the university, the state, or some other public body, or a private agency. Generally speaking, black students have been most able to get their demands accepted on campuses where the public, or the government, in effect, as guardian of the public interest, is least able to affect the campus situation. Although privately-operated institutions most often fit this situation, many such institutions now heavily rely on government funds to operate and thus their internal affairs are subject to careful scrutiny by the government. Antioch College, a privately-controlled institution, is a case in point. In 1968, Antioch officials acceded to the *separatist* demands of black students by establishing a dormitory restricted to the black students and by creating a curriculum in Afro-American studies. Inasmuch as such segregated facilities and educational programs were against the law, the government threatened to withdraw its substantial financial support of this institution. The government agreed, however, to withhold its decision until it examined the results from an experimental plan in which white students would be allowed to join the all-black dormitory if they wished. None, however, applied so that the dormitory remains segregated in *fact,* though not by law. When this case is finally settled, it will set the precedent for the freedom of other institutions that rely heavily on government funds to establish similar facilities and programs solely for the benefit of black students.

The fact that black students are able to affect the living conditions and educational curricula at colleges throughout America may only give the illusion of success. The educational system in America is bound to change in the seventies because the majority of students are beginning to see that their educational training is not relevant to their needs and desires. The development of courses in Afro-American studies will only be one of many changes to occur, and will undoubtedly happen with or without the insistence of many black students. Moreover, if one were to evaluate the programs that black students have been able to get adopted at white educational institutions by their ability to redistribute power and wealth in America, then they by no means qualify as victories, certainly not in the immediate future. The substance of educational programs is simply too far removed and too different from economic and political affairs to have much immediate impact on them. As in the case of the pursuits by black youths in urban ghettoes, we may have to wait many years to see whether the new Afro-American studies programs so affect the consciousness of black and white youths that they produce genuine changes in the American way of life.

part VI

COMPARATIVE PERSPECTIVES ON YOUTH AND POLITICS IN AMERICA

Where the contemporary politics of young people in America stand in relation to those of other young people is to be sought not merely in looking at history, but also in examining what has happened to youth at present in other nations. The object of such a comparison is partly to provide a means for assessing the uniqueness of the American situation and partly to determine the more general principles involved in the political activism of young people.

These issues are treated at length by the two articles included in this section. In the first one, Seymour Martin Lipset examines the characteristics of the politics of youth in the developing nations of the world. After an extensive study of many countries, Lipset concludes that "it may be said that where the society, the university and the student are committed to the fullest development of research and teaching in an atmosphere of academic freedom, and where adequate resources are available in the form of faculty, libraries, laboratories, and financial support, students are less likely to engage in political activities . . ."

The article by Raymond Aron, on the other hand, analyzes and compares the quality of student politics among nations that basically are industrialized, including the United States, Germany, and France. Aron believes that there are common threads underlying the student activism in many of these nations, among them the emergence of a new generation untouched by the effects of

World War II, the democratization of higher education, and the general growth of technology in society. Yet, he also believes that there are certain cultural and national differences, and comments on these with particular regard to the French student uprisings in 1968.

19

UNIVERSITY STUDENTS
AND POLITICS IN
UNDERDEVELOPED COUNTRIES

THE UNIVERSITY
IN UNDERDEVELOPED COUNTRIES [1]

The tasks of the universities in the underdeveloped countries of the world are fundamentally not very different from what they are in more highly developed societies. They must transmit in a more differentiated and more specific way the cultural heritage—the history, the scientific knowledge, the literature—of their society and of the world culture of which their society is a part; they must train persons who will become members of the elites of their societies to exercise skills in science, technology, management, and administration; they must cultivate the capacity for leadership and a sense of responsibility to their fellow countrymen, and they must train them to be constructively critical, to be able to initiate changes while appreciating what they have inherited. The universities must contribute new knowledge to the world's pool of knowledge and must stimulate in some of the students, at least, the desire to become original contributors to this pool, as well as equipping them with the knowledge and discipline which, given adequate endowment, will enable them to do so. Regardless of whether the university system seeks to educate only a very small fraction of the stratum of university age or a quite large proportion, these tasks remain the indispensable minimum. A university system which fails to perform these functions, however useful it might be in other respects, is not doing its job. It will become parasitic on the university systems of other countries and will be unable to cope with the tasks of national development.

From *Minerva* 3, no. 1 (Autumn 1964): 15–56; reprinted by permission of the author.

[1] There are also a number of recent articles, books, and theses concerned with issues of students and politics. Probably the best source for these materials is Philip G. Altbach, ed., *Select Bibliography on Students, Politics, and Higher Education* (Cambridge: Center for International Affairs, Harvard University, 1967).

In the underdeveloped countries, the role of the universities is especially important because the elites of the modern sector of the society are drawn very largely from the reservoir of persons with university training. There is no class of indigenous business enterprises who, without university training, have taken or are likely to be allowed to take the main responsibility for economic development—as they did in Europe and America in the nineteenth century. There is no class of highly skilled artisans from whom significant technological innovations will come forth. There is very little research in most new states, apart from the little that is done in universities—although the balance is now beginning to change in favor of nonuniversity research establishments. Much of the intellectual journalism, e.g., analytical commentary on public policy, emanates from the universities. Thus the universities alone must not only produce much of the elite which must modernize the society, but they are also almost solely responsible for the conduct of intellectual life in general in their own countries. A substantial proportion of the political elite, too, is bound to emerge from the ranks of university graduates, even in a time of populistic politics.

The universities of the underdeveloped countries bear the burden of being in an age of nationalism, institutions part of whose task it is to propagate a universal culture and to contribute to its growth, while simultaneously cultivating and developing the indigenous, actual or potential national culture and enhancing national life. The task of interpreting the indigenous cultural inheritance through linguistics, anthropology, sociology, historiography, literary history, and criticism must also be conducted according to standards and procedures of universal validity. Not only do the substance and procedure of university study partake of universality, but they are from the beginning of the modern age, and still at present, derived from the accomplishments of academics and amateurs of the Western, Central, and Northern European culture area, including the North American, the very areas of the world against which the twentieth-century nationalism of Asia, Africa, and Latin America is asserting itself. The situation is not made easier politically and pedagogically by the fact that in Africa, and in major areas of Asia, university teaching and scientific writing are still conducted in the languages of the former colonial powers. Even where this is not so, a university to perform its functions well must still, and will for some time to come, depend on books and periodicals written and printed in the metropolitan countries. Moreover, the universities of the underdeveloped countries must still share the performance of their tasks with the metropolitan universities, which for much of the world carry the major responsibility for advanced training in science and scholarship.[2]

---

2 Systematic inquiry into the problems of overseas students has scarcely begun. Some pioneer works are Amar Kumar Singh, *Indian Students in Britain* (London and Bombay: Asia Publishing Co., 1963), and Prodosh Aich, *Farbige unter Weissen* (Berlin and Cologne: Kiepenheuer und Witsch, 1962). These books have been summarized in the following articles: Amar Kumar Singh, "Indian Students in Britain," *Minerva* 1,

Under these circumstances, the universities are bound to be subject to pressure from their politically sensitive fellow countrymen and from the opinion of their academic colleagues overseas. They will also be under pressure from their own student bodies, who at the most sensitive and reactive stage of life are being subjected to a discipline which is alien to their own indigenous social and cultural traditions and on their performance on which, assessed by "alien standards," their future will largely depend. Universities to be successful must form a community which embraces students as well as teachers and research workers. Universities must develop a culture of their own. This culture must go beyond the bodies of specific knowledge which are taught and cultivated and extend to a vague ethos of attitudes and sensibilities, of standards and canons of judgment which must be assimilated and cannot be explicitly taught.[3]

It is difficult enough to infuse such a culture into a new generation even in societies where the culture of the university is more or less integral to the indigenous culture. It is even more so in underdeveloped countries, where it is still in greater or lesser measure an alien culture, alien to the background from which the students come.

The central tasks of the university cannot be performed without the assimilation of the student body into the university community, which is a graded community, inevitably hierarchical by virtue of differences in age and competence. This task is not an easy one, but on its effective performance depends the success of the university in the performance of its essential functions.

University students are not, however, merely prospective members of the elites of their countries. Particularly in the underdeveloped countries, university students do not just prepare themselves for future roles in public life; they play a significant part in the political life of their countries even during their student period. The intensity of the university students' political activity is in some sense a measure of the failure of the

---

no. 1 (Autumn 1962): 43–53, and Prodosh Aich, "Asian and African Students in West German Universities," *Minerva* 1, no. 4 (Summer 1963): 439–52. Cf. also J. M. Meijer, *Knowledge and Revolution: The Russian Colony in Zurich (1870–1873), A Contribution to the Study of Russian Populism* (Assen: Van Gorcum and Comp., 1955); Claire Selltiz et al., *Attitudes and Social Relations of Foreign Students in the United States* (Minneapolis: University of Minnesota Press, 1963); Ralph Beals and Norman Humphrey, *No Frontier to Learning: The Mexican Student in the United States* (Minneapolis: University of Minnesota Press, 1957); John W. Bennett, Herbert Passin, and Robert McKnight, *In Search of Identity: The Japanese Overseas Scholar in America and Japan* (Minneapolis: University of Minnesota Press, 1958); Richard D. Lambert and Marvin Bressler, *Indian Students on an American Campus* (Minneapolis: University of Minnesota Press, 1956); Richard Morris, *The Two-Way Mirror: National Status in Foreign Students' Adjustment* (Minneapolis: University of Minnesota Press, 1960); John Useem and Ruth Hill Useem, *The Western Educated Man in India* (New York: Dryden Press, 1955).

3 Michael Polanyi has best described the nature of this community, particularly the mode by which "tacit knowledge" is communicated. Cf. *Personal Knowledge* (London: Routledge and Kegan Paul, 1958); *Science, Faith and Society* (London: Oxford University Press, 1946; reprinted Chicago University Press, 1964); and "The Republic of Science: Its Political and Economic Theory," *Minerva* 1, no. 1 (Autumn 1962): 54–73.

university as an academic community. This is not necessarily and always so, but it does seem to be so in the underdeveloped countries where universities operate under severe handicaps of unfavorable traditions and a paucity of resources, human and financial, and where student politics are frequently associated with the rejection of the intellectual leadership of the faculty of the universities.

Quite apart from the influence of the life of the university itself on the students' disposition toward politics, the position of the student in an underdeveloped society is itself conducive to political preoccupations. For one thing, the modern educated classes of the former colonial countries of Asia and Africa were the creators of the political life of their countries. University students and, where there were no universities, secondary school students, played important roles as adjuncts to the movements for independence. Students at overseas universities became nationalists in the course of their sojourn in a foreign country, and they organized political bodies which, at least in the case of the African countries, were the first steps toward independence. Much of the political life of the colonial period allowed little freedom in terms of normal political activity, and strikes and demonstrations became major forms of political activity. Students were ideally suited, by the disposition of adolescence in situations of relatively safe rebellion against authority, for such activities. The political tradition then engendered has persisted into independence.

Their self-consciousness as a distinctive group with high status and with relative immunity from severe repression has also continued into independence. In societies where learning has been associated with religion and earthly authority, students, as aspirants to that learning, have enjoyed great respect. University students, too, are quite often the offspring of families of some eminence in their respective countries. Their status as kinsmen of the incumbent elites, and as prospective members of the elite themselves, affords them a special position among oppositional groups. They tend to be confident that the harsh suppression to which other opposition groups are subject will not fall to their lot. This, too, encourages their entry into the political sphere.

It should also be pointed out that public opinion in underdeveloped countries is not constituted by the views of a large and educated middle class of professional and business men and women. Because of the small size of the educated middle class, students in certain underdeveloped countries make up a disproportionately large section of the bearers of public opinion; their various affinities of education, class, and kinship with the actual elites give them an audience which students in more developed countries can seldom attain.

Finally, university students in underdeveloped countries are the heirs of a European tradition of student politics. In Germany and Russia, student politics gave much animation to the movement for national renewal and progress in the nineteenth century.[4] In France, too, in the nineteenth

---

[4] Cf. Armad Coquart, *Dmitri Pisarev (1840–1888) et l'idéologie du nihilisme russe* (Paris: Institut d'Études Slaves de l'Université de Paris, 1946), pp. 24–44; Martin Malia,

and twentieth centuries, university students have been significantly drawn toward revolutionary, agitational, and demonstrative politics. The traditions of European liberalism, rationalism, and nationalism found their main recipients in underdeveloped countries, within the ranks of the educated classes. All these movements have left behind a precipitate which has entered into the nationalist and oppositional politics of the underdeveloped countries, both those which have recently been colonial and those long independent.

Endemic to all progressive societies has been a tension between the intellectuals, religious and secular, who seek to transmit and affirm traditional views and those engaged in research and artistic creativity whose roles require them to criticize, revise, and supplant tradition. The latter value new discoveries and innovation, not the reproduction, copying, or transmission of old discoveries and ideas. Originality, departure from what is established and officially accepted, is a central value in the outlook of the modern intellectual. More generally, in the tradition of the intellectual classes of Western society, there are important currents of long duration and great intellectual value which have set the intellectuals against established authority.[5] These include scientism, romanticism, revolutionary apocalypticism, and populism. These traditions largely form the characteristic outlook of the intellectuals outside universities. Universities have been institutions established by or supported by the authoritative center of society—political and ecclesiastical—and they have been more integrated into the tasks of training young persons for careers connected with the central functions of society and culture. But they, too, by their stress on scientific discipline and detachment from the idols of the market place, have nurtured a critical attitude. Especially in the social sciences has there been a tension between the affirmation of the dominant systems of practices and beliefs and a critical attitude toward those systems.[6]

It is this antitraditional outlook of modern Western intellectual life which has found reception among the intellectuals of the underdeveloped

Alexander Herzen and the Birth of Russian Socialism: 1812–1855 (Cambridge, Mass.: Harvard University Press, 1961), Ch. 4, pp. 57–68; Valentin Gitermann, *Geschichte Russlands* (Hamburg: Europäische Verlagsanstalt GmbH, 1949), vol. 3, part 8, Chapters 2 and 4, pp. 212–52 and 272–301; Karl Griewank, *Deutsche Studenten und Universitäten in der Revolution von 1848* (Weimar: Hermann Bohlaus Nachfolger, 1949); Carl Brinkmann, *Der Nationalismus und die deutschen Universitäten im Zeitalter der deutschen Erhebung* (Heidelberg: Carl Winters Universitätsbuchhandlung, 1932).

[5] Cf. Edward Shils, "The Intellectuals and the Powers," *Comparative Studies in Society and History* 1, no. 1 (1958): 15–21.

[6] Cf. Robert Waelder, who writes that antagonism between intellectuals and the dominant institutions and classes has existed

> "To some degree . . . in all societies in which intellectuals have enjoyed the freedom of expression. Since the days of the Sophists, they have been in the habit of questioning and challenging the values and the assumptions that were taken for granted in their societies. . . . Intellect tends to question and thereby to undermine dogma and tradition. The act of understanding, said the historian of science Charles Coulston Gillespie, is an act of alienation. . . . Alienation is an aspect of emancipation."

"Protest and Revolution against Western Societies," in Morton A. Kaplan, ed., *The Revolution in World Politics* (New York: John Wiley, 1962), p. 15.

countries, and it provides the point of departure of the youngest generation of intellectuals in those countries.

A not unimportant factor which has encouraged the presence of critical,
antitraditional opinions and groups on campuses is the tradition of corporate autonomy of the university, which became established on the European continent in the Middle Ages. The norm has become strong enough
in recent years in the United States, and for a longer time in Great Britain
and France, to protect the freedom of social scientists and others to present
views in writing and in the lecture halls, which are antithetical to the economic, political, and religious views of those who govern the university or
the society. In tsarist Russia, university autonomy operated at times to
allow the adult sections of illegal revolutionary groups to hold meetings
in university precincts, without interference by the police. In Venezuela,
in recent years, terrorists have exploited this tradition of university autonomy by using the university precincts as a sanctuary from the police.
Seemingly, the recognition that a university must have freedom if it is
to carry out its function as a source of innovation has been more powerful
in many countries than the threat such freedom might pose to the political and economic self-interest of the dominant elites.

The way in which such norms arise has been described in the case of
Meiji Japan, whose late nineteenth-century leaders imitated Humboldt
and the Prussian educational reformers in consciously recognizing the
need to differentiate between the "indoctrination" function of primary
education and the "creative" role of the universities in fostering research
and training leaders. The initial educational ordinances drawn up by
the Minister of Education, Arinori Mori, in the 1880s were explicitly concerned with such distinctions. He

> believed that primary education, by being based on the doctrines of Japanese
> nationalism and militarism, would help teach the people to be loyal to the
> state while they were still in the formative period of their lives. But he also
> believed that if education were limited to the primary level, leaders could
> not be produced with sufficient grasp of science and technology to contribute
> to the prosperity of the nation. He was therefore convinced that, in both
> research and instruction, universities and professional schools should assume
> the task of preparing such leaders and that *sufficient and appropriate freedom
> should be allowed for this purpose.* . . .[7]

It is, therefore, not surprising that university students, when they develop political concerns, should be more radical than the classes from
which they come even in the underdeveloped nations. In the United
States, where, until recently, university students have not played a notable
part in public or political affairs, they are much more prone to favor the

---

[7] Michio Nagai, "The Development of Intellectuals in the Meiji and Taisho Periods,"
Journal of Social and Political Ideas in Japan 2, no. 1 (April 1964): 29. Although Mori
favored freedom within the Imperial University of Tokyo, "he was convinced that
what was taught in Tokyo University should not be conveyed to the masses since too
much free thought among the masses might pose a threat to the regime."

Democratic party and to support liberal and even socialist measures than is the middle class in general.[8] Likewise, in Britain and most European countries, the leftist parties are considerably stronger among university students than they are in the rest of the middle class.

STUDENTS AND POLITICS IN COMMUNIST COUNTRIES

The situation in the various communist countries, of course, has been quite different, particularly in Stalin's time. Public oppositional politics have rarely been possible. It is noteworthy, however, that students and intellectuals have played a major role in the movements to liberalize the totalitarian regimes. This was especially true in Poland and Hungary in 1956. In Poland the chief critical magazine was a student journal, *Po Prostu* (Plain Talk), which served as the main rallying point for the liberal elements as long as it was allowed to exist.[9] In Hungary, also, the university student body was a major force in the groups leading the uprising.[10] In the Soviet Union, intellectuals, particularly young ones, including students, have played a major role in demands for reform, insisting on more freedom and more intellectual integrity. A former student of Moscow University now living abroad reports that while

> it is difficult to give exact figures, . . . my estimate of the proportion of Soviet students whose political discontent was revealed during the thaw of 1956 would be from one-fourth to one-third of the total. With the exception

---

8 Unpublished data from an ongoing American study of student attitudes in several colleges and universities in different parts of the United States reveal that students by and large are more likely to prefer the Democratic party, and for this preference to increase from their first year in university onward. Study of Selected Institutions, Center for the Study of Higher Education, University of California, Berkeley. Many studies reveal the effect of education, especially at the university level, in reducing prejudice and increasing liberal and tolerant attitudes. See, for example, Charles Herbert Stember, *Education and Attitude Change* (New York: Institute of Human Relations Press, 1961); and Samuel A. Stouffer, *Commission, Conformity, and Civil Liberties* (Garden City: Doubleday, 1955), pp. 89–108. Evidence for Britain is provided in a British Gallup youth poll conducted in 1959. For Germany, a comparison of party preferences among university students, in Jürgen Habermas et al., *Student und Politik* (Neuwied am Rhein und Berlin: Hermann Luchterhand Verlag, 1961), p. 290, with those of university-educated voters in .Wolfgang Hirsch-Weber and Klaus Schütz, *Wähler und Gewählte* (Berlin und Frankfurt a.M.: Verlag Franz Vahlen GmbH, 1957), p. 309, reveals a higher preference among students for the Social Democratic party.

9 See Flora Lewis, *The Polish Volcano* (London: Secker and Warburg, 1959), pp. 67–69, 134–35. *Po Prostu* was shut down in October 1957, one year after the demonstrations which had opened the way to liberalization. Students rioted for four days in vain protest; pp. 255–56. See also William R. McIntyre, "Students' Movements," *Editorial Research Reports* 2, no. 23 (11 December 1957): 915–16.

10 The first demonstrations in Hungary in 1956 were those of the university students. Student organizations were also the first groups formed breaking openly with Communist party control. See Paul Kecskemeti, *The Unexpected Revolution: Social Forces in the Hungarian Uprising* (Stanford University Press, 1961), pp. 79–82, 106–9.

of the professional activists, the remaining played the familiar role of "the masses": their attitude toward the political avant-garde was sometimes sympathetic, sometimes uncomprehending, but rarely hostile.[11]

During 1956–1957, following the 20th Party Congress, there were open attacks on the leadership of the Young Communist League, with demands for more freedom and democracy:

> Illegal and semilegal student journals with such characteristic titles as *Heresy* and *Fresh Voices* began to appear; they discussed art and ideology, ridiculed socialist realism, and attacked the local Komsomol leaders. Wall newspapers began to print "undesirable articles. . . ." Finally during the Hungarian uprising an account of the events, as gathered from a British Broadcasting Company [*sic*] broadcast, was posted on a bulletin board in the University of Moscow. . . .[12]

In Communist China, the year 1957 witnessed the "Hundred Flowers" campaign, in which criticism was openly encouraged by Mao Tse-tung and other party leaders. The results startled the regime, since for five weeks it was exposed to a barrage of sharp attacks by older intellectuals and students. As one Frenchman present in China during this period reported: "What really shook the party was a feeling that it faced the loss of its control over the youth. Young people brought up under communist rule had become the loudest in denouncing the party which had vested its hopes in them." [13]

Some indication of the nature of the criticism may be found in the pamphlet, *Look! What Kind of Talk Is This?* published by a party organization, the Peking Student Union, on June 14, 1957, as a collection of critical attitudes to be dealt with in reindoctrination sessions. The statements so presented "are not anti-socialist; they are anti-party, anti-Kuomintang, anti-imperialist, anti-Stalin, pro-Tito." [14]

There is, of course, no reliable way of estimating the extent of critical sentiments and behavior among university students in communist (or even other, more accessible) countries from evidence concerning protests which have become known. While such sentiments and actions are extremely important, it may be that most of the students passively support the status

---

[11] David Burg, "Observations on Soviet University Students," *Daedalus*, no. 3 (Summer 1960): 530.

[12] Ibid., pp. 530–31; see also Walter Z. Laqueur and George Lichtheim, *The Soviet Cultural Scene 1956–1957* (New York: Frederick A. Praeger, 1958), pp. 215–20.

[13] René Goldman, "The Rectification Campaign at Peking University: May–June 1957," *The China Quarterly* 12 (October–December 1962): 139. For a report by a participant, see Tang Chu-kuo, *The Student Anti-Communist Movement in Peiping* (Taipei: Asian People's Anti-Communist League, 1960).

[14] Dennis Doolin, ed., *Communist China; The Politics of Student Opposition* (Stanford: The Hoover Institution on War, Revolution and Peace, 1964), p. 14. This publication contains a verbatim translation of the pamphlet published by the Peking Student Union.

quo. Survey data based on samples of total student populations gathered in Warsaw in 1958 and 1961, and in Zagreb in 1961, do not, however, support this hypothesis. The Polish data clearly indicate that the bulk of the students were socialist, anti-Marxist, favorable to freedom and civil liberties, and egalitarian (as indicated by support for a narrow range in the distribution of income), and that 45 percent had played an active role in the anti-Stalinist demonstrations of October 1956. Less than one-quarter (24 percent) approved of the activities of the communist youth organization, and 72 percent voiced dissatisfaction with them. Sixty-eight percent favored some sort of socialism, but only 13 percent identified themselves as Marxists, and 68 percent indicated clear opposition to Marxism.[15] A survey of Yugoslav students at the University of Zagreb suggests greater support for the official ideology. Over half (53 percent) stated that they accepted Marxism fully while another 19 percent indicated partial acceptance. On the other hand, when asked their opinion of the leaders of the official League of Students, less than half (43 percent) approved of them, while 53 percent would have preferred other leaders. And 26 percent of the respondents indicated that they sometimes thought they would be "more satisfied" if they could live abroad.[16]

The history of student politics in the countries of Eastern Europe and China still arouses old memories and calls forth corresponding responses from the present rulers of these countries. The efforts of students and intellectuals were of notable importance in undermining precommunist regimes in these countries, and current efforts at their suppression may be consciously related to an awareness of that history.[17] In his classic study

---

[15] See Stefan Nowak, "Social Attitudes of Warsaw Students," *Polish Sociological Bulletin,* nos. 1–2 (3–4) (January–June 1962): 91–103; Stefan Nowak and Anna Pawelczynska, "Les attitudes idéologiques des etudiantes de Varsovie," *Esprit* 26, no. 11 (1958): 699–707; Stefan Nowak, "Factors Determining Egalitarianism of Warsaw Students," *American Sociological Review* 25, no. 2 (1960): 219–31; Anna Pawelczynska and Stefan Nowak, "World Outlook of Students in a Period of Stabilization," *Polish Perspectives,* V (February 1962), no. 2, pp. 38–50; Zofia Jozefowicz, Stefan Nowak, and Anna Pawelszynska, "Students: Myth and Reality," *Polish Perspectives* 1, nos. 7–8 (July–August 1958): 21–28; and "Students: Their Views on Society and Aspirations," *Polish Perspectives* 1, Nos. 11–12 (November–December 1958): 31–43.

[16] Study conducted by Professor V. Serdar, preliminary results of which were published in Mirko Martic, "Student i Zagrebackog sveucilista u svijetlu jednog anketnog istrazivanja," *Nase Teme* (Zagreb), no. 2 (1961).

[17] Socialists and others face the dilemma in the emerging world. In Burma it may be recalled that it "was from the university students' union that the AFPFL (socialist) government sprang, and that precedent was ironically ominous: for the communists had made inroads among the students. The Rangoon Students' Union and the All-Burma Federation Students' Unions, both of which were captured by the communists, were much stronger than the Democratic Students' Organization sponsored by the socialists. The situation deteriorated to such an extent that the government felt obliged in October 1956 to ban student unions in schools." Saul Rose, *Socialism in Southern Asia* (London: Oxford University Press, 1959), p. 142. Similarly in Venezuela, the social-democratic government of Betancourt and Leoni has been led by men who had themselves entered politics via the student movement and who played a major part as student leaders in undermining reactionary and authoritarian regimes. They are now faced by a student movement in which communists play a significant role.

of tsarist Russia, set consciously in a Tocquevillian framework, Leroy-Bealieu noted:

> The schools . . . have always been the hotbeds of radicalism and the higher the school, the more imbued with the revolutionary spirit the young people who graduate therefrom. . . . Science and education, no matter how watchful the supervision they are subjected to—by the wants which they create, by the confidence in right and reason which they inspire, by the curiosity they arouse and the comparisons they suggest—invincibly predispose to criticism, to free investigation, hence to liberalism, to the spirit of innovation.[18]

The university students in particular were among the few to engage in demonstrations demanding freedom and major economic reforms from the mid-nineteenth century on. Many of these early protests began as struggles for greater rights for students within the universities and then widened their objectives as they met with repression. A report by a faculty commission of the University of Moscow, written in 1901, traced the causes and nature of every student disorder back to the 1850s. It

> noted that since 1887 they had become almost annual. . . . This upward trend of student disorders was confirmed by statistics on expulsions from the university, which had doubled in the six years from 1894 to 1899, as compared to the preceding seven years. During the later period, a total of 1,214 students were expelled from the University of Moscow. . . .[19]

Student strikes and demonstrations became even more prevalent after 1899, reaching a climax in 1905, when the universities were closed by the government.

> In 1901, the workers were to learn the value of the street demonstrations from students. These demonstrations, first organized by the university stu-

---

[18] Anatole Leroy-Beaulieu, *The Empire of the Tsars and the Russians*, Part II: "The Institutions" (New York: G. P. Putnam's Sons, 1894), pp. 486–87. He documents these contentions with reference to statistical data on the background of those revolutionists who had been arrested, which showed that four-fifths had received higher or secondary education, most of them in government schools, and that a "statistical list of 1880 shows four-fifths of the agitators arrested by the police to have been nobles, sons of priests, of functionaries and officers, of merchants or city 'notables,' only 20 per cent were small employees, working people, and peasants." See his footnotes on pp. 485 and 486. Cf. also Gabor Kiss, *Die gesellschaftspolitische Rolle der Studentenbewegung im vorrevolutionären Russland* (München: Georg Heller Verlag, 1963). Joseph Conrad, *Under Western Eyes* (London: J. M. Dent, 1955), is one of the classic treatments, perhaps the greatest, of Russian student politics under the *ancien régime*. On the beginnings of the student movement, cf. Franco Venturi, *Il populismo russo*, vol. 1, ch. VIII, "Il movimenta studentesco," pp. 366–85 and *passim*. Alexander Herzen in his *My Past and Thoughts*, vol. 1, trans. Constance Garnett (London: Chatto and Windus, 1924) presents a beautiful account of the political sensitivity of the Russian university students of the 1830s.

[19] See George Fischer, *Russian Liberalism* (Cambridge, Mass.: Harvard University Press, 1958), pp. 53–56. Fischer points out that in Russia before 1905, when the lower classes were quiescent, students were the one group which had "the numbers and the hardiness to stand up physically to government force."

dents of St. Petersburg . . . spread rapidly to other universities and were promptly joined by sympathetic workers and other elements of the urban population.[20]

The freedom which was won by the students for themselves, in the form of autonomy given to the universities in 1905, helped facilitate revolutionary disturbances.

The student movement was being led by a group of extreme radicals, mostly Social Democrats and some Socialist Revolutionaries and others. . . . Overriding the liberal professors who sought a return to normal academic life, the students opened the doors of the universities to mass meetings of the workers. Since the police could not enter the universities except at the request of the university council, these meetings were held in complete freedom. Here, in closed quarters, revolutionary speeches were made and strikes organized; here the revolutionary parties made their plans without interference.[21]

Sixty years ago, Bernard Pares included students, with the intelligentsia, as the carriers of the revolutionary outlook in tsarist Russia. His analysis emphasized some of the determinants that have been pointed to in recent analyses of the politics of university students in underdeveloped countries:

The universities, long the fortress of criticism, had united within their walls a number of young men who were never again in all their lives to meet so many of their fellows under the inspiration of a common ideal. Here they were stilll young in heart and brain, and as yet unhampered by the practical concerns of life. They did not represent any ruling class; naturally, their interests were quite as much social as political; and students or ex-students, especially those who crossed the frontier, might be expected to carry on a scheme of social propagandism as whole-hearted and as all-embracing as any other of the enthusiasms of the Russian nature. The universities were by their merits, as by their defects, a very focus of revolution.[22]

In China, students played a major role in the downfall of the Manchu Dynasty at the turn of the century. In large numbers, they backed Sun Yat-sen and helped spread radical ideas of modernization and democracy

[20] Jacob Walkin, *The Rise of Democracy in Pre-Revolutionary Russia* (New York: Frederick A. Praeger, 1962), pp. 188–89.

[21] Ibid., pp. 129–32. Autonomy was withdrawn in 1911; police broke up meetings within the universities and mass expulsions of students, as well as dismissal of professors, occurred.

[22] Bernard Pares, *Russia between Reform and Revolution* (New York: Schocken Books, 1962), pp. 180–81. This book was first published in 1907. For a detailed discussion of the situation on the Russian intelligentsia and their political roles, see pp. 161–282. As Francis B. Randell, the author of the "Introduction" to this edition, states: ". . . we read this book because the Russia it presents is so much like so many backward countries today, poor but slowly rising modern economies. . . . Its *intelligentsia* was a classic example of the nationalist intellectual movement to be found in every backward country. Pares' book is relevant to our many discussions of 'the problem of development' in the many little Russias of the world": p. xi.

throughout the country.[23] Later, with the overthrow of the monarchy in 1911, university students rallied around the ideas of Ch'en Tu-hsiu, a professor at Peking, who called, in effect, for a thoroughly democratic and egalitarian society. Student politics reached a climax in May 1919, when the huge student demonstration which began in Peking inaugurated the second Chinese Revolution. "The movement spread across the country. In it a new note sounded when workers in factories struck in support of the student demands for a new regime." [24] Many of the intellectuals and students who took part in these movements, including Ch'en Tu-hsiu, were to be among the founders of the Chinese Communist party in 1921. Student movements, demonstrations, and strikes played a major role in undermining Chiang Kai-shek during the 1930s as well. They tended to favor a united front between the Kuomintang and the communists.[25] In December 1931, a mass student demonstration in the capital, Nanking, demanded immediate united resistance to Japan. After this the student movement turned increasingly to the left and the Kuomintang attempted to suppress it. Again at the end of 1935 and in 1936, massive student demonstrations played an important role in pressing the government to accept the new United Front strategy of the communists and "the effect of the postwar [World War II] student riots was to hasten the downfall of Chiang's government and the communist victory." [26]

Historical patterns of student politics comparable to the Russian and Chinese cases may be described for other communist states. Although communist ideology forbids the party from acknowledging the fact that university students have provided both the initial leadership and a large part of the mass base in countries in which the party has taken power on its own, the facts bear out this assertion. That the Castro movement developed from student activities in the University of Havana is well recognized. Less well known is the fact that the Communist party of Cuba, itself, was founded after a massive student demonstration in the University of Havana. José Antonio Mella and other expelled student leftists founded the party in 1925.[27] The first Vietnamese communist movement, the Association of Vietnamese Revolutionary Young Comrades, was founded by Ho Chi Minh in 1925 from among "large numbers of young men who had escaped from the repressions following the Hanoi Students' Movement in 1925." Among those veterans of the 1925 Student Movement who joined the communists following its suppression was Pham Van Dong, now Prime Minister of the Democratic Republic of Vietnam.[28]

---

23 Wen-han Kiang, *The Chinese Student Movement* (New York: King's Crown Press, 1948).

24 Harold Isaacs, *The Tragedy of the Chinese Revolution* (Stanford University Press, 1961), pp. 53–55.

25 H. Seton-Watson, *The Pattern of Communist Revolution* (London: Methuen, 1953), pp. 190–91.

26 John Israel, *The Chinese Student Movement, 1927–1937* (Ph.D. thesis, History Department, Harvard University, 1963), p. 146.

27 Eduardo Suárez Rivas, *Un pueblo crucificado* (Miami: n.p., 1964), p. 21.

28 Hoang Van Chi, *From Colonialism to Communism* (New York: Praeger, 1964), p. 43.

The Yugoslav Communist party also secured a large proportion of its leadership from the student movement. Before World War II, the communist student organization (SKOJ) was much larger than the rest of the movement, and its members played a major role in the partisan resistance.[29]

UNIVERSITY STUDENTS IN
UNDERDEVELOPED COUNTRIES

In the underdeveloped or emerging countries, the critical attitude of the educated stratum resembles the reactions of intellectuals in precommunist Russia and China. Their concern is, from a nationalist standpoint, with the modernization of their country, which would permit it to take its place with the leading countries of the modern world. The long absence of sovereignty adds only a complication to the responses to social, economic, political, and cultural backwardness vis-à-vis the then dominant centers of modern civilization. Great Britain, France, Germany—these were the models of modernity, and it was the retrograde position of their own country in comparison with one of these countries or with a vague composite image of all of them which provided the point of departure for the radical criticism of their own countries. Where their own countries were under colonial rule, it was only a simple step to link the backwardness of the country with the interests and intentions of the ruling foreign power.[30] The attraction of the foreign model was associated with a revulsion against the backwardness of indigenous institutions. At the same time, the politicized students and their older intellectual confrères were nationalists, and they could not lightly accept their own xenophilia and their own implicit denial of the vitality of their own indigenous inheritance.[31]

---

[29] Joseph Broz Tito, *Report to the 5th Congress CPY* (Belgrade, Yugoslavia, 1948), pp. 27–34.

[30] Edward Shils, "Political Development in the New States," *Comparative Studies in Society and History* 2, no. 3 (1960): 272–77. A similar situation existed even in independent Japan. The early appeal of Marxism to Japanese intellectuals, which underlies its success after 1945, is related to its provision of a universalistic justification for Japanese nationalism. As Yuzuru Okada puts it: "Many intellectuals were driven by a desire for Japan to catch up with, or even surpass, the West. For them Marxism represented a system that derived from, and was critical of, the social, political, and cultural systems of the West. It appeared to present them with a model of a society of utopian proportions, far exceeding any society that existed at that time in the West. They felt that if they could create a socialist state in Japan, their nation, at a single stroke, would be ahead of the nations of Europe and America. They were emotionally challenged by the *possibility* of achieving socialism before any nation of the Western world." "Introduction" to special issue dealing with "Japanese Intellectuals," *Journal of Social and Political Ideas in Japan* 2, no. 1 (April 1964): 4. Joseph Ben-David points out that in eighteenth-century France the model to be emulated was Britain, while Germans later sought to copy France. See "Professions in the Class System of the Present Day Societies," *Current Sociology* 12, no. 3 (1963–1964): 273.

[31] The "memory" of exploitation by the colonial power is still strong in the consciousness of many of the younger generation, even those born after independence.

As Seton-Watson has noted, the disproportion between the modern education imparted by the universities in Eastern Europe during the nineteenth and early twentieth centuries and the backwardness of the rest of the nation made sensitive young people painfully aware of the cultural and economic backwardness of their own country.

> They belonged to the nineteenth or twentieth centuries. But their less fortunate compatriots in the villages were living in the eighteenth or sixteenth centuries. . . . They felt themselves obliged to serve their peoples, to raise them to their level, and to fight against all those who had, or appeared to have, an interest in keeping them in their backward state.[32]

And the same reforming tendencies which emerged in the universities of Eastern Europe have been paralleled in Latin America:

> From the [Latin American] university, came the liberal movements of the 19th century and the progressive movements—Christian or Marxist—of the 20th century. Naturally the ideological *avant garde* did not escape conflicts with the conservatives and the beneficiaries of older socio-political structures. And as these latter held power in the previous generation, there was an effort—unavowed but real—of the political elite to halt the spreading influence of the university.[33]

The concern with modernization and development has gone hand in hand with the international stratification system, in which the elite of each nation makes international comparisons and uses international standards to locate themselves as higher or lower with respect to various characteristics which are accorded international prestige.[34] The elites of the emerging nations see themselves and their countries as parts of the suppressed strata of the world though they themselves may be among the well-to-do not only within their own country but even by a world standard. Awareness or concern with the inferior position of the nation is most acute

---

Thus there is a tendency for the former colonial power to be viewed with mixed feelings, as the source of intellectual prestige and recognition, as well as the former subjugator of the nation, who still exploits the country economically. In Latin America the United States has played this role for students and intellectuals who have seen her, with considerable justice at times, as an economic exploiter. Recent surveys of students in Iran and Pakistan reveal a negative image of the major former colonial powers, Britain and France, while these students, particularly the Pakistani, are much more favorable to the U.S.A. and Russia. *Student Survey in Pakistan* (Bielefeld: E.M.N.I.D., 1963); *Teheran University Student Survey: Attitudes and Aspirations* (Teheran: National Institute of Psychology, 1963).

[32] H. Seton-Watson, op. cit., pp. 8–9.

[33] León Cortinas Peláez, "Autonomy and Student Co-Government in the University of Uruguay," *Comparative Education Review* 7, no. 2 (1963): 166.

[34] See especially Gustavo Lagos, *International Stratification and Underdeveloped Countries* (Chapel Hill: University of North Carolina Press, 1963); Edward Shils, "Metropolis and Province in the Intellectual Community" in N. V. Sovani and V. M. Dandakar, ed., *Changing India* (Bombay: Asia Publishing Co., 1961), pp. 275–94 and R. Waelder, op. cit., pp. 17–18.

among those who have received or are receiving a university education, since the culture which that conveys is so obviously part of a universal culture and the university community has such close ties with the international community of scholars and universities.[35] Many of its leaders have been trained in the more advanced, higher-ranking nations, and hence are more likely to be especially prone to feelings of national inferiority.[36] Those who seek to maintain traditional institutions within the country, who favor only moderate change, are perceived as reinforcing the inferior status of the country.

Thus the conflict between the values of intellectuals and students and of traditional institutions is intensified with an increase in national concern for modernization and for the international position of the country. Although the inherent logic of modern university education is in principle at variance with traditional values even in culturally and linguistically more or less homogeneous countries, the conflict becomes more pronounced in new states where the university and modern cultures are either at present or in the recent past of patent foreign origin and where the language of intellectual communication so often is one which is alien to the indigenous culture.

The behavior of universities and intellectuals in developing countries should not be perceived solely or even primarily as merely a reaction to changes instigated by others. Rather, as John Friedman has argued, the "modern" intellectuals must be placed alongside those directly concerned with economic innovation as the principal agents of social change and economic growth. "The one is active in the realm of values and ideas, the

---

35 The general problem has been conceptualized by Edward Shils as part of the general phenomenon of the tension which exists between the intellectual metropolis and province. The writer or scholar in nineteenth-century Eastern Europe sought recognition from Paris or Germany. Then and today, the principal intellectual capitals of Western Europe, and increasingly in recent decades, those of the United States, have "exercised an irresistible fascination on certain strata of the societies outside the European centre, and the situation was not made any easier to bear by the often explicit derogation of their own culture and society which its admirers encountered . . . in the works and attitudes of intellectuals of the foreign culture to which they were attracted." Edward Shils, "The Prospects for Intellectuals," *Soviet Survey*, no. 29 (July–September 1959): 86; see also his "The Traditions of Intellectual Life," *International Journal of Comparative Sociology* 1, no. 2 (1960): 180–83.

36 The intelligentsia of the underdeveloped countries are those "who are experiencing internal conflict between allegiance to traditional cultures and the influence of the modern West. . . . An understanding of the intelligentsia can perhaps most readily be gained by examining the case of the 'returned student.' In China particularly, this term has been used to denote the many thousands of young people who produced a powerful ferment within their country after their return from studies abroad. The same pattern occurred in many other countries. It did not matter whether a student had actually studied in a Western country; many took on the characteristics of the 'returned student' simply after exposure to Western culture in . . . schools of their own country." Klaus Mehnert, "The Social and Political Role of the Intelligentsia in the New Countries," in Kurt London, ed., *New Nations in a Divided World* (New York: Frederick A. Praeger, 1963), pp. 122–23. Cf. also Y. C. Wang, "Intellectuals and Society in China, 1860–1949," *Comparative Studies in Society and History* 3, no. 4 (1961): 325–426, and his forthcoming book on the "foreign-returned Chinese student."

other in the realm of technology and organisation. But the actions of both will tend to undermine the established order of things." [37]

The university trained "modern" intellectual has three essential tasks, "each of which is essential to the process of cultural transformation: he mediates new values, he formulates an effective ideology, and he creates an adequate, collective [national] self-image." [38] These place him in direct conflict with the traditionalist forces in his nation. Thus one of the central tasks of the study of the social requisites for development is the analysis of the conditions which influence the responses of the intellectuals and university students. It is interesting to note that the late C. Wright Mills, in his more direct concern with facilitating political revolution, also suggested that students and intellectuals, rather than the working class, may be an "immediate radical agency of change." As a sociologist, he urged the need "to study these new generations of intellectuals (including university students) around the world as real live agencies of historic change." [39]

THE UNIVERSITY SITUATION AND THE CONFLICT OF GENERATIONS

The behavior of university students in underdeveloped countries, while to some degree identical with or derivative from the characteristics of adult intellectuals in those countries, is also a function of certain elements peculiar to the situation of the university student. University students live on the boundary between the last stage of adolescence, with its freedom from the burdens of adult responsibility, and the first stages of adulthood, with its complex of pressing tasks and difficult decisions. University students are generally at an age which is defined as biologically adult; many nonstudents of the same age have often already entered upon adult activities, married, earn money and spend it as they wish. Students are often at the age where they may vote and marry, and many do both. Yet few university students earn all their livelihood; many remain financially dependent on their parents, and the society at large still treats them in many ways as irresponsible adolescents, permitting and even approving of a certain amount of sowing of "wild oats." They may even violate the laws in various minor ways without being punished. In many societies the university is responsible for student conduct, and the corporate autonomy of the university is often a symbol, as well as a bulwark, of the

---

37 John Friedman, "Intellectuals in Developing Societies," *Kyklos* 8, no. 4 (1964): 514.

38 Ibid., p. 524.

39 C. Wright Mills, *Power, Politics and People* (New York: Ballantine Books, 1963), pp. 256–59. Mills detailed the many actions by university students as key sources of political opposition and denigrated the political potential of the working class. In discussing the politics of students and intellectuals, he called for "detailed comparative studies of them": p. 257.

immunity of the students from external authority on their dependent condition.[40]

Max Weber in his great lecture on "Politics as a Vocation" observed that youth has a tendency to follow "a pure ethic of absolute ends," while maturity is associated with "an ethic of responsibility." The advocate of the first fears that any compromise on matters of principles will endanger the "salvation of the soul"; the proponent of the second fears that an unwillingness to confront the complex "realities of life" may result in "the goals . . . [being] damaged and discredited for generations, because responsibility for *consequences* is lacking." [41] Thus, if some university students are inclined to be irresponsible with respect to the norms of adult society, they are also inclined to be idealistic. They have not established a sense of affinity with adult institutions; experience has not hardened them to imperfection. Their libidos are unanchored; their capacity for identification with categories of universal scope, with mankind or the oppressed or the poor and miserable, is greater than it was earlier or than it will be later in life. Their contact with the articulated moral and political standards of their society is abstract; they encounter them as principles promulgated by older persons, as impositions by authority, rather than as maxims incorporated into and blurred by their own practice. Increasingly in the modern world, which includes the highly educated sector of the emerging nations, equality, efficiency, justice, and economic well-being are presented as the values of the good society. Poverty, racial discrimination, caste systems, social inequality, administrative and political corruption, and cultural backwardness are all violations of such principles.[42] In all countries, of course, reality is usually at variance with principles, and young persons, especially those who have been indulged in adolescence and are alienated from the authority of their elders or of their parents, teachers, and other rulers of the institutional system, feel this strongly. Educated young people everywhere consequently tend disproportionately to support idealistic movements which take the ideologies or values of the adult world more seriously than does the adult world itself.[43] Youthful idealism, even when it leads to rejection of adult prac-

40 As Edwin Lieuwen has pointed out in discussing the participation of the Venezuelan students in revolutionary politics on many occasions in the history of the country: "The autonomous status of the universities has provided the students special licence to participate freely in politics, particularly in revolutionary activities." Edwin Lieuwen, *Venezuela* (London: Oxford University Press, 1961), p. 164.

41 Max Weber, *Essays in Sociology,* ed. and trans. H. H. Gerth and Wright Mills (New York: Oxford University Press, 1946), pp. 126–27.

42 As Talcott Parsons puts it, youth are "inculcated with the major values of the society. . . . However good the current society may be from various points of view, *it is not good enough to meet their standards.*" See "Youth in the Context of American Society," in Erik H. Erikson, ed., *Youth: Change and Challenge* (New York: Basic Books, 1963), p. 117.

43 For an analysis of both the elements of self-interest and the idealism in student movements in Europe, see Frank A. Pinner, "Student Trade-Unionism in France, Belgium, and Holland," *Sociology of Education* 37, no. 3 (1964): 177–99; and Raymond Aron, "Some Aspects of the Crisis in the French Universities," *Minerva* 2, no. 3 (Spring 1964), pp. 279–85.

tices, is often "expected and respected. . . . [Thus] in Latin America . . . the young are surrounded by a mystique which seems to make people believe all their views are somehow 'purer' and less corrupt than those of their elders." [44] The propensity of highly and even moderately educated youth to be radical, and of older persons to be conservative, is not peculiar to either advanced or underdeveloped countries. Within conservative as well as left-wing groups or parties, youth movements or affiliates tend to give the adult organization trouble by their tendency to demand that the party or church live up to its principles.[45]

In underdeveloped societies, the institutions such as the family, church, and school, through which young men and women have had to pass before they entered the university, are usually concerned with transmitting the culture already accepted by the elders rather than inculcating into them a culture which is only in a barely incipient state. An approximately similar situation exists even in "modern" societies, but the situation is much more acute in societies in which most of the older generation lives in a traditional indigenous culture much different from the culture the young person encounters in his contacts with the modern sector of his own society. The resulting hostility against the efforts of authority to impose on him a culture with which he has no sympathy disposes him to accept an anti-authoritarian political culture once he becomes interested in political things.[46]

The older generations are more attached to traditional norms regarding topics such as familial authority, women's rights, authority, religion, etc., than are the younger. Differences in attitudes are also linked to education; the better educated favor "modern" values.[47] University students

---

44 Luigi Einaudi, "The Drama of the Latin American Student Movement" (unpublished paper, 1961), p. 2. Eisenstadt suggests that societies may "evolve an image of youth as the purest manifestation and repository of ultimate cultural and social values." S. N. Eisenstadt, "Archetypal Patterns of Youth," in Erik H. Erikson, op cit., p. 27.

45 See Eric Josephson, *Political Youth Organizations in Europe, 1900–1950; A Comparative Study of Six Radical Parties and Their Youth Auxiliaries* (Ph.D. dissertation, Columbia University, 1960).

46 Karl Mannheim has located the concerns of "adolescents and early adults, particularly students" for major political or social concerns beyond their personal interests, in the "uncertainty and doubt" which results when "one's questions outrun the scope of one's inherited answers." This occurs when the youth learns that there are other values and ways of life different from those urged on him by his family. In seeking distance from his primary environment, "with a sense of liberation . . . the adolescent discovers alternative interpretations and new values. Self-assertion and defiance accompany this new experience." This contact with a variety of possibilities not taught within the family is confusing, and rather than remain in a state of doubt, many youths seek a new certainty in beliefs which are opposed to those taught at home. "Intellectual fanaticism is not the product of a tacitly accepted heritage, but the expression of an anxiety to end the wear and tear of a state of suspense by the adoption of a categorical creed." Karl Mannheim, *Essays on the Sociology of Culture* (New York: Oxford University Press, 1956), pp. 163–64.

47 See Seymour M. Lipset, "Political Cleavages in 'Developed' and 'Emerging' Polities," in Erik Allardt and Yrjö Littunen, eds., *Cleavages, Ideologies and Party Systems: Contributions to Comparative Political Sociology* (Helsinki: The Westermarck Society, 1964). For a detailed account of sources of generational conflict between students and

being both younger and more highly educated are specially inclined to diverge from the prescriptions of tradition in their cultural and political beliefs.[48]

It is common for social movements and most parties in developing countries, especially when they are out of power, to have programs which correspond to many of the vague aspirations and resentments of the younger educated generations.[49]

The most dramatic recent demonstrations of university students as the most aggressive proponents of "modern" values have occurred in Korea, Bolivia, South Vietnam, and the Sudan, where students together with the army have undone governments. The Syngman Rhee regime in Korea was finally overthrown in 1960 as a result of student demonstrations, and similar activities have been directed against the military regime in 1964.[50] This latter year has witnessed the downfall of governments in the other three countries following demonstrations begun by students.

The need of a younger generation to establish its independence corresponds to the tactic of revolutionary movements to seek recruits among those who are not yet integrated into the institutional system. Revolutionary movements give young people an idealistic rationale for breaking with

---

their parents in the China of 1935–1937 based on questionnaires filled out by 1164 university students, see Olga Lang, *Chinese Family and Society* (New Haven, Conn.: Yale University Press, 1946), pp. 283–96.

[48] Joseph Fischer, "Universities and the Political Process in Southeast Asia," *Pacific Affairs* 36, no. 1 (1963): 13.

[49] Frederick W. Frey writes: "Having spoken of student activities, one can hardly avoid mentioning the very pronounced 'youth culture' which pervades portions of Turkish life. Mustafa Kemal proclaimed youth 'the owner and guardian of the revolution'—a fact which some segments of Turkish youth will let no one ignore." "Education: Turkey," in Robert E. Ward and Dankwart Rustow, eds., *Political Modernization in Japan and Turkey* (Princeton, N.J.: Princeton University Press, 1964), p. 235. The conflict of generations and its consequences for politics in Latin America is discussed in Carlos Alberto Floria, "Ideas e ideales políticos de los jóvenes latinoamericanos," *Occidente* 17, no. 139 (August 1962): 12–17. For empirical research on this topic for Latin America, specifically Uruguay, see Isaac Ganon et al., *Nuestro estudiante contemporáneo* (mimeographed, Instituto de Ciencias Sociales, Facultad de Derecho y Ciencias Sociales; Universidad de la República, Montevideo, Uruguay, 1964), pp. 38–62. Concerning students in Panama, and Latin America generally, as "the only group exerting continuous pressure for socio-economic and governmental reform . . .", see Daniel Goldrich, *Radical Nationalism: The Political Orientations of Panamanian Law Students* (East Lansing: Bureau of Social and Political Research, Michigan State University, 1961).

[50] "The students constituted one of the most modernized groups in Korean society, for they grew up after independence and during the period of the massive American military and diplomatic presence. The older people's attitudes had been formed during the Yi dynasty and under Japanese colonial rule. Thus the students were more quick than the general public to feel, perhaps only vaguely and unconsciously, that the process of modernisation was at standstill. They also had a less fatalistic attitude towards the abuse of power by the government. To their more modern minds, Rhee's maneuvers during the election seemed like anachronistic 'absurdities,' as they put it, whereas to the adults, they appeared as merely the most recent manifestations of age-old and inevitable phenomena. The adults suffered more directly from Rhee's repressions than did the students who had no family or economic responsibilities, yet it was the students who acted, not the wage-earners of the professional class." William A. Douglas, "Korean Students and Politics," *Asian Survey* 3, no. 12 (1963): 586.

their families, which may be defined as part of the reactionary system. The higher the degree of parental control exercised before youth leave home for university, the more violent the need to demonstrate "autonomy" once they are "free." [51]

Resistance to the pressure of adult authorities which try to impel them toward the burdens of adulthood, of regular employment, regular family life, etc., is intensified by uncertainty as to whether the roles toward which they are being impelled will actually be available. The poor employment prospects for university-educated youth in many underdeveloped countries enlarge the reservoir of late adolescent rebellion from which revolutionary politics can draw support.

Students engaged in the courses of study which entail something like apprenticeship for a definite profession, e.g., engineering, medicine, and preparation for secondary school teaching, where employment prospects are fair, are likely to be less rebellious than students in courses of study without determinate destinations and in which the pattern of instruction does not require personal contact between teachers and students. The most insecure of all are those without specific aims or prospects and who therefore will have to compete with multitudes of other arts graduates, equally poorly qualified, for a small number of inconsequential posts.[52]

---

[51] Hypotheses such as these have been presented to account for the rebelliousness of German youth before World War I, and for Latin American and Japanese students in more recent periods. Walter Laqueur, *Young Germany* (New York: Basic Books, 1962), p. 5; Robert Havighurst, "Latin American and North American Higher Education," *Comparative Education Review* 4, no. 3 (1961): 180.

[52] The existing data bearing on the subject are fragmentary and inconclusive. Thus a comparison of the student supporters of four Indian political parties—Communist, Socialist, Congress, and the conservative, communal Jan Sangh—reveals, as might be expected, that "commerce" is the subject most frequently studied by those with more conservative party choice, while students in "sociology, economics and anthropology" incline more toward the left. The combined group "philosophy, psychology and education" gives the communists much less support vis-à-vis the other parties than any other. Students in the sciences (about a fifth of the sample) seem evenly distributed among the various political positions. Bureau of Social Science Research, *Political Attitudes of Indian Students* (Washington: The American University, 1955), p. 47. In the National University of Colombia, the students in the Faculties of Law and Economics appear to be much more to the left than those in "education, psychology and sociology," who in turn are more radical than those in the natural sciences. K. Walker, "Determinants of Castro Support among Latin American University Students" (paper presented at the Seventh Latin American Congress of Sociology; Bogotá, Colombia, 13–19 July 1964), and Robert C. Williamson, "El estudiante colombiano y sus actitudes" (Bogotá: Facultad de Sociología, Universidad Nacional de Colombia, 1962), p. 49. On the other hand, in a study of the students in three faculties in the University of Buenos Aires, Silvert and Bonilla indicate that "the economics group stand well below exact sciences in degree of political activity, and most of the details of such participation just a little below even medicine." The science students were much more likely to report having participated in a street rally or having attended a party meeting than the economists. Kalman Silvert and Frank Bonilla, *Education and the Social Meaning of Development: A Preliminary Statement* (New York: American Universities Field Staff, 1961), pp. 127–28. See also Seymour M. Lipset, op. cit.; and K. Walker, op. cit., pp. 18–19. In student elections in recent years in Buenos Aires, it has become clear that the most radical faculty by far is letters and philosophy, which includes the large

In the past decade the rapid expansion of the university student population in much of Asia has increased this source of student insecurity. Unemployment or low-status employment awaits many graduates.[53]

The ecological concentration of universities within a limited area, bringing together many young men and women in a similar situation in life and isolating them for the most part from the motley routine of adult life, contributes to the perpetuation of student restlessness. This is as true of universities in underdeveloped countries as it is of those in advanced countries.

Like a vast factory, a large campus brings together great numbers of people in similar life situations, in close proximity to each other, who can acquire a sense of solidarity and wield real power. In Tokyo there are over 200,000 students on the various campuses in the city; the comparable figures for Peking and Calcutta are about 100,000; in Mexico City there are over 65,000; and in Buenos Aires, there are close to 70,000 students in the university. It is relatively easy to reach students; leaflets handed out at the campus gates will usually do the job. These facilitate quick communication, foster solidarity, and help to arouse melodramatic action. The organization of campus life at the new African universities, as well as in the colleges and universities of India and Pakistan, even where the numbers run only into a few thousand, has the same results. The politicians' awareness that students have contributed so much in the past to the independence movements and to revolutionary movements makes them appreciate the students' political potential in the politics of the immediate present.[54] They are aware of their value in increasing the size

---

Department of Sociology. In Mexico, a detailed study based on interviews in nine universities indicates considerable variation in political opinion among the different faculties. Within the large National University in Mexico City the economics faculty, which includes sociology, was by far the most leftist, with law second. Commerce, engineering and medical students tended to respond more conservatively. *A Study of Opinions of University Students in Mexico* (Mexico City: International Research Associates, 1964), pp. 16–19, 40–43, 123–32.

[53] Justus M. Van der Kroef, "Asian Education and Unemployment: The Continuing Crisis," *Comparative Education Review* 7, no. 2 (1963): 173–80, and Edward Shils, "Indian Students," *Encounter* 17, no. 3 (September 1961): 12–20. Lorraine D. Eyde, "Characteristics and Problems of Indian Universities and Their Students," *The International Review of Education* 9, no. 4 (1963–1964): 461–76. The classic treatment of this subject is to be found in Walter Kotschnig, *Unemployment in the Learned Professions* (New York and London: Oxford University Press, 1938). See also Philip Altbach, "Japanese Students and Japanese Politics," *Comparative Education Review* 7, no. 2 (1963): 182, and M. Shimbori, "Zengakuren: A Japanese Case Study of a Student Political Movement," *Sociology of Education* 37, no. 2 (1964): 233–34.

[54] In Egypt, "students were virtually a distinct social class wooed by the government and opposition parties alike." Morroe Berger, *The Arab World Today* (Garden City: Doubleday, 1962), p. 311. ". . . all the major political parties in Venezuela today originated in university groups. . . . Soon after the present Venezuelan political parties came into existence in the 1930s and 1940s, they appointed directors of student activities who recruited supporters not only in the universities but also in the *liceos*, or high schools." S. Walter Washington, "Student Politics in Latin America: The Venezuelan Example," *Foreign Affairs* 37, no. 3 (1959): 465.

of demonstrations and of the heat which can be given to demonstrations by their youthful excitability.[55]

THE POLITICAL SITUATION
IN THE COUNTRY AT LARGE

In large measure, student political behavior is anticipatory adult political behavior, particularly in developing countries, where even student demands for better universities, teachers, and research facilities are part of the struggle for national development. Consequently, student behavior will often reflect the state of adult politics, even if in a more extreme reformist fashion.

For the most part, "being dynamic" is the main element in the student political demands addressed to the authorities of their respective countries. "Being dynamic" means making dramatic exertions in the direction of modernity. This entails Draconic measures against "remnants of neo-colonialism," against chiefs, against foreign enterprisers, having a rapid rate of economic growth and scoring "anticolonialist" points in the international arena of the United Nations. Governments which give an air of going about their business in a tough-minded and aggressive way appear dynamic. In Iran, students criticize the regime as conservative, while many identify the military government in Pakistan as dynamic. This is clearly brought out in surveys of student opinion in both countries, which asked identical questions. In Iran only 8 percent believe that the standard of living is going up for the people, as contrasted with 52 percent in Pakistan.[56]

Two surveys of "francophone" African students studying in French universities report that majorities of those interviewed stated that there is a conflict of views and/or interests between themselves personally, or the youth of their country generally, and their governments.[57] The pro-

---

[55] An official communist journal, for example, calls attention to the need "to look at the experience gained in the University of Rome, which, with its enrolment of 50,000, not only is a big cultural centre, but represents the greatest concentration of young people in the country." Giovanni Berlinguer, "In the University of Rome," *World Marxist Review* 6, no. 2 (February 1963): 60. "Of all the political parties, the Japan Communist Party has worked assiduously on students, who are very apparently regarded as an important target of the party's activities." Lawrence H. Battistini, *The Postwar Student Struggle in Japan* (Tokyo: Charles Tuttle, 1956), p. 145. Lucien Pye notes that in Asia generally "it is the students and the intelligentsia who are seen as likely candidates for communism" by the communist parties. See Lucien Pye, *Guerrilla Communism in Malaya* (Princeton, N.J.: Princeton University Press, 1956), p. 38.

[56] See *Teheran University Study: Attitudes and Aspirations* (Teheran: National Institute of Psychology, 1963), p. 19; and *Student Survey in Pakistan* (Bielefeld: E.M.N.I.D., 1963), pp. 89–90.

[57] One study which asked whether the respondent himself was in conflict with his government indicates that two-thirds have such a sense of difference. J.-P. N'Diaye, *Enquête sur les étudiants noirs en France* (Paris: Réalités Africaines, 1963), p. 224. The study which asked whether respondents see a "basic disagreement of aims or interests between the youth of your country and the leaders of your government" reports that 51 percent see such a conflict. *The African Students in France* (Paris: Institut Français d'Opinion Publique, 1962), p. 48.

portions indicating such differences were lower among those from the two countries with avowedly radical regimes, Guinée and Mali, than from students from other mainland African states.[58] However, one investigation which also included students from the Malagasy Republic (Madagascar) found that they had the least disagreement with their regime.

The characteristics of the dominant elites, and the connections between those elites and the universities, influence the degree of identification with, or opposition to, government policy by the university community at large, or subsections within it. In his analysis of Japanese educational developments since the Meiji Restoration, Ronald Dore points out that the original opposition to government policies came from the staff and students of the less well-connected private universities which were identified with the various "outgroups" among the middle classes in the larger society. The imperial (state) universities were close to the government and supplied the large majority of the higher civil servants and political leaders of the Restoration period.

By the twenties, when industrialists began to exercise more influence on Japanese life, both staff and students began to be attracted by revolutionary ideologies which demanded drastic social changes. In the post-World War II period of rapid growth, prosperous capitalism, and bourgeois domination of parliament, Dore suggests, the private universities have become much more identified with the regime than the state universities. The latter

> have preserved the "devotion-to-high-principle" strain in the Confucian scholar-ruler tradition of the oligarchy and remain the home of the politically minded intellectual—now typically "alienated" and forming the nucleus of political opposition.[59]

The extent of concern with politics among students in different countries is in part a function of the degree of tension in the larger polity. It has been argued that the

> apparent greater student interest in national politics among Latin American students is probably a reflection of more general political uncertainty and

---

[58] Although neither study reports on the content of the attitudes of the more critical students, one might hypothesize that the critical students in the more communist-oriented states would espouse a more liberal position, would feel state power as too coercive—much as in the communist states of Europe; while students from other countries should make their criticism from the collectivist extreme, which is more common among politicized students in nontotalitarian countries.

[59] Ronald P. Dore, "Education: Japan," in R. E. Ward and D. Rustow, eds., *Political Modernization in Japan and Turkey* (Princeton University Press, 1964), pp. 180–87. He is, of course, writing chiefly of the leading state and private universities.

instability in Latin America. . . . Thus national politics become a matter of concern to everybody.[60]

Where, in a condition of political tension, the existing adult elites and counter-elites are ill-organized and ineffectual, student organizations are likely to become more important in the political sphere.

> . . . if young persons can gain sufficient influence to change on occasion the course of national political life, then . . . other power centres must be in such disarray as to elevate the relative power of any organized group.[61]

Thus, countries in which governments may be toppled by the political action of the military are often the same nations in which student activity is of major significance. Korea, Bolivia, the Sudan, and South Vietnam are the most recent cases in point.

THE STUDENT WITHIN THE UNIVERSITY

Academic standards are relevant. The greater the pressure placed on students to work hard to retain their position in university or to obtain a good appointment after graduation, the less they will participate in politics of any kind. Such an emphasis on rigorous training will be related to some extent to the professionalization of the teaching staff. Where the staff is part-time, as in most of Latin America, students will be more inclined to give their attention to nonacademic concerns, including politics. Students are also more available for politics in universities which do not hold the undergraduates to a demanding syllabus. This is the case in Japan and India. Within the university, of course, similar variations hold. Fields such as the natural sciences, which generally require more concentrated study and work than the arts subjects or the social sciences, will inhibit the inclination of students toward politics. Where there is sufficient concern for standards of instruction and student numbers are accordingly restricted to a level compatible with adequate instruction, as in engineering and medical faculties in India, student indiscipline is less marked.

An analysis of the behavior of Indian students which seeks to account for differences among universities indicates that the colleges with better

---

60 R. Havighurst, "Latin American and North American Higher Education," *Comparative Education Review* 4, no. 3 (1963): 180; or as Kalman Silvert has put it: "The Latin American university student is the child of his parents." "Continuity and Change in Latin America: The University Student," in John J. Johnson, ed., *Continuity and Change in Latin America* (Stanford University Press, 1964), p. 225. Parsons argues that the absence of "generalized ideological commitment" among American students reflects "the general political characteristics of the society, which has been a relatively stable system with a strong pluralistic character." "Youth in the Context of American Society," in Erik H. Erikson, ed., op. cit., p. 113.

61 Kalman Silvert, "The University Student," in John J. Johnson, ed., op. cit., p. 217.

trained and more devoted staffs experience relatively few incidents of student indiscipline. The students most likely to be involved in such activities appear to come from the arts faculties of institutions and departments of low standing, which require low per capita investment, which do not inculcate into the student a sense of self-esteem in the pursuit of knowledge and which offer fewer employment opportunities.[62]

The weak concern for academic standards in India is reflected in the admission standards of many of the larger universities which admit students, some suggest a majority, who do not have the background to carry on university level work.

> . . . the Vice-Chancellor of one of the greatest and oldest universities in India . . . recognized the futility of his university's task but suggested that it nevertheless fulfilled a social function. "We keep tens of thousands of young people off the streets," he said, "and instead of letting them become delinquents we turn them, instead, into communists.[63]

That it is possible to restrain student political activity is suggested by a recent study of the Arab world which reports that in ". . . Egypt and Syria, recently, the regime has been . . . successful in curbing political activities by increasing the number of examinations, stiffening the requirements to stay enrolled, trying to emphasize science and technology. . . ."[64]

Nonetheless, efforts to raise standards in an atmosphere impregnated with traditions of student agitation may themselves arouse unrest and political activity. The student generation which is subjected to demands for greater exertion may find their chances to gain a degree reduced. In various parts of Asia there have been

> spectacular student demonstrations in recent years, some of them with disturbing political overtones, . . . apparently caused by well-intended government measures to up-grade the curriculum. For example, a recent outburst of student agitation in Pakistan stemmed from the government's attempt to implement the report of the country's Educational Commission pointing the way to a lengthening and improvement of a number of curricula. But stiffer and tougher courses proved burdensome not only on those without the intellectual qualifications, but also on those with but slender means; and angry demonstrations, student strikes and walk-outs, even destruction of campus property, have been the result.[65]

---

[62] Edward Shils, "Indian Students," loc. cit., and Myron Weiner, *The Politics of Scarcity* (University of Chicago Press, 1962), pp. 184–85.

[63] Chanchal Sarkar, *The Unquiet Campus: Indian Universities Today* (Calcutta: The Statesman, 1960), p. 6; another detailed discussion of the nature and sources of student indiscipline may be found in Margaret Cormack, *She Who Rides a Peacock: Indian Students and Social Change* (New York: Frederick A. Praeger, 1961), especially, pp. 174–212.

[64] M. Berger, *The Arab World Today* (Garden City, N.Y.: Doubleday, 1962), p. 333.

[65] Justus M. Van der Kroef, op. cit., p. 178.

In Venezuela, in a deliberate effort to reduce student opposition politics, the University of Caracas adopted a "no repeating rule" in 1963, which provided that a student who failed more than twice was to be dropped permanently from the rolls of the university. This rule, however, was not enforced until the crisis of mid-May 1964, in which the police violated traditional university autonomy in order to arrest students accused of acts of terrorism. When the Rector responded to violent demonstrations against these arrests by announcing that the "no repeating rule" would be strictly enforced, a student strike designed to force the repeal of the rule developed, supported by both communist and Christian democratic student groups. The demonstrations and strike failed, however, when the university administration made it clear that if they continued, all students would be faced with the loss of a year's credit. Much of the success of these efforts to impose more exigent standards depends on the determination of university administrators and the attitude of the public. That students in their opposition to higher standards may be supported by a public which is concerned mainly with increasing the production of university graduates is indicated in Dr. Karve's account from India:

> It has happened that when the result of a particular examination was rather strict and a larger number of candidates than usual failed, public agitation in the newspapers and on the platform has been known to have taken place as a protest against the "massacre of the innocents." [66]

Where universities follow the historic Bologna practices of student participation in the government of the university through elections to university bodies, one may expect more political activity among students. In Latin American universities, "generally about one-third of the governing body are students.[67]

> The ideal of the university as a republic in microcosm has been central to student ideology in Latin America since the launching of the Cordoba University Reform Movement in Argentina in 1918 . . . in Latin America the student is used to exercising, or at least demands as his right, a much greater role in the conduct of university affairs than would be dreamed of on a U.S. campus.[68]

University issues such as the quality of teaching, the extent of library facilities, and the character of dormitories are linked in these situations to larger political matters.

Perhaps the best example of the way in which the concern of a student movement for a specifically academic demand, namely, the improvement of the quality of education, may have widespread political consequences is, of course, the famous Latin American University Reform Movement

---

[66] D. D. Karve, "Universities and the Public in India," *Minerva* 1, no. 3 (Spring 1963): 268.

[67] R. Havighurst, op. cit., pp. 176, 178–79.

[68] Frank Bonilla, "The Student Federation of Chile: 50 Years of Political Action," *Journal of Inter-American Studies* 2, no. 3 (1960): 312.

which began in the University of Cordoba in Argentina in 1918. It spread through much of Latin America, demanding a greater emphasis on the social and physical sciences and changes in the university government so as to give increased power to representatives of the staff and students. But regardless of its success in changing the university, the Reform Movement politicized university life in many Latin American countries. Robert Alexander reports: "there is no doubt that after 1918 each generation of students passed on to the next what had become a tradition of intense political activity by an appreciable part of the student body." [69]

The location of a university in or near a capital encourages political activity because national political organizations and personalities are more on the minds of students and are also more available as the foci of thought, agitation, and demonstration. Staff members are likewise more politicized, and students are more accessible to political agitators. Thus it was that Bengal, and particularly Calcutta, became the first center of student political agitation—Calcutta was the capital of the British Raj until 1912.

Latin America, Burma, and Japan testify to a similar relationship. "With few exceptions the only student organisations that historically have had important roles in political life (in Latin America) are those of the major national universities established in the capital cities." [70] Student political activity may soon become as high in provincial as in metropolitan universities, however, since those in the less prestigious institutions may feel the need to be politically involved to validate their claim to equal distinction. In Japanese student movements

> leadership is taken by students of the leading universities (located in Tokyo and Kyoto), and most of the participants belong to them. At the same time students in the minor leagues may feel that they must follow the example

[69] Robert Alexander, *Today's Latin America* (Garden City: Doubleday Anchor Books, 1962), p. 199. Perhaps the best collection of materials in English in the University Reform Movement is a book of articles by various Latin American scholars and participants in the movement; *University Reform in Latin America, Analyses and Documents,* published by the International Student Conference; no editor, no place, or date of publication indicated. A basic collection of documents on the movement is Gabriel del Mazo, ed., *La reforma universitaria,* vols. 1–3 (Buenos Aires: Ed. El Ateneo, 1946). A sampling of some of the large literature on the university, its problems and the Reform Movement, is the following: Gabriel del Mazo, *La reforma universitaria y la universidad latinoamericana* (Corrientes, República Argentina: Universidad Nacional de Nordeste, 1957); A. Grompone, *Universidad oficial y universidad viva* (Mexico, D. F.: Biblioteca de Ensayos Sociológicos, Universidad Nacional, n. d.); Luis Alberto Sánchez, *La universidad latinoamericana* (Guatemala City: Editorial Universitaria de Guatemala, 1949); Roberto Mac-Lean y Estenos, *la crisis universitaria en Hispano-América* (Mexico, D.F.: Biblioteca de Ensayos Sociológicos, Universidad Nacional, n. d.); and Lucio Mendieta y Núñez and José Gómez Robleda, *Problemas de la universidad* (Mexico, D.F.: Biblioteca de Ensayos Sociológicos, Universidad Nacional, n. d.); and Foción Febres Cordero, *Reforma universitaria* (Caracas: Universidad Central de Venezuela, 1959). Recent assessments of the Latin American University are found in Abraham Rabotnikov, "Panorama de la universidad latinoamericana," *Cultura Universitaria,* nos. 83–84 (April–September 1963): 82–101; and Rudolph P. Atcon, "The Latin American University," *Die Deutsche Universitätzeitung,* No. 2 (February 1962): 9–48.

[70] Kalman Silvert, op. cit., p. 212.

set by those in the major leagues in order to assure themselves that they are university students too. Thus the same type of movement spreads easily all over the country, and federation is readily accomplished under the leadership of the students in leading universities.[71]

Earlier it was noted that the larger the university, the greater the absolute number of those with dispositions to political activity and the stronger their mutual support, organization, and resources. Larger student bodies will also heighten the tendency toward the formation of an autonomous student culture resistant to the efforts of the university administration to control it. Large universities in capital cities are, therefore, especially prone to agitation and demonstrative student politics. The massive demonstrations mounted in Tokyo in opposition to the Mutual Security Treaty between Japan and the United States; in Seoul against the treaty between Japan and Korea; in Buenos Aires against a Bill providing for state support of private (Catholic) universities; in Warsaw and Budapest demanding more freedom; in Paris against the Algerian war; and many others in recent years have been associated with the existence of large universities located in major metropolitan centers, often national capitals, in which students have provided an easily mobilizable population available for opposition to authority.

The greater the number of years the student spends at the university, the greater the likelihood of student political activity. Tenure may be determined not only by actual number of scheduled course years, but by rules pertaining to requirements for a degree. Where the university system permits students to "hang around" for years, to finish at their own discretion, one may find the phenomenon of the professional student, from whose ranks political leaders are likely to be recruited. Shils points to those Indians who

> live on in the university or college hostels, not registered, not studying, having nothing academic about them except their residence and their associates. Older, tougher, more ingenious, often seductively attractive, these "professional" students are often the catalysts who agitate lambs into lions.[72]

Such a system also permits political parties to maintain paid agents on campus, as occurs in India, Latin America, and elsewhere.

> The possibility of making a career of being a student over an extended period by moving from one practically autonomous "faculty" to another, and the extended courses taken by many students, so that the presence of students over 30 years of age does not cause any lifted eyebrows, is a circumstance favorable to the unremarked continuous presence of such agents who have other motives than to get an education.[73]

---

[71] M. Shimbori, "Zengakuren: A Japanese Case Study of a Student Political Movement," *Sociology of Education* 37, no. 21 (1964): 232.

[72] Edward Shils, "Indian Students," loc. cit., p. 17.

[73] E. Wight Bakke, "Students on the March: The Cases of Mexico and Colombia," *Sociology of Education* 37, no. 3 (1964): 204.

Whether students live at home with their families, in university halls of residence, or in "digs" will affect their involvement in politics in particular. The common life in a hostel or hall of residence or dormitory enhances the formation of common student attitudes, a consciousness of kind, and the readiness to mobilize for organized activity. The *Cité Universitaire* in Paris clearly has facilitated student political activity in recent years. This proposition assumes, of course, that these common residential arrangements are not attended by strict supervision by adults, where the wardens or other university or college officials stand *in loco parentis*. The relative peacefulness of student life in British and American universities is partly a function of the strength of a tradition in which the teaching staff takes on responsibility for the surveillance and supervision of the students' affairs. The provision of hostels on the continental and Indian styles, where it occurs against a tradition of an almost complete laissez-faire attitude on the part of the teaching staff vis-à-vis the students, only contributes to turning the halls of residence into centers of agitation.

Living in digs and cafés, in the pattern of the major Latin continental countries, France and Italy, is frequently associated with the emergence of an autonomous political culture among the students and that culture is usually agitational and extremist.

Living at home prolongs the authority of the family over the student and tends to insulate him from university influences.[74] The Indian student study cited earlier indicates that the more conservative the political party, the more likely were its supporters to live with parents or relatives while attending university, while a disproportionate number of more leftist students lived in hostels or in a "private lodge." [75] In Japan, with its strong radical student movement, the centers of activity are in

the metropolitan areas, especially Tokyo, [which] have the largest proportion of students who are far from home and live either in a dormitory or in a lodging. They are freer as well as lonelier than students who live at home. Their marginality is greater, and they are less controlled—a favorable condition again for student movements.[76]

Similarly, a survey of student political leaders in Santiago, Chile, reports that the "greater freedom of action of students from the provinces, many of whom escape strict parental control for the first time on coming to the university also helps to explain the prominence of provincials." [77]

The quality of the relationships between students and their teachers

---

74 For evidence of this in relation to Colombia, see K. Walker, "Determinants of Castro Support among Latin American University Students," pp. 16–17, cited footnote 52 above. Cf. also the *Calcutta University Commission 1917–1919 Report,* 12 volumes (Calcutta: Government of India Press, 1919).

75 Bureau of Social Science Research, *Political Attitudes of Indian Students* (Washington: The American University, 1955), p. 46.

76 M. Shimbori, op. cit., p. 233.

77 Frank Bonilla, *Students in Politics: Three Generations of Political Action in a Latin-American University* (Ph.D. thesis, Department of Social Relations, Harvard University, 1959), p. 253. A study of former communists in four countries, the United

depends in part on the traditions which have developed within the various university systems and on the student/staff ratio. Where there is a drastic separation between students and teachers, where teachers have other than university employment, or where there is a very great number of students per staff member, the staff will have less direct influence on student behavior than where the relationship is more that of the apprentice working closely with the master. The relationship between teachers and students is, of course, not exclusively determined by the number of students a teacher must teach. The deference accorded to university teachers within their society will to some extent affect their influence on students. The eminence of teachers in the world of science and scholarship, their interest in their own subjects and their academic self-esteem based on their belief in the worthiness of their calling and accomplishment are additional factors which determine whether students become integrated into the structure of the university as an intellectual community connected with the center of its society or whether they will become attached to an autonomous and more or less alienated student community. Frank Bonilla has said that the relatively low level of competence of professors in Brazil and the consequent lack of respect for them by students is one of the factors which "occasionally makes for excesses and for a hyper-politicization of academic issues" in that country.[78] An eminent Indian administrator and educator writing of the sources of student indiscipline attributes much responsibility to the fact that "teachers today do not command the respect and affection of their pupils to the extent they did in the past" and suggests various devices to raise the social status of academics.[79]

States, England, France and Italy, points to a comparable causal pattern in describing the conditions under which many joined the party while in university. "It is certainly true that at the time of joining the party their condition might have been accurately described as 'alienated.' In many cases they were away from home for the first time, adapting to a new setting, exposed to confusing impressions, rejective and iconoclastic with regard to their pasts, and confronted with a political world [during the 1930s] in which militance might readily have appeared to be an appropriate attitude." Gabriel Almond, *The Appeals of Communism* (Princeton, N.J.: Princeton University Press, 1954), p. 215.

[78] Frank Bonilla, "Education and Political Development in Brazil: Growth toward Nationhood" (mimeographed paper, Conference on Education and Political Development, Lake Arrowhead, California, 25–29 June 1962), pp. 13–14. For a general analysis of the way in which large classes, overcrowding, and lack of scholarly resources alienate Latin American students from university life, see Gabriel del Mazo, "La nueva crisis de las universidades latino-americanas," *Panoramas* 2, no. 10 (July–August 1965): 95–111.

[79] See Humayun Kabir, *Education in New India* (London: Allen and Unwin, 1956), pp. 151–66. Shils has detailed the decline in status, influence and income of Indian academic and other intellectuals since independence. He cites the fact "that in Bombay University more than one-half of the teaching staff had been at one time or another approached by students or friends or kinsmen of students with the intention of obtaining special favors in connection with examinations in return for payment, . . . [as showing] how little respect intellectual life and the standards in which it rests enjoy in the Indian middle classes." Edward Shils, *The Intellectual between Tradition and Modernity: The Indian Situation* (The Hague: Mouton and Co., 1961), p. 107.

The high cost of living in large towns and the lack of financial support or opportunity for employment clearly generate student dissatisfaction and unrest in India and Burma, although this does not determine whether their unrest will take a political form or will express itself in other forms of indiscipline. Student poverty fosters and intensifies resentment which frequently focuses on questions of fees, hostel, and food charges, etc. The main themes of the resentments of impoverished students, particularly in countries without traditions of part-time student employment or without opportunities for it, are easily adaptable to the major themes of conventional extremist political agitation. Part-time student employment does not really fit into the traditions of university life in most countries —students in underdeveloped countries either come from or aspire to a style of life in which learning and manual work are thought to be incompatible—nor does it fit into the economic situation of those countries. There is, therefore, no remedy for student poverty except further subsidy, or the refusal of admission to indigent students, which is contrary to every assumption of present-day public life and raises serious questions of policy as to how to deal with unemployed secondary school-leavers.

ALTERNATIVE ACTIVITIES

Participation in politics is an alternative to other forms of extracurricular activity.

> In Colombia and Mexico, where the extracurriculum is virtually non-existent, at least in the public universities, satisfaction of this leadership ambition must focus on participation in university management and in the opportunity to stimulate, organize and inspire student group action.[80]

In the United States, organized sports were expressly introduced into colleges and universities to divert the adolescent energy which in many college communities had gone into brawls and "town and gown" riots. Conscious but unsuccessful efforts to manipulate the situation similarly so as to diminish the energy available for political activity have been attempted by some American-run universities in the Arab world:

> American universities in the Near East have tried to reduce their [student] political activity, which takes the form of demonstrations and strikes, by providing more opportunities for extracurricular activities such as athletics

---

[80] E. W. Bakke, op. cit., p. 203. "In most Near Eastern universities, . . . students have no organized extracurricular activities and little or no personal contact with teachers. . . . Thus, . . . the excess energy of Near Eastern students is easily sucked into the political vacuum." Dankwart Rustow, "Politics and Westernization in the Near East," in Richard Nolte, ed., *The Modern Middle East* (New York: Atherton Press, 1963), p. 89. An analysis of student life in British universities reports there "are about 200 intercollegiate clubs and societies in Oxford and probably three or four times as many in colleges." Ferdynand Zweig, *The Student in the Age of Anxiety* (London: Heinemann, 1963; New York: Free Press, 1964), p. 23.

and clubs of many kinds. The logic behind this policy has been that such hitherto neglected aspects of Arab campus life might drain off the students' political energies into other channels. But this American technique has not worked. The new activities have only given the students additional stages upon which to play their political roles, more opportunities to disagree with one another, more arenas in which to extend their political attitudes on the campus.[81]

In Japan also, during the 1920s, in a conscious effort to counter the growth of student radicalism, "political societies were banned in the universities, sports were encouraged instead, and the puritanical restrictions on high school love affairs were relaxed in an effort to divert student energies to less dangerous channels." [82] The traditional pattern could not, however, be overcome.

The mere provision of opportunity for extracurricular activities does not, then, guarantee that all or even most students will make a satisfactory social adjustment. In all societies, some, for reasons of personality, inadequate income, or family background, will find themselves to be "outsiders." Political groups simultaneously gratify the resentment of "outsiders" and give them a dignified position in the course of their activities.

Much of the time which male university students in Western countries do not devote to study or to student societies is devoted to attending to young women. Where the tradition of marriage by arrangement prevails, and women are isolated from men before marriage, this opportunity does not exist. Even the small proportion of young women in the student body in such societies live within this tradition. They are more carefully watched over by custodians and the young men are too shy and too gauche. That this is not a minor student concern is dramatically revealed in a recent study of Asian students:

> In a series of samples of over 1500 students in four South-East Asian universities who were asked: "What has been the most serious personal problem which has adversely affected your university studies?", over 80 percent answered: "Troubles with the opposite sex." This did not mean troubles with females with whom relationships had been established but rather the inability to initiate any relationships at all with them. The stories are legion of Rangoon University male students who for months follow, from a distance, female students they admire in the hope that somehow they might be introduced to them. The initiation of the faintest and least erotic heterosexual relationships in Asian universities is hampered by inhibition and uncertainty.[83]

---

81 M. Berger, op. cit., p. 333.
82 Ronald P. Dore, op. cit., p. 185.
83 Joseph Fischer, "The University Student in South and South-East Asia," *Minerva* 2, no. 1 (Autumn 1963): 49; and Benjamin Schlesinger, "Student Unrest in Indian Universities," *Comparative Education Review* 6, no. 3 (1963): 221.

As a result, students have more time and energy than they can or are willing to use on their studies and they have no satisfactory outlet for them. Their sexual propensities exist in a vacuum.[84] The vacuum is sometimes filled by restless and freely floating hostility and sometimes by the precipitation of that hostility into a political form.

PATTERNS OF RECRUITMENT TO UNIVERSITIES

There has been an increase in the proportion of university students in underdeveloped countries coming from lower middle class, village, and even peasant families, although the last are still very rare. Students from these backgrounds tend to be less sophisticated, less at ease in the languages of academic discourse. Despite what seems to be their great seriousness in the pursuit of a "career" through attendance at university, they have more difficulties in settling down. Their pecuniary as well as cultural poverty places them under a great strain. Just what this contributes to the extreme politicization of university students is uncertain. It surely causes distress, but whether distress gives rise to extremist political attitudes is not settled. Bonilla believes that it does have such a consequence, at least for Chile.

> . . . important segments of student leadership come from lower middle- and working-class families, from the provinces and from among first-generation Chileans (though only 3.2 percent of the population were foreign-born, 31 percent of the student leaders had at least one foreign-born parent). In an extremely class-conscious country, all of these are groups with a marked status disadvantage. They are the groups bearing the brunt of existing inequities, the ones with the most to gain from social and political reforms and the individuals most likely to be caught up in the competition for status.[85]

Surveys of Brazilian [86] and Panamanian law students also suggest that lower class origins tend to render students more political. Brazilian students of lower status background were more likely to believe that such activities should be engaged in regularly than were students from more privileged families.[87] A study of student attitudes conducted at the University of Ibadan, Nigeria, in 1960, revealed that students whose fathers had lower status occupations were more likely to be affiliated to a politi-

---

[84] Edward Shils, "Indian Students," loc. cit., p. 19.

[85] F. Bonilla, *Students in Politics*, cited footnote 77 above, p. 253.

[86] Ronald L. Scheman, "The Brazilian Law Student: Background, Habits, Attitudes," *Journal of Inter-American Studies* 5, no. 3 (1963): 252.

[87] On the other hand, students from middle-class backgrounds were found to be more politically active than those from upper- or lower-class backgrounds. The meaning of these divergent results is obscure.

cal party, and among the affiliated those from lower status backgrounds were more likely to be politically active.[88]

The study of Panamanian law students, which distinguished between "radical nationalists," those who strongly favored nationalization of the Canal, and "moderates," those who felt less strongly about or who opposed nationalization, supports the hypothesis regarding the class correlates of radicalism. The more radical students disproportionately came from rural or small town backgrounds and low-income families. Their "backgrounds were marginal in a few significant respects which suggest that they may feel relatively deprived in status." [89] And an analysis of Brazilian student opinion in a number of universities reported that lower family income tends to be associated with more leftist views.[90] A survey among college students in various parts of China in 1937 revealed that students in the lowest income group, primarily sons of small landlords and peasants, were most likely to have "radical," essentially communist, political sympathies.[91]

We may wish to distinguish between societies in which admission to university is easy and those in which it is difficult; whether there is mass education, as in the United States, the Philippines, Puerto Rico, or Argentina, in which almost anyone who wants to enter a university may

---

[88] William John Hanna, "Students" in James S. Coleman and Carl G. Rosberg, Jr., eds., *Political Parties and National Integration in Tropical Africa* (Berkeley: University of California, 1964), pp. 419, 421.

[89] Daniel Goldrich, *Radical Nationalism: The Political Orientations of Panamanian Law Students* (East Lansing: Bureau of Political and Social Research, Michigan State University, 1961), pp. 7, 9, 19.

[90] *Student Study* (São Paulo: Instituto de Estudos Sociais e Economicos, 1963), *passim*. As noted earlier, Gabriel Almond reported that in terms of "class, ethnic or regional origin" European former communists who joined the party while in university in various countries were of relatively low social status (op. cit., p. 215). Within a communist nation, Poland, it is interesting to note that the same variable is associated with support for economic egalitarianism, although the operating communist order and ideology stress the need for inequality of income and university students aspire to the financially more rewarding positions. Thus, a Polish study reports, "the higher the position of the student's parents, the less he is in favour of economic equality." S. Novak, "Social Attitudes of Warsaw Students," loc. cit., p. 100. And in Japan, an analysis of students at the University of Tokyo completed in 1957 found that support for the leftist Zengakuren was associated with lower family socioeconomic status. M. Ozaki, "The Third Generation," unpublished translation. It should be noted that almost all students at Tokyo University are from middle-class or higher-class families. There are few children of workers or peasants there. In Iran also, ideological politics is reported to have "its major appeal among students, especially those students of lower middle class connections." Leonard Binder, *Iran: Political Development in a Changing Society* (Berkeley: University of California Press, 1962), p. 215.

On the other hand, a survey of the opinions of students in three families at the University of Buenos Aires indicated that although the differences correlated with mobility are small, the "upwardly mobile elements seem inclined to attach less importance to politics than the stable." K. H. Silvert and Frank Bonilla, *Education and the Social Meaning of Development: A Preliminary Statement* (New York: American Universities Field Staff, 1961), p. 104.

[91] Olga Lang, *Chinese Family and Society* (New Haven, Conn.: Yale University Press, 1946), pp. 317–18.

do so; and where education is "elitist," based on the assumption that universities should admit only a relatively small elite who meet stringent criteria and have passed through a rigorous system of elimination in the lower schools, as in Britain and the former British African colonies.

Elitist systems tend to assure those who succeed in reaching university a guaranteed place in the upper levels of society. To enter, remain in, and graduate from systems of higher education is all-important. Relatively few drop out through failure or other reasons. Students may realistically expect to enter the elite and thus they tend to identify with the existing one. One may anticipate, therefore, that elitist systems will be less productive of student political unrest than those which do not offer secure paths to success. A study of Nigerian and Sierra Leonean students attending the University College of Sierra Leone [92] provides striking evidence of elite status expectations in two countries where university students form a tiny minority of their age group. When asked: "By the time you are 45, how active are you likely to be in the political life of your country as a whole?" 49 percent of the Nigerians said they would be active and 24 percent expected to be cabinet ministers or members of the legislature (25 percent). Sierra Leoneans were somewhat less sanguine about high-level political careers, but only 35 percent of them reported that they did not expect to play any significant political role, as contrasted with 27 percent among the Nigerians.[93] This is not simply a function of better intellectual and social qualifications on admission or of better prospects after graduation. The pattern of teaching in the "elitist" systems is much more conducive to the incorporation of the student into the university community as a part of the central institutional system. Residence in halls with intimate contact with teachers serving *in loco parentis,* smaller classes, tutorial arrangements, isolation in a part of the country not far from, but not easily accessible to, the capital city, as well as a generally patrician, non-populistic, social and political culture all contribute to this result.[94]

The situation of the Egyptian, Japanese, and Indian students, on the other hand, may be cited to illustrate the consequence of a policy of unlimited admission. In these nations, attendance at university has "skyrocketed" since independence, far outstripping the rise in suitable job opportunities. Malcolm Kerr suggests that in Egypt it

---

[92] It should be pointed out that Fourah Bay College is the oldest institution of higher education in Africa south of the Sahara. It has produced a larger proportion of older administrators, the cultural, ecclesiastical and political elites of West Africa than any other institution in that part of the world.

[93] Dwaine Marvick, "Higher Education in the Development of Future West African Leaders: A Survey of the Perspectives of Students at Fourah Bay College, Freetown, Sierra Leone" (mimeographed paper presented at the Conference on Education and Political Development held at Lake Arrowhead, California, 25–29 June 1962), Table 17, p. 33.

[94] At the same time, the students of the University of Ghana, which meets all the criteria of "elitist" education, seem, according to many observers, to be quite alienated from the government of their country.

is this explosive compound of the high aspirations and self-conscious dignity instilled by university education on the one hand and the frustration and deception imposed by the conditions of the market, that has made university students and graduates a continuing revolutionary force. . . .[95]

Their current support for Nasser rests on his commitment "to provide them with opportunities for successful careers."
In Japan:

Since the end of the war there has been a very spectacular increase in the total number of students enrolled in the higher schools and universities. . . . The proportion of economically poor students has increased at a much higher rate than has the total number of students. . . . The family of the poor student invariably makes a supreme economic sacrifice to get him through college. Nevertheless, only about half of the more than 120 thousand students who graduate annually from the universities are able to find jobs which are in any way commensurate with their level of aspirations and ambitions. With each passing year, it can be anticipated that there will be a steady increase in the number of unemployed or "improperly" employed university graduates who will be disssatisfied with their lot.[96]

The phenomena of increasing university enrollments and a decreasing prospect of access to elite positions for large numbers of university graduates has also occurred to some extent in Latin America. José Enrique Miguens refers to the consequent

deep impression that they are not needed by their societies, that not only are they employed in marginal occupations with minimal [economic] rewards, but they are not accorded gratitude or other forms of social esteem beyond some stylistic flattery in the way they are addressed.[97]

CONCLUDING OBSERVATIONS

This chapter has attempted to analyze some of the conditions under which university students, above all university students in underdeveloped countries, reject incorporation into the university as an intellectual community and refuse to accept the existing political and social order of which the university is a part in the political sphere. It has sought also to account for the radical orientation, usually socialist, of their political outlook and activity. It has considered the factors which help account for

---

95 Malcolm Kerr, "Education and Political Development in Egypt: Some Problems of Political Socialization" (mimeographed paper for the Conference on Education and Political Development held at Lake Arrowhead, California, 25–29 June 1962), pp. 25–27; see also M. Berger, op. cit., p. 333.

96 L. H. Battistini, *The Postwar Student Struggle in Japan* (Tokyo: Charles Tuttle, 1956), pp. 141–42.

97 José Enrique Miguens, "Radiografías de las juventudes latinoamericanas," *Occidente* 17, no. 141 (Octboer 1962): 20.

variations in the direction and intensity of student political orientations, including cultural and social characteristics of underdeveloped countries, the characteristics of the universities in such countries, and the characteristics of the students themselves.

In general it may be said that where the society, the university, and the student are committed to the fullest development of research and teaching in an atmosphere of academic freedom, and where adequate resources are available in the form of faculty, libraries, laboratories, and financial support, students are less likely to engage in political activities and more likely to allow themselves to be assimilated into the corporate life of the university as an institution devoted to the interpretation of what is inherited, the discovery of new truths, and the training of students to do both of these and to prepare themselves for careers based on these activities. On the other hand, even when these conditions are present, there is an inherent tendency for students to take a critical attitude toward the status quo. This critical attitude is the product of a tradition of criticism and alienation, and of the rebellious attitude of youth toward their elders in modern societies; it is also a product of the application of the presumed standards of advanced countries to the behavior of present elites and the societies they govern.[98]

Many protest movements directed at changes in the university constitution and amenities are not always linked to demands for political changes. Indeed, much of the student indiscipline in some underdeveloped countries has become quite apolitical. Some of it expresses grievances about the conditions of life and study and some of it expresses an amorphous dissatisfaction and hostility with immediate authoritative institutions, without political objects or legitimations. It is particularly important to notice that even though radical and extremist attitudes and actions occur frequently among highly politicized students, many students are not very politicized, and some of them, insofar as they have political attitudes at all, are conservative, moderate, or liberal. Thus, a study conducted among students in twenty-two universities and colleges throughout China in 1937, a period when student radical activity was at its height, revealed wide

---

[98] Although in the main student politics in the underdeveloped societies tend to be "leftist," there are significant variations from this tendency. Despite their education in more modern orientations within the university, many if not most students in such societies have grown up in traditional surroundings, and some of them disapprove of changes which threaten to alter radically the values with which they were raised. Some evidence for this is contained in a report on surveys conducted in Pakistan, Iran, Thailand, and Malaysia, in which students were asked whether a group of nations including Great Britain, France, West Germany, Japan, the United States, and Russia were "too much on the side of reform," "too much on the side of having things as they are," or "about right in their attitudes." The United States and Russia, despite their obvious ideological differences, were seen as excessively *favorable to reform* more often than were the other nations listed. *Student Survey in Pakistan* (Bielefeld: E.M.N.I.D., 1963); *Teheran University Study: Attitudes and Aspirations* (Teheran: National Institute of Psychology, 1963); *Malayan Student Study* (Bangkok: Coordination Center for Southeast Asian Studies, 1963); and *Student Study—Thailand* (Bangkok: Coordination Center for Southeast Asian Studies, 1963).

variation in student ideological orientations. Of some 1160 students, 10 percent were "conservative," 14 percent "fascist," 12 percent "democratic," 10 percent "Christian," 19 percent "radical" (communist), and 16 percent "nationalist." [99] In India, a sample of students from ten universities, when asked to give their preferred choice of government among a number of alternatives, opted 23 percent in favor of parliamentary democracy as in England, 15 percent for democracy as in the United States, 18 percent for democratic socialism, 6 percent for the Soviet type of socialism, 21 percent for people's democracy as in new China, and 10 percent for "dictatorship." [100] And when asked their views concerning civil liberties for minority groups, 36 percent of these students indicated agreement with the statement, "Steps should be taken right away to outlaw the Communist party," as contrasted with 52 percent who opposed such an action and 9 percent who could not make up their minds.[101]

Other countries in Asia in fact reveal considerable political conservatism among university students. Thus a study of opinions in four universities in the Philippines reports that the overwhelming majority gave very pro-American responses in answer to questions concerning the nature of the American social system or about correspondence of the interests of the Philippines and the United States, while much antagonism was evidenced toward both the Soviet Union and Communist China. Almost two-thirds indicated "satisfaction" with the way American "private companies operated their business in the Philippines.[102]

In Malaysia, a study of student opinion at the University of Malaya reported that, when asked to state their preference for government or private ownership of industry, the respondents divided into three almost equal parts, for a mixed system, for private ownership, and for government ownership. Seventy percent reported having a good opinion of Great Britain and the United States, as contrasted with only 14 percent favorable to the Soviet Union and 7 percent to Communist China.[103]

In Thailand similar questions answered by students of Thammasát University resulted in even more conservative responses. Forty-five percent of the Thai students favored private ownership of industry as contrasted to 25 percent for government ownership and 27 percent "mixed" replies. They were also more pro-American than the Malaysians (86 percent) and more hostile to the Soviet Union and Communist China.[104]

In Latin America too there is substantial evidence that radical and extremist views are far from the only ones to be found among university

---

[99] Recomputed from data in Table XV in Olga Lang, op. cit., p. 316.

[100] *The Indian Student* (Washington, D.C.: Bureau of Social Science Research, 1954), p. 40. One has the impression that since the beginning of the present decade, the proportion in the last two categories has diminished considerably, without any compensating incorporation into the university community.

[101] Ibid., p. 43.

[102] Private, unpublished survey of student opinion in the Philippines.

[103] *Malayan Student Study* (Bangkok: Coordination Center for Southeast Asian Studies, 1963), pp. 27, 32.

[104] *Student Study—Thailand* (Bangkok: Coordination Center for Southeast Asian Studies, 1963), pp. 38, 45.

students. Most recently there has been a decline of the Reformista vote in elections at the University of Buenos Aires, and across the Andes, in the Chilean University elections, a loss of votes for the leftist coalition, FRAP.[105] In Brazil, students, when asked to give their opinions of capitalism, divided almost evenly: 50 percent answered positively, while 47 percent were negative. Conversely, 26 percent stated that communism is "good" while 68 percent thought it was "bad." [106] A Mexican study based on interviews with students in nine universities also reports considerable ideological diversity, although as a group they seemed much more favorable to socialism than their compeers in Argentina or Brazil. When asked their opinions of socialism, 57 percent answered "very good" or "good" as contrasted with 10 percent who had negative answers. A comparable question about "communism" revealed 25 percent favorable and 40 percent negative. And "capitalism" as a system was approved by 29 percent and termed as "bad" or "very bad" by over 40 percent of those replying.[107]

A recent survey of students in Colombian universities also points to the diversity of political attitudes among students. The large majority expressed dissatisfaction with all parties, including the left-wing liberals and the communists. Of those with preferences, about half favored the parties of government coalition, the official liberals and the conservatives. The communists were backed by 11 percent of those who expressed an opinion, or 4 percent of the total sample. But though Colombian students may not identify with any specific reformist or communist ideology, it is important to note that there is a relationship between their satisfaction with their own society and their political opinions. The more dissatisfied students were the least likely to have a preference for any party.[108]

The discrepancy between the image of university students in developing countries as predominantly leftist and the data reported in various opinion surveys points to the existence of large numbers of students who are indifferent to politics or who, whatever their preferences, do not have intense feelings about political things. The Brazilian study, cited earlier, reports that among students who state that they are "very interested" in politics, 60 percent have negative attitudes toward capitalism, while among those reporting that they "are not at all interested in politics," only 16 percent are anticapitalist. However, 55 percent of the politically apathetic group indicate hostility to communism, as contrasted with but 37 percent anti-communist among the very interested.[109] The Mexican study suggests a comparable pattern among students in that country.

---

[105] On diversity among Argentinian students in the past see Kalman Silvert, *The Conflict Society: Reaction and Revolution in Latin America* (New Orleans: The Hauser Press, 1961), p. 166.

[106] *Student Study* (São Paulo: Instituto de Estudos Sociais e Economicos, 1963), responses to question 10 (pages are unnumbered).

[107] *A Study of Opinions of University Students in Mexico* (Mexico City: International Research Associates, 1964), pp. 16–19.

[108] "En minoría absoluta los universitarios que tienen interés por la política," *El Tiempo* (7 June 1964), p. 7. This study was done under the direction of Professor Istvan Mustog of the Pontificia Universidad Javeriana, Bogotá.

[109] *Student Study* (São Paulo: Instituto de Estudos Sociais e Economicos, 1963).

Whatever the qualitifications which have to be introduced into the picture drawn in the preceding pages, the fact remains that university students in underdeveloped countries constitute a significant proportion of the rebellious elements in their respective societies.[110] As such they play an important part in political life. But what happens to their political rebelliousness when they cease to be students?

Writing about what happened to the revolutionary students of tsarist Russia of sixty years ago after they had left university, Bernard Pares raised this question and suggested an answer:

> What becomes of the ex-student? In fact, he very often ceases to be a reformer when he ceases to be a student, that is, when he becomes a man. He begins to get experience of life and he leaves his ideals behind him. This . . . discounts the political value of the student's ideals. . . . Friends of reason and of liberty must be grateful to the universities for offering at least the nucleus of a protest of principle. In a word, one has much less reason to quarrel with the spirit of self-sacrifice amongst the students than with the instinct of self-interest which so many of them have shown when they passed into the ranks of officialdom.[111]

Yet it is doubtful whether Pares was right concerning the adult behavior of student revolutionaries in Russia. Ten years after he wrote, political movements largely led and staffed by alumni of student protest overturned tsarist autocracy. Today in many countries, local political experts agree with Pares about the lack of long-term consequences of student radicalism on participants after graduation. In Japan, where there is general agreement that student socialists turn conservative after securing employment leading to positions in business or government, opinion surveys show that more university graduates vote for leftist rather than for conservative parties and that there is a larger socialist vote among the "management and professionals" category than among manual workers.[112] A Japanese sociologist informed the author that a confidential survey conducted among a sample of young business executives (under 40) reported that a majority voted for the left-wing Socialist party. In India, also survey data show disproportionate backing for the more

---

110 Thus even in the Philippines, students stand out as a group which contribute "many of the active members of the [communist] party and the participants in front organizations." George E. Taylor, *The Philippines and the United States* (New York: Frederick A. Praeger, 1964), pp. 278, 285.

111 B. Pares, *Russia between Reform and Revolution* (New York: Schocken Books, 1962), pp. 197–98.

112 Research Society on Japanese Social Structure, "Special Traits of White-Collar Workers in Large Urban Areas," *Journal of Social and Political Ideas in Japan* 1, no. 2 (August 1963): 78; Z. Suetuna, H. Aoyama, C. Hyashi, and K. Matusita, "A Study of Japanese National Character, Part II," *Annals of the Institute of Statistical Mathematics* (Tokyo), Supplement II (1961): 54; Robert A. Scalapino and Junnosuke Masumi, *Parties and Politics in Contemporary Japan* (Berkeley: University of California Press, 1961), p. 177.

leftist tendencies among the university-educated.[113] As in tsarist Russia and the China of some decades past, leftist ideologies, socialism, and current varieties of socialism or communism have been strong among the elite because these political tendencies are symbolically associated with modernization, rapid economic development, and ultimately with equality, all of these being objectives favored by the well educated. Capitalism is perceived as being linked to foreign influences, traditionalism, and slow growth. Hence many of the younger and better schooled members of the elites, including business executives, often look with favor on or at least are not hostile to leftist tendencies. Such patterns are more common in Asia and Africa than they are in Latin America, but they seem to exist in most of the nations of the "third world."

THE NEED FOR FUTURE RESEARCH

It is clear that if we are to understand the effects of modern education on the dynamics of change in these countries, it is important not only to study what happens to the student within universities, but also the way in which those who have had a "modern" education and who have become part of the intellectual classes conceive of their society and its system of authority after they have left university.[114] As yet, however, there are even fewer reliable data concerning the attitudes of the adults of the intellectual classes than concerning students.

Our observations of the political effects of university education, or simply of the political correlates of university education, are still in a very primitive state. Indeed, the entire study of universities and their role in the development of the society, polity, economy, and culture of their countries is still to be undertaken systematically. There are multitudes of questions requiring answers, but there are few answers. We know little about the influence of the patterns of university organization or the types of courses of study best fitted to train young people to become responsible and effective incumbents of elite positions in countries which seek to modernize themselves. The influence of university studies, patterns of recruitment, modes of teaching, on intellectual, professional, political, and cultural standards and aspirations, or the assimilation of

---

113 See Indian Institute of Public Opinion, *Monthly Public Opinion Surveys* 2 (January–April 1957): 9–14; 4 (June–September 1959): 73; 8 (February 1963): 5. However, it should be noted that the Congress party is dominant among all educational strata. Among those with a "post-graduate" education, 61 percent favored the Congress party and 11 percent the communists in 1963. In 1959, before the Chinese War, support for communism among the educated was much higher.

114 It has been suggested that the process of becoming more conservative takes time, and that it may be concealed in many reports of opinion related to education since the bulk of the well educated in the merging nations are young. An Indian report on communist adherents in Lucknow supports this suggestion. The better educated were the most likely to be communists, but younger college graduates (under 40) gave the communists more support (25 percent) than did the older (15 percent). *The Indian Student* (Washington, D.C.: Bureau of Social Science Research, 1954), p. 8.

students into the various spheres of adult activity is still *terra incognita*. Nor are we better informed about the influence of family background, modes of preuniversity education and intragenerational relationships on academic and political performance at the university and after graduation.

One major hypothesis of great practical importance asserts that the intense involvement of students in politics is least likely where their universities have very high standards, adequate study and research facilities, and a teaching staff deeply committed to teaching and research. Still, the factual basis for this hypothesis is very fragmentary and vague. A really scientific answer would require the comparison of institutions which are similar with respect to size, location, pattern of student recruitment, and characteristics of the environing society, but different with respect to their standards, teaching and research staff, library, laboratory provision, etc. Such comparisons between universities within a society should be supplemented by international comparisons, in order to determine the extent to which national variations in culture and in student political traditions account for variations in the extent and character of student political activity.

One could go on multiplying the illustrations of significant research which should be conducted into the role of universities, university teachers, and university students in the life of their societies. In the foregoing chapter, I have taken only one small section of this vast and still uncharted domain and attempted to summarize some of the available historical and sociological studies, some quite rigorously quantitative, some impressionistic, some very general, some very particular, and many of them not readily comparable, bearing on this small section. The illumination brought to it by ordering these data should, I hope, be accepted not only for the substantive insight it affords but as an argument for the necessity of more systematic research into the nature and functions of universities in the modern world.

20

STUDENT REBELLION:
VISION OF THE FUTURE
OR ECHO FROM THE PAST?

RAYMOND ARON

In order to limit my subject and to concentrate on the most interesting or familiar cases, I shall not discuss Latin-American universities, for two reasons. These universities have known student unrest for a long time, and have granted their students a role in the administration—a right which is demanded by some protesters and which is spreading throughout the West. Secondly, the relative underdevelopment, the influence of the United States, the example of Cuba, and the mediocrity and authoritarianism of a great many established regimes suggest probable interpretations. Similarly, African universities give their students a Western education, separate them from their milieu, teach them criticism and the critical spirit. How could the students fail to perceive the gap between the society they live in and the society whose ideal plan has been taught them through the culture they have received? How could they fail to revolt when the best jobs, those in government bureaucracy, are held by the preceding generation, and when economic progress offers graduates, most of them nonscientific, no chance of promotion in the private sector?

I shall therefore limit myself to student revolts in the industrialized countries, in the United States, Western Europe, and Japan. A question that arises immediately is, To what extent do the students revolt in Eastern Europe, in the Socialist countries, and, where they do, is this the same phenomenon as in the industrialized, democratic, and liberal countries? A first observation is that there have been no student revolts in the Soviet Union; student revolts have taken place only in Poland, where they were brutally put down, and in Czechoslovakia, where they were an integral part of a national movement. In order to enter college it is not enough merely to have graduated from secondary school; a college accepts only a small percentage of those who apply to it. For this reason

From *Political Science Quarterly* 84, no. 2 (June 1969): 289–310; adapted from the text of Professor Aron's Joseph Wunsch lecture delivered at the Technion, Israel Institute of Technology, Haifa, Israel, in 1969; reprinted by permission of the author, the Academy of Political Science, and the Technion.

students in the strict sense of the word constitute a privileged minority, which is not to say that this minority does not deserve its privileges by virtue of its intellectual or academic abilities or accomplishments. In the Soviet Union, up to now, those excluded from college seem more inclined to protest than the students themselves.

And in any case, the Polish and Czech student revolts, and probably those of all students in countries of the Soviet type, are closer to the revolts of nineteenth-century liberal students than they are to the revolt of libertarian, utopian, or Marxist students in democratic countries. Czech students are attacking neither professors nor university institutions as such; in agreement with their professors (at least the majority of them), they are demanding democratic freedoms and, above all, the right to the truth. Is it any surprise that the dialogue between the extremists of West Berlin and the Czech students ended in the discovery of disagreement? Educated in the harsh school of despotism by that merciless teacher called reality (to paraphrase the famous passage of Thucydides), the Czech students, through one of their spokesmen, ultimately both justified and condemned the spoiled children of the consumer society with this stinging retort: "Your educational system must indeed be deplorable since it produces idiots like you."

All polemics aside, it seems obvious to me after the slight contact I have had with Czech students or intellectuals that they do not belong to the same psycho-social type as the leftists of France or Germany. They know what they want; anti-utopians, they demonstrate a sense of reality, a sobriety of attitude and thought, a discipline of reflection and action, which make them differ almost point for point from the protesters of the West.

An observer will probably reply that the young people of the West and the East are united in their dissatisfaction, and that according to a logic of emotions if not of ideas, one group is attacking the lack of so-called formal or bourgeois freedoms while the other group, which enjoys these freedoms, wants to go beyond them to direct or "participatory" democracy. But even if one accepts the opposition between a liberal revolt in the East and a libertarian revolt in the West, it remains to be demonstrated that the apparently libertarian revolt does not, like the revolts of the Soviets in 1917, conceal a totalitarian intention or, regardless of its intentions, a totalitarian ending.

I

Let us omit Eastern Europe and the Socialist countries and concentrate our attention on revolts in the United States, Europe, and Asia, in industrialized countries with democratic and liberal governments. The frequency and violence of the revolts vary from one country to the next. Up to now the universities of Great Britain, which number fewer than 250,000 students and have excellent working conditions on the whole, have, although they have not been spared, not suffered such violent attacks as those of France or West Germany. The London School of Economics, the institution most like those on the continent, has been most seriously disturbed. The storm is raging through Italian universities, which are the least modernized in Western Europe. German universities, especially in certain departments, are the victims of an endemic anarchy which gives rise to enough sporadic violence so that the government is contemplating measures on the federal level (although education is in the hands of the *Länder*). In France the students triggered a social explosion in May 1968. The American students provided the example at Berkeley.

In spite of differences in these revolts which may be attributed to the structure of the universities or the political climate, they seem to have two common features, the singular combination of university revolt and political revolt (or revolution) and the technique of action.

This technique, which was employed at Berkeley if not for the first time, at least for the first time in a spectacular manner and in the eyes of the world, is derived from the method employed in the struggle for civil rights. It might be called the "search for symbolic illegality" or, at least in the first phase, "nonviolent violence": violence because of the refusal to obey the law and the occupation of places, nonviolence by the rejection of arms and sometimes even passivity in the face of police intervention. In fact, this nonviolence does not last, it lapses first into violence against things and then into violence pure and simple, although up to now it has not escalated to the use of firearms or the desire to kill.

Symbolic illegality—the interruption of classes and the occupation of buildings—has the function of provocation. It generally occurs on the occasion of an incident—more or less important, sometimes ridiculous—in university life. It is a question of forcing the authorities into a position where they must choose between giving in at the risk of losing face and resisting or even punishing at the risk of a confrontation. In the event of an open conflict between the extremists and the authorities, a mass of students—in the United States about one-third of the student body—which is somewhat sympathetic to the extremists without belonging to them or approving of their methods, will go over to the active minority. Provocation-repression-indignation-confrontation: the vicious circle is encountered virtually everywhere with minor variations.

Provocation can lead to two different results; it is inspired by two different states of mind, although the two are usually combined. Either provocation as conceived and desired by the leaders is a means of bringing about a confrontation, or provocation becomes an end in itself. The demonstrators want to live the experience of the demonstration: the "happening" of Anglo-Americans becomes a sort of existential transfiguration of the *chahut* (rumpus) which is traditional in French secondary schools and little known or unknown in Great Britain and the United States. The first alternative corresponds to political action, the second is closer to the hippies. Curiously enough, extreme politicization joins with retreat from society in a common rejection of the world as it is.

This community of technique is explained neither by an international conspiracy nor even by imitation. It results from the very nature of the university, an institution which is without means of force and which is normally based on the discipline or voluntary obedience of the students. In the United States the universities, ensconced on campuses, have small police forces at their disposal and function according to a legality. Even in the United States, defiance of the law and the police involves only a minimum of risks. Nonviolent violence is eminently well suited to this kind of institution. The scuffle or the riot represents the extreme form of physical violence in places where, theoretically, the word reigns and reason rules.

The other characteristic common to all student movements, namely, the combination of academic revolt and political revolt, the simultaneous demand for a new university and a new society, is harder to explain. In a certain sense this phenomenon constitutes the crux of the problem under discussion. Students who took part in national or liberal struggles in the last century were attacking the government, not the professors or the administrators of the universities. Thus it is a question of two phenomena coming together and interacting: on the one hand, all through the West a new left, a new revolutionary extremism is emerging; on the other hand, this extremism, which is a force among students, is exploiting a crisis in the universities which is present in all Western countries in varying degrees. These two separate but related phenomena require an explanation that is relevant to the Western world, since they are encountered from Berkeley to West Berlin, on the Pacific coast as well as by the wall that bisects the ancient capital of the Reich. Let us begin with the observation—which is not yet an explanation—that the historical climate has changed. A new generation is entering on the scene which is defined not by its civil status but by the historical conjuncture which it perceives as it arrives at consciousness. The postwar period is coming to a close. Young people born between 1945 and 1950, the turbulent generation of today, have not had any authentic experience with war or cold war. Hitler and Stalin are no more to them than historical figures, almost as remote and almost as alien to their world as Wilhelm II or Nicholas II. It is a generation strangely devoid of historical awareness, at least in its noisier representatives. There is a danger that everything will begin all over again because in their eyes everything begins with them.

II

The historical climate has changed because the world has changed. Even in Europe the sense of an outside threat has practically disappeared— wrongly or rightly, it matters little. Hardly anybody dares to use the expression "free world" any more, unless ironically. For some twenty years Westerners have justified themselves while opposing the Soviet Union. The liberal democracies did not pretend to perfection; at least they paid some respect to the fundamental freedoms, without necessarily being hell-bent in the race for prosperity. According to the famous statement the liberal democracies, modest when they observed themselves, proud when they compared themselves to others, defended themselves against Marxism-Leninism with a good conscience. This kind of defense no longer impresses the young generation, who compare our societies with their stated goals, their proclaimed ideals, rather than with the so-called Socialist societies.

During the postwar period, as a result of the rivalry between the two great powers, between the two Europes, the productivist ideology dominated people's minds. The Soviet Union boasted a rate of growth superior to that of the capitalist countries; the latter took up the challenge and there followed the "miracles" of Germany, Italy, and Japan. Without despotism and without a planned economy, the neocapitalist regimes advanced just as fast (and in the case of Japan even faster) than the Soviet Union and the countries of Eastern Europe; and in the last few years the rate of growth of the Socialist economies has diminished. But this competition no longer interests the "activists" of the young generation. They see the affluent society as a gift of the gods, a permanent acquisition: what's the point of worrying about it? Henceforth it is beyond affluence that there lie spaces to be explored, riches to be discovered. What spaces? What riches? No one knows. The future belongs to action, not to foresight: it must be forged, not imagined. For the future which our young revolutionaries want is prefigured by no existing society.

The economic progress of the last twenty-five years, which is the most rapid and most continuous in the history of the world, has led to a spiritual crisis. The war in Vietnam, the islands of poverty in the richest country in the world, racial tensions, the deterioration of the cities, feed American self-criticism, and the same facts provide arguments for those who continue to perceive the world in terms of the Marxist-Leninist categories and for whom the United States, last bastion of capitalism, center of imperialism, is the final embodiment of evil. This does not mean that the Soviet Union automatically becomes the embodiment of good. Both despotic, as was once again demonstrated by the military intervention in Czechoslovakia of August 1968, and "bourgeoisified," with a new class of technicians and bureaucrats separated from the mass by their way of life and their authority, the Soviet Union no longer arouses the boundless hopes, the fervor of idealists in search of the absolute. Here and there, in Italy and in France, she retains her troops and her organization. She leaves the field open to the New Left.

This conjuncture of historical circumstances, both material and spiritual, encompasses all the countries in the West. But beyond these causes, which are as general as the phenomenon to be explained, a more penetrating analysis would uncover causes limited to a single country, causes which would partly account for the specific characteristics which the phenomenon presents in that particular country. In the United States civil rights and the war in Vietnam furnished subjects of discussion and then of protest within the universities, discussions and protests which expanded into a total interrogation of American civilization. At the same time the university system, in spite of the considerable resources at its disposal, is also beginning to suffer from numbers. At Berkeley, a campus of over 25,000 students, size necessitates organization which in turn creates an anonymity in interpersonal relations which is a prefiguration of the anonymity and alienation which the rebels denounce in modern society.

In Germany the generation that fills the amphitheaters of the schools is the first one which no longer lives with the obsession, the specter of Hitler. The students whom I met in 1953 when I spent several weeks in Tübingen as *Gastprofessor* were reacting to their still recent ordeal with skepticism, the rejection of illusions or ideologies. The condition imposed on Eastern Germans, the constant flow of refugees from the eastern sector protected them from the Soviet temptation. Young people between the ages of nineteen and twenty-three today, born after the catastrophe, have discovered a world which has already emerged from the cold war. They are arriving at political awareness in a Germany which is economically powerful and politically powerless—the economic power leaves them indifferent, the political powerlessness forbids all national ambition. They find West Germany socially conservative, in spite or because of its prosperity: are they revolting, twenty years after the fact because of the cold war, against the generation responsible for National Socialism or, like their counterparts in other countries, against the banality of a society which seems utterly dedicated to the accumulation of things?

In Japan it may be the same combination of material progress and political dependence which explains the violence of the student revolts and the popularity of Marxist ideas. Is youth *without sword or crysanthemum* looking for something to hold on to, devoid as they are of national ambition or religious faith?

In France and Italy the university crisis in the strict sense of the term —the lack of facilities, the vain attempt to accommodate an increasing number of students in the traditional structures—has, outside any political revolt, created a climate of demands which is propitious to the enterprises of the activist minority. Finally, the decline of the two churches, the Catholic and the Communist, in France probably even more than in Italy, has opened intellectual milieus, professors or students, to the influence of the New Left. Let us now turn to the New Left and to the minorities of activists or extremists.

III

In the United States, as in West Germany, many empirical studies have been devoted to students and their revolts. Certain results emerge which, without imposing an interpretation, suggest various hypotheses. The number of extremists properly speaking, the number of those who are militant members of the German SDS (*sozialistische deutsche Studenten*) or the American SDS (*Students for a Democratic Society*) or say that they are in agreement with them is small, about 5 percent of the total number of students. In France, according to a recent poll, about 12 percent of the students are supposed to have said that they favored revolutionary action within the universities rather than reform of the universities themselves, but I doubt that this 12 percent constitutes the equivalent of the SDS of West Germany or that of the United States.

This small proportion of true revolutionaries does not deprive them of all representative value. In the first place, in any historical period and especially in a revolutionary period, a minority may express the spirit of the time, may translate into actions the ideas or the underlying desire of a generation. After all, it is still true, as Marx has written, that revolutions have been the work of minorities and that sometimes these minorities were really carrying out a task secretly desired by the majority, a task that was recognized after the fact as in agreement with the interest and aspirations of the majority. Moreover, the same empirical studies reveal that approximately one-third of the students feel a certain sympathy for the SDS, at any rate a sympathy that is sufficiently lively that these students join its ranks or demonstrate some solidarity in the event of a confrontation. A certain awareness of a "class based on age" among the students erases differences of origin or ideology and gives the activists opportunities for action, a margin for maneuvering.

The majority of these extremists of the New Left come from bourgeois families (what in the United States would be called upper middle-class families), families whose ideas are called liberal on the other side of the Atlantic and leftist in Germany or France. They were raised not according to authoritarian methods, but, on the contrary, in a style of extreme tolerance, according to the method which Americans call permissive. A psychoanalyst might suggest that they are revolting less against the father than against the absence of the father. In any case, it seems irrefutable that this generation of rebels has not suffered the oppression of tyrannical parents but, on the contrary, the lack, the void which results from the absence of opposition, resistance, or difficulties. Perhaps they were oppressed in a subtle sense, because they were the spoiled children of fathers who acted like brothers in a society whose abundance lowered the value of effort for young people born on the right side of the tracks and almost assured them of success from the cradle.

These rebels are unequally distributed among the students of various disciplines. In the United States and Germany the humanities and social sciences "produce" more of them than the natural sciences; mathematics produces more than physics or chemistry; few are found among engineers. It goes without saying that neither the discipline nor the teachers bear the responsibility for the revolutionary exploits of their students. Students choose their fields of study because of their interests or passions. Do they become revolutionaries because they study sociology or do they choose sociology because they want to be revolutionaries? The teachers provide them with the concepts, the theory, and facilitate its application, and this may be all.

Circumstances differ from one country to the next. In France until recent years students of sociology rarely belonged to the elite. Older, on the average, than in the other disciplines, without definite vocation, they had sought and found refuge in a newly introduced discipline on the margin of the old university. In Great Britain sociology has undergone rapid expansion over the last few years, and it furnishes the largest contingent of protesters. In France at least, the sociologists seem to include representatives of the two groups which are inclined to revolt: children of good families who have become indifferent to social success and money and children of modest families who are already aware of their lack of mobility or opportunities for advancement. Similarly, also in France, sociologists seem given to the extreme politicization of the German or American SDS as well as to the twentieth-century bohemianism of the hippies.

There is a large percentage of Jews among the leaders of these movements; according to the studies done, 40 percent of SDS leaders are Jewish. I do not know any statistics for France, but everyone is aware that a few Jews played the major roles in the events of last May. Overrepresentation of the Jewish intelligentsia in movements of political protest is not a modern innovation. In the United States, where the Jewish community has won its place, and an important place, students coming from Jewish families present in an extreme degree all those characteristics which sociologists find underlying the revolt of the "children of liberal parents," who have critical minds and noble souls and who are more interested in justice than in making money (at least, if we take them at their word). They invoke different ideologies in different countries, and even within the same country. They also present certain similarities. Aggressively visible, with long hair and dirty clothes, sometimes personally unclean, they make certain statements or manifest certain feelings: they denounce bureaucracy, Soviet as well as capitalist, they want participatory democracy, they are opposed to the values of the business bourgeoisie, work or money, they rail against specialization and want to give free rein to emotions and creativity. Thus they seem to be rebelling against the exigencies of the scientific culture and to be nostalgic for the culture of the past or already anticipating a postscientific culture beyond the productivist obsession and the reign of computers. This revolt with its nostalgic tone in spite of its futurist pretentions suggests an interpretation which would emphasize the reciprocal ignorance of the two cultures as an underlying cause of the spiritual crisis of today.

Without trying to point out all the specifically national traits within the context of a study which must necessarily be brief, let us indicate a few differences that are immediately visible.

IV

First of all, in France and only in France have the disturbances started by a small number of *enragés* in a new liberal-style university spread first to all the other universities and next to the factories. Only in France has symbolism—fall of the Sorbonne = fall of capitalism or violation of the magisterial taboo = violation of all social authorities—seemed to endow the students with a revolutionary capacity, or at least a destructive capacity, which has not manifested itself anywhere else. I have written a short book analyzing the reasons for the uniqueness of the French situation, of which some are historical and others imputable to the present organization of society. The revolutionary scheme is still inscribed in the collective unconscious; teachers who had taught and sung the French revolutions, and above all the Revolution of 1789, the true and great one, have not been able to resist the temptation to take part in the revolution offered them, or seemingly offered them, by their students. In creating general assemblies in which teachers and students were intermingled, in sitting down in the midst of their students, the professors enjoyed the illusion of living their night of August 4. They diverted against the authorities the wrath of the young, to which the authorities replied by diverting onto the teaching body the wrath of the public, young and old alike.

Since there is only one university in France it was completely carried away by the storm, whereas in New York disturbances on one campus do not necessarily spread to neighboring campuses. Besides, the labor unions, weak and divided as they are, succeeded neither in preventing the spread of the movement that began in Nanterre and the Sorbonne nor in retaining control of it. Harassed on the left by various Marxist groups and threatened by the higher bid of the CFDT, the Communist-inspired unions attempted simultaneously to safeguard their claim to revolutionary dignity and to prevent any attempt at insurrection. France lacks those buffers provided in West Germany and the United States by labor unions, which make demands but are antirevolutionary, which resolutely prefer neocapitalism to Sovietism or to revolutionary utopia.

Why do students attack both the university and the society at the same time? As far as ideological structure is concerned, I think the uniqueness of the French situation has to do with the extreme politicization of the rebels, their loyalty to Marxism (or rather to the various Marxisms), a combination of esotericism, literary Byzantinism, and the propensity, at least verbally, to Castroist violence or to cultural revolution (inspired by a Maoism more imagined than experienced). Aside from the anarchist-inspired *Mouvement du 22 mars* led by Cohn-Bendit, the two groups which played the most important role (*Jeunesse communiste révolutionnaire* and *Fédération des étudiants révolutionaires*), sometimes by applying the old stratagem of infiltrating other organizations, invoked Trotskyism. The Maoists (*Union des étudiants communistes-marxistes-léninistes*) followed rather than took the initiative.

Of course all these militants proclaimed the same principles of "participatory democracy" or "direct democracy," but they acted or believed they acted according to the Leninist method of the soviets: direct democracy, but democracy manipulated by organized activists. Although they may have been sincere in their conviction that a Leninist type of revolution would not this time lead to Stalinism, they nevertheless acted in the spirit of the "soviets everywhere," with the ambition, perhaps childish but authentic, of seizing power. The French New Left is defined in relation to the Communist party, which controls the largest central union and receives twenty to 25 percent of the votes in elections, much more than either the German or the American New Lefts. Ideologically, the French New Left is struggling with the Communist party for monopoly of the revolutionary idea and Marxist truth. It dominates the PSU (*Parti socialiste unifié*), a party of intellectuals which gleans some 5 percent of the votes in general elections, is split into several factions, but has some influence over all of the intelligentsia, including civil servants. In the universities the strength of the New Left has less to do with the membership of 15 to 10 percent of the students than with the support of a probably higher fraction of teachers (especially among the young teachers, assistant professors, and associate professors). The action committees responsible for the sporadic disturbances of the past few months which here and there paralyze the functioning of the universities all remain in contact with instructors, without which contact they would very soon disappear or be reduced to impotence.

In France few of the rebels had read Herbert Marcuse before May 1968, and even today they do not identify themselves with his teaching and his inspiration to the extent that their counterparts in the United States and West Germany do. To be sure, they, too, are antibureaucratic; they, too, denounce manipulation by the mass media, the dehumanization caused by organization, technology, computers; they, too, are trying to give the revolution "supreme hope and supreme thought," the added dimension of a new mankind and not simply a new mode of production. But precisely because the French New Left includes more intellectuals than workers, it wants to work for political revolution and not merely a cultural revolution. It refuses to face the obvious fact that if the students and intellectuals succeeded in enlisting the working-class masses which today are still under the influence of the Communist party, it is the latter which would inevitably seize power after the collapse of legal or bourgeois power. The French New Left is forced by its rivalry with the Communist party to be political, to make permanent use of the Marxist vocabulary. This rivalry condemns it, perhaps, to play in spite of itself the game of the Communist party, "objective ally" of the Gaullist regime against the troublemakers and heir to this regime in the unlikely event of its demise.

In the United States the SDS is opposed to the establishment or the power elite, to those responsible for the unjust destiny imposed on the blacks. On the political level the presidential election of 1968 must have increased the sense of alienation of the rebels. Between two "professionals," one committed to Johnson, the other representing the Eisenhower era, they saw no difference that gave any meaning to their choice. For Senator Eugene McCarthy a number of students had agreed to shave and bathe, in other words, to re-enter the system in order to devote themselves to a cause. Perhaps Robert Kennedy would have inspired similar results. For the time being the revolt, in spite of its political inspiration and objectives, seldom goes beyond the confines of the campuses, and although it uses Marxist or para-Marxist language, it remains primarily cultural.

The meaning of this cultural revolt is more easily discerned on the other side of the Atlantic. In France the organizations of businesses or universities retain too many authoritarian characteristics which are contradictory to the exigencies of rationality and efficiency for one to be able to clearly distinguish the meaning of the revolt, to tell whether it is against an oligarchy of another age or against a triumphant technocracy. In the United States discrimination operates automatically, as it were. The rebels take their distance with regard to the traditional values of the middle class—the cult of work, of success measured in terms of money or social prestige. They refuse to become a part of the milieu, to adjust to it; they dream of expressing their uniqueness or of creating. Wrongly or rightly they denounce society, and indeed the university itself, as an obstacle to authentic existence.

The young people in France, hostile to consumer society, were in their own way expressing a nostalgia of identical inspiration: neither production nor material success represents the final objective for the collectivity or for the individual. For the individual it is a question of living, of realizing himself, of obeying a higher morality than that of effort and productivity. But the French protest, coming out of bourgeois milieus, retains an element of ambivalence, because affluence can be discerned on the horizon, although at a considerable distance from the present reality. In the United States the transfiguration of indefinite growth into the common good is more inclined to seem absurd than in a France undergoing modernization. There, the rejection of the Puritan and capitalist ethic may foreshadow the societies of the near or distant future.

The German SDS owes a great deal to the critical theory of the Marxists of Frankfort, especially to Herbert Marcuse and his book *One-Dimensional Man*. What a strange destiny for this professor, so typical of Weimarian Germany with his mixture of Freudianism and Marxism, whom the extremists of today recognize as their intellectual master. A grandfather for lack of a father! These Socialists of the sixties fill the universities with their uproar and the streets with riots prepared in advance. They have already crossed the boundaries of the universities and are expanding into an extraparliamentary opposition (*ausser parlementarische Opposition*). They, too, are given to invective against enslavement by manipulation, against conditioning by the media of mass communication, while continuing to perceive the world through Marxist ideas (American imperialism, the possibility of collusion between the two imperialisms or the two hegemonies, etc.).

The demands of students vary in their details from one country to another or even, in the United States, from one university to another. Nevertheless two tendencies seem rather widespread, one concerning the content of instruction, the other concerning the organization of the university. The German youth who is a member of SDS does not want to become a *Fachidiot*, an idiot specialist. A number of American students are demanding from their colleges an expansion of general education, greater freedom of choice among the courses offered. Cohn-Bendit made similar statements at Nanterre. In the second place, students everywhere in great numbers are demanding power or participation in power. The term "student power" is becoming the equivalent of "worker power" or "black power." Students, and not merely the extremists, are determined to be *heard,* whether it is a question of pedagogical methods or even of the material being taught. But do the extremists and *enragés* want to improve the functioning of the university, become part of the system, or, by destroying the power of administrators (trustees or regents) or professors, do they want to offer a kind of prefiguration of other victories over other powers? The revolution in the university, against the adults and the theoretical possessors of knowledge, symbolizes the revolution in society.

From these facts, deeds, or words, what interpretation can be made? Let me begin by repeating the warning I gave at the outset: I do not claim to possess the truth. The significance of a historical movement like this one will only gradually emerge; I shall merely suggest some hypotheses, some directions for research.

V

Two causes of student unrest, one historical, the other sociological, seem obvious. This revolt marks the end of the postwar period and the appearance of a generation whose perception of the world is in many respects radically different from that of the preceding generation. In the second place, these student revolts are the result of a critique of the universities and of higher education which has come out of democratization.

Initially one is surprised at the similarity of the revolts, given the diversity of situations in the universities. But certain probable explanations immediately come to mind. In the United States the percentage of students in relation to each age group greatly exceeds the same percentage in any European country, but the number of students in France has tripled in the last ten years. Overcrowding, the mass phenomenon, the anonymity of interpersonal relations have become worse in Paris than in any American university. In this sense the situation is the same in spite of the discrepancy in figures or percentages.

Moreover, the problem created by the number of students depends on the degree of economic development, on the social context. There is no reason to believe that students who denounce the consumer society and refuse to become a part of it do not feel an unconscious anxiety about the future. What is the significance of the degrees to which they aspire? What chances do they have for a career? All observers have been struck by the conjunction in these movements of two categories of students, the first group brilliant, almost assured of success, the second group, on the contrary, comparatively old, without a clear vocation, having chosen disciplines of refuge like sociology or psychology which are close to their personal preoccupations but without sure opportunities. In France this reality appears clearly, since students of the *Ecole Normale Supérieure* on the one hand (the cream of the French university system) and students of sociology on the other hand, many of them mediocre, have swelled the ranks of the *enragés.*

Perhaps there is a general significance in this conjunction of extremely talented students and students with a premonition of failure. The college diploma does not have the same prestige, the same value as a principle of social differentiation or hierarchy, precisely because of democratization. The college degree is becoming the equivalent of the *baccalauréat* of twenty years ago. Admission itself is becoming less and less significant. Only the Great Schools are escaping this devaluation because they refuse to appreciably lengthen the list of applicants accepted, a "Malthusianism" for which nobody blames them, which is not inspired by generous sentiments, but which does give fortunate candidates certain guarantees. The fact that democratization arouses more or less violent reactions at the two extremes, in the winners and the losers, the first in quest of a great cause and new values, the second translating their own resentment and confusion into invectives against the social order—this meeting of contraries only seems paradoxical. The first are trying to go beyond a success that requires no effort, the second are revolting against their disappointed hopes, which they conceal beneath a language of universal pretentions.

Similarly, it is possible to combine the historical explanation—the end of the postwar period, the first generation not to have experienced the World War and the postwar period—with the sociological explanation —the number of students, the democratization of the universities, and the necessary reorganization of these old institutions. At this point there arises once again a question already indicated but each time postponed: to what extent do the social and academic causes of these disturbances differ from one country to another? To what extent do certain similarities betray observers into error? I shall confine myself to a few brief observations. Up to now the most aristocratic universities, those least open to large numbers of students, those of Great Britain, though they have not escaped the wave of protest, have comparatively speaking been spared. But does the moderation of students, their civilized style, have to do with the solidity of the structure, the human scale of British universities, or with the characteristics of British life itself? In the United States the troubles began in a so-called multiversity on a huge campus where the administration tends toward the rationality of vast organizations and where students were experiencing that anonymity in human relations which is characteristic of those organizations against which the young, desirous of community, participation, personal expression, and creativity, are drawing up a bill of indictment.

In Italy graduates coming out of the universities are encountering a situation of unemployment which also threatens French graduates in certain fields (total lack of jobs or jobs which the graduates consider unworthy of them). In a sense this may be a general problem: what is the fate of the failures, the "drop-outs," in a democratized system of education? I should add, although once again I hesitate to interpret, that in France at least, the range of salaries is relatively more open than in the United States and in other countries of Western Europe, which may serve to restrict the employment opportunities of graduates, especially those in literary fields (or which reveals the irrelevance of the graduates to the needs of the economy).

In Italy, France, and West Germany the university crisis has just as much effect on relations among teachers as it does on relations between teachers and students. The position of full-fledged professors, *ordinarius* in Germany, titulars in France, or mandarins as their enemies call them, appears all the more unacceptable to the younger teachers because the younger group has grown enormously in the last few years. In France especially, there has been an increase in assistants, head assistants, and instructors without any corresponding increase in the opportunities for permanent staff positions. The professional demands of the assistants and instructors, as well as their age, have made them sensitive to student protests. Sometimes they have served as intermediaries between the rebels and the old teachers; sometimes they encourage the revolt.

VI

Beyond a generation in quest of a crusade, beyond students disillusioned by facile success or premature failure, beyond old edifices that are bursting because they are too small for the crowds that fill them, are we in the presence of a movement of historical significance? What are we to think of what certain German writers regard as an original version of a *Jugendbewegung?* Is it a counter-revolution or a revolution?

No one can choose unhesitatingly between these two views. If we consider the ideologies of the movement, we find few original ideas. Either the students invoke the authority of Marcuse, and in this case they hark back to what I call the Weimarian grandfather, the man who could neither retain nor dismiss the Marxism of his youth and who, in a Marxist vocabulary, expresses a romantic protest against modernity, technology, and manipulation. Or they identify imaginatively with Che Guevara, the bearded partisan, both soldier and adolescent, who went from country to country bearing the good news of the worldwide revolt of the oppressed. But what affinity is there between this struggle and the management of an affluent industrial society? Or they dream of Mao and the Cultural Revolution, the Red Guard mobilized against the party bureaucrats. But here again, in what way does this revolution, more imagined than experienced, correspond to the present situation in France or West Germany? A revolution as envisioned by Marcuse, Mao, or Castro requires first of all a seizure of power, a violent break with the established order, followed by a qualitative mutation of man and of society which the Weimarian grandfather hopes for without believing in it.

These young people no longer look to the Soviet Union as the embodiment of their revolutionary desires. They have gone beyond, or think they have gone beyond Marxism-Leninism, although they have retained some essential elements of this philosophy, above all a certain image of the historical world which is dominated by the tentacular, omnipresent "imperialist monster," the United States. In the Soviet Union they condemn the bureaucratic degeneration which Marcuse implicitly recognizes, since in theory he criticizes both of the advanced industrial societies. But does rationalized modern business tolerate "participatory democracy," that watchword of the New Left? Does technology stifle or promote individual expression? Rationalized organization naturally tends to become authoritarian, or to seem authoritarian to those who are part of it even if, especially if, there is no flesh and blood creature at the top of the hierarchy. The domination or oppression that is denounced is identified with machines rather than with human beings.

Here we encounter the fundamental ambiguity of this revolt, which is nostalgic in its ideologies and its vocabulary, but futurist when it announces certain aspirations which industrial society has not satisfied and which the very progress of modernity may make it possible to realize. So far student rebels have neither invented nor developed anything. Their themes of protest, their visions of the future seem to be borrowed from writers long-since buried in obscurity like the pre-Marxist Socialists, especially the French ones, Proudhon or Fourier. These utopians, or those whom Marx baptized as such, do not deserve the scorn which the Bolsheviks and their fellow travelers heaped on them for many years, but neither do they bring us a message that is directly translatable into practice. Fourier's thought, like Marcuse's, expresses a rejection of the reality principle, the demand for an existence entirely ruled by the pleasure principle. As a reaction to technological discipline or to the quasi sanctification of the economic (or consumer) society, the resurrection of the pre-Marxists has historical significance: it marks a moment in the dialectical evolution of modernity. Experience has shown that the revolutions that called themselves and aspired to be Socialist did not suddenly alter the conditions of human existence. Thus the rebels no longer dream of collective ownership of the instruments of production but of a new mankind and a cultural transfiguration.

Do students who do not have any authentic experience in science feel this dissatisfaction more strongly than others? Possibly. Would a better balanced education which would combine an initiation in disciplined knowledge with the tradition of the humanities help to cure this melancholy or this passionate and sometimes nihilistic dream? I hesitate to give an answer. As far as I can see, the historians cite three kinds of precedents: the youth movements in Germany, the French romantics of 1830, who did not discover a cause worthy of them on a scale with the great revolution, republican liberty, and Napoleonic grandeur, and the thirties radicals, most of whom leaned toward fascism or national revolution, but who shared with today's protesters their intransigence, their taste for violence (which today is more symbolic than physical), and their sweeping, unconditional rejection of existing society. Members of youth movements, romantics, and national revolutionaries are recruited at the two extremes, among the idealists, who cannot adjust to what they find mediocre even when this mediocrity entails high social status and success, and among the embittered, who are proletarians in the original sense in spite of years spent in secondary schools and even in colleges.

Is it technological society, scientific civilization that calls forth this revolt? I would be inclined to correct the wording of this question or at least complete it to read technological society at a moment when a new generation is living in quest of its mission and of a great cause, and when secularization is gradually overtaking all institutions, including some whose centuries-old vocation seemed to protect them, the churches, particularly the Catholic church. Today, in the aftermath of Vatican II, a number of Catholics are talking as if their fidelity did not require belief in the supernatural. Some, like the students, are investing in the revolution and in violence a faith which has become, so to speak, unemployed. The authority of bishops or of the Pope, of the hierarchy in possession of dogmatic truth, is no longer safe from criticism and even rejection. Men of the church share the fate of scholars in the university. Are scientists alone able to escape this interrogation?

I said at the beginning of this paper that I was simply going to raise questions, to which I would give only partial and hesitant answers. The students, a majority of them coming from the literary disciplines or the social sciences, are playing the major role in a revolt which extends beyond the university to attack the institutions of scientific society: rational organization and the obsessional concern with output, production, wealth, and consumption. Nostalgic for a bygone culture, they are reviving old utopias, but they act according to methods incompatible with democratic rules, methods which stir sad memories in men of my generation. Must we tolerate these methods because these young people are disturbing calm certainty and intellectual complacency, because in spite of everything they are expressing not only the dissatisfactions of spoiled children but a hope for spiritual liberation beyond submission to the necessities of science as applied to production?

Here, in a single question, is the problem that concerns me, the problem which the events raise for us all: Can a revolt of the violent in the name of a libertarian ideal in a liberal society, open the way to the future? Can it help to humanize the authoritarian organizations of a liberal society? Or will it lead, directly or indirectly, either of itself or by the reaction it will bring about, to a repetition of the tragedies of yesterday, even before they have ceased to haunt our minds? Those who want to go beyond liberalism always run the risk of returning to a previous stage.

Men born at the beginning of the century have learned this lesson by bitter experience; will they succeed in transmitting it to a generation which is in danger of repeating history because they do not know it?

part VII

TOWARDS A THEORY OF YOUTH POLITICAL ACTIVISM IN AMERICA

There is as yet no single theory of political activism among youth, much less a theory of the broader topic of political socialization. Thus, it would be presumptuous to make great claims for the articles included in this last section. All three, however, represent something of a beginning, especially because they attempt to draw together and integrate the three central approaches to studying the politics of youth in America: the historical, the social psychological, and the comparative.

The first article is by Kenneth Keniston. Like Jeanne Block and her colleagues, Keniston believes that it is necessary to distinguish between activism and other forms of response among youth, in particular, alienation. He also suggests a scheme of four conditions that produce political activism among young people.

Political activism among young people in America in the 1960s confounded most analysts, as we have noted elsewhere in this book. It fit neither past patterns of rebellious behavior nor did it appear to have any immediate political antecedents. Instead, as Richard Flacks points out, it was the product of an almost unique configuration of events and conditions in American society, some of which were psychological, others historical. In a perceptive analysis of white student radical politics in the 1960s, Flacks claims that a new breed of youth emerged in the 1960s, "a 'liberated' generation: affluence has freed them, at least for a period of time, from some of the anxieties and preoccupations which have been the defining features of American middle-class social character."

Aside from Flacks and Keniston the other major analyst of youth political activism in America is Lewis Feuer. In the selection from Feuer's work, *The Conflict of Generations,* we find an attempt to combine insights from psychology, history and sociology. Feuer argues that youth activism, in particular, student movements, rest on a *generational consciousness* and, further, that such movements are doomed to failure.

21

THE SOURCES OF
STUDENT DISSENT

KENNETH KENISTON

The apparent upsurge of dissent among American college students is one of the more puzzling phenomena in recent American history. Less than a decade ago, commencement orators were decrying the "silence" of college students in the face of urgent national and international issues; but in the past two or three years, the same speakers have warned graduating classes across the country against the dangers of unreflective protest, irresponsible action and unselective dissent. Rarely in history has apparent apathy been replaced so rapidly by publicized activism, silence by strident dissent.

This "wave" of dissent among American college students has been much discussed. Especially in the mass media—popular magazines, newspapers and television—articles of interpretation, explanation, deprecation and occasionally applause have appeared in enormous numbers. More important, from the first beginnings of the student civil rights movement, social scientists have been regular participant-observers and investigators of student dissent. There now exists a considerable body of research that deals with the characteristics and settings of student dissent. To be sure, most of these studies are topical (centered around a particular protest or demonstration), and some of the more extensive studies are still in varying stages of incompletion. Yet enough evidence has already been gathered to permit tentative generalizations about the varieties, origins and future of student dissent in the nineteen sixties.

In the remarks to follow, I will attempt to gather together this evidence (along with my own research and informal observations) to provide tentative answers to three questions about student dissent today. First, what is the nature of student dissent in American colleges? Second, what are the sources of the recent "wave of protest" by college students? And third, what can we predict about the future of student dissent?

From *Journal of Social Issues* 23, no. 3 (July 1967): 108–16; reprinted and abridged by permission of the author and the Society for the Psychological Study of Social Issues.

TWO VARIETIES OF DISSENT

Dissent is by no means the dominant mood of American college students. Every responsible study or survey shows apathy and privatism far more dominant than dissent.[1] On most of our twenty-two hundred campuses, student protest, student alienation and student unrest are something that happens elsewhere, or that characterizes a mere handful of "kooks" on the local campus. However we define "dissent," overt dissent is relatively infrequent and tends to be concentrated largely at the more selective, "progressive," and "academic" colleges and universities in America. Thus, Peterson's study of student protests finds political demonstrations concentrated in the larger universities and institutions of higher academic calibre, and almost totally absent at teachers colleges, technical institutes and non-academic denominational colleges.[2] And even at the colleges that gather together the greatest number of dissenters, the vast majority of students—generally well over 95 percent—remain interested onlookers or opponents rather than active dissenters. Thus, whatever we say about student dissenters is said about a very small minority of America's six million college students. At most colleges, dissent is not visible at all.

Partly because the vast majority of American students remain largely uncritical of the wider society, fundamentally conformist in behavior and outlook, and basically "adjusted" to the prevailing collegiate, national and international order, the small minority of dissenting students is highly visible to the mass media. As I will argue later, such students are often distinctively talented; they "use" the mass media effectively; and they generally succeed in their goal of making themselves and their causes highly visible. Equally important, student dissenters of all types arouse deep and ambivalent feelings in nondissenting students and adults—envy, resentment, admiration, repulsion, nostalgia and guilt. Such feelings contribute both to the selective overattention dissenters receive and to the often distorted perceptions and interpretations of them and their activities. Thus, there has developed through the mass media and the imaginings of adults a more or less stereotyped—and generally incorrect—image of the student dissenter.

The Stereotyped Dissenter

The "stereotypical" dissenter as popularly portrayed is both a Bohemian and political activist. Bearded, be-Levi-ed, long-haired, dirty and

---

1 See, for example, "Campus, 1965," *Newsweek*, 22 March 1965; J. Katz, "The Learning Environment: Social Expectations and Influences" (paper presented at the American Council of Education, Washington, D.C., 1965); Richard E. Peterson, *The Scope of Organized Student Protest in 1964–65* (Princeton, N.J.: Educational Testing Service, 1966); M. Reed, "Student Non-Politics, or How to Make Irrelevancy a Virtue," *The American Student* 1, no. 3 (1966): 7–10; and Jeanne Block, Norma Haan, and M. Brewster Smith, "Activism and Apathy in Contemporary Adolescents," in *Contributions to the Understanding of Adolescence,* ed. J. F. Adams (Boston: Allyn & Bacon, 1968).

2 Peterson, *The Scope of Organized Student Protest in 1964–65.*

unkempt, he is seen as profoundly disaffected from his society, often in-fluenced by "radical" (Marxist, Communist, Maoist, or Castroite) ideas, an experimenter in sex and drugs, unconventional in his daily behavior. Frustrated and unhappy, often deeply maladjusted as a person, he is a "failure" (or as one U. S. Senator put it, a "reject"). Certain academic communities like Berkeley are said to act as "magnets" for dissenters, who selectively attend colleges with a reputation as protest centers. Further-more, dropouts or "nonstudents" who have failed in college cluster in large numbers around the fringes of such colleges, actively seeking pre-texts for protest, refusing all compromise and impatient with ordinary democratic processes.

According to such popular analyses, the sources of dissent are to be found in the loss of certain traditional American virtues. The "break-down" of American family life, high rates of divorce, the "softness" of American living, inadequate parents, and, above all, overindulgence and "spoiling" contribute to the prevalence of dissent. Brought up in undis-ciplined homes by parents unsure of their own values and standards, dissenters channel their frustration and anger against the older generation, against all authority, and against established institutions.

Similar themes are sometimes found in the interpretaions of more scholarly commentators. "Generational conflict" is said to underly the motivation to dissent, and a profound "alienation" from American so-ciety is seen as a factor of major importance in producing protests. Then too, such factors as the poor quality and impersonality of American col-lege education, the large size and lack of close student-faculty contact in the "multiversity" are sometimes seen as the latent or precipitating fac-tors in student protests, regardless of the manifest issues around which students are organized. And still other scholarly analysts, usually men now disillusioned by the radicalism of the 1930s, have expressed fear of the dogmatism, rigidity and "authoritarianism of the left" of today's stu-dent activists.

Activism and Alienation

These stereotyped views are, I believe, incorrect in a variety of ways. They confuse two distinct varieties of student dissent; equally important, they fuse dissent with maladjustment. There are, of course, as many forms of dissent as there are individual dissenters; and any effort to counter the popular stereotype of the dissenter by pointing to the existence of distinct "types" of dissenters runs the risk of oversimplifying at a lower level of abstraction. Nonetheless, it seems to me useful to suggest that student dissenters generally fall somewhere along a continuum that runs between two ideal types—first, the political activist or protester, and second, the withdrawn, culturally alienated student.

The activist. The defining characteristic of the "new" activist is his participation in a student demonstration or group activity that concerns itself with some matter of general political, social or ethical principle.

Characteristically, the activist feels that some injustice has been done, and attempts to "take a stand," "demonstrate" or in some fashion express his convictions. The specific issues in question range from protest against a paternalistic college administration's actions to disagreement with American Vietnam policies, from indignation at the exploitation of the poor to anger at the firing of a devoted teacher, from opposition to the Selective Service laws which exempt him but not the poor to—most important—outrage at the deprivation of the civil rights of other Americans.

The initial concern of the protester is almost always immediate, ad hoc and local. To be sure, the student who protests about one issue is likely to feel inclined or obliged to demonstrate his convictions on other issues as well.[3] But whatever the issue, the protester rarely demonstrates because his *own* interests are jeopardized, but rather because he perceives injustices being done to *others* less fortunate than himself. For example, one of the apparent paradoxes about protests against current draft policies is that the protesting students are selectively drawn from that subgroup *most* likely to receive student deferments for graduate work. The basis of protest is a general sense that the selective service rules and the war in Vietnam are unjust to others with whom the student is identified, but whose fate he does not share. If one runs down the list of "causes" taken up by student activists, in rare cases are demonstrations directed at improving the lot of the protesters themselves; identification with the oppressed is a more important motivating factor than an actual sense of immediate personal oppression.

The anti-ideological stance of today's activists has been noted by many commentators. This distrust of formal ideologies (and at times of articulate thought) makes it difficult to pinpoint the positive social and political values of student protesters. Clearly, many current American political institutions like de facto segregation are opposed; clearly, too, most students of the New Left reject careerism and familism as personal values. In this sense, we might think of the activist as (politically) "alienated." But this label seems to me more misleading than illuminating, for it overlooks the more basic *commitment* of most student activists to other ancient, traditional and credal American values like free speech, citizen's participation in decision-making, equal opportunity and justice. In so far as the activist rejects all or part of "the power structure," it is because current political realities fall so far short of the ideals he sees as central to the American creed. And in so far as he repudiates careerism and familism, it is because of his implicit allegiance to other human goals he sees, once again, as more crucial to American life. Thus, to emphasize the "alienation" of activists is to neglect their more basic allegiance to credal American ideals.

One of these ideals is, of course, a belief in the desirability of political and social action. Sustained in good measure by the successes of the student civil rights movement, the protester is usually convinced that dem-

---

[3] Paul Heist, "The Dynamics of Student Discontent and Protest" (paper read at the American Psychological Association Meetings, 1966).

onstrations are effective in mobilizing public opinion, bringing moral or political pressure to bear, demonstrating the existence of his opinions, or, at times, in "bringing the machine to a halt." In this sense, then, despite his criticisms of existing political practices and social institutions, he is a political optimist. Moreover, the protester must believe in at least minimal organization and group activity; otherwise, he would find it impossible to take part, as he does, in any organized demonstrations or activities. Despite their search for more truly "democratic" forms of organization and action (e. g., participatory democracy), activists agree that group action is more effective than purely individual acts. To be sure, a belief in the value and efficacy of political action is not equivalent to endorsement of prevalent political institutions or forms of action. Thus, one characteristic of activists is their search for new forms of social action, protest and political organization (community organization, sit-ins, participatory democracy) that will be more effective and less oppressive than traditional political institutions.

The culturally alienated. In contrast to the politically optimistic, active, and socially-concerned protester, the culturally alienated student is far too pessimistic and too firmly opposed to "the System" to wish to demonstrate his disapproval in any organized public way.[4] His demonstrations of dissent are private: through nonconformity of behavior, ideology and dress, through personal experimentation and above all through efforts to intensify his own subjective experience, he shows his distaste and disinterest in politics and society. The activist attempts to change the world around him, but the alienated student is convinced that meaningful change of the social and political world is impossible; instead, he considers "dropping out" the only real option.

Alienated students tend to be drawn from the same general social strata and colleges as protesters. But psychologically and ideologically, their backgrounds are often very different. Alienated students are more likely to be disturbed psychologically; and although they are often highly talented and artistically gifted, they are less committed to academic values and intellectual achievement than are protesters. The alienated student's real campus is the school of the absurd, and he has more affinity for pessimistic existentialist ontology than for traditional American activism. Furthermore, such students usually find it psychologically and ideologically impossible to take part in organized group activities for any length

---

4 The following paragraphs are based on the study of culturally-alienated students described in my *The Uncommitted: Alienated Youth in American Society* (New York: Harcourt, Brace & World, 1965). For a more extensive discussion of the overwhelmingly antipolitical stance of these students, see K. Keniston, "The Psychology of Alienated Students" (Paper read at the American Psychological Association, 1966); Francis J. Rigney and L. D. Smith, *The Real Bohemia* (New York: Basic Books, 1961); William Arthur Watts and D. Whittaker, "Some Socio-Psychological Differences Between Highly-Committed Members of the Free Speech Movement and the Student Population at Berkeley," *Applied Behavioral Science* 2 (1966): 41–62; and D. Whittaker and W. A. Watts, "Personality and the Value Attitudes of Intellectually-Disposed, Alienated Youth" (paper presented at the American Psychological Association Meetings, 1966).

of time, particularly when they are expected to assume responsibilities for leadership. Thus, on the rare occasions when they become involved in demonstrations, they usually prefer peripheral roles, avoid responsibilities and are considered a nuisance by serious activists.

Whereas the protesting student is likely to accept the basic political and social values of his parents, the alienated student almost always rejects his parents' values. In particular, he is likely to see his father as a man who has "sold out" to the pressures for success and status in American society: he is determined to avoid the fate that overtook his father. Toward their mothers, however, alienated students usually express a very special sympathy and identification. These mothers, far from encouraging their sons towards independence and achievement, generally seem to have been oversolicitous and limiting. The most common family environment of the alienated-student-to-be consists of a parental schism supplemented by a special mother-son alliance of mutual understanding and maternal control and depreciation of the father.[5]

In many colleges, alienated students often constitute a kind of hidden underground, disorganized and shifting in membership, in which students can temporarily or permanently withdraw from the ordinary pressures of college life. The alienated are especially attracted to the hallucinogenic drugs like marijuana, mescalin and LSD, precisely because these agents combine withdrawal from ordinary social life with the promise of greatly intensified subjectivity and perception. To the confirmed "acid head", what matters is intense, drug-assisted perception; the rest—including politics, social action and student demonstrations—is usually seen as "role-playing." [6]

The recent and much-publicized emergence of "hippie" subcultures in several major cities and increasingly on the campuses of many selective and progressive colleges illustrates the overwhelmingly apolitical stance of alienated youth. For although hippies oppose war and believe in interracial living, few have been willing or able to engage in anything beyond occasional peace marches or apolitical "human be-ins". Indeed, the hip-

---

[5] Kenneth Keniston, *The Uncommitted.*

[6] The presence among student dissenters of a group of "nonstudents"—that is, dropouts from college or graduate school who congregate or remain near some academic center—has been much noted. In fact, however, student protesters seem somewhat *less* likely to drop out of college than do nonparticipants in demonstrations, and there is no evidence that dropping out of college is in any way related to dissent from American society. On the contrary, several studies suggest that the academically gifted and psychologically intact student who drops out of college voluntarily has few distinctive discontents about his college or about American society. If he is dissatisfied at all, it is with himself, usually for failing to take advantage of the "rich educational opportunities" he sees in his college. The motivations of students dropping out of college are complex and varied, but such motivations more often seem related to personal questions of self definition and parental identification or to a desire to escape relentless academic pressures, than to any explicit dissent from the Great Society. Thus, although a handful of students have chosen to drop out of college for a period in order to devote themselves to political and societal protest activities, there seems little reason in general to associate the drop-out with the dissenter, whether he be a protester or an alienated student. The opposite is nearer the truth.

pies's emphasis on immediacy, "love" and "turning-on," together with his basic rejection of the traditional values of American life, innoculates him against involvement in long-range activist endeavors, like education or community organization, and even against the sustained effort needed to plan and execute demonstrations or marches. For the alienated hippie, American society is beyond redemption (or not worth trying to redeem); but the activist, no matter how intense his rejection of specific American policies and practices, retains a conviction that his society can and should be changed. Thus, despite occasional agreement in principle between the alienated and the activists, cooperation in practice has been rare, and usually ends with activists accusing the alienated of "irresponsibility," while the alienated are confirmed in their view of activists as moralistic, "up-tight," and "un-cool."

Obviously, no description of a type ever fits an individual perfectly. But by this rough typology, I mean to suggest that popular stereotypes which present a unified portrait of student dissent are gravely oversimplified. More specifically, they confuse the politically pessimistic and socially uncommitted alienated student with the politically hopeful and socially committed activist. To be sure, there are many students who fall between these two extremes, and some of them alternate between passionate search for intensified subjectivity and equally passionate efforts to remedy social and political injustices. And as I will later suggest, even within the student movement, one of the central tensions is between political activism and cultural alienation. Nonetheless, even to understand this tension we must first distinguish between the varieties of dissent apparent on American campuses.

Furthermore, the distinction between activist and alienated students as psychological types suggests the incompleteness of scholarly analyses that see social and historical factors as the only forces that "push" a student toward one or the other of these forms of dissent. To be sure, social and cultural factors are of immense importance in providing channels for the expression (or suppression) of dissent, and in determining *which* kinds of dissenters receive publicity, censure, support or ostracism in any historical period. But these factors cannot, in general, change a hippie into a committed activist, nor a SNCC field worker into a full-time "acid-head." Thus, the prototypical activist of 1966 is not the "same" student as the prototypical student bohemian of 1956, but is rather the politically aware but frustrated, academically oriented "privatist" of that era. Similarly, as I will argue below, the most compelling alternative to most activists is not the search for kicks or sentience but the quest for scholarly competence. And if culturally-sanctioned opportunities for the expression of alienation were to disappear, most alienated students would turn to private psychopathology rather than to public activism.

Stated more generally, historical forces do not ordinarily transform radically the character, values and inclinations of an adult in later life. Rather, they thrust certain groups forward in some eras and discourage or suppress other groups. The recent alternation in styles of student dissent in America is therefore not to be explained so much by the malleability of individual character as by the power of society to bring activists into the limelight, providing them with the intellectual and moral instruments for action. Only a minority of potential dissenters fall close enough to the midpoint between alienation and activism so that they can constitue a "swing vote" acutely responsive to social and cultural pressures and styles. The rest, the majority, are characterologically committed to one or another style of dissent.

THE SOURCES OF ACTIVISM

What I have termed "alienated" students are by no means a new phenomenon in American life, or for that matter in industrialized societies. Bohemians, "beatniks" and artistically-inclined undergradutes who rejected middle-class values have long been a part of the American student scene, especially at more selective colleges; they constituted the most visible form of dissent during the relative political "silence" of American students in the 1950s. What is distinctive about student dissent in recent years is the unexpected emergence of a vocal minority of politically and socially active students.[7] Much is now known about the characteristics of such students, and the circumstances under which protests are likely to be mounted. At the same time, many areas of ignorance remain.

It is abundantly clear that no single factor will suffice to explain the increase of politically-motivated activities and protests on American campuses. Even if we define an activist narrowly, as a student who (a) acts together with others in a group, (b) is concerned with some ethical, social, ideological or political issue, and (c) holds liberal or "radical" views, the sources of student activism and protest are complex and interrelated. At least four kinds of factors seem involved in any given protest. First, the individuals involved must be suitably predisposed by their personal backgrounds, values and motivations. Second, the likelihood of protest is far greater in certain kinds of educational and social settings. Third, socially-directed protests require a special cultural climate, that is, certain distinctive values and views about the effectiveness and meaning of demonstrations, and about the wider society. And finally, some historical situations are especially conducive to protests. . . .

[EDITOR'S NOTE: *At this point in his article, Keniston turns to discuss the empirical results that relate to the four factors underlying student protests. Similar results may be found in this reader in Section V, The Development of Activism and Rebellion.*]

---

[7] Student activism, albeit of a rather different nature, was also found in the 1930s. For a discussion and contrast of student protest today and after the Depression, see Seymour M. Lipset, "Student Opposition in the United States," *Government and Opposition* 1 (1966): 351–74.

22

THE LIBERATED GENERATION:
AN EXPLORATION OF THE
ROOTS OF STUDENT PROTEST

RICHARD FLACKS

As all of us are by now aware, there has emerged, during the past five years, an increasingly self-conscious student movement in the United States. This movement began primarily as a response to the efforts by southern Negro students to break the barriers of legal segregation in public accommodations—scores of northern white students engaged in sympathy demonstrations and related activities as early as 1960. But as we all know, the scope of the student concern expanded rapidly to include such issues as nuclear testing and the arms race, attacks on civil liberties, the problems of the poor in urban slum ghettoes, democracy and educational quality in universities, the war in Vietnam, conscription.

This movement represents a social phenomenon of considerable significance. In the first place, it is having an important direct and indirect impact on the larger society. But secondly it is significant because it is a phenomenon which was unexpected—unexpected, in particular, by those social scientists who are professionally responsible for locating and understanding such phenomena. Because it is an unanticipated event, the attempt to understand and explain the sources of the student movement may lead to fresh interpretations of some important trends in our society.

From *Journal of Social Issues* 23, no. 3 (July 1967): 52–63; reprinted and abridged by permission of the author and the Society for the Psychological Study of School Issues.

The research reported here stemmed from a coalescence of interests of the author and of Professor Bernice Neugarten of the Committee on Human Development of the University of Chicago. The author's interests were primarily in the student movement and the families and social backgrounds of student activists. Professor Neugarten's interests have been primarily in the relations between age-groups in American society. The plan to gather parallel data from students and their parents accordingly provided a welcome opportunity for collaboration. The research has been supported in part by grant #MH 08062, National Institute of Mental Health; in part by grants from the Carnegie Fund for the Advancement of Teaching and the Survey Research Center of The University of Michigan. I wish to thank Professor Neugarten, Charles Derber and Patricia Schedler for their help in preparing this manuscript; its flaws are entirely my own responsibility.

RADICALISM AND THE YOUNG
INTELLIGENTSIA

In one sense, the existence of a radical student movement should not be unexpected. After all, the young intelligentsia seem almost always to be in revolt. Yet if we examine the case a bit more closely I think we will find that movements of active disaffection among intellectuals and students tend to be concentrated at particular moments in history. Not every generation produces an organized oppositional movement.

In particular, students and young intellectuals seem to have become active agents of opposition and change under two sets of interrelated conditions:

[1] When they have been marginal in the labor market because their numbers exceed the opportunities for employment commensurate with their abilities and training. This has most typically been the case in colonial or underdeveloped societies; it also seems to account, in part, for the radicalization of European Jewish intellectuals and American college-educated women at the turn of the century.[1]

[2] When they found that the values with which they were closely connected by virtue of their upbringing no longer were appropriate to the developing social reality. This has been the case most typically at the point where traditional authority has broken down due to the impact of Westernization, industrialization, modernization. Under these conditions, the intellectuals, and particularly the youth, felt called upon to assert new values, new modes of legitimation, new styles of life. Although the case of breakdown of traditional authority is most typically the point at which youth movements have emerged, there seems, historically, to have been a second point in time—in Western Europe and the United States —when intellectuals were radicalized. This was, roughly, at the turn of the century, when values such as gentility, laissez faire, naive optimism, naive rationalism and naive nationalism seemed increasingly inappropriate due to the impact of large scale industrial organization, intensifying class conflict, economic crisis and the emergence of total war. Variants of radicalism waxed and waned in their influence among American intellectuals and students during the first four decades of the twentieth century.[2]

---

1 Lewis Coser, *Men of Ideas* (New York: Free Press, 1965); Edward Shils, "The Intellectuals in the Political Development of New States," *World Politics* 12 (1960): 329–68; Thorstein Veblen, "The Intellectual Pre-eminence of Jews in Modern Europe," in *Thorstein Veblen*, ed. B. Rosenberg (New York: Crowell, 1963).

2 Daniel Aaron, *Writers on the Left* (New York: Avon, 1965); Shmuel Eisenstadt, *From Generation to Generation* (Glencoe, Ill.: Free Press, 1956); Christopher Lasch, *The New Radicalism in America* (New York: Knopf, 1965).

If these conditions have historically been those which produced revolts among the young intelligentsia, then I think it is easy to understand why a relatively superficial observer would find the new wave of radicalism on the campus fairly mysterious.

In the first place, the current student generation can look forward, not to occupational insecurity or marginality, but to an unexampled opening up of opportunity for occupational advance in situations in which their skills will be maximally demanded and the prestige of their roles unprecedentedly high.

In the second place, there is no evident erosion of the legitimacy of established authority; we do not seem, at least on the surface, to be in a period of rapid disintegration of traditional values—at least no more so than a decade ago when sociologists were observing the *exhaustion* of opportunity for radical social movements in America.[3]

In fact, during the Fifties sociologists and social psychologists emphasized the decline in political commitment, particularly among the young, and the rise of a bland, security-oriented conformism throughout the population, but most particularly among college students. The variety of studies conducted then reported students as overwhelmingly unconcerned with value questions, highly complacent, status-oriented, privatized, uncommitted.[4] Most of us interpreted this situation as one to be expected given the opportunities newly opened to educated youth, and given the emergence of liberal pluralism and affluence as the characteristic features of postwar America. Several observers predicted an intensification of the pattern of middle-class conformism, declining individualism, and growing "other-directedness" based on the changing styles of childrearing prevalent in the middle class. The democratic and "permissive" family would produce young men who knew how to cooperate in bureaucratic settings, but who lacked a strongly rooted ego-ideal and inner control![5] Although some observers reported that some students were searching for "meaning" and "self-expression," and others reported the existence of "subcultures" of alienation and bohemianism on some campuses,[6] not a single observer of the campus scene as late as 1959 anticipated the emer-

---

3 Daniel Bell, *The End of Ideology* (New York: Free Press, 1962); and Seymour Lipset, *Political Man, the Social Bases of Politics* (Garden City, N.Y.: Doubleday Anchor, 1960).

4 Philip Jacob, *Changing Values in College* (New York: Harper & Bros., 1957); and Rose, Goldsen et al., *What College Students Think* (Princeton, N.J.: Van Nostrand, 1960).

5 Daniel Miller and G. E. Swanson, *The Changing American Parent* (New York: John Wiley, 1958); U. Bronfenbrenner, "The Changing American Child: A Speculative Analysis," *Merrill-Palmer Quarterly* 7 (1961): 73–85; and Erik Erikson, *Childhood and Society* (New York: W. W. Norton, 1963), pp. 306–25.

6 Kenneth Keniston, *The Uncommitted* (New York: Harcourt Brace Jovanovich, 1965); Martin Trow, "Student Cultures and Administrative Action," in *Personality Factors of the College Campus*, ed. R. Sutherland et al. (Austin: Hogg Foundation for Mental Health, 1962); and Theodore Newcomb and R. Flacks, *Deviant Subcultures on a College Campus* (Washington, D.C.: U. S. Office of Education, 1963).

gence of the organized disaffection, protest and activism which was to take shape early in the Sixties.

In short, the very occurrence of a student movement in the present American context is surprising because it seems to contradict our prior understanding of the determinants of disaffection among the young intelligentsia.

A REVOLT OF THE ADVANTAGED

The student movement is, I think, surprising for another set of reasons. These have to do with its social composition and the kinds of ideological themes which characterize it.

The current group of student activists is predominantly upper middle class, and frequently these students are of elite origins. This fact is evident as soon as one begins to learn the personal histories of activist leaders. Consider the following scene at a convention of Students for a Democratic Society a few years ago. Toward the end of several days of deliberation, someone decided that a quick way of raising funds for the organization would be to appeal to the several hundred students assembled at the convention to dig down deep into their pockets on the spot. To this end, one of the leadership, skilled at mimicry, stood on a chair, and in the style of a Southern Baptist preacher, appealed to the students to come forward, confess their sins and be saved by contributing to SDS. The students did come forward, and in each case the sin confessed was the social class or occupation of their fathers. "My father is the editor of a Hearst newspaper, I give $25!" My father is Assistant Director of the —————— Bureau, I give $40." "My father is dean of a law school, here's $50!"

These impressions of the social composition of the student movement are supported and refined by more systematic sources of data. For example, when a random sample of students who participated in the anti-Selective Service sit-in at the University of Chicago Administration Building was compared with a sample composed of nonprotesters and students hostile to the protest, the protesters disproportionately reported their social class to be "upper middle," their family incomes to be disproportionately high, their parents' education to be disproportionately advanced. In addition, the protesters' fathers' occupations were primarily upper professional (doctors, college faculty, lawyers) rather than business, white collar, or working class. These findings parallel those of other investigators.[7] (Braungart, 1966). Thus, the student movement represents the disaffection not of an underprivileged stratum of the student population but of *the most advantaged* sector of the students.

One hypothesis to explain disaffection among socially advantaged youth would suggest that, although such students come from advantaged backgrounds, their academic performance leads them to anticipate down-

---

[7] R. G. Braungart, "Social Stratification and Political Attitudes" (unpublished manuscript, Pennsylvania State University, 1966).

ward mobility or failure. Stinchombe, for example, found high rates of quasi-delinquent rebelliousness among middle-class high school youth with poor academic records.[8] This hypothesis is not tenable with respect to college student protest, however. Our own data with respect to the antidraft protest at Chicago indicate that the grade point average of the protesters averaged around B— B+ (with 75 percent of them reporting a B— or better average). This was slightly higher than the grade point average of our sample of nonprotesters. Other data from our own research indicate that student activists tend to be at the top of their high school class; in general, data from our own and other studies support the view that many activists are academically superior, and that very few activists are recruited from among low academic achievers. Thus, in terms of *both* the status of their families of origins *and* their own scholastic performance, student protest movements are predominantly composed of students who have been born to high social advantage and who are in a position to experience the career and status opportunities of the society without significant limitations.

THEMES OF THE PROTEST

The positive correlation between disaffection and status among college students suggested by these observations is, I think, made even more paradoxical when one examines closely the main value themes which characterize the student movement. I want to describe these in an impressionistic way here; a more systematic depiction awaits further analysis of our data.

Romanticism

There is a strong stress among many Movement participants on a quest for self-expression, often articulated in terms of leading a "free" life—i.e., one not bound by conventional restraints on feeling, experience, communication, expression. This is often coupled with aesthetic interests and a strong rejection of scientific and other highly rational pursuits. Students often express the classic romantic aspiration of "knowing" or "experiencing" "everything."

Anti-authoritarianism

A strong antipathy toward arbitrary rule, centralized decision-making, "manipulation." The anti-authoritarian sentiment is fundamental to the widespread campus protests during the past few years; in most cases, the protests were precipitated by an administrative act which was interpreted as arbitrary, and received impetus when college administrators continued to act unilaterally, coercively or secretively. Anti-authoritarianism is manifested further by the styles and internal

---

[8] Arthur Stinchcombe, *Rebellion in a High School* (Chicago: Quadrangle, 1964).

processes within activist organizations; for example, both SDS and SNCC have attempted to decentralize their operations quite radically and members are strongly critical of leadership within the organization when it is too assertive.

Egalitarianism, Populism

A belief that all men are capable of political participation, that political power should be widely dispersed, that the locus of value in society lies with the people and not elites. This is a stress on something more than equality of opportunity or equal legal treatment; the students stress instead the notion of "participatory democracy"—direct participation in the making of decisions by those affected by them. [Three] common slogans—"One man, one vote"; "Let the people decide"; "Power to the People."

Anti-dogmatism

A strong reaction against doctrinaire ideological interpretations of events. Many of the students are quite restless when presented with formulated models of the social order, and specific programs for social change. This underlies much of their antagonism to the varieties of "old left" politics, and is one meaning of the oft-quoted (if not seriously used) phrase: "You can't trust anyone over thirty."

Moral purity

A strong antipathy to self-interested behavior, particularly when overlaid by claims of disinterestedness. A major criticism of the society is that it is "hypocritical." Another meaning of the criticism of the older generation has to do with the perception that (a) the older generation "sold out" the values it espouses; (b) to assume conventional adult roles usually leads to increasing self-interestedness, hence selling-out, or "phoniness." A particularly important criticism students make of the university is that it fails to live up to its professed ideals; there is an expectation that the institution ought to be *moral*—that is, not compromise its official values for the sake of institutional survival or aggrandizement.

Community

A strong emphasis on a desire for "human" relationships, for a full expresson of emotions, for the breaking down of interpersonal barriers and the refusal to accept conventional norms concerning interpersonal contact (e.g., norms respecting sex, status, race, age, etc.). A central positive theme in the campus revolts has been the expression of the desire for a campus "community," for the breaking down of aspects of impersonality on the campus, for more direct contact between students and faculty. There is a frequent counterposing of bureaucratic norms to communal norms; a testing of the former against the latter. Many of the students involved in slum projects have experimented with attempts to achieve a "kibbutz"-like community amongst themselves, entailing communal living and a strong stress on achieving intimacy and resolving tensions within the group.

Anti-institutionalism

A strong distrust of involvement with conventional institutional roles. This is most importantly expressed in the almost universal desire among the highly involved to avoid institutionalized careers. Our data suggest that few student activists look toward careers in the professions, the sciences, industry or politics. Many of the most committed expect to continue to work full-time in the "movement" or, alternatively, to become free-lance writers, artists, intellectuals. A high proportion are oriented toward academic careers—at least so far the academic career seems still to have a reputation among many student activists for permitting "freedom."

Several of these themes, it should be noted, are not unique to student activists. In particular, the value we have described as "romanticism"— a quest for self-expression—has been found by observers, for example Kenneth Keniston,[9] to be a central feature of the ideology of "alienated" or "bohemian" students (see also Keniston's article in this issue). Perhaps more important, the disaffection of student activists with conventional careers, their low valuation of careers as important in their personal aspirations, their quest for careers outside the institutionalized sphere— these attitudes toward careers seem to be characteristic of other groups of students as well. It is certainly typical of youth involved in "bohemian" and aesthetic subcultures; it also characterizes students who volunteer for participation in such programs as the Peace Corps, Vista and other full-time commitments oriented toward service. In fact, it is our view that the dissatisfaction of socially advantaged youth with conventional career opportunities is a significant social trend, the most important single indicator of restlessness among sectors of the youth population. One expression of this restlessness is the student movement, but it is not the only one. One reason why it seems important to investigate the student movement in detail, despite the fact that it represents a small minority of the student population, is that it is a symptom of social and psychological strains experienced by a larger segment of the youth—strains not well understood or anticipated heretofore by social science.

If some of the themes listed above are not unique to student activists, several of them may characterize only a portion of the activist group itself. In particular, some of the more explicitly political values are likely

---

[9] Kenneth Keniston, "Social Change and Youth in America," in *The Challenge of Youth,* ed. E. Erikson (Garden City, N.Y.: Doubleday Anchor, 1965).

to be articulated mainly by activists who are involved in radical organizations, particularly Students for a Democratic Society, and the Student Nonviolent Coordinating Committee. This would be true particularly for such notions as "participatory democracy" and deep commitments to populist-like orientations. These orientations have been formulated within SDS and SNCC as these organizations have sought to develop a coherent strategy and a framework for establishing priorities. It is an empirical question whether students not directly involved in such organizations articulate similar attitudes. The impressions we have from a preliminary examination of our data suggest that they frequently do not. It is more likely that the student movement is very heterogeneous politically at this point. Most participants share a set of broad orientations, but differ greatly in the degree to which they are oriented toward ideology in general or to particular political positions. The degree of politicization of student activists is probably very much a function of the kinds of peer group and organizational relationships they have had; the underlying disaffection and tendency toward activism, however, is perhaps best understood as being based on more enduring, pre-established values, attitudes and needs.

SOCIAL-PSYCHOLOGICAL ROOTS OF STUDENT PROTEST: SOME HYPOTHESES

How, then, can we account for the emergence of an obviously dynamic and attractive radical movement among American students in this period? Why should this movement be particularly appealing to youth from upper-status, highly educated families? Why should such youth be particularly concerned with problems of authority, of vocation, of equality, of moral consistency? Why should students in the most advantaged sector of the youth population be disaffected with their own privilege?

It should be stressed that the privileged status of the student protesters and the themes they express in their protest are not *in themselves* unique or surprising. Student movements in developing nations—e.g., Russia, Japan and Latin America—typically recruit people of elite background; moreover, many of the themes of the "new left" are reminiscent of similar expressions in other student movements.[10] What is unexpected is that these should emerge in the American context at this time.

Earlier theoretical formulations about the social and psychological sources of strain for youth, for example the work of Parsons, Eisenstadt, and Erikson [11] are important for understanding the emergence of self-conscious oppositional youth cultures and movements. At first glance, these theorists, who tend to see American youth as relatively well-integrated into the larger society, would seem to be unhelpful in providing

---

[10] Seymour Lipset, "University Students and Politics in Underdeveloped Countries," *Comparative Education Review* 10 (1966): 132–62.

[11] Talcott Parsons, "Youth in the Context of American Society," in *The Challenge of Youth*, ed. Erikson.

a framework for explaining the emergence of a radical student movement at the present moment. Nevertheless, in developing our own hypotheses we have drawn freely on their work. What I want to do here is to sketch the notions which have guided our research; a more systematic and detailed exposition will be developed in future publications.

What we have done is to accept the main lines of the argument made by Parsons and Eisenstadt about the social functions of youth cultures and movements. The kernel of their argument is that self-conscious subcultures and movements among adolescents tend to develop when there is a sharp disjunction between the values and expectations embodied in the traditional families in a society and the values and expectations prevailing in the occupational sphere. The greater the disjunction, the more self-conscious and oppositional will be the youth culture (as for example in the situation of rapid transition from a traditional-ascriptive to a bureaucratic-achievement social system).

In modern industrial society, such a disjunction exists as a matter of course, since families are, by definition, particularistic, ascriptive, diffuse, and the occupational sphere is universalistic, impersonal, achievement-oriented, functionally specific. But Parsons, and many others, have suggested that over time the American middle-class family has developed a structure and style which tends to articulate with the occupational sphere; thus, whatever youth culture does emerge in American society is likely to be fairly well-integrated with conventional values, not particularly self-conscious, not rebellious.[12]

The emergence of the student movement, and other expressions of estrangement among youth, leads us to ask whether, in fact, there may be families in the middle class which embody values and expectations which do *not* articulate with those prevailing in the occupational sphere, to look for previously unremarked incompatibilities between trends in the larger social system and trends in family life and early socialization.

The argument we have developed may be sketched as follows:

First, on the macrostructural level we assume that two related trends are of importance: one, the increasing rationalization of student life in high schools and universities, symbolized by the "multiversity," which entails a high degree of impersonality, competitiveness and an increasingly explicit and direct relationship between the university and corporate and governmental bureaucracies; two, the increasing unavailability of coherent careers independent of bureaucratic organizations.

Second, these trends converge, in time, with a particular trend in the development of the family; namely, the emergence of a pattern of familial relations, located most typically in upper middle class, professional homes, having the following elements:

(a)   a strong emphasis on democratic, egalitarian interpersonal relations

(b)   a high degree of permissiveness with respect to self-regulation

---

12 Parsons, "Youth in the Context of American Society."

(c)   an emphasis on values *other than achievement;* in particular, a stress on the intrinsic worth of living up to intellectual, aesthetic, political, or religious ideals.

Third, young people raised in this kind of family setting, contrary to the expectations of some observers, find it difficult to accommodate to institutional expectations requiring submissiveness to adult authority, respect for established status distinctions, a high degree of competition, and firm regulation of sexual and expressive impulses. They are likely to be particularly sensitized to acts of arbitrary authority, to unexamined expressions of allegiance to conventional values, to instances of institutional practices which conflict with professed ideals. Further, the values embodied in their families are likely to be reinforced by other socializing experiences—for example, summer vacations at progressive children's camps, attendance at experimental private schools, growing up in a community with a high proportion of friends from similar backgrounds. Paralleling these experiences of positive reinforcement, there are likely to be experiences which reinforce a sense of estrangement from peers or conventional society. For instance, many of these young people experience a strong sense of being "different" or "isolated" in school; this sense of distance is often based on the relative uniqueness of their interests and values, their inability to accept conventional norms about appropriate sex-role behavior, and the like. An additional source of strain is generated when these young people perceive a fundamental discrepancy between the values espoused by their parents and the style of life actually practiced by them. This discrepancy is experienced as a feeling of "guilt" over "being middle class" and a perception of "hypocrisy" on the part of parents who express liberal or intellectual values while appearing to their children as acquisitive or self-interested.

Fourth, the incentives operative in the occupational sphere are of limited efficacy for these young people—achievement of status or material advantage is relatively ineffective for an individual who already has high status and affluence by virtue of his family origins. This means, on the one hand, that these students are less oriented toward occupational achievement; on the other hand, the operative sanctions within the school and the larger society are less effective in enforcing conformity. It seems plausible that this is the first generation in which a substantial number of youth have both the impulse to free themselves from conventional status concerns *and can afford to do so.* In this sense they are a "liberated" generation; affluence has freed them, at least for a period of time, from some of the anxieties and preoccupations which have been the defining features of American middle-class social character.

Fifth, the emergence of the student movement is to be understood in large part as a consequence of opportunities for prolonged interaction available in the university environment. The kinds of personality structures produced by the socializing experiences outlined above need not necessarily have generated a collective response. In fact, Kenneth Keniston's recently published work on alienated students at Harvard suggests that students with similar characteristics to those described here were identifiable on college campuses in the Fifties. But Keniston makes clear that his highly alienated subjects were rarely involved in extensive-peer relationships, and that few opportunities for collective expressions of alienation were then available. The result was that each of his subjects attempted to work out a value-system and a mode of operation on his own.[13]

What seems to have happened was that during the Fifties, there began to emerge an "alienated" student culture, as students with alienated predispositions became visible to each other and began to interact. There was some tendency for these students to identify with the "Beat" style and related forms of bohemianism. Since this involved a high degree of disaffiliation, "cool" noncommitment and social withdrawal, observers tended to interpret this subculture as but a variant of the prevailing privatism of the Fifties. However, a series of precipitating events, most particularly the southern student sit-ins, the revolutionary successes of students in Cuba, Korea and Turkey, and the suppression of student demonstrations against the House Un-American Activities Committee in San Francisco, suggested to groups of students that direct action was a plausible means for expressing their grievances. These first stirrings out of apathy were soon enmeshed in a variety of organizations and publicized in several student-organized underground journals—thus enabling the movement to grow and become increasingly institutionalized. The story of the emergence and growth of the movement cannot be developed here; my main point now is that many of its characteristics cannot be understood solely as consequences of the structural and personality variables outlined earlier—in addition, a full understanding of the dynamics of the movement requires a "collective behavior" perspective.

Sixth, organized expressions of youth disaffection are likely to be an increasingly visible and established feature of our society. In important ways, the "new radicalism" is *not* new, but rather a more widespread version of certain subcultural phenomena with a considerable history. During the late nineteenth and early twentieth century a considerable number of young people began to move out of their provincial environments as a consequence of university education; many of these people gathered in such locales as Greenwich Village and created the first visible bohemian subculture in the United States. The Village bohemians and associated young intellectuals shared a common concern with radical politics and, influenced by Freud, Dewey, etc., with the reform of the process of socialization in America—i.e., a restructuring of family and educational institutions.[14] Although many of the reforms advocated by this group were only partially realized in a formal sense, it seems to be the case that the values and style of life which they advocated have be-

---

[13] Keniston, "Social Change and Youth in America," and Kenneth Keniston, "The Sources of Student Dissent," *Journal of Social Issues* 23, no. 3 (July 1967): 108–37.

[14] Lasch, *The New Radicalism in America;* and Coser, *Men of Ideas.*

come strongly rooted in American life. This has occurred in at least two ways: first, the subcultures created by the early intellectuals took root, have grown and been emulated in various parts of the country. Second, many of the *ideas* of the early twentieth century intellectuals, particularly their critique of the bourgeois family and Victorian sensibility, spread rapidly; it now seems that an important defining characteristic of the college-educated mother is her willingness to adopt child-centered techniques of rearing, and of the college educated couple that they create a family which is democratic and egalitarian in style. In this way, the values that an earlier generation espoused in an abstract way have become embodied as *personality traits* in the new generation. The rootedness of the bohemian and quasi-bohemian subcultures, and the spread of their ideas with the rapid increase in the number of college graduates, suggests that there will be a steadily increasing number of families raising their children with considerable ambivalence about dominant values, incentives and expectations in the society. In this sense, the students who engage in protest or who participate in "alienated" styles of life are often not "converts" to a "deviant" adaptation, but people who have been socialized into a developing cultural tradition. Rising levels of affluence and education are drying up the traditional sources of alienation and radical politics; what we are now becoming aware of, however, is that this same situation is creating new sources of alienation and idealism, and new constituencies for radicalism.

23

THE SOURCES AND TRAITS
OF STUDENT MOVEMENTS

LEWIS FEUER

WHAT ARE STUDENT MOVEMENTS?
THEIR DEFINITION AND CHARACTER

The history of civilization bears witness to certain universal themes. They assert themselves in every era, and they issue from the deepest universals in human nature. Every age sees its class struggles and imperialistic drives, just as every age sees its ethical aspirations transcend economic interest. Every society has among its members examples of all the varieties of motivation and temperament; it has its scientists and warriors, its entrepreneurs and withdrawers. Thus, too, generational conflict, generational struggle, has been a universal theme of history.

Unlike class struggle, however, the struggle of generations has been little studied and little understood. Class conflicts are easy to document. Labor movements have a continuous and intelligible history. Student movements, by contrast, have a fitful and transient character, and even seem lacking in the substantial dignity which a subject for political sociology should have. Indeed the student status, to begin with, unlike that of the workingman, is temporary; a few brief years, and the quantum-like experience in the student movement is over. Nevertheless, the history of our contemporary world has been basically affected by student movements. Social revolutions in Russia, China, and Burma sprang from student movements, while governments in Korea, Japan, and the Sudan have fallen in recent years largely because of massive student protest. Here, then, is a recurrent phenomenon of modern times which challenges our understanding.

Generational struggle demands categories of understanding unlike those which enable us to understand the class struggle. Student movements, unlike those of workingmen, are born of vague, undefined emo-

From *The Conflict of Generations* by Lewis S. Feuer, pp. 10–35; copyright 1969 by Lewis S. Feuer, Basic Books, Inc., Publishers, New York; reprinted and abridged by permission of the publisher.

tions which seek for some issue, some cause, to which to attach themselves. A complex of urges—altruism, idealism, revolt, self-sacrifice and self-destruction—searches the social order for a strategic avenue of expression. Labor movements have never had to search for issues in the way in which student movements do. A trade union, for instance, calls a strike because the workingmen want higher wages, better conditions of labor, shorter hours, more safety measures, more security. A trade union is a rational organization in the sense that its conscious aims are based on grievances which are well understood and on ambitions which are clearly defined. The wage demands and the specific grievances of workingmen are born directly of their conditions of life. Their existence determines their consciousness, and in this sense the historical materialism of Karl Marx is indeed the best theoretical framework for explaining the labor movement. The conflict of generations, on the other hand, derives from deep, unconscious sources, and the outlook and philosophy of student movements are rarely materialistic. If labor seeks to better its living conditions as directly as possible, student movements sacrifice their own economic interests for the sake of a vision of a nobler life for the lowliest. If historical materialism is the ideology of the working class, then historical idealism is the ideology of student movements. If "exploitation" is the master term for defining class conflict, then "alienation" does similar service for the conflict of generations. In this book, we shall be concerned with the nature of student movements, and how their aims, methods, tactics, philosophies, achievements, and failures are related to their origin in a generational struggle which seeks to merge itself with the dominant social struggle of its time.

What is a student movement? It is not a fraternity, or a social club, or an organization of the freshman, sophomore, junior, or senior class, or an academic society, although under certain circumstances it may enlist such groups into its activities. We may define a student movement as a combination of students inspired by aims which they try to explicate in a political ideology, and moved by an emotional rebellion in which there is always present a disillusionment with and rejection of the values of the older generation; moreover, the members of a student movement have the conviction that their generation has a special historical mission to fulfill where the older generation, other elites, and other classes have failed.

Countries like Britain and the United States have virtually never (until recently) had student movements. Britain has had a strong labor movement but no student movement.[1] The United States in the thirties had weak stirrings toward a student movement. In recent years there has been a renewed striving for one and its virtual emergence. But in the sense in which Russia in the latter part of the nineteenth century, China

---

[1] Whether Britain's generational equilibrium will now be seriously disrupted is an open question. See Jim Daly, "Labour's Lost Students," *Socialist Commentary* (July 1963): 8–10. Also, on the political moderation of Britain's students, see Ferdynand Zweig, *The Student in the Age of Anxiety: A Survey of Oxford and Manchester Students* (London: William Heinemann, 1963), pp. 42–46, 116–19, 198–99.

in 1917, Burma in 1936, Korea in 1960, and Japan in 1960 had their student movements, Britain and the United States did not. Student movements are a sign of a sickness, a malady in society. They arise from conditions which have made for a breakdown in the "generational equilibrium" of the society and are reinforced by a mass apathy in which the initiative for political action devolves upon the intellectual elite.

The inner dynamic of student movements leads them to an attempt to "politicalize" all the university's activities. To "politicalize" the university means more than having all students take intelligent, informed stands on political issues. What is sought, rather, is that every activity in the university be linked with, infused by, and subordinated to the alienated ideology of the student movement. The students' work, friendships, readings, play, pleasures, the theater and concerts he attends must all be imbued somehow with the ethos of the student movement. No activity can then be regarded as neutral in the conflict of generations. In Moscow, for instance, in the early 1890s, the student activists resented the privileged existence of the Moscow student orchestra and choir, the only student activities permitted by the authorities. The nonpolitical character of these highly popular musical activities was a challenge to their ideology. By a series of maneuvers, they managed to capture administrative control of both the orchestra and choir and began using them as bases for propagandist activities.[2] The authorities thereupon dissolved these agencies of musical politics. In Berkeley, in 1966, a student writer characterized vividly what he called "the life styles of the political fraternity members": "The radical political fraternity has taken a hint from the old saw that a family that prays together stays together, and believes that a movement that screws together glues together. Or, to be specific, that Socialists who sleep together creep together."[3]

THE BASIC TRAITS OF STUDENT MOVEMENTS: JUVENOCRACY, FILIARCHY, INTELLECTUAL ELITISM

A student movement thus is founded upon a coalescence of several themes and conditions. It tends to arise in societies which are gerontocratic—that is, where the older generation possesses a disproportionate amount of economic and political power and social status. Where the influences of religion, ideology, and the family are especially designed to strengthen the rule of the old, there a student movement, as an uprising of the young, will be most apt to occur. As against the gerontocracy, a student movement in protest is moved by a spirit of what we may call *juvenocracy*. If an element of patriarchy prevails in most governments, the student

---

2 Michael T. Florinsky, *Russia: A History and an Interpretation,* vol. 2 (New York: Macmillan, 1953), p. 1164.

3 David Kamen, "The New Left—The New Fraternity," *The Daily Californian* 10 (August 1966):10.

movement by contrast is inspired by a will to *filiarchy*. Gerontocratic societies, however, have often existed without experiencing a revolt of the younger generation. A gerontocratic order is not a sufficient condition for the rise of a student movement. Among other factors, there must also be present a feeling that the older generation has failed. We may call this experience the process of the "de-authoritization" of the old. A student movement will not arise unless there is a sense that the older generation has discredited itself and lost its moral standing. The Chinese student movement which was born in May 1919 thus issued from a tremendous disillusionment with the elder statesmen who, in the students' eyes, had capitulated with shameful unmanliness to the Japanese demands at Versailles. The Japanese student movement which arose after the Second World War was based on the emotional trauma which the young students had experienced in the defeat of their country. Traditional authority was de-authoritized as it never had been before; their fathers, elders, teachers, and rulers were revealed as having deceived and misled them. Japan in 1960 was far more technologically advanced than it had been in the twenties, and also far more democratic. Yet because in 1960 the psychological hegemony of the older generation was undermined, there arose a large student movement, whereas there had been little unrest among students in earlier and more difficult years.

A student movement, moreover, tends to arise where political apathy or a sense of helplessness prevails among the people. Especially where the people are illiterate will the feeling exist among the young that the political initiative is theirs. The educated man has an inordinate prestige in a society of illiterates. He is a master of the arts of reading and writing, and a whole world of knowledge and the powers of expression are at his command. Throughout human history, whenever people of a society have been overwhelmingly illiterate and voiceless, the intellectual elite has been the sole rival for political power with the military elite. The intellectual elite, under such conditions, constitutes a class of managerial or administrative intellectuals. Several thousand years ago an Egyptian father told his son, "Put writing in your heart that you may protect yourself from hard labor of any kind. The scribe is released from manual tasks: it is he who commands." [4] Ibn Khaldun, sociologist of the fourteenth century, meditating on his life's observations in the North African countries, was on this question as on so many others the great precursor. "When the Arabs conquered many lands, founded their empire," he noted, "the state needed many clerks." Whereas at the beginning of a dynasty, as well as its end, "the sword plays a more important part than the pen," it was otherwise when the state was flourishing. The requirements of administration brought the intellectual elite to the fore; intellectuals have always staffed the bureaucracy: "For all this it is to the pen that he [the ruler] must look for help, hence their importance increases." [5]

---

[4] V. Gordon Childe, "Social Worlds of Knowledge," *Hobhouse Memorial Lectures, 1941–1950* (London, 1952), p. 21.

[5] *An Arab Philosophy of History: Selections from the Prolegomena of Ibn Khaldun*, trans. Charles Issawi (London, 1950), pp. 116–17.

In China, where the intellectual class ruled for two thousand years, their awareness of their community of interest as the elite most fit to govern was incorporated in the people's wisdom and sociological common sense, their proverbs:

> Without leaving his study, a Bachelor of Arts may understand the affairs of the empire.
> As a student—under one man; in office—over ten thousand.
> All scholars are brethren.[6]

Student movements are especially prone to occur in countries which have known such a tradition of intellectual elitism.

A student movement is the most mobile and tense section of the intellectual elite. It usually differs in its ethic and motivation from the mature, elder intellectuals; for within the ranks of the intellectual class itself, a sharp cleavage along generational lines usually takes place, quite apart from economic factors. In the early 1900s, for instance, Russian Social Revolutionaries declared that the chief difference between them and the new democratic liberals had nothing to do with class origins or affiliations with the bourgeoisie; they claimed indeed "that the awakening democratic liberal movement was really not tied to the bourgeoisie at all—that it represented, rather, an older generation of the intelligentsia, the members of which were related to the revolutionaries as 'fathers' to 'sons.'" It was a question, they wrote, of a liberalism which "unites only the 'fathers' of the intelligentsia, while the 'sons' constitute confirmed fighters for the revolution. . . . The 'fathers' are distinguished from us by the moderation of their tactics and demands. . . ."[7] Moreover, the fathers as established professional men and bureaucrats, as members of the Establishment, have often become realists, forsworn illusions, and made the inevitable accommodations of ideals to actualities which their existence requires. The student movement is rather an idea in its purity, a Platonic Idea seeking for a brief period an entry into time. Sometimes student movements have been called the "striking force" of the intellectual elite. A "striking force" it is because students, in the nature of things, congregate in campuses, classrooms, and academic halls. A student audience or crowd is the easiest one in the world to assemble. They are not dispersed over distances as peasants are, and their studies are rarely so demanding that they do not have time on their hands. They are not bound and exhausted by work schedules as workers are, and they usually have no families to support. Nevertheless, the student movement's relationship to the adult section of the intellectual elite is an ambiguous and shifting one. Where an oppressive military elite rules the country, where the avenues of democratic politics have been closed, the young and

---

6 Rev. W. Scarborough, *A Collection of Chinese Proverbs,* rev. ed. Rev. C. Wilfred Allen (Shanghai, 1926), pp. 74–75.

7 See Leopold H. Haimson, *The Russian Marxists and the Origins of Bolshevism* (Cambridge, Mass.: Harvard University Press, 1955), pp. 149–50.

old of the intellectual elite will tend to make common cause. But where the elder intellectuals share power with the military elite, or where the possibilities of political compromise have opened themselves for the elders, a divergence between the generations of intellectuals makes itself felt.

A student movement, however, is not solely what is called a youth movement. It has in addition the component of intellectualism. The students are above all intellectuals, persons with ideas, ideas which they embrace with the full fervor of fresh discovery. A new idea has all the poetry, involvement, and purity of a first love. The students are pure ideologists whose consciousness determines their existence more wholly than that of any other group. They are not adult professionals, who in innumerable ways have allowed reality to determine their ideas. It was the young Joseph Djugashvili, later Stalin, who shortly after he was expelled from the Tbilisi Theological Seminary for his political activities noted how the students' condition exempted their consciousness from material determination: "Until they have plunged into the sea of life and have occupied a definite social position, the students, being young intellectuals, are more inclined than any other category to strive for ideals which call them to fight for freedom. Be that as it may, at the present time the students are coming out in the 'social' movement almost as leaders, as the vanguard." [8] In Japan in 1960, cynical politicians and functionaries would still concede that the Zengakuren activists were of "pure heart." The students, at an age when emotions are most sincerely altruistic, expressed an ethical and political idealism which compelled respect.

THE MIDDLE-CLASS ORIGIN OF STUDENTRIES

Student movements, like the studentries from which they arise, are almost always constituted in largest part of children of the middle classes. It is a striking sociological truth that unless the social composition of a studentry is arbitrarily determined by the political authority, it will tend, whether in capitalist or socialist countries, to be predominantly middle class. The class backgrounds of the students of the world are thus remarkably similar. In France, for instance, in 1958, 63 percent of the students came from the middle classes (professionals, managers, government officials, craftsmen, tradesmen, farm proprietors), 19 percent were from the upper classes (employers, owners, stockholders), while only 4 percent were from the proletariat (industrial and farm laborers).[9]

In socialist Yugoslavia, the studentry in 1958 was likewise predominantly middle class. The percentage was 53.5 percent, excluding peasants'

---

8 J. V. Stalin, "The Russian Social-Democratic Party and Its Immediate Tasks" (1901), trans. from the Georgian, in J. V. Stalin, *Works*, vol. 1 (Moscow, 1952), p. 22.

9 World University Service, *Economic Factors Affecting Access to the University* (Geneva, 1961), pp. 176–77.

sons; and if peasants were included as proprietors in the middle class, the percentage rose to 80.8 percent. Of course, the middle class now consisted mostly of the new, bureaucratic class; only 12.4 percent of the studentry, however, came from the working class, despite the socialistic economy. The intellectuals and state employees who composed only 13 percent of the population provided disproportionately more than 45 percent of the studentry; whereas the workers, who comprised 27 percent of the population, contributed only 12.4 of the studentry. The peasantry were the majority (60 percent) of the Yugoslav people, yet the percentage of peasants' sons among the students was only 27.30 percent.[10]

Communist Poland had a distribution of students much like that of Yugoslavia; the majority of its studentry derived from the "new middle class." [See Table 1.]

TABLE 1. Social Origin of Polish Studentry (1957-1958)

Class	Percentage of Studentry
Workers	26.2
Peasants	21.7
Intelligentsia (trade, others)	52.1

Source: World University Service, *Economic Factors Affecting Access to the University* (Geneva, 1961), p. 53.

The social origin of students in Sweden was much similar to the Polish; the Swedish students derived predominantly from "the families of teachers and those in government service." [See Table 2.]

TABLE 2. Social Origin of Swedish Studentry (1956)

Class		Percentage of Studentry
I	Proprietors, managers, higher officials	43.2
II	Farmers, elementary school teachers, lower officials, shopkeepers	38.8
III	Workers	17.2
IV	Miscellaneous	0.8

Source: Same as Table 1, p. 69.

The studentries of the backward, or industrially underdeveloped countries likewise were predominantly from the middle classes. In other words, the degree of technical development in a country no more affected the primacy of the middle class in its universities than did the type of

---

10 Ibid., p. 112.

social system. The University of Indonesia, for instance, in 1958 drew 46.4 percent of its studentry from the children of professors, persons in free occupations, officers, entrepreneurs, and high civil servants; 41.5 percent from the children of secondary school teachers, middle businessmen, middle civil servants, and pensioners; and 12.1 percent from elementary school teachers, lower civil servants, noncommissioned officers, and small peasants. At least 87.9 percent of Indonesia's studentry was drawn from its middle or upper class; the lowest classes were virtually unrepresented. This despite President Sukarno's socialism and "guided democracy." [11]

The Indonesian percentages were much like those of Turkey, 36 percent of whose studentry in 1959 was drawn from the upper classes, 57 percent from the middle classes, and only 7 percent from the lower class. In India, likewise, most of the students came from the middle and higher income classes, though the average income of the middle class was low.[12] The studentry of Japan, the most industrially developed of the Asian countries, was also drawn predominantly from the middle and upper classes. Only 2.9 percent of Japanese students were children of skilled workers, while the middle income group contributed 35.5 percent and the upper income group 34.5 percent of the studentry.[13]

The Danish, Swiss, and Dutch all have middle-class studentries, despite the influence in other ways of their respective social democratic and democratic philosophies. The children of academics indeed provided the largest groups in these studentries. In Denmark, as many as 34.2 percent of the students at the time of the survey were children of professors and teachers, while only 8.2 percent came from the working class. The Swiss studentry in 1960 was overwhelmingly middle class: 83 percent were children of employers, managers, public officials, professionals, professors, teachers, and white collar employees; 13 percent were children of independent tradesmen, handicraftsmen and farmers; and only 3.7 percent were children of industrial and agricultural laborers. In the Netherlands in 1954–1955 the higher classes provided 47 percent of the studentry, the middle classes 46 percent, and the lower class (workers, policemen, clerks, state office workers) only 7 percent. The German studentry in 1955–1956 was drawn largely from families in which the parents were civil servants and lawyers (38.8 percent), businessmen and managers (17.4 percent), and doctors and pharmacists (6 percent). In Britain, after almost five years under a Labour government, only 7 percent of students at Oxford and Cambridge were the sons of manual "workers," though the percentage reached 20 percent in the "red brick" universities. Only the Korean studentry in 1953 was predominantly (76 percent) from the lower income group, but that only because so many of the students' families had been uprooted by the war which ended that year.[14]

---

11 Ibid., p. 120.

12 Ibid., p. 102a, 86.

13 Ibid., p. 107.

14 Ibid., p. 17, 58, 34, 36, 150, 80. A Survey by the Canadian Union of Students, published in 1966, found that 48 percent of the students gave their father's occupation

Student movements arising out of such studentries have except in rare instances been composed of sons and daughters of the middle class, brought up with the culture and values of the middle class, its tensions, outlook, and hopes, and reacting to their origins with various degrees of "alienation." . . .

THE BACK-TO-THE-PEOPLE SPIRIT IN STUDENT MOVEMENTS

From the combination of youth, intellectuality, and altruistic emotion, there arise certain further basic traits of student movements. In the first place, a student movement, unlike a labor movement, has at its inception only a vague sense of its immediate goals; indeed, its "ultimate aims" are usually equally inchoate. A trade union, as we have mentioned, comes into being because a group of workers have certain specific grievances relating to wages, hours and conditions of work, seniority rights, safety precautions. It is only with difficulty that political propagandists can get workers to think in generic terms of opposing the "system." A student movement, on the other hand, arises from a diffused feeling of opposition to things as they are. It is revolutionary in emotion to begin with, and because its driving energy stems largely from unconscious sources, it has trouble defining what it wants. It tries to go from the general to the particular, and to find a justifying bill of grievances; what moves it at the outset, however, is less an idea than an emotion, vague, restless, ill-defined, stemming from the unconscious. A Japanese student leader of many years' standing, Shigeo Shima, remarked, "One cannot understand the student movement if one tries to understand it in terms of the labor movement. The strength of the student movement lies in its energy of consciousness trying to determine existence, instead of the other way around." [15] An intellectual has been defined as a person whose consciousness determines his existence; [16] in the case of the young intellectuals of a student movement we might add further that their ideological consciousness is founded on the emotional unconscious of generational revolt.

The student movement strives further to fill the role of the conscience of society. In a gerontocracy, the older generation embodies the powers of the cultural conscience. A student movement, however, is an instrumentality of psychological revolution; in a world where the fathers have been de-authorized, the sons step forward as the self-anointed bearers of authority. People then pay tribute to the students as the only group in society who can speak their minds honestly. We might call this process a "displacement of the superego." Toshio Kamba, whose daughter was

---

as professional, managerial, or proprietory, and that Canadian students by and large "bear the characteristics of the middle and upper classes of Canadian society." See *University Affairs* 7, no. 4 (April 1966): 10.

[15] See Lewis S. Feuer, *The Conflict of Generations* (New York: Basic Books, 1969), p. 201.

[16] Lewis S. Feuer, *The Scientific Intellectual* (New York: Basic Books, 1963), p. ix.

killed when the Japanese students forced the Diet grounds in 1960, described this reverence of Japanese society towards its new student super-ego:

> Nobody will deny that the feeling in the students' life is the purest. It is difficult for the average man to express his pure mind. When we are mindful of our situation or of future censure, we scarcely dare to speak our opinion frankly even if we are sure that our opinion is right. The students are favored, for they can express and act on their opinions frankly. . . . The students have a natural wisdom, for they are pursuing their studies, seeking the truth. . . . So long as the student has wisdom, he knows spontaneously what he should do.[17]

The students are strategically placed for taking the initiative and acting on their beliefs. "Only students can do it, because they need not worry about their earnings at all." Organized society, moreover, is prepared to grant students liberties they would allow no other group. In Japan (as in the United States), the courts have shown an unusual reluctance to pass judgment on students involved in a variety of incidents, riots, and disturbances. The cases drag on for years, and the tribunals become the occasions for friendly interchange between the judges, prosecutors, defense lawyers, and students, as they view and review the photographic slides of the incidents. The student is perceived as society's naïve child acting on the ideas which it has been taught, and society is embarrassed by the children who quote to it its ideals; the students who only recently have been children have not yet been conditioned to act slavishly. "The students," said Toshio Kamba, "have fewer social bonds, so that they can do with free will what they think right."

A student movement thus tends to take its stand as the pure conscience of the society; it is concerned with ideal issues, not, like an economic movement, with the material, bread-and-butter ones. Every student movement, however, also has a populist ingredient. A student movement always looks for some lowly oppressed class with which it can psychologically identify itself. Whether it be to the peasantry, the proletariat, or the Negro, the students have a tremendous need to offer themselves in a self-sacrificial way, to seek out an exploited group on whose behalf their sacrifices will be made. Conceiving of themselves as deceived, exploited sons, they feel a kinship with the deceived and exploited of society as a whole. The back-to-the-people spirit is at once the most distinctive, noblest, and most self-destructive trait within student movements. The populist ingredient separates the student movement sharply from what we might call student syndicalism. The latter embraces the variety of student organizations which are primarily devoted to matters relating to student well-being, such as mutual aid, transportation, examination

---

[17] Toshio Kamba, *Saigo No Bisho* [Last Smile] (Tokyo, 1960). All passages quoted from this book are adapted from a manuscript translation kindly given to me by the author.

schedules, housing, and tuition. Student syndicates may even engage in demonstrations against the government, especially where the universities are state institutions. A student syndicate is, however, an example of studentism pure and simple; it is preoccupied with the normal interests of the student elite, and is devoid of the back-to-the-people motif. As such, it lacks an essential psychological characteristic of student movements.

As fathers and sons argued in Russia in 1860, so they have debated in other countries and times. There is no principle of cumulative historical experience; rare is the generation that is spared the mistakes of its predecessor. In Japan in 1959, Toshio Kamba argued with his activist daughter Michiko as he saw her reenacting the back-to-the-people spirit which had swept through the Russian youth almost a hundred years before. He recalled the somber outcomes of terrorism and self-destruction. He pleaded with his daughter, "You members of Zengakuren are foolish. . . . Is there no other means . . . ? Do you say that such destructive action, the most pathetic, is also the most heroic? If you say so, I venture to reply that you are following in the footsteps of the Narodniks, and that the heroism and leadership of that intelligentsia culminated in Bolshevism." When his daughter spoke of the need for a new vanguard party, and of the historic mission of the intellectuals to guide the workers, the father replied in vain, "That is the theory, but if the students take the leadership of the political movement, it will be as it was with the intelligentsia who played the central role before Lenin's advent." [18]

The populist and elitist moods in student movements can merge into a morbid self-destructive masochism as they did, for instance, among the Russian students. The burden of guilt which a generation in revolt takes upon itself is immense, and it issues in perverse and grotesque ways. Nevertheless, something would be lost in our understanding of student movements if we were to see in them solely a chapter of history written on an abnormal theme. For student movements, let us remember, are the most sincerely selfless and altruistic which the world has seen. A student is a person who, midway between childhood and maturity, is imbibing the highest ideals and hopes of the human cultural heritage; moreover, he lives in comradeship with his fellow-students. The comradeship of students is usually the last communal fellowship he will experience. The student feels that he will then enter into a maelstrom of competitive and bureaucratic pseudoexistence; he has a foreboding that he will become alienated from the self he now is. Articulate by education, he voices his protest. No edict in the world can control a classroom. It is everywhere the last free forum of mankind. Students meet together necessarily, think together, laugh together, and share a common animus against the authorities. The conditions of student existence remain optimal for spontaneous rebellion. When the absolutism of the Czar stifled the nascent democratic strivings in a culturally backward people, the universities stood as isolated fortresses of relatively free expression. As Lenin wrote in 1903, "The ac-

---

[18] Ibid., p. 12.

tual conditions of social life in Russia render (soon we shall have to be saying: rendered) extremely difficult any manifestation of political discontent except through the universities." [19]

The students' age, moreover, is the age of friendship and the fullness of love, And in this setting, feelings of sympathy for the deprived, the suffering, and the underdog are spontaneous and natural. The collectivity of student youth lives on long hours of talk into the night. The Zenga-kuren leaders Kitakoji and Kurokawa were always referring to their "heated discussions." The populist ingredient, in Japan as in America, also made "folk singing" a kind of hymnal ritual for the student movement. The Utagoe Undo (Group Singing Movement), founded in 1950, acquired great popularity among Zengakuren activists. Then, too, almost every student movement, in its filiarchical revolt, has had a commitment to struggle for "the emancipation of women," especially in the realm of sexual freedom. Michiko Kamba thus confided to her mother "that she would like to get into the emancipation movement in the future," and Zengakuren in 1954, impressed by the increasing militancy of women students' societies, adopted demands for an end to discrimination against women, and for the abolition of unreasonable restrictions on dormitory privileges.

The student movement is almost like a secret society of sons and daughters banded against the father. Here student comradeship can flourish. The secret society is like a voluntary family, a new "primary group," in which one chooses anew one's brothers and sisters. Its confidences cannot yield to those of the natural family. Student movements tend to choose a secret society form of organization not because of any political necessity but precisely because it marks the generational separation. Children have always reveled in secret groups with secret passwords precisely because these establish their mark of independence in conspiracy against the adults. A kindly and "permissive" father tells how he learned that his daughter Michiko had been a Communist: "She joined the Communist party at the end of the freshman year, I think. . . . As she had never shown the slightest sign of it to my family, we learned it for the first time at the memorial service of the Zengakuren soon after her death." Nor had the father known that shortly before her junior year Michiko had broken with the Communist party: " 'I will make my way in the direction I think right,' " she had said, "and rose up from my seat, throwing them my party badge." . . .

WHAT IS A GENERATION?

A student movement is a generational movement. What then is a generation? Marx never answered at length what he meant by a class, and the concept of a generation is equally elusive. "What makes people members

---

[19] V. I. Lenin, "The tasks of Revolutionary Youth" (1903), in Lenin, *Collected Works*, vol. 7, trans. Abraham Fineberg and Naomi Jochel (Moscow, 1961), p. 53.

of one and the same age group? It is not simply the coexistence in the same period," said the political scientist, Sigmund Neumann. "Contemporaries are not merely people born in the same year. . . . What identifies them as people of one generation is decided by their common experiences, the same decisive influence, similar historical problems." [20] Generations, he believed, could be divided according to essential impressions received around the age of seventeen.

We might well distinguish between biological generations and cultural-political ones. In the biological sense, fathers and sons always succeed each other, but their modes of life and standpoints under peaceful conditions may be much the same; the generations in the biological sense do not then have a political significance. When does a "generation" become a sociopolitical phenemenon? A generation in the sociological sense consists of persons in a common age group who in their formative years have known the same historical experiences, shared the same hopes and disappointments, and experienced a common disillusionment with respect to the elder age groups, toward whom their sense of opopsition is defined.

Often a generation's consciousness is shaped by the experience of what we might call the "generational event." To the Chinese Communist students of the early thirties, for instance, it was the "Long March" with Mao Tse-tung; that was what one writer called their "unifying event." [21] More than class origin, such an historical experience impresses itself on the consciousness of a student movement. The depression, the struggle against fascism, the ordeals of the civil rights agitation—all these were generational events; they demarcated a generation in its coming of age.

In Berkeley in 1964 the student movement said, "You can't trust anyone over thirty." They were not as exclusive as Pyotr Tkachev; expelled in 1861 from St. Petersburg at the age of seventeen, he advocated the execution of all over twenty-five. Mikhailovsky, a generation later, made the age of thirty-five the dividing line.[22] On the other hand, the Spanish student movement included all up to forty-five among the youth; but in Tunisia today, twenty-five is the year of youth's end. The length of a generation is socially determined. At Berkeley, for instance, its duration was set by the graduate student years. But the character of the historical experience was most important.

Social generations follow upon each other more rapidly in critical times than in others. In Germany, after the First World War, there was

[20] Sigmund Neumann, "The Conflict of Generations in Contemporary Europe," *Vital Speeches of the Day* 5 (1939): 623–28.

[21] Donald W. Klein, "The 'Next Generation' of Chinese Communist Leaders," *China Quarterly*, no. 12 (October–December 1962): 73.

[22] On Pyotr Tkachev, see Michael Karpovich, "A Forerunner of Lenin: P. N. Tkachev," *The Review of Politics* 6 (1944): 336–50; Dinko Tomasic, *The Impact of Russian Culture on Soviet Communism* (Glencoe, Ill.: Free Press, 1953), p. 267; Abraham Yarmolinsky, *Road to Revolution: A Century of Russian Radicalism* (New York: Macmillan, 1959), p. 146; Max Nomad, *Apostles of Revolution* (New York, 1961), p. 218; Albert L. Weeks, *The First Bolshevik: A Political Biography of Peter Tkachev* (New York: New York University Press, 1968), p. 64. Mikhailovsky's statement is cited in V. I. Lenin, *What is to be Done?* (New York, 1932), p. 166.

a notably rapid succession of generations. A generational system can become even more differentiated than a class system. Just as a class system can evolve with multiple levels from upper-upper to lower-lower, so *repeated historical crises within a short interval of time* can multiply the political generations which exist at any given time. Thus, the First World War differentiated generations in somewhat the following pattern. First was the prewar generation, comprised of people born before 1890, whose education was complete and whose careers had been formed before the war started. For them the war was an interruption. Second was the war-participant generation. As Neumann described it, "To them the war meant the great, formative experience. Admirable or brutal, it was in their blood. It could never leave them. This was the 'younger generation' called upon to make postwar history." It was superimposed on a prewar vanguard youth movement which had already articulated a protest against "the artificial and corrupt style of bourgeois society." What had been "a burgher's secession of a middle-class youth" was "surprised and overtaken by the war." A massive political traumatic event amplified the wave of the normal generational conflict. Even as a depression accentuates the class struggle with its increased unemployment, so any world event which imposes a diversity of experience on the generations, especially one which imposes a burden of trauma on one generation and not others, tends to divide society, to intensify generational conflict, and upset the generational equilibrium: "Those who returned were cynics and skeptics. They had lost connection with their profession, with their family, with civil society. . . . They had just left school, ready to carve out lives of their own, enthusiastically open to a world to be conquered. So they joined the army, these young volunteers. War became their calling." Many were worn out by their ordeal, and later, "silent, impenetrable . . . distrusted the noisy and petty world of busy people they returned to." Others were embittered. Years later the Nazi revolution became their cause as they sought in anguish and unreason to recover a meaning for their lives. In this sense fascism, as Neumann pointed out, was "the revolution of the war generation par excellence."

The third successor generation in Germany was composed of the war's adolescent nonparticipants, many of whose fathers were away at the front. They went on with their studies, followed professions. "It sometimes seemed to their elders that they took after the grandfathers. Indeed they often locked hands with them over the heads of the preceding generation." This postwar youth was not impressed by the paramount event of the recent past—war. "They had no headaches. Economics, techniques, sport —those interested them. . . . They did not want to reform the world. They wanted to live. The motorcycle was the embodiment of their ambitions. . . . If there was a great experience comparable to the roar which impressed this problemless generation, it was the inflation. . . ." [23] This generation was driftwood. The Nazi revolution drew them later into an alliance with the disillusioned war generation.

---

[23] Neumann, "The 'Next Generation' of Chinese Communist Leaders," p. 625.

What keeps generational consciousness most intense is the sense of generational martyrdom, the actual experience of one's fellow-students assaulted, killed, imprisoned, by armed deputies of the elder generation. Whether in Russian, Chinese, or Latin American universities, or at Berkeley, the actual physical clash made students frenzied with indignation. The youthful adolescent resents the elders' violence especially for its assault upon his new manhood. Student movements make of their martyrs the high symbols of a common identity. The Iranian Students' Association, for example, published a leaflet in their exile to commemorate "Student Day" for three of their comrades. Its language was that of the martyrology of generational consciousness:

STUDENTS MASSACRED

On December 7th, 1953, the armed forces of the post-coup d'etat government invaded the Tehran University. Some soldiers entered a classroom and threatened to kill the professor . . . As the terrified students started to run away the soldiers opened fire with their machine guns in the hallway and wounded many students and killed three.

. . . The students were going to demonstrate against the government on December 9th, 1953, the day that Vice-President Richard M. Nixon was going to visit Iran and its "free" people. . . .

The three students, Ghandchi, Bozorgnia and Shariatrazavi, died, but their memory and their heroic sacrifice will forever remain with us to guide the student movement of Iran. To honor their memories and to rededicate ourselves to the cause for which they gave their lives, this day will always be honored. . . .[24]

Every student movement has cherished similar memories of brothers whom their fathers destroyed. . . .

GENERATIONAL CONSCIOUSNESS AND GENERATIONAL STRUGGLE

Student movements are founded on *generational consciousness* in the same basic sense in which workers' movements are founded on class consciousness. Curiously, generational consciousness was not clearly recognized as a mainspring in social change in modern times until the first stirrings of the Russian student movement. It was in Russia that men became dated by their generations; one was a man of the "forties," the "sixties," the "eighties." Rudin, in Turgenev's novel of that name, for instance, as Kropotkin says, "was a man of the 'forties,' nurtured upon Hegel's philosophy, and developed under the conditions which prevailed under Nicholas I, when there was no possibility whatever for a thinking

---

[24] Leaflet of the Iranian Students' Association of Northern California, December 1963.

man to apply his energy, unless he chose to become an obedient functionary of an autocratic, slave-owning state." [25]

Now just as there are conditions which make for the importance of class consciousness in history, so there are conditions, as in Russia, during the nineteenth century, which bring generational consciousness to the fore. At other times the consciousness of generation may be comparatively recessive. When Ortega y Gasset came to the conclusion in 1914 "that the generation was the fundamental concept in history," no one else in Europe, he says, was talking about this concept. [26] The categories of economic determinism had so shaped the perceptions of social scientists that they tended to be unaware of generational conflict. Twenty years later, however, socialist professors in Germany, experiencing the Nazi student uprising in their universities, rediscovered the concept of the generation. [27]

Generational consciousness, however, is generally not strong enough to bind students and workers of the same age. Young workers, aware that the students constitute the members of a future upper class, aware of student elitism, always remain suspicious of young redeemers. During the tense agitational years in the 1890s in St. Petersburg, for instance, although working-class and student activists were usually from the same age group, the twenties, they were separated, as Richard Pipes has noted, by deep psychological barriers. The workers, despite their years, were hardened and matured; they had been earning their bread from their early teens. They were hungry for knowledge as well, "but they resented practical advice tendered them by bookish, naïve students. The fact that, come June, the students abandoned the worker circles and left for the summer for their parental homes and country houses, while the workers had to keep on working," separated the two worlds. "Every summer, when, as the workers sarcastically used to say, 'the revolution scattered to the dachas,' there occurred a crisis in the circle movement." [28]

The psychological cleavage between workers and students of the same age has in all societies a simple basis. The young worker has generally been directing his emotional energies for several years into the struggle for existence. Whatever generational resentments he has felt, he has had to divert all his aggressive energies into the struggle for survival. He dismisses the issues of generational conflict, because he can afford no surplus energy with which to brood upon them. Moreover, he stands already as an adolescent the equal to his father, often earning as much or more. He is

[25] Peter Kropotkin, *Ideals and Realities in Russian Literature* (New York, 1905), p. 97.

[26] José Ortega y Gassett, *Man and Crisis*, trans. Mildred Adams (New York: Norton, 1958), p. 51.

[27] Karl Mannheim, "The Problem of Generations," in *Essays on the Sociology of Knowledge*, ed. Paul Kecskemeti, 2d ed. (London: Oxford University Press, 1952), pp. 276–320.

[28] Richard Pipes, *Social Democracy and the St. Petersburg Labor Movement, 1885–1897* (Cambridge, Mass.: Harvard University Press, 1963), p. 11.

not irritated by a dependence relationship prolonged unnaturally into manhood. His grievances are definable and real: low wages, long hours, poor working conditions, fear of unemployment, fear of a life always at the bottom. The existence of the young worker determines his consciousness; the class struggle moves him, not generational struggle.

Generational consciousness is a phenomenon far different from class consciousness, with which, however, it can merge in great social crises. How different generational consciousness is can be seen if we try to write a Generational Manifesto on the analogue of the Communist Manifesto:

> The history of all hitherto existing society is the history of generational struggles. Old and young, fathers and sons, aged masters and young apprentices, aged employers and young laborers, old professors and young students have since the primal parricide contended with each other for the mastery of society. Every revolutionary movement has been heralded by an uprising of the young. Young Russia, Young China, Young Turkey, and even Young England. The fight continues uninterrupted, now hidden, now open; thus far it has never ended with a clear triumph for the young, for by the time they have won, they have become middle-aged. Only in recent times, with the rise of great student communities brought about by the new affluence, has it become genuinely possible for the student movement as the vanguard of the young to take decisive power.

Now such a Generational Manifesto would contain considerable truth, yet it would not be likely to win as much assent from common-sense sociology as the Communist Manifesto. For class struggles have a tangible referent; they are struggles over the distribution of income, struggles over wages, surplus value, profits, rents, over the material goods of life. Class consciousness is a response to the fact of class differences; the latter are socially grounded, the creation of society, and therefore with a certain man-madeness about them. The differences of age, on the other hand, are biological. Particular classes can be abolished, as the feudal lords were, yet society continues to exist without them. Generations, however, are part of the permanent nature of social existence. Moreover, class struggles are animated by the desire to abolish economic exploitation. Can one say that generational struggles are motivated by a desire to abolish a generational mode of exploitation?

Quite the contrary. Generational struggles often arise among students living in relative material comfort but who feel themselves driven by an ethical compulsion; the student movements give allegiance to absolute ethical conceptions of justice and right, and judge the older generation and their society in the light of these conceptions. The older generation finds itself removed as the keeper of society's conscience. In this curious way, ethical ideas become an instrument of generational struggle, the means by which the young discredit the old. If we ask for the mechanism in social change by means of which ethical ideas usually enter history, and make themselves felt, that mechanism is usually generational struggle. "Social progress," writes Otto Rank, "is essentially based upon this opposition between the two generations." [29] This is a productive duality in human history; the young, in their aggressive struggle against the old, are imbued with an altruistic devotion for the lowliest in society.

Student movements are a manifestation, furthermore, of the trauma of adolescence, which is, in large measure, a trauma of renunciation; the young man must renounce his bookish dreams and ideals and come to terms with reality. He must in other words accept an alienation of part of his self; he must give up part of himself. Not only must he give up a variety of interests to concentrate on a particular craft and job; he must also surrender the egalitarianism of the young group, the comradeship, the friendship. The student movement is a protest against the alienation from self which the social system exacts.

Thus, generational consciousness first appears as a historical force with the romantic movement, as in France, for instance, with the "generation of 1830." No one in the sixteenth, seventeenth, or eighteenth centuries would have used such terminology, but now it became common. Generational conflict was not conceived, however, as involving primarily the activism of student movements. Ortega y Gasset, for example, emphasized the role of the "generation of '98" in the Spanish Renaissance, but assigned little importance to student movements. The basic conflict, according to Ortega, was the one between the age group of thirty to forty-five and that of forty-five to sixty; these two groups, he held, comprised "historic reality" at any given moment; the younger men had ideas, whereas the older had power. The youth under thirty, however, was described by Ortega as being in a "formidably egotistical stage of life" and as not exercising a "positive historic role." "He plays at creating things—for example, he entertains himself by publishing youth reviews—he plays at busying himself with problems of the collective type, and at times with such passion and such heroism that anyone ignorant of the secrets of human life would be led to believe that his preoccupation was genuine. But in truth, all this is a pretext for concerning himself with himself. . . ." [30] A Spanish student manifesto of 1930 entitled "The Conquest of the State" did indeed give a liberal duration to its "generation": "Those Spaniards over forty-five cannot participate actively in our works." [31]

This play of students with "collective problems," with their own political organizations and journals, has indeed its egocentricity, yet its movement alters history, overturns governments, and brings death to

---

[29] Otto Rank, *The Myth of the Birth of the Hero and Other Writings,* trans. F. Robbins and Smith Ely Jelliffe, ed. Philip Freund (New York, 1964), p. 68.

[30] Ortega y Gassett, *Man and Crisis,* pp. 51, 56–57. See also his *The Modern Theme,* trans. James Cleugh (New York, 1933), pp. 14–17; Helene Weyl, "José Ortega y Gassett," *University of Toronto Quarterly* (June 1937): 470.

[31] The Federación Universitaria Española, from its inception in January 1927, contrasted the pessimists of '98 with the new spirit of youth. A student strike in Madrid, on behalf of their expelled leader Sbert, was a principal factor in the overthrow of the dictatorship of Primo de Rivera in 1930. See David Jato, *Rebelión de los Estudiantes* (Madrid, 1953), Ch. 1.

ministers and students alike. Moreover, one can have generational equilibrium as well as a generational struggle; we must ask, therefore, what accounts for the breakdown of generational equilibrium and the emergence of overt struggle? Age differences in and of themselves do not necessitate the outbreak of generational confiict and the heightening of generational consciousness.

There can be little doubt that the French Revolution and its Napoleonic aftermath were the prime factors in the disruption of the generational equilibrium in Europe. In their wake came not only the German movement of Karl Follen but also the Young Italy of Giuseppe Mazzini. No previous age in European history would have so honored the word "Young"; youth, with its romantic enthusiasm, displaced the old with its felt mission to rule. Secret societies of the young appeared; they brooded on death and suicide. Giuseppe Mazzini became famous throughout all Europe in the first half of the nineteenth century as its preeminent youth leader. Mazzini's work and his movement showed indeed all the traits which later student movements more fully exhibited. At the Royal College of Genoa which he attended, the students "were principally preoccupied with the problem of how to overthrow authority." They learned they could do so "if only they were bold enough." They organized secret societies, were thrown into the school "dungeon," and scratched odes to liberty or despair on the walls. "The great thing was to belong to a secret society," with its passwords, gestures, handshakes. A day before he was sixteen years old, in 1820, at the University of Geneva, Giuseppe helped organize a disturbance in the University Church over some trivial question of seating arrangements; he enjoyed his first arrest. The next year, in a more back-to-the-people spirit, he and his fellow-students demonstrated on behalf of the Carbonari revolt in Piedmont. They said of Mazzini that "he was born to be a Carbonaro," a member of the secret society of lumpenproletarian vagabonds and cultured aristocratic intellectuals which seized power for a few months in several Italian towns. Mazzini and his fellow-students read Byron and Rousseau; he wept at the sorrows of Goethe's suicidal hero Werther. But self-destruction was more than romantic fantasy for the young student activists. Mazzini's close friend, the student Jacopo Ruffini, killed himself in disillusionment over the betrayal of comrades in Young Italy; his eldest brother too killed himself as a student at Geneva. Young Italy drew its barrier between the generations; it excluded those over forty from its ranks and avowed that its sense of mission was not only to liberate the Italian people from foreign oppression but to liberate themselves from the old. They took to conspiracy and terrorism. Mazzini told Charles Albert of Sardinia, "Blood calls for blood, and the dagger of the conspirator is never so terrible as when sharpened upon the touchstone of a martyr." Thus the student movement was under compulsion to superimpose the irrational patterns of its generational revolt on the movement for an independent Italian nation. In 1834 Mazzini tried to found Young Europe, an international organization of youth extending on a continental scale the emotional patterns and principles of Young Italy. It failed; no students' international has ever lasted unless it was supported by the funds of guiding elderly politicians, for the student experience is too transient to provide the basis for a continuing international union.[32]

It was during the political reaction after the French Revolution that generational consciousness first became pronounced. "The young generation," writes George Brandes, "had heard in their childhood of the great events of the Revolution, had known the Empire, and were the sons of heroes or of victims." Now they saw the new order, bourgeois, timid, colorless, middle class. An earlier youth had gone through Europe creating with its armies a new Europe and a new dream of freedom. Now the bourgeoisie ruled, with its omnipotence of economic interests, the pursuit of money. The romantic "school" emerged, and it was indeed a school, for it issued out of the feelings of protest on the part of students against the social environment. The young found themselves speaking a common language "unknown to the rest of their contemporaries." They lived with enthusiasm, and with an awe and reverence for each other, unlike their bourgeois elders. "These young Romanticists," says Brandes, "felt like brothers, like fellow-conspirators; they felt that they were the sharers in a sweet and invigorating secret. . . ." They were generation-conscious; their aim was to overturn tradition, conformity, order, formalism; they wanted passion, life, blood. Marx's famous metaphor of taking Hegel's dialectic which was standing on its head, and turning it right side up, was typical of the left Hegelian graduate students (the Doctors' Club) whom he had known at Berlin in his youth.[33] The chroniclers of the Old Testament had made use of the concept "generation," but theirs was primarily a static usage: "And so-and-so begat so-and-so. . . ." Generational consciousness, in the sense of involving an antagonism, first came into existence when the hopes of the French Revolutionary era were unfulfilled, and those of the Restoration period were de-authoritized in the eyes of the young. Thus arose "the generation of 1830." [34]

Generational consciousness, it should be emphasized, can prove more potent than any bond of ideological unity with elder radicals. The young Marxists of the Japanese Zengakuren, for instance, in 1964 felt no sense of emotional unity with the elder generation in the Socialist party. As Masatake Ono, the head of the latter's Student Policies Department, noted, "The number of students holding membership in the Japan Socialist party is so small that there is no action corps that puts into practice the policies formulated by the JSP Student Policies Department." The party itself in its twenty years' history to 1965 had never taken the initiative in the student movement. The primary reason for this separation of

---

[32] See E. E. Y. Hales, *Mazzini and the Secret Societies: The Making of a Myth* (London: Eyre and Spottiswoode, 1956), pp. 29, 40, 42, 84, 64, 62.

[33] Karl Marx, *Capital: A Critique of Political Economy,* trans. S. Moore and E. Aveling (Chicago, 1906), p. 25.

[34] George Brandes, *Main Currents in Nineteenth Century Literature,* vol. 5, *The Romantic School in France* (New York, 1906), pp. 2–15.

the party from the students was "that the party's 'grownups' hardly understand the importance of the student movement and the social influence it wields." [35] Between the generations, as Bernard Shaw said in *Misalliance,* "there's a wall ten feet thick and ten miles high."

---

[35] Mitsuo Nakamura, "Renovationist Parties and the Student Movement," *Keizai Hyoron* (December 1964), trans. in *Summaries of Selected Japanese Magazines* (Tokyo: American Embassy, 15 March, 1965), p. 15.